Thackray's 2019 Investor's Guide

THACKRAY'S
2019
INVESTOR'S
GUIDE

Brooke Thackray MBA, CIM, CFP

Published in 2018 by: MountAlpha Media:

alphamountain.com

ISBN13: 978-1-989125-00-7

Printed and Bound by Webcom Ltd.

To my wife Jane

Acknowledgments

This book is the product of many years of research and could not have been written without the help of many people. I would like to thank my wife, Jane Steer-Thackray, and my children Justin, Megan, Carly and Madeleine, for the help they have given me and their patience during the many hours that I have devoted to writing this book. Thanks must be given to Austin Ip for helping me source and filter a lot of the data in this book. Special mention goes to Jane Stiegler, my proofreader and editor, for the countless hours she spent helping with formatting and editing this book.

INTRODUCTION

2019 THACKRAY'S INVESTOR'S GUIDE
Technical Commentary

The seasonal strategies that I have included in my previous books have proven to be very successful. The buy and sell dates are based upon iterative comparisons of different time periods measured by gain and frequency of success. Although the buy and sell dates are the optimal dates on which seasonal investors should focus on making their investment decisions, the markets have different dynamics from year to year, shifting the optimal buy and sell dates. Combining technical analysis with seasonal trends helps to adjust the decision process, allowing seasonal investors to enter and exit trades early or late, depending on market conditions.

The universe of technical indicators and techniques is huge. It is impossible to use all of the indicators. Only a small number of indicators and techniques that suit an investment style should be used. In the case of seasonal investing, a lot of long-term indicators provide little benefit. For example, the standard Moving Average Convergence Divergence (MACD), is too slow to be of use in shorter term seasonal strategies. In this book I have chosen to illustrate three technical indicators that can provide value in fine-tuning the dates for seasonal investing: Full Stochastic Oscillator (FSO), Relative Strength Index (RSI) and Relative Strength. The indicators are used in conjunction with the price pattern and moving averages of the security being considered. Investors must remember that technical analysis is not absolute and there will be exceptions when utilizing indicators and price patterns.

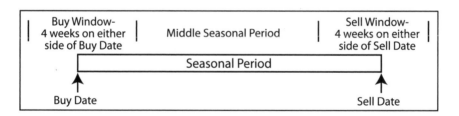

To combine technical indicators with seasonal trends, it is best that the indicators be used within the windows of the buy and sell dates. The indicators should be ignored outside the seasonal buy/sell windows. An exception to this occurs when an indicator gives a signal during its middle seasonal period, which is in the seasonal period, but after the buy window and before the sell window. In this case a technical signal can support selling a full position based upon a fundamental breakdown in the price action of a security. By itself, a FSO or RSI indicator showing weakness in a security during its middle seasonal period, does not necessarily warrant action, it can be used to support a decision being made in conjunction with underperformance relative to the broad market, or a major price action break.

Below are short descriptions of three technical indicators that can be used with seasonal analysis. Full evaluation of the indicators and their uses with seasonal analysis is beyond the scope of this book.

Full Stochastic Oscillator (FSO)

A stochastic oscillator is a range bound momentum indicator that tracks the location of the close price relative to the high-low range, over a set number of periods. It tracks the momentum of price change and helps to indicate the strength and direction of price movement.

I have found that generally the best method to combine the FSO with seasonal trends is to buy an early partial position when the FSO turns up above 20 within four weeks of the seasonal buy date. Additionally, the best time to sell an early partial position occurs when the FSO turns below 80, within four weeks of the seasonal exit date.

Relative Strength Index (RSI)

The RSI is a momentum oscillator that measures the speed and change of price movements. I have found that the best method to combine the RSI with seasonal trends is to buy an early partial position when the RSI turns up above 30 within four weeks of the seasonal buy date. The best time to sell an early partial position occurs when the RSI turns below 70, within four weeks of the seasonal exit date. Compared with the FSO, the RSI is less useful as it is slower and gives too few signals in the buy/sell windows.

Relative Strength

Relative strength calculates the performance of one security versus another security. When the relative strength is increasing, it indicates the seasonal security is outperforming. When the relative strength is declining, the seasonal security is underperforming. When a downward trend line is broken to the upside by the performance of the seasonal security, relative to the benchmark, this is a positive signal. This action carries a lot of weight and can justify a full early entry into a position if other technical evidence is positive. Likewise, if an upward trend line is broken to the downside, a negative technical signal is given and can justify a full early exit from a position if other technical evidence is negative.

THACKRAY'S 2019 INVESTOR'S GUIDE

You can choose great companies to invest in and still underperform the market. Unless you are in the market at the right time and in the best sectors, your investment expertise can be all for naught.

Successful investors know when they should be in the market. Very successful investors know when they should be in the market, and the best sectors in which to invest. *Thackray's 2019 Investor's Guide* is designed to provide investors with the knowledge of when and what to buy, and when to sell.

The goal of this book is to help investors capture extra profits by taking advantage of the seasonal trends in the markets. This book is straightforward. There are no complicated rules and there are no complex algorithms. The strategies put forward are intuitive and easy to understand.

It does not matter if you are a short-term or long-term investor, this book can be used to help establish entry and exit points. For the short-term investor, specific periods are identified that can provide profitable opportunities. For the long-term investor best buy dates are identified to launch new investments on a sound footing.

The stock market has its seasonal rhythms. Historically, the broad markets, such as the S&P 500, have a seasonal trend of outperforming during certain times of the year. Likewise, different sectors of the market have their own seasonal trends of outperformance. When oil stocks tend to do well in the springtime before "driving season," health care stocks tend to underperform the market. When utilities do well in the summertime, industrials do not. With different markets and different sectors having a tendency to outperform at different times of the year, there is always a place to invest.

Until recently, investors did not have access to the information necessary to analyse and create sector strategies. In recent years there have been a great number of sector Exchange Traded Funds (ETFs) and sector indexes introduced into the market. For the first time, investors are now able to easily implement a sector rotation strategy. This book provides a seasonal road map of what sectors tend to do well at different times of the year. It is a first of its kind, revealing new sector-based strategies that have never before been published.

In terms of market timing there are ample strategies in this book to help determine the times when equities should be over or underweight. During a favorable time for the market, investments can be purchased to overweight equities relative to their target weight in a portfolio (staying within risk tolerances). During an unfavorable time, investments can be sold to underweight equities relative to their target.

A large part of the book is devoted to sector seasonality – the underpinnings for a sector rotation strategy. The most practical rotation strategy is to create a core part of a portfolio that represents the broad market and then set aside an allocation to be rotated between favored sectors from one time period to the next.

It does not makes sense to apply any investment strategy only once with a large investment. Seasonal strategies are no exception. The best way to apply an investment strategy is to use a disciplined methodology that allows for diversification and a large enough number of investments to help remove the anomalies of the market. This reduces risk and increases the probability of a long term gain.

Following the specific buy and sell dates put forth in this book would have netted an investor large, above market returns. To "turbo-charge" gains, an investor can combine seasonality with technical analysis. As the seasonal periods are never exactly the same, technical analysis can help investors capture the extra gains when a sector turns up early, or momentum extends the trend.

IMPORTANT: Strategy Buy and Sell Dates
The beginning date of every strategy period in this book represents a full day in the market; therefore, investors should buy at the end of the preceding market day. For example the *Biotech Summer Solstice* seasonal period of strength is from June 23rd to September 13th. To be in the sector for the full seasonal period, an investor would enter the market before the closing bell on June 22nd. If the buy date landed on a weekend or holiday, then the buy would occur at the end of the preceding trading day.

The last day of a trading strategy is the sell date. For example, the Biotech sector investment would be sold at the end of the day on September 13th. If the sell date is a holiday or weekend, then the investment would be sold at the close on the preceding trading day.

What is Seasonal Investing?

In order to properly understand seasonal investing in the stock market, it is important to look briefly at its evolution. It may surprise investors to know that seasonal investing at the broad market level, i.e. Dow Jones or S&P 500, has been around for a long time. The initial seasonal strategies were written by Fields (1931, 1934) and Watchel (1942), who focused on the *January Effect*. Coincidentally, this strategy is still bantered about in the press every year.

Yale Yirsch Senior has been largely responsible for the next stage in the evolution, producing the *Stock Trader's Almanac* for more than forty years. This publication focuses on broad market trends such as the best six months of the year and tendencies of the market to do well depending on the political party in power and holiday trades.

In 2000, Brooke Thackray and Bruce Lindsay wrote, *Time In Time Out: Outsmart the Market Using Calendar Investment Strategies*. This work focused on a comprehensive analysis of the six month seasonal cycle and other shorter seasonal cycles in the broad markets such as the S&P 500.

Seasonal investing has changed over time. The focus has shifted from broad market strategies to taking advantage of sector rotation opportunities – investing in different sectors at different times of the year, depending on their seasonal strength. This has created a whole new set of investment opportunities. Rather than just being "in or out" of the market, investors can now always be invested by shifting between different sectors and asset classes, taking advantage of both up and down markets.

Definition – Seasonal investing is a method of investing in the market at the time of the year when it typically does well, or investing in a sector of the market when it typically outperforms the broad market such as the S&P 500.

The term seasonal investing is somewhat of a misnomer, and it is easy to see why some investors might believe that the discipline relates to investing based upon the seasons of the year – winter, spring, summer and autumn. Other than some agricultural commodities where the price is often correlated to growing seasons, generally seasonal investment strategies use the calendar as a reference for buy and sell dates. It is usually a specific event, i.e. Christmas sales, that occurs on a recurring annual basis that creates the seasonal opportunity.

The discipline of seasonal investing is not restricted to the stock market. It has been used successfully for a number of years in the commodities market. The opportunities in this market tend to be based upon changes in supply and/or demand that occur on a yearly basis. Most commodities, especially the agricultural commodities, tend to have cyclical supply cycles, i.e., crops are harvested only at certain times of the year. The supply bulge that occurs at the same time every year provides seasonal investors with profit opportunities. Recurring increased seasonal demand for commodities also plays a major part in providing opportunities for seasonal investors. This applies to most metals and many other commodities, whether the end-product is industrial or consumer based.

Seasonal investment strategies can be used with a lot of different types of investments. The premise is the same, outperformance during a certain period of the year based upon a repeating event in the markets or economy. In my past writings I have developed seasonal strategies that have been used successfully in the stock, commodity, bond and foreign exchange markets. Seasonal investing is still relatively new for most markets with a lot of new opportunities waiting to be discovered.

How Does Seasonal Investing Work?

Most stock market sector seasonal trends are the result of a recurring annual catalyst: an event that affects the sector positively. These events can range from a seasonal spike in demand, seasonal inventory lows, weather effects, conferences and other events. Mainstream investors very often anticipate a move in a sector and incorrectly try to take a position just before an event takes place that is supposed to drive a sector higher. A good example of this would be investors buying oil just before the cold weather sets in. Unfortunately, their efforts are usually unsuccessful as they are too late to the party and the opportunity has already passed.

By the time the anticipated event occurs, a substantial amount of investors have bought into the sector – fully pricing in the expected benefit. At this time there is little potential left in the short-term. Unless there is a strong positive surprise, the sector's outperformance tends to slowly roll over. If the event produces less than its desired result, the sector can be severely punished.

So how does the seasonal investor take advantage of this opportunity? "Be there" before the mainstream investors, and get out before they do. Seasonal investors usually enter a sector two or three months before an event is anticipated to have a positive effect on a sector and get out before the actual event takes place. In essence, seasonal investors are benefiting from the mainstream investor's tendency to "buy in" too late.

Seasonality in the markets occurs because of three major reasons: money flow, changing market analyst expectations and the *Anticipation-Realization Cycle*. First, money flows vary throughout the year and at different times of the month. Generally, money flows increase at the end of the year and into the start of the next year. This is a result of year end bonuses and tax related investments. In addition, money flows increase at month end from money managers "window dressing" their portfolios. As a result of these money flows, the months around the end of the year and the days around the end of the month, tend to have a stronger performance than the other times of the year.

Second, the analyst expectations cycle tends to push markets up at the end of the year and the beginning of the next year. Stock market analysts tend to be a positive bunch – the large investment houses pay them to be positive. They start the year with aggressive earnings for all of their favorite companies. As the year progresses, they generally back off their earnings forecast, which decreases their support for the market. After a lull in the summer and early autumn months, they start to focus on the next year with another rosy forecast. As a result, the stock market tends to rise once again at the end of the year.

Third, at the sector level, sectors of the market tend to be greatly influenced by the *Anticipation-Realization Cycle*. Although some investors may not be familiar with the term "anticipation-realization," they probably are familiar with the concept of "buy the rumor – sell the fact," or in the famous words of Lord Rothschild "Buy on the sound of the war-cannons; sell on the sound of the victory trumpets."

The *Anticipation-Realization Cycle* as it applies to human behavior has been much studied in psychology journals. In the investment world, the premise of this cycle rests on investors anticipating a positive event in the market to drive prices higher and buying in ahead of the event. When the event takes place, or is realized, upward pressure on prices decreases as there is very little impetus for further outperformance.

A good example of the *Anticipation-Realization Cycle* takes place with the "conference effect." Very often large industries have major conferences that occur at approximately the same time every year. Major companies in the industry often hold back positive announcements and product introductions to be released during the conference.

Two to three months prior to the conference, seasonal investors tend to buy into the sector. Shortly afterwards, the mainstream investors anticipate "good news" from the conference and start to buy in. As a result, prices are pushed up. Just before the conference starts, seasonal investors capture their profits by exiting their positions. As the conference unfolds, company announcements are made (realized), but as the potential good news has already been priced into the sector, there is little to push prices higher and the sector typically starts to rolls over.

The same *Anticipation-Realization Cycle* takes place with increased demand for oil to meet the "summer driving season", increased sales of goods at Christmas time, increased demand for gold jewellery to meet the autumn and winter demand, and many other events that tend to drive the outperformance of different sectors.

Does Seasonal Investing ALWAYS Work?

The simple answer to the above question is "No." There is not any investment system in the world that works all of the time. When following any investment system, it is probability of success that counts. It has often been said that "being correct in the markets 60% of the time will make you rich." Investors tend to forget this and become too emotionally attached to their losses. Just about every investment trading book states that investors typically fail to let their profits run and cut their losses quickly. I concur. In my many years in the investment industry, the biggest mistake that I have found with investors is not being able to cut their losses. Everyone wants to be right, that is how we have been raised. Investors feel that if they sell at a loss they have failed, and as a result, often suffer bigger losses by waiting for their position to trade at profit.

With any investment system, investors should let probability work for them. This means that investors should be able to enter and exit positions capturing both gains and losses without becoming emotionally attached to any positions. Emotional attachment clouds judgement, which leads to errors. When all of the trades are put together, the goal is for profits to be larger than losses in a way that minimizes risks and beats the market.

If we examine the winter oil stock trade, we can see how probability has worked in an investor's favor. This trade is based upon the premise that at the tail end of winter, the refineries drive up demand for oil in order to produce enough gas for the approaching "driving season" that starts in the spring. As a result, oil stocks tend to increase and outperform the market (from February 25th to May 9th). The oil stock sector, represented by the NYSE Arca Oil Index (XOI), has been very successful at this time of year, producing an average return of 7.2% and beating the

XOI vs S&P 500 1984 to 2018			
Feb 25	positive		
to May 9 S&P 500	XOI		Diff
1984	1.7 %	5.6 %	3.9 %
1985	1.4	4.9	3.5
1986	6.0	7.7	1.7
1987	3.7	25.5	21.8
1988	-3.0	5.6	8.6
1989	6.3	8.1	1.8
1990	5.8	-0.6	-6.3
1991	4.8	6.8	2.0
1992	0.9	5.8	4.9
1993	0.3	6.3	6.0
1994	-4.7	3.2	7.9
1995	7.3	10.3	3.1
1996	-2.1	2.2	4.3
1997	1.8	4.7	2.9
1998	7.5	9.8	2.3
1999	7.3	35.4	28.1
2000	4.3	22.2	17.9
2001	0.8	10.2	9.4
2002	-1.5	5.3	6.9
2003	12.1	5.7	-6.4
2004	-3.5	4.0	7.5
2005	-1.8	-1.0	0.8
2006	2.8	9.4	6.6
2007	4.2	10.1	5.8
2008	2.6	7.6	5.0
2009	20.2	15.8	-4.4
2010	0.5	-2.3	-2.8
2011	3.1	-0.6	-3.7
2012	-0.8	-13.4	-12.5
2013	7.3	3.8	-3.5
2014	1.7	9.1	7.4
2015	0.3	1.2	1.1
2016	6.7	11.1	4.4
2017	1.3	-4.0	-5.2
2018	-1.8	15.4	17.2
Avg	3.0 %	7.2 %	4.2 %
Fq > 0	77 %	83 %	77 %

S&P 500 by 4.2%, from 1984 to 2018. In addition it has been positive 29 out of 35 times. Investors should always evaluate the strength of seasonal trades before applying them to their own portfolios.

If an investor started using the seasonal investment discipline in 1984 and chose to invest in the winter-oil trade, they would have been very happy with the results. If an investor started using the strategy in 2010 a loss would have occurred following the strategy. The fact that the strategy did not produce gains in 2010, 2011 and 2012, does not mean that the seasonal trade no longer works. All seasonal trades go through periods, sometimes multiple years where they do not work. An investor can start any methodology of trading at the "wrong time," and be unsuccessful in a particular trade. In fact, if an investor started the oil-winter trade in 1990 and had given up in the same year, they would have missed the following successful twelve years. Investors have to remember that it is the final score that counts, after all of the gains have been weighed against the losses.

In practical terms, investors should not put all of their investment strategies in one basket. If one or two large investments were made based upon seasonal strategies, it is possible that the seasonal methodology might be inappropriately evaluated and its use discontinued. A much more prudent strategy is to use a larger number of strategic seasonal investments with smaller investments. The end result will be to put the seasonal probability to work with a much greater chance of success.

Measuring Seasonal Performance

How do you determine if a seasonal strategy has been successful? Many people feel that ten years of data is a good sample size, others feel that fifteen years is better, and yet others feel that the more data the better. I tend to fall into the camp that, if possible, it is best to use fifteen or twenty years of data for sectors and more data for the broad markets, such as the S&P 500. Although the most recent data in almost any analytical framework is the most relevant, it is important to get enough data to reflect a sector's performance across different economic conditions. Given that historically the economy has performed on an eight year cycle, four years of expansion and then four years of contraction, using a short data set does not provide for enough exposure to different economic conditions.

A data set that is too long can run into the problem of older data having too much of an influence on the numbers when fundamental factors affecting a sector have changed. It is important to look at trends over time and assess if there has been a change that should be considered in determining the dates for a seasonal cycle. Each sector should be judged on its own merit. The analysis tables in this book illustrate the performance level for each year in order to provide the opportunity for readers to determine any relevant changes.

In order to determine if a seasonal strategy is effective there are two possible benchmarks, absolute and relative performance. Absolute performance measures if a profit is made and relative performance measures the performance of a sector in relationship to a major market. Both measurements have their merits and depending on your investment style, one measurement may be more valuable than another. This book provides both sets of measurement in tables and graphs.

It is not just the average percent gain of a sector over a certain time period that determines success. It is possible that one or two spectacular years of performance skew the results substantially (particularly with a small data set). The frequency of success is also very important: the higher the percentage of success the better. Also, the fewer large drawdowns the better. There is no magic number (percent success rate) per se of what constitutes a successful strategy. The success rate should be above fifty percent, otherwise it would be better to just invest in the broad market. Ideally speaking a strategy should have a high percentage success rate on both an absolute and relative basis. Some strategies are stronger than others, but that does not mean that the weaker strategies should not be used. Prudence should be used in determining the ideal portfolio allocation.

Illustrating the strength of a sector's seasonal performance can be accomplished through either an absolute yearly average performance graph, or a relative yearly average performance graph. The absolute graph shows the average yearly cumulative gain for a set number of years. It lets a reader visually identify the strong periods during the year. The relative graph shows the average yearly cumulative gain for the sector relative to the benchmark index.

Both graphs are useful in determining the strength of a particular seasonal strategy. In the above diagram, the top graph illustrates the average year for the NYSE Arca Oil Index (XOI) from 1984 to 2017. Essentially it illustrates the cumulative average gain if an investment were made in the index. The steep rising line starting in January/February shows the overall price rise that typically occurs in this sector at this time of year. In May the line flattens out and then rises very modestly starting in July.

The bottom graph is a ratio graph, illustrating the strength of the XOI Index relative to the S&P 500. It is derived by dividing the average year of the XOI by the average year of the S&P 500. When the line in the graph is rising, the XOI is outperforming the S&P 500, and vise versa when it is declining. This is an important graph and should be used in considering seasonal investments because the S&P 500 is a viable alternative to the energy sector. If both markets are increasing, but the S&P 500 is increasing at a faster rate, the S&P 500 represents a more attractive opportunity. This is particularly true when measuring the risk of a volatile sector relative to the broad market. If both investments were expected to produce the same rate of return, generally the broad market is a better investment because of its diversification.

Who Can Use Seasonal Investing?

Any investor from novice to expert, from short-term trader to long-term investor can benefit from using seasonal analysis. Seasonal investing is unique because it is an easy to understand system that can be used by itself or as a complement to another investment discipline. For the novice it provides an easy to follow strategy that makes intuitive sense. For the expert it can be used as a stand-alone system or as a complement to an existing system.

Seasonal investing is easily understood by all levels of investors, which allows investors to make rational decisions. This may seem obvious, but it is very common for investors to listen to a "guru of the market", be impressed and blindly follow his advice. When the advice works there is no problem. When the advice does not work investors wonder why they made the investment in the first place. When investors do not understand their investments it causes stress, bad decisions and a lack of "stick-to-it ness" with any investment discipline. Even expert investors realize the importance of understanding your investments. Peter Lynch of Fidelity Investments used to say "Never invest in any idea that you can't illustrate with a crayon." Investors do not need to go that far, but they should understand their investments.

Novice investors find seasonal strategies very easy to understand because they are intuitive. They do not have to be investing for years to understand why seasonal strategies work. They understand that an increase in demand for gold every year at the same time causes a ripple effect in the stock market pushing up gold stocks at the same time every year.

Most expert investors use information from a variety of sources in making their decisions. Even experts that primarily use fundamental analysis can benefit from using seasonal trends to get an edge in the market. Fundamental analysis is a very crude tool and provides very little in the way of timing an investment. Using seasonal trends can help with the timing of the buy and sell decisions and produce extra profit.

Seasonal investing can be used by both short-term and long-term investors, but in different ways. For short-term investors it provides a complete trade – buy and sell dates. For long-term investors it can provide a buy date for a sector of interest.

Combining Seasonal Analysis with other Investment Disciplines

Seasonal investing used by itself has historically produced above average market returns. Depending on an investor's particular style, it can be combined with one of the other three investment disciplines: fundamental, quantitative and technical analysis. There are two basic ways to combine seasonal analysis with other investment methodologies – as the primary or secondary method. If it is used as a primary method, seasonally strong time periods are established for a number of sectors and then appropriate sectors are chosen based upon fundamental, quantitative or technical screens. If it is used as a secondary method, sector selections are first made based upon one of three methods and then final sectors are chosen based upon which ones are in their seasonally strong period.

Technical analysis is an ideal mate for seasonal analysis. Unlike fundamental and quantitative analysis, which are very blunt timing tools at best, seasonal and technical analysis can provide specific trigger points to buy and sell. The combination can turbo-charge investment strategies, adding extra profits by fine-tuning entry and exit dates.

Seasonal analysis provides both buy and sell dates. Although a sector in the market can sometimes bottom on the exact seasonal buy date, it more often bottoms a bit early or a bit late. After all, the seasonal buy date is based upon an average of historical performance. Depending on the sector, buying opportunities start to develop approximately one month before and after the seasonal buy date. Using technical analysis gives an investor the advantage of buying into a sector when it turns up early or waiting when it turns up late. Likewise, technical analysis can be used to trigger a sell signal when the market turns down before or after the sell date.

The sell decision can be extended with the help of a trailing stop-loss order. If a sector has strong momentum and the technical tools do not provide a sell signal, it is possible to let the sector "run." When a trailing stop-loss is used, a profitable sell point is established. If the price continues to run, then the selling point is raised. If, on the other hand, the price falls through the stop-loss point, the position is sold.

Sectors of the Market

Standard & Poor's has done an excellent job in categorizing the U.S. stock market into its different parts. Although the demand for this service initially came from institutional investors, many individual investors now seek the same information. Knowing the sector breakdown in the market allows investors to see how different their portfolio is relative to the market. As a result, they are able to make conscious decisions on what parts of the stock market to overweight based upon their beliefs of which sectors will outperform. It also helps control the amount of desired risk.

Standard & Poor's uses four levels of detail in its Global Industry Classification Standard (GICS$^©$) to categorize stock markets around the world. From the most specific, it classifies companies into sub-industries, industries, industry groups and finally economic sectors. All companies in the Standard & Poor's global family of indices are classified according to the GICS structure.

This book focuses on the U.S. market, analysing the trends of the venerable S&P 500 index and its economic sectors and industry groups. The following diagram illustrates the index classified according to its economic sectors.

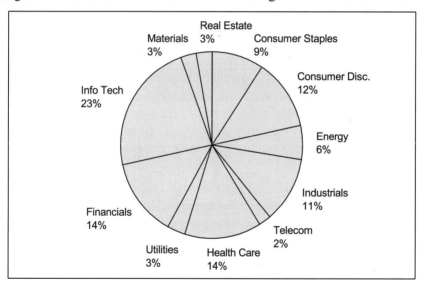

Standard and Poor's, Understanding Sectors, June 30, 2017

For more information on Standard and Poor's Global Industry Classification Standard (GICS$^©$), refer to www.standardandpoors.com

Investment Products –
Which One Is The Right One?

There are many ways to take advantage of the seasonal trends at the broad stock market and sector levels. Regardless of the investment products that you currently use, whether exchange traded funds, mutual funds, stocks or options, all can be used with the strategies in this book. Different investments offer different risk-reward relationships and return potential.

Exchange Traded Funds (ETFs)

Exchange Traded Funds (ETFs) offer the purest method of seasonal investment. The broad market ETFs are designed to track the major indices and the sector ETFs are designed to track specific sectors without using active management. Relatively new, ETFs are a great way to capture both market and sector trends. They were originally introduced into the Canadian market in 1993 to represent the Toronto stock market index. Shortly afterward they were introduced to the U.S. market and there are now hundreds of ETFs to represent almost every market, sector, style of investing and company capitalization. Originally ETFs were mainly of interest to institutional investors, but individual investors have fast realized the merits of ETF investing and have made some of the broad market ETFs the most heavily traded securities in the world.

An ETF is a single security that represents a market, such as the S&P 500; a sector of the market, such as the financial sector; or a commodity, such as gold. In the case of the S&P 500, an investor buying one security is buying all 500 stocks in the index. By investing into a financial ETF, an investor is buying the companies that make up the financial sector of the market. By investing into a gold commodity ETF, an investor is buying a security that represents the price of gold.

ETFs trade on the open market just like stocks. They have a bid and an ask, can be shorted and many are option eligible. They are a very low cost, tax efficient method of targeting specific parts of the market.

Mutual Funds

Mutual funds are a good way to combine market or sector investing with active management. In recent years, many mutual fund companies have added sector funds to accommodate an increasing appetite in this area.

As the seasonal strategies put forward in this book have a short-term nature, it is important to make sure that there are no fees (or a nominal charge) for getting into and out of a position in the market.

Stocks

Stocks provide an opportunity to make better returns than the market or sector. If the market increases during its seasonal period, some stocks will increase dramatically more than the index. Choosing one of the outperforming stocks will greatly enhance returns; choosing one of the underperforming stocks can create substantial loses. Using stocks requires increased attention to diversification and security selection.

Options

Disclaimer: Options involve risk and are not suitable for every investor. Because they are cash-settled, investors should be aware of the special risks associated with index options and should consult a tax advisor. Prior to buying or selling options, a person must receive a copy of Characteristics and Risks of Standardized Options and should thoroughly understand the risks involved in any use of options. Copies may be obtained from The Options Clearing Corporation, 440 S. LaSalle Street, Chicago, IL 60605.

Options, for more sophisticated investors, are a good tool to take advantage of both market and sector opportunities. An option position can be established with either stocks or ETFs. There are many different ways to use options for seasonal trends: establish a long position on the market during its seasonally strong period, establish a short position during its seasonally weak period, or create a spread trade to capture the superior gains of a sector over the market.

THACKRAY'S 2019 INVESTOR'S GUIDE

CONTENTS

JANUARY

	MONDAY	TUESDAY	WEDNESDAY

WEEK 01	31	**1** 30
		
		 CAN Market Closed -
		       New Year's Day
		
		 USA Market Closed -
		       New Year's Day
			2 29

WEEK 02	**7** 24	**8** 23	**9** 22
WEEK 03	**14** 17	**15** 16	**16** 15
WEEK 04	**21** 10 USA Market Closed- Martin Luther King Jr. Day	**22** 9	**23** 8
WEEK 05	**28** 3	**29** 2	**30** 1

THURSDAY		FRIDAY	
3	28	**4**	27
10	21	**11**	20
17	14	**18**	13
24	7	**25**	6
31		1	

FEBRUARY

M	T	W	T	F	S	S
				1	2	3
4	5	6	7	8	9	10
11	12	13	14	15	16	17
18	19	20	21	22	23	24
25	26	27	28			

MARCH

M	T	W	T	F	S	S
				1	2	3
4	5	6	7	8	9	10
11	12	13	14	15	16	17
18	19	20	21	22	23	24
25	26	27	28	29	30	31

APRIL

M	T	W	T	F	S	S
1	2	3	4	5	6	7
8	9	10	11	12	13	14
15	16	17	18	19	20	21
22	23	24	25	26	27	28
29	30					

MAY

M	T	W	T	F	S	S
		1	2	3	4	5
6	7	8	9	10	11	12
13	14	15	16	17	18	19
20	21	22	23	24	25	26
27	28	29	30	31		

JANUARY SUMMARY

S&P500 Cumulative Daily Gains for Avg Month 1950 to 2018

	Dow Jones	S&P 500	Nasdaq	TSX Comp
Month Rank	6	6	1	4
# Up	43	41	29	21
# Down	25	27	17	12
% Pos	63	60	63	64
% Avg. Gain	0.9	0.9	2.4	1.0

Dow & S&P 1950-2017, Nasdaq 1972-2017, TSX 1985-2017

Prob. of Daily Gain

♦ Over the last ten years, the stock market in January has had some large moves up or down on a number of occasions. The S&P 500 has on four occasions either gained or lost more than 5% ♦ In January there is typically a lot of sector rotation. ♦ Small caps tend to perform well. ♦ The technology sector finishes its seasonal period. ♦ The industrials, materials, metals and mining sectors start the second part of their seasonal periods. ♦ The retail sector starts its strongest seasonal period.

BEST / WORST JANUARY BROAD MKTS. 2009-2018

BEST JANUARY MARKETS
- Nasdaq (2012) 8.0%
- Nasdaq (2018) 8.0%
- Nikkei 225 (2013) 7.2%

WORST JANUARY MARKETS
- Russell 2000 (2009) -11.2%
- Nikkei 225 (2009) -9.8%
- Russell 2000 (2016) - 8.8%

Index Values End of Month

	2009	2010	2011	2012	2013	2014	2015	2016	2017	2018
Dow	8,001	10,067	11,892	12,633	13,861	15,699	17,165	16,466	19,864	26,149
S&P 500	826	1,074	1,286	1,312	1,498	1,783	1,995	1,940	2,279	2,824
Nasdaq	1,476	2,147	2,700	2,814	3,142	4,104	4,635	4,614	5,615	7,411
TSX Comp.	8,695	11,094	13,552	12,452	12,685	13,695	14,674	12,822	15,386	15,952
Russell 1000	447	589	713	726	832	996	1,112	1,070	1,265	1,562
Russell 2000	444	602	781	793	902	1,131	1,165	1,035	1,362	1,575
FTSE 100	4,150	5,189	5,863	5,682	6,277	6,510	6,749	6,084	7,099	7,534
Nikkei 225	7,994	10,198	10,238	8,803	11,139	14,915	17,674	17,518	19,041	23,098

Percent Gain for January

	2009	2010	2011	2012	2013	2014	2015	2016	2017	2018
Dow	-8.8	-3.5	2.7	3.4	5.8	-5.3	-3.7	-5.5	0.5	5.8
S&P 500	-8.6	-3.7	2.3	4.4	5.0	-3.6	-3.1	-5.1	1.8	5.6
Nasdaq	-6.4	-5.4	1.8	8.0	4.1	-1.7	-2.1	-7.9	4.3	7.4
TSX Comp.	-3.3	-5.5	0.8	4.2	2.0	0.5	0.3	-1.4	0.6	-1.6
Russell 1000	-8.3	-3.7	2.3	4.8	5.3	-3.3	-2.8	-5.5	1.9	5.4
Russell 2000	-11.2	-3.7	-0.3	7.0	6.2	-2.8	-3.3	-8.8	0.3	2.6
FTSE 100	-6.4	-4.1	-0.6	2.0	6.4	-3.5	2.8	-2.5	-0.6	-2.0
Nikkei 225	-9.8	-3.3	0.1	4.1	7.2	-8.5	1.3	-8.0	-0.4	1.5

January Market Avg. Performance 2009 to 2018[1]

Dow	-0.9%
S&P 500	-0.5%
Nasdaq	0.2%
TSX Comp (CAN)	-0.3%
Russell 1000 (Lg Cap)	-0.4%
Russell 2000 (Sm Cap)	-1.4%
FTSE 100	-0.9%
Nikkei 225	-1.6%

Interest Corner Jan[2]

	Fed Funds %[3]	3 Mo. T-Bill %[4]	10 Yr %[5]	20 Yr %[6]
2018	1.50	1.46	2.72	2.83
2017	0.75	0.52	2.45	2.78
2016	0.50	0.33	1.94	2.36
2015	0.25	0.02	1.68	2.04
2014	0.25	0.02	2.67	3.35

(1) Russell Data provided by Russell (2) Federal Reserve Bank of St. Louis- end of month values (3) Target rate set by FOMC (4)(5)(6) Constant yield maturities.

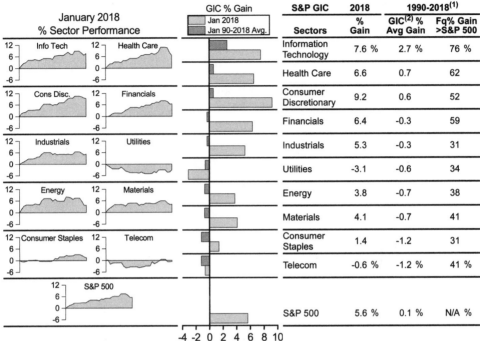

S&P GIC Sectors	2018 % Gain	1990-2018[1] GIC[2] % Avg Gain	Fq% Gain >S&P 500
Information Technology	7.6 %	2.7 %	76 %
Health Care	6.6	0.7	62
Consumer Discretionary	9.2	0.6	52
Financials	6.4	-0.3	59
Industrials	5.3	-0.3	31
Utilities	-3.1	-0.6	34
Energy	3.8	-0.7	38
Materials	4.1	-0.7	41
Consumer Staples	1.4	-1.2	31
Telecom	-0.6 %	-1.2 %	41 %
S&P 500	5.6 %	0.1 %	N/A %

Sector Commentary

♦ In January 2018, the S&P 500 was positive as investors pushed the stock market higher as analysts increased their estimates of corporate earnings based upon the tax reform being implemented. ♦ The cyclical sectors of the stock market were the big winners, with the consumer discretionary sector producing a return of 9.2% and the technology sector producing a return of 7.6%. ♦ Utilities and telecom, both defensive sectors, were the only two major sectors to produce a loss in January. ♦ The consumer staples sector produced a relatively small gain of 1.4%, compared to the S&P 500's gain of 5.6%. ♦ Although the overall performance for the stock market was positive in January, the last few days were negative for most sectors as investors became concerned about market valuations and rising interest rates.

Sub-Sector Commentary

♦ The retail sub-sector produced a large gain of 15.4% as the tax reform was expected to drive consumer spending higher. ♦ The semi-conductor, biotech and banking sub-sectors also produced large gains above 8%. ♦ Investors generally rewarded higher beta sub-sectors.

SELECTED SUB-SECTORS[3]			
SOX (1995-2018)	8.7 %	3.6 %	58 %
Silver	2.2	3.1	69
Home-builders	-3.0	2.5	59
Biotech (1993-2018)	8.8	2.0	58
Gold	4.2	1.8	59
Railroads	1.8	1.1	55
Automotive & Components	-0.1	0.6	48
Steel	5.3	0.4	48
Retail	15.4	0.3	55
Pharma	1.6	-0.1	55
Transportation	2.3	-0.1	48
Banks	8.1	-0.2	48
Agriculture (1994-2018)	7.2	-0.5	40
Chemicals	3.9	-0.7	41
Metals & Mining	5.2	-0.9	41

(1) Sector data provided by Standard and Poors (2) GIC is short form for Global Industry Classification (3) Sub Sector data provided by Standard and Poors, except where marked by symbol.

BARNES & NOBLE— READ YOUR GAINS

Barnes & Noble has had some serious competition from Amazon over the years. Despite Amazon's negative influence on its stock price, Barnes & Noble has displayed fairly consistent seasonality. It tends to be positive from October 28th to November 28th, in the same period as the overall retail sector.

Investors buying Barnes & Noble stock in November, ahead of the busy shopping season, tend to push up the stock price at this time.

Barnes and Noble tends to perform poorly from November 29th to January 30th, as investors anticipate the slow sales early in the upcoming year.

Barnes & Noble tends to perform well from January 31st until March 26th. This period of seasonal strength is similar to the retail period of seasonal strength, which lasts from late January until mid-April.

It is interesting to note that the frequency of positive returns for Barnes & Noble's periods of seasonal strength are not higher than the S&P 500's frequency of positive returns. In other words, when Barnes & Noble outperforms in its seasonal periods, on average the gains are large.

BKS- stock symbol for Barnes & Noble, which trades on the NYSE, adjusted for splits.

Gain % & Fq % Positive BKS vs. S&P 500 1994/95 to 2017/18
Negative Short [ ]   Positive Long [ ]

Year	Jun 4 to Oct 27 S&P 500	BKS	Oct 28 to Nov 28 S&P 500	BKS	Nov 29 to Jan 30 S&P 500	BKS	Jan 31 to Mar 26 S&P 500	BKS	Compound Growth S&P 500	BKS
1994/95	1.2	20.2	-2.5	-1.3	3.2	2.2	6.9	4.8	8.9	-19.3
1995/96	8.9	27.5	4.6	0.7	3.9	-28.1	3.6	32.2	22.6	23.7
1996/97	5.0	-4.2	7.7	-9.5	3.9	-4.4	0.8	21.9	18.4	20.0
1997/98	3.7	18.1	8.9	22.5	2.6	2.6	12.3	23.6	30.2	20.7
1998/99	-1.6	-16.0	11.9	20.7	7.3	8.3	0.3	-12.7	18.5	12.1
1999/00	-0.2	-27.0	9.3	10.2	-4.0	-11.4	12.3	5.1	17.5	63.6
2000/01	-6.6	-16.9	-3.2	54.6	2.8	-10.6	-16.1	1.5	-22.0	102.8
2001/02	-12.4	11.1	2.2	-26.4	-1.3	21.3	2.2	-5.4	-9.7	-51.3
2002/03	-13.7	-26.7	4.6	5.9	-10.0	-26.5	3.0	12.3	-16.4	90.5
2003/04	6.1	24.2	2.6	16.7	6.9	2.0	-2.0	-6.9	14.1	-19.3
2004/05	0.8	8.3	5.1	-19.9	-1.0	19.2	0.0	6.7	4.9	-36.6
2005/06	-1.4	-10.2	6.7	18.0	2.2	4.4	1.4	8.7	8.9	35.1
2006/07	6.9	5.2	0.7	-4.5	3.0	-0.8	0.6	0.4	11.6	-8.3
2007/08	-0.1	-8.3	-4.3	0.2	-7.7	-18.1	-1.1	4.3	-12.7	33.6
2008/09	-38.4	-43.9	5.6	-7.1	-7.9	4.1	0.9	42.8	-39.5	83.2
2009/10	14.1	-33.9	2.6	42.0	-1.6	-28.3	8.6	31.0	25.2	219.5
2010/11	7.2	-19.4	0.6	0.3	7.3	3.5	2.9	-40.6	19.1	-31.2
2011/12	-1.2	-37.5	-7.2	49.9	10.1	-30.9	7.9	21.1	8.9	226.6
2012/13	10.5	-3.3	-0.1	8.1	6.5	-16.7	4.1	21.2	22.4	58.0
2013/14	7.3	-33.8	2.7	12.9	-0.7	-19.0	3.3	50.8	12.9	171.0
2014/15	1.9	11.8	5.4	12.2	-3.5	0.6	3.1	-3.2	6.9	-4.8
2015/16	-2.3	-18.9	1.2	2.3	-7.2	-33.3	4.9	39.6	-3.7	126.2
2016/17	1.6	-10.0	3.2	22.2	3.6	-21.0	2.8	-14.0	11.7	39.8
2017/18	5.8	3.6	1.8	4.1	7.4	-35.8	-5.8	3.1	9.0	40.5
Avg. %	0.1	-7.5	2.9	9.8	1.1	-9.0	2.4	10.3	7.0	49.8
Fq%>0	58	38	79	75	58	42	83	75	75	71

BKS - Avg. Year 1994 to 2017

BKS / S&P 500 Rel. Strength- Avg Yr. 1994-2017

Barnes & Noble Performance

BKS Monthly Performance (1994-2017)

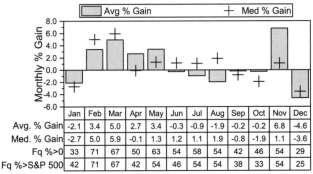

	Jan	Feb	Mar	Apr	May	Jun	Jul	Aug	Sep	Oct	Nov	Dec
Avg. % Gain	-2.1	3.4	5.0	2.7	3.4	-0.3	-0.9	-1.9	-0.2	-0.2	6.8	-4.6
Med. % Gain	-2.7	5.0	5.9	-0.1	1.3	1.2	1.1	1.9	-0.8	-1.9	1.1	-3.6
Fq %>0	33	71	67	50	63	54	58	54	42	46	54	29
Fq %>S&P 500	42	71	67	42	54	46	54	54	38	33	54	25

BKS 5 Year (2013-2017) % Gain

BKS Performance 2017-2018

Relative Strength, % gain vs. S&P 500

Market Indices & Rates
Weekly Values**

Stock Markets	2017	2018
Dow	19,964	25,296
S&P500	2,277	2,743
Nasdaq	5,521	7,137
TSX	15,496	16,349
FTSE	7,210	7,724
DAX	11,599	13,320
Nikkei	19,454	23,715
Hang Seng	22,503	30,815

Commodities	2017	2018
Oil	53.99	61.44
Gold	1175.9	1317.2

Bond Yields	2017	2018
USA 5 Yr Treasury	1.92	2.29
USA 10 Yr T	2.42	2.47
USA 20 Yr T	2.73	2.64
Moody's Aaa	3.91	3.50
Moody's Baa	4.66	4.23
CAN 5 Yr T	1.13	1.97
CAN 10 Yr T	1.73	2.15

Money Market	2017	2018
USA Fed Funds	0.75	1.50
USA 3 Mo T-B	0.53	1.39
CAN tgt overnight rate	0.50	1.00
CAN 3 Mo T-B	0.44	1.07

Foreign Exchange	2017	2018
EUR/USD	1.05	1.20
GBP/USD	1.23	1.36
USD/CAD	1.32	1.24
USD/JPY	117.02	113.05

JANUARY

M	T	W	T	F	S	S
	1	2	3	4	5	6
7	8	9	10	11	12	13
14	15	16	17	18	19	20
21	22	23	24	25	26	27
28	29	30	31			

FEBRUARY

M	T	W	T	F	S	S
					1	2	3
4	5	6	7	8	9	10
11	12	13	14	15	16	17
18	19	20	21	22	23	24
25	26	27	28			

MARCH

M	T	W	T	F	S	S
					1	2	3
4	5	6	7	8	9	10
11	12	13	14	15	16	17
18	19	20	21	22	23	24
25	26	27	28	29	30	31

From 1994 to 2017, the best months on average for Barnes & Noble have been November, February and March. The worst performing periods have been December, January and June through October.

Over the last five years, Barnes & Noble has generally followed its seasonal pattern. The exception has been the stronger than average performance in June.

In late 2017 and early 2018, Barnes & Noble was negative in its weak seasonal period and positive in its strong seasonal period that starts in late January and lasts until March.

AT&T— DON'T HANG UP ON GAINS

①LONG (Sep3-Oct3) ②SHORT (Jan3-Feb23)
③LONG (Nov15-Dec22) ④SHORT(Oct4-Oct25)

AT&T has its origins as a monopoly phone company, but is now the world's largest telecommunications company competing directly with other companies providing similar services.

The seasonal trends for AT&T are similar to the overall telecom industry. AT&T tends to perform poorly from January 3rd to February 23rd. This is the time period when cyclical companies tend to outperform slower growing, higher yielding companies such as AT&T.

From September 3rd to October 3rd, AT&T tends to outperform the S&P 500 as this is the time period when investors look for more stability in their portfolios.

From October 4th to October 25th, AT&T tends to perform poorly as investors transition back into the stock market at this time and tend to seek high growth stocks.

From November 15th to December 22nd, AT&T tends to perform well as investors anticipate an increase in mobile subscriptions coming into the busy holiday season.

T - stock symbol for AT&T which trades on the NYSE, adjusted for splits.

Gain % & Fq % Positive AT&T vs. S&P 500 1990 to 2017
Negative Short ▭ / Positive Long ▭

Year	Jan 3 to Feb 23 S&P 500	AT&T	Sep 3 to Oct 3 S&P 500	AT&T	Oct 4 to Oct 25 S&P 500	AT&T	Nov 15 to Dec 22 S&P 500	AT&T	Compound Growth S&P 500	AT&T
1990	-9.9	-18.2	-3.5	9.4	-0.4	-0.7	3.5	6.8	-10.3	39.1
1991	12.0	-2.5	-2.8	2.7	-0.1	-0.2	-2.6	4.6	6.1	10.3
1992	-1.4	-11.7	-1.8	0.7	0.9	-3.3	4.2	13.8	1.8	32.3
1993	-0.2	0.0	0.0	-3.9	0.6	-3.7	0.4	8.0	0.8	7.6
1994	0.9	-9.6	-2.0	0.9	-0.1	-3.9	-1.4	-2.1	-2.5	12.5
1995	6.0	2.2	3.3	9.5	0.0	3.2	3.9	4.9	13.7	8.7
1996	6.2	-4.1	6.3	6.4	1.2	-0.8	1.8	4.1	16.2	16.2
1997	8.8	7.8	4.0	11.9	-2.4	4.2	2.7	11.5	13.5	10.1
1998	6.5	2.2	1.2	25.0	6.8	-8.7	6.9	10.4	23.1	46.8
1999	3.4	-2.7	-2.8	7.2	0.8	-13.7	2.9	-1.6	4.3	23.1
2000	-7.4	-26.7	-6.2	16.3	-4.3	9.8	-5.6	-20.0	-21.5	6.4
2001	-2.9	-1.3	-5.4	12.9	2.6	-15.8	0.3	5.0	-5.5	38.9
2002	-5.6	-7.7	-10.6	-11.9	9.6	14.5	-0.9	15.6	-8.4	-6.2
2003	-6.7	-28.3	0.8	0.5	-0.1	1.5	4.1	7.8	-2.3	37.0
2004	2.9	-8.2	1.2	0.5	-3.2	-5.1	2.1	-2.7	2.9	11.2
2005	-1.7	-6.3	0.7	0.4	-2.5	-1.1	2.8	2.6	-0.8	10.8
2006	3.2	14.1	1.8	3.0	3.6	5.5	1.3	6.1	10.1	-11.3
2007	2.3	3.5	4.5	5.1	-1.6	-2.2	0.9	5.4	6.1	9.3
2008	-6.5	-14.7	-14.0	-12.8	-20.2	-12.2	-0.2	1.7	-36.0	14.2
2009	-20.2	-22.9	3.1	4.5	5.3	-3.0	2.2	6.3	-11.5	40.6
2010	-1.8	-11.4	5.2	5.2	3.4	-1.6	5.0	2.4	12.1	21.8
2011	4.0	-4.6	-6.4	0.4	11.8	0.9	0.2	1.6	9.0	5.7
2012	8.4	0.7	3.2	4.2	-2.6	-9.6	5.5	-0.3	14.9	13.0
2013	3.6	1.9	2.8	-0.6	4.8	4.6	1.6	-2.5	13.4	-9.3
2014	0.2	-6.2	-1.7	1.5	-0.2	-4.2	1.9	-5.7	0.2	5.9
2015	2.5	-0.1	0.1	-0.6	6.3	3.4	0.8	6.5	10.0	2.4
2016	-6.0	6.8	-0.9	-0.4	-0.8	-10.0	4.5	18.2	-3.5	20.7
2017	5.6	-1.4	2.3	5.3	0.8	-15.2	4.1	15.5	13.4	42.0
Avg. %	0.2	-5.3	-0.6	3.7	0.7	-2.4	1.9	4.4	2.5	16.4
Fq%>0	57	29	54	79	54	32	82	75	64	89

AT&T - Avg. Year 1990 to 2017

AT&T/ S&P 500 Rel. Strength- Avg Yr. 1990-2017

AT&T Performance

AT&T Monthly Performance (1990-2017)

	Jan	Feb	Mar	Apr	May	Jun	Jul	Aug	Sep	Oct	Nov	Dec
Avg. % Gain	-3.0	-1.0	1.8	1.1	0.1	0.9	0.5	-2.3	3.0	1.0	1.2	2.3
Med. % Gain	-2.5	-1.1	2.2	1.3	-0.6	1.1	0.8	-2.3	3.0	1.3	-0.3	2.3
Fq %>0	36	43	61	61	39	68	57	32	71	54	46	61
Fq %>S&P 500	21	36	43	46	36	64	46	39	68	43	43	54

AT&T 5 Year (2013-2017) % Gain

AT&T Performance 2017-2018

Relative Strength, % gain vs. S&P 500

Market Indices & Rates
Weekly Values**

Stock Markets	2017	2018
Dow	19,886	25,803
S&P500	2,275	2,786
Nasdaq	5,574	7,261
TSX	15,497	16,308
FTSE	7,338	7,779
DAX	11,629	13,245
Nikkei	19,287	23,654
Hang Seng	22,937	31,413

Commodities	2017	2018
Oil	52.37	64.30
Gold	1190.4	1326.8

Bond Yields	2017	2018
USA 5 Yr Treasury	1.90	2.35
USA 10 Yr T	2.40	2.55
USA 20 Yr T	2.71	2.71
Moody's Aaa	3.90	3.50
Moody's Baa	4.63	4.43
CAN 5 Yr T	1.13	1.97
CAN 10 Yr T	1.72	2.17

Money Market	2017	2018
USA Fed Funds	0.75	1.50
USA 3 Mo T-B	0.53	1.43
CAN tgt overnight rate	0.50	1.00
CAN 3 Mo T-B	0.45	1.15

Foreign Exchange	2017	2018
EUR/USD	1.06	1.22
GBP/USD	1.22	1.37
USD/CAD	1.31	1.25
USD/JPY	114.49	111.06

JANUARY

M	T	W	T	F	S	S
	1	2	3	4	5	6
7	8	9	10	11	12	13
14	15	16	17	18	19	20
21	22	23	24	25	26	27
28	29	30	31			

FEBRUARY

M	T	W	T	F	S	S
				1	2	3
4	5	6	7	8	9	10
11	12	13	14	15	16	17
18	19	20	21	22	23	24
25	26	27	28			

MARCH

M	T	W	T	F	S	S
				1	2	3
4	5	6	7	8	9	10
11	12	13	14	15	16	17
18	19	20	21	22	23	24
25	26	27	28	29	30	31

From 1990 to 2017, January, February and August were on average the worst performing months of the year for AT&T. September and December the best performing months. Over the last five years, AT&T has generally followed its long-term seasonal pattern.

In 2017, AT&T produced a compound growth rate of 42.0% in its seasonal periods. In 2017 and 2018, four out of five seasonal periods were successful. This compares favorably to the S&P 500 which produced a compound growth rate of 13.4% in the same periods.

SILVER — SHINES IN LATE DECEMBER
December 27- February 22

The seasonal period for silver has been adjusted to focus on the strongest part of the beginning of the year with the best return profile.

Silver is often thought of as the poor man's gold. Silver has a lot of similar properties to gold as it is a store of value and is used for jewelery and industrial purposes.

5.5% gain and
positive 71% of the time

One of the major differences between silver and gold is the proportion of production that is used for industrial purposes. A very small amount of gold is used in industrial products due to its price. In comparison, a large portion of silver's production is used for industrial products because of its relatively low price, giving silver both base metal and precious metal properties.

Silver - Avg. Year 1984 to 2017

Silver / S&P 500 Rel. Str. - Avg Yr. 1984 - 2017

Gold and silver have a high degree of price correlation, with silver typically mirroring the direction of gold's price changes. When gold increases in price, silver typically increases in price and vice versa. Despite this relationship, the seasonal profiles for gold and silver are different because of silver's use in industrial products.

Silver* vs. S&P 500
1983/84 to 2017/18

Dec 27 to Feb 22	S&P 500	Silver	Positive Diff
1983/84	-5.5%	6.6%	12.1%
1984/85	7.7	-6.4	-14.1
1985/86	8.4	1.7	-6.7
1986/87	15.6	2.6	-13.0
1987/88	5.4	-5.1	-10.5
1988/89	4.7	-2.9	-7.6
1989/90	-6.1	-5.6	0.5
1990/91	10.5	-10.4	-21.0
1991/92	1.6	5.2	3.6
1992/93	-1.0	-2.8	-1.8
1993/94	0.9	2.7	1.8
1994/95	5.5	0.1	-5.4
1995/96	7.3	9.2	1.9
1996/97	6.1	8.2	2.1
1997/98	10.4	7.9	-2.5
1998/99	3.7	13.7	9.9
1999/00	-7.3	1.0	8.2
2000/01	-4.7	-3.8	0.9
2001/02	-5.2	-2.1	3.1
2002/03	-4.7	0.5	5.2
2003/04	4.4	15.5	11.1
2004/05	-2.2	9.7	11.8
2005/06	1.9	12.1	10.2
2006/07	2.8	14.0	11.2
2007/08	-9.7	25.0	34.7
2008/09	-11.8	38.8	50.6
2009/10	-1.6	-5.1	-3.4
2010/11	4.7	13.1	8.5
2011/12	7.3	16.6	9.3
2012/13	6.8	-4.6	-11.4
2013/14	-0.3	12.1	12.4
2014/15	1.0	3.6	2.6
2015/16	-5.6	5.6	11.2
2016/17	4.4	14.4	10.0
2017/18	0.9	1.8	0.9
Avg	1.6%	5.5%	3.9%
Fq > 0	63%	71%	69%

Although the period of seasonal strength for silver finishes in late February, under favorable conditions of rising base metal prices, silver can perform well into late March.

Historically, when silver has corrected sharply in December, it has often rallied strongly at the beginning of its seasonal period. This phenomenon has taken place over the last five years.

 Source: Bank of England- London PM represents the close value of silver in afternoon trading in London.

Silver Performance

Silver Monthly Performance (1984-2017)

	Jan	Feb	Mar	Apr	May	Jun	Jul	Aug	Sep	Oct	Nov	Dec
Avg. % Gain	2.6	2.0	2.5	0.1	-0.8	-2.1	1.5	-0.7	1.4	-1.4	0.6	-0.1
Med. % Gain	2.6	0.1	-0.2	-2.1	1.0	-2.9	0.7	-0.7	1.3	-1.0	-1.2	-1.0
Fq %>0	62	53	47	38	53	32	56	44	56	41	38	41
Fq %>S&P 500	62	50	47	35	41	32	62	41	71	29	44	41

Silver 5 Year (2013-2017) % Gain

Silver Performance 2017-2018

Relative Strength, % gain vs. S&P 500

From 1984 to 2017, January and February on average have been strong months of the year for silver. However, only January is a top ranked month on a median basis. The median for February is "flat." In other words, a few large returns have skewed the average upwards in February. Over the same yearly period, the weakest month of the year has been June.

Over the last five years, silver has followed its general seasonal trend, as January and February have been the strongest months for silver. In both 2017 and 2018, silver was positive in its seasonal periods.

WEEK 03

Market Indices & Rates
Weekly Values**

Stock Markets	2017	2018
Dow	19,827	26,072
S&P500	2,271	2,810
Nasdaq	5,555	7,336
TSX	15,548	16,353
FTSE	7,198	7,731
DAX	11,630	13,434
Nikkei	19,138	23,808
Hang Seng	22,886	32,255

Commodities	2017	2018
Oil	52.42	63.37
Gold	1200.6	1335.0

Bond Yields	2016	2017
USA 5 Yr Treasury	1.95	2.45
USA 10 Yr T	2.48	2.64
USA 20 Yr T	2.79	2.78
Moody's Aaa	3.97	3.58
Moody's Baa	4.69	4.28
CAN 5 Yr T	1.13	2.03
CAN 10 Yr T	1.75	2.24

Money Market	2017	2018
USA Fed Funds	0.75	1.50
USA 3 Mo T-B	0.50	1.44
CAN tgt overnight rate	0.50	1.25
CAN 3 Mo T-B	0.44	1.18

Foreign Exchange	2017	2018
EUR/USD	1.07	1.22
GBP/USD	1.24	1.39
USD/CAD	1.33	1.25
USD/JPY	114.62	110.77

JANUARY

M	T	W	T	F	S	S
	1	2	3	4	5	6
7	8	9	10	11	12	13
14	15	16	17	18	19	20
21	22	23	24	25	26	27
28	29	30	31			

FEBRUARY

M	T	W	T	F	S	S
				1	2	3
4	5	6	7	8	9	10
11	12	13	14	15	16	17
18	19	20	21	22	23	24
25	26	27	28			

MARCH

M	T	W	T	F	S	S
				1	2	3
4	5	6	7	8	9	10
11	12	13	14	15	16	17
18	19	20	21	22	23	24
25	26	27	28	29	30	31

TJX TJX COMPANIES INC.
January 22nd to March 30th

TJX is an off-price apparel and home fashion retailer that typically reports its fourth quarter earnings in approximately the third week of February. The company, like the retail sector, benefits from investors expecting positive results from the Christmas season.

In 2018, TJX during its seasonally strong period, outperformed the retail sector and outperformed the S&P 500. Over the long-term, TJX has typically outperformed the retail sector when the sector has been positive, making it an excellent complement to a retail sector investment during retail's strong seasonal period that also starts in January.

TJX's period of seasonal strength is similar to the seasonal period for the retail sector. The best time to invest in TJX has been from January 22nd to March 30th. From 1990 to 2018, investing in this period has produced an average gain of 11.9%, which is substantially better than the average 1.9% performance of the S&P 500. It is also important to note TJX has been positive 76% of the time during this period.

11.9% gain & positive 76% of the time

Equally impressive is the amount of times TJX has produced a large gain, versus a large loss in its seasonal period. In the last twenty-nine years, TJX has only had one loss of 10% or greater. In the same time period, TJX has had thirteen gains of 10% or greater.

Jan 22 to Mar 30	S&P 500	Retail	TJX
1990	0.2%	6.3%	6.7%
1991	13.3	21.7	61.9
1992	-2.3	1.7	17.0
1993	3.8	3.0	21.7
1994	-6.1	-0.1	-2.8
1995	8.1	9.7	-6.9
1996	5.5	19.7	43.6
1997	-1.1	10.4	-0.3
1998	12.6	19.7	25.4
1999	5.3	16.5	18.9
2000	3.2	5.1	35.4
2001	-13.6	1.7	16.4
2002	1.8	4.7	2.9
2003	-2.7	6.6	-6.7
2004	-1.8	5.4	3.5
2005	1.2	-0.6	-1.6
2006	3.1	4.5	3.8
2007	-0.7	-2.7	-10.2
2008	-0.8	1.4	13.1
2009	-6.3	8.1	29.0
2010	5.1	12.5	17.2
2011	3.5	3.5	6.1
2012	7.1	12.9	19.3
2013	5.6	6.2	4.5
2014	0.8	-2.7	-0.2
2015	2.7	12.5	6.8
2016	10.4	10.2	16.0
2017	4.3	5.4	5.7
2018	-6.0	1.6	3.4
Avg	1.9%	7.1%	11.9%
Fq > 0	66%	86%	76%

TJX* vs. Retail vs. S&P 500
1990 to 2018
(Positive)

It is interesting to note that the seasonally strong period for TJX ends before April, one of the strongest months of the year for the stock market. It is possible that by the end of March, after a typically strong run for TJX, the full value of TJX's first quarter earnings report has already been priced into the stock and investors look to other companies in which to invest. This is particularly true if the economy and the stock market are in good shape. On the other hand, in a soft economy, consumers favor off-price apparel companies such as TJX. In this scenario, TJX is more likely to rally past the end of its seasonal period in March, allowing seasonal investors to continue holding TJX until it starts to show signs of weakness.

TJX - Avg. Year 1990 to 2017

TJX / S&P 500 Relative Strength - Avg Yr. 1990 - 2017

ⓘ * TJX - stock symbol for The TJX Companies Inc. which trades on the NYSE, adjusted for stock splits.

TJX Performance

TJX Monthly Performance (1990-2017)

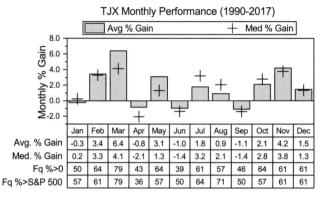

	Jan	Feb	Mar	Apr	May	Jun	Jul	Aug	Sep	Oct	Nov	Dec
Avg. % Gain	-0.3	3.4	6.4	-0.8	3.1	-1.0	1.8	0.9	-1.1	2.1	4.2	1.5
Med. % Gain	0.2	3.3	4.1	-2.1	1.3	-1.4	3.2	2.1	-1.4	2.8	3.8	1.3
Fq %>0	50	64	79	43	64	39	61	57	46	64	61	61
Fq %>S&P 500	57	61	79	36	57	50	64	71	50	57	61	61

TJX 5 Year (2013-2017) % Gain

TJX Performance 2017-2018

Relative Strength, % gain vs. S&P 500

Market Indices & Rates
Weekly Values**

Stock Markets	2017	2018
Dow	20,094	26,617
S&P500	2,295	2,873
Nasdaq	5,661	7,506
TSX	15,576	16,239
FTSE	7,184	7,666
DAX	11,814	13,340
Nikkei	19,467	23,632
Hang Seng	23,361	33,154

Commodities	2017	2018
Oil	53.17	66.14
Gold	1184.9	1353.2

Bond Yields	2016	2017
USA 5 Yr Treasury	1.94	2.47
USA 10 Yr T	2.49	2.66
USA 20 Yr T	2.80	2.79
Moody's Aaa	3.95	3.58
Moody's Baa	4.68	4.26
CAN 5 Yr T	1.14	2.06
CAN 10 Yr T	1.78	2.26

Money Market	2017	2018
USA Fed Funds	0.75	1.50
USA 3 Mo T-B	0.52	1.41
CAN tgt overnight rate	0.50	1.25
CAN 3 Mo T-B	0.45	1.20

Foreign Exchange	2017	2018
EUR/USD	1.07	1.24
GBP/USD	1.26	1.42
USD/CAD	1.32	1.23
USD/JPY	115.10	108.58

JANUARY

M	T	W	T	F	S	S
	1	2	3	4	5	6
7	8	9	10	11	12	13
14	15	16	17	18	19	20
21	22	23	24	25	26	27
28	29	30	31			

FEBRUARY

M	T	W	T	F	S	S
			1	2	3	
4	5	6	7	8	9	10
11	12	13	14	15	16	17
18	19	20	21	22	23	24
25	26	27	28			

MARCH

M	T	W	T	F	S	S
				1	2	3
4	5	6	7	8	9	10
11	12	13	14	15	16	17
18	19	20	21	22	23	24
25	26	27	28	29	30	31

From 1990 to 2017, March has been the best month for TJX on an average, median and frequency basis. March is the core part of the seasonal period for TJX, which lasts from January 22nd to March 30th. The seasonal trade falls off sharply in April and investors should consider exiting early if weakness is evident. Over the last five years, March has been one of the better performing months. TJX performance was also strong in November when other retails stocks on average perform well.

In 2018, TJX performed well in its seasonal period and continued to perform well after its seasonal period ended.

CVX CHEVRON
February 1st to May 5th

Chevron is one of the world's largest integrated energy companies with upstream and downstream operations. The company benefits from the seasonality of the energy sector, which tends to perform better in the time period from late February into early May. This energy seasonal period tends to be driven by the increased demand for oil in late spring, which is driven by the "driving season" that starts in late May on Memorial Day.

7.6% gain & positive 86% of the time

Chevron has a seasonal period that starts earlier than the energy sector, with its period starting February 1st and ending May 5th. In this period, from 1990 to 2018, Chevron produced an average gain of 7.6% and was positive 86% of the time. It outperformed the S&P 500, 66% of the time.

CVX* vs. S&P 500
1990 to 2018

Feb 1 to May 5	S&P 500	CVX	Diff
1990	2.8%	0.4%	-2.5%
1991	10.7	8.4	-2.3
1992	2.0	7.5	5.5
1993	1.3	19.2	17.9
1994	-6.3	-6.8	-0.6
1995	10.6	9.2	-1.3
1996	0.9	9.2	8.3
1997	5.6	5.7	0.0
1998	13.8	15.3	1.5
1999	5.3	34.3	29.0
2000	2.7	8.5	5.8
2001	-7.3	12.1	19.4
2002	-5.0	6.8	11.8
2003	8.3	4.3	-4.0
2004	-0.9	9.3	10.2
2005	-0.7	-2.0	-1.3
2006	3.6	5.0	1.4
2007	4.7	8.8	4.1
2008	2.1	14.9	12.8
2009	9.4	-6.8	-16.2
2010	8.6	11.2	2.6
2011	3.8	8.1	4.3
2012	4.3	0.6	-3.7
2013	7.8	7.2	-0.5
2014	5.7	12.3	6.6
2015	4.7	5.3	0.6
2016	5.7	17.3	11.6
2017	5.3	-5.0	-10.3
2018	-5.7	0.1	5.8
Avg	3.6%	7.6%	4.0%
Fq > 0	79%	86%	66%

CVX - Avg. Year 1990 to 2017

CVX / S&P 500 Relative Strength - Avg Yr. 1990 - 2017

Chevron is an integrated oil company with a diversified portfolio of assets. As a result, it tends to be more secure compared to many highly leveraged exploration and production oil companies.

If the energy sector declines late in a year and into the next year, and then starts to show initial signs of strength, investors are often first attracted to integrated energy companies. Chevron is one of the companies that benefits from early interest in the energy sector.

Chevron also benefits from investors rotating out of higher beta energy companies into more defensive integrated energy companies, which often occurs towards the end of the seasonal period for the energy sector.

Although Chevron has a similar seasonal period as the energy sector, it can provide value at the beginning and end parts of the energy seasonal trade by generally having more stability than most other companies in the energy sector.

CVX- stock symbol for Chevron Corporation, which trades on the NYSE, adjusted for stock splits.

Chevron Performance

CVX Monthly Performance (1990-2017)

	Jan	Feb	Mar	Apr	May	Jun	Jul	Aug	Sep	Oct	Nov	Dec
Avg. % Gain	-2.2	1.2	3.7	2.6	-0.0	-0.2	1.2	-0.5	1.4	0.4	-0.6	2.1
Med. % Gain	-2.3	2.0	2.4	3.1	0.0	0.3	1.4	-0.2	0.9	-0.5	0.1	2.2
Fq %>0	25	68	71	64	50	50	64	50	64	46	50	64
Fq %>S&P 500	36	50	64	71	39	54	61	57	71	39	32	61

CVX 5 Year (2013-2017) % Gain

CVX Performance 2017-2018

Relative Strength, % gain vs. S&P 500

Market Indices & Rates Weekly Values**

Stock Markets	2017	2018
Dow	20,071	25,521
S&P500	2,297	2,762
Nasdaq	5,667	7,241
TSX	15,476	15,606
FTSE	7,188	7,443
DAX	11,651	12,785
Nikkei	18,918	23,275
Hang Seng	23,129	32,602
Commodities	2017	2018
Oil	53.83	65.45
Gold	1215.2	1331.2
Bond Yields	2017	2018
USA 5 Yr Treasury	1.93	2.58
USA 10 Yr T	2.49	2.84
USA 20 Yr T	2.82	2.97
Moody's Aaa	4.04	3.73
Moody's Baa	4.73	4.42
CAN 5 Yr T	1.11	2.14
CAN 10 Yr T	1.77	2.36
Money Market	2017	2018
USA Fed Funds	0.75	1.50
USA 3 Mo T-B	0.51	1.48
CAN tgt overnight rate	0.50	1.25
CAN 3 Mo T-B	0.47	1.20
Foreign Exchange	2017	2018
EUR/USD	1.08	1.25
GBP/USD	1.25	1.41
USD/CAD	1.30	1.24
USD/JPY	112.61	110.17

JANUARY

M	T	W	T	F	S	S
	1	2	3	4	5	6
7	8	9	10	11	12	13
14	15	16	17	18	19	20
21	22	23	24	25	26	27
28	29	30	31			

FEBRUARY

M	T	W	T	F	S	S
					1	2	3
4	5	6	7	8	9	10
11	12	13	14	15	16	17
18	19	20	21	22	23	24
25	26	27	28			

MARCH

M	T	W	T	F	S	S
					1	2	3
4	5	6	7	8	9	10
11	12	13	14	15	16	17
18	19	20	21	22	23	24
25	26	27	28	29	30	31

From 1990 to 2017, February, March and April have been the best three month contiguous period on an average, median and frequency basis. January was the weakest month of the year. With the worst month of the year being juxtaposed with the start of the strong seasonal period in the following month, selecting the best entry point with technical analysis is important. Over the last five years, Chevron has followed its overall seasonal period with the strongest months being February, March and April, and weakest month being January.

In 2017, Chevron was negative in its seasonal period. In 2018, Chevron was positive in its seasonal period.

FEBRUARY

	MONDAY	TUESDAY	WEDNESDAY
WEEK 05	28	29	30
WEEK 06	**4** 24	**5** 23	**6** 22
WEEK 07	**11** 17	**12** 16	**13** 15
WEEK 08	**18** 10 CAN Market Closed - Family Day USA Market Closed - Presidents' Day	**19** 9	**20** 8
WEEK 09	**25** 3	**26** 2	**27** 1

THURSDAY	FRIDAY
31	**1** 27
7 21	**8** 20
14 14	**15** 13
21 7	**22** 6
28	1

MARCH

M	T	W	T	F	S	S
				1	2	3
4	5	6	7	8	9	10
11	12	13	14	15	16	17
18	19	20	21	22	23	24
25	26	27	28	29	30	31

APRIL

M	T	W	T	F	S	S
1	2	3	4	5	6	7
8	9	10	11	12	13	14
15	16	17	18	19	20	21
22	23	24	25	26	27	28
29	30					

MAY

M	T	W	T	F	S	S
		1	2	3	4	5
6	7	8	9	10	11	12
13	14	15	16	17	18	19
20	21	22	23	24	25	26
27	28	29	30	31		

JUNE

M	T	W	T	F	S	S
					1	2
3	4	5	6	7	8	9
10	11	12	13	14	15	16
17	18	19	20	21	22	23
24	25	26	27	28	29	30

FEBRUARY
S U M M A R Y

	Dow Jones	S&P 500	Nasdaq	TSX Comp
Month Rank	8	9	8	5
# Up	40	38	25	21
# Down	28	30	21	12
% Pos	59	56	54	64
% Avg. Gain	0.4	0.1	0.7	1.0

Dow & S&P 1950-2017, Nasdaq 1972-2017, TSX 1985-2017

S&P500 Cumulative Daily Gains for Avg Month 1950 to 2018

♦ Historically, over the long-term, February has been one of the weaker months of the year for the S&P 500. After positive returns for eight consecutive years, the S&P 500 returned to its seasonal trend of a weak February in 2018. ♦ Small caps tend to outperform in February. ♦ The energy sector typically starts to outperform in late February, which helps to boost the S&P/ TSX Composite. ♦ The consumer discretionary sector tends to be one of the better performing sectors.

BEST / WORST FEBRUARY BROAD MKTS. 2009-2018

BEST FEBRUARY MARKETS
♦ Nikkei 225 (2012) 10.5%
♦ Nasdaq (2015) 7.1%
♦ Nikkei (2015) 6.4%

WORST FEBRUARY MARKETS
♦ Russell 2000 (2009) -12.3%
♦ Dow (2009) -11.7%
♦ S&P 500 (2009) -11.0%

Index Values End of Month

	2009	2010	2011	2012	2013	2014	2015	2016	2017	2018
Dow	7,063	10,325	12,226	12,952	14,054	16,322	18,133	16,517	20,812	25,029
S&P 500	735	1,104	1,327	1,366	1,515	1,859	2,105	1,932	2,364	2,714
Nasdaq	1,378	2,238	2,782	2,967	3,160	4,308	4,964	4,558	5,825	7,273
TSX Comp.	8,123	11,630	14,137	12,644	12,822	14,210	15,234	12,860	15,399	15,443
Russell 1000	400	607	736	756	841	1,041	1,173	1,067	1,311	1,501
Russell 2000	389	629	823	811	911	1,183	1,233	1,034	1,387	1,512
FTSE 100	3,830	5,355	5,994	5,872	6,361	6,810	6,947	6,097	7,263	7,232
Nikkei 225	7,568	10,126	10,624	9,723	11,559	14,841	18,798	16,027	19,119	22,068

Percent Gain for February

	2009	2010	2011	2012	2013	2014	2015	2016	2017	2018
Dow	-11.7	2.6	2.8	2.5	1.4	4.0	5.6	0.3	4.8	-4.3
S&P 500	-11.0	2.9	3.2	4.1	1.1	4.3	5.5	-0.4	3.7	-3.9
Nasdaq	-6.7	4.2	3.0	5.4	0.6	5.0	7.1	-1.2	3.8	-1.9
TSX Comp.	-6.6	4.8	4.3	1.5	1.1	3.8	3.8	0.3	0.1	-3.2
Russell 1000	-10.7	3.1	3.3	4.1	1.1	4.5	5.5	-0.3	3.6	-3.9
Russell 2000	-12.3	4.4	5.4	2.3	1.0	4.6	5.8	-0.1	1.8	-4.0
FTSE 100	-7.7	3.2	2.2	3.3	1.3	4.6	2.9	0.2	2.3	-4.0
Nikkei 225	-5.3	-0.7	3.8	10.5	3.8	-0.5	6.4	-8.5	0.4	-4.5

February Market Avg. Performance 2009 to 2018[1]

Dow	0.8%
S&P 500	0.9%
Nasdaq	1.9%
TSX Comp (CAN)	1.0%
Russell 1000 (Lg Cap)	1.0%
Russell 2000 (Sm Cap)	0.9%
FTSE 100	0.8%
Nikkei 225	0.5%

Interest Corner Feb[2]

	Fed Funds % [3]	3 Mo. T-Bill % [4]	10 Yr % [5]	20 Yr % [6]
2018	1.50	1.65	2.87	3.02
2017	0.75	0.53	2.36	2.70
2016	0.50	0.33	1.74	2.19
2015	0.25	0.02	2.00	2.38
2014	0.25	0.05	2.66	3.31

(1) Russell Data provided by Russell (2) Federal Reserve Bank of St. Louis- end of month values (3) Target rate set by FOMC (4)(5)(6) Constant yield maturities.

S&P GIC	2018	1990-2018[1]	
Sectors	% Gain	GIC[2] % Avg Gain	Fq% Gain >S&P 500
Materials	-5.5 %	1.4 %	59 %
Consumer Discretionary	-3.6	1.1	72
Energy	-11.3	0.8	45
Consumer Staples	-7.8	0.8	48
Industrials	-4.3	0.5	48
Information Technology	-0.1	0.3	55
Financials	-3.0	0.1	66
Health Care	-4.6	-0.4	38
Utilities	-4.4	-1.0	28
Telecom	-7.1 %	-1.0 %	38 %
S&P 500	-3.9 %	0.2 %	N/A %

Sector Commentary

♦ In February 2018, all of the major sectors of the stock market were negative as the stock market corrected sharply. ♦ Investors had become nervous that stock market valuations had become too rich and that rising interest rates were going to take their toll on the economy and stock market. ♦ The sector results for the month do not truly indicate the volatility for the month as the S&P 500 bottomed in early February. ♦ The technology sector fell sharply at the beginning of February and then rallied sharply later in the month. Overall, the sector ended with a nominal loss of 0.1%. ♦ The energy sector produced a large loss of 11.3%, setting itself up well for the core of its strong seasonal period in March and April.

Sub-Sector Commentary

♦ In February 2018, the Homebuilders sector corrected sharply on fears of an economic slowdown, producing a loss of 12.3%. ♦ Likewise, the automotive and transportation sectors both produced a loss of 6.4%.

SELECTED SUB-SECTORS[3]			
SOX (1995-2018)	0.0 %	2.8 %	63 %
Silver	-4.6	2.5	52
Retail	-0.9	1.9	72
Metals & Mining	-4.3	1.7	52
Chemicals	-5.6	1.6	69
Gold	-2.0	1.2	48
Steel	-2.3	0.8	55
Agriculture (1994-2018)	-3.3	0.7	52
Automotive & Components	-6.4	0.5	45
Transportation	-6.4	0.5	52
Railroads	-4.6	0.4	45
Banks	-2.9	0.2	59
Homebuilders	-12.3	0.0	59
Pharma	-4.5	-0.4	38
Biotech (1993-2018)	-4.5	-0.9	50

RETAIL – POST HOLIDAY BARGAIN
SHOP Jan 21st and RETURN Your Investment Apr 12th

Historically, the retail sector has outperformed from January 21st until April 12th. From 1990 to 2018, during its seasonally strong period, the retail sector produced an average gain of 8.1%, compared with the S&P 500's average gain of 2.4%. Not only has the retail sector had greater gains than the broad market, but it has also outperformed it on a fairly regular basis: 79% of the time.

5.8% extra & 79% of the time better than the S&P 500

Jan 21 to Apr 12	S&P 500	Positive Retail	Diff
1990	1.5 %	9.7 %	8.1 %
1991	14.5	29.9	15.4
1992	-2.9	-2.7	0.2
1993	3.5	-0.6	-4.0
1994	-5.8	2.0	7.8
1995	9.1	7.4	-1.8
1996	4.1	19.7	15.7
1997	-5.0	6.0	11.0
1998	13.5	20.1	6.6
1999	8.1	23.4	15.2
2000	1.5	5.8	4.3
2001	-11.8	-0.5	11.3
2002	-1.5	6.7	8.2
2003	-3.7	6.5	10.3
2004	0.6	6.7	6.1
2005	1.1	-1.6	-2.7
2006	2.1	3.4	1.3
2007	1.2	-0.7	-1.9
2008	0.6	3.5	3.0
2009	6.4	25.1	18.7
2010	5.1	15.5	10.4
2011	2.7	4.4	1.7
2012	5.5	12.1	6.6
2013	6.9	10.1	3.2
2014	-1.3	-7.1	-5.8
2015	3.9	15.5	11.5
2016	10.9	9.7	-1.2
2017	3.2	4.6	1.4
2018	-5.2	1.6	6.8
Avg.	2.4 %	8.1 %	5.8 %
Fq > 0	72 %	79 %	79 %

Retail Sector vs. S&P 500 1990 to 2018

Retail Sector - Avg. Year 1990 to 2017

Retail / S&P 500 Relative Strength - Avg Yr. 1990 - 2017

Most investors think that the best time to invest in retail stocks is before Black Friday in November. Yes, there is a positive seasonal cycle at this time, but it is not as strong as the cycle from January to April.

The worst month for retail sales is January. Consumers are all shopped out from the holiday season. Investors start becoming attracted to the sector as the prospect of increasing spring sales unfolds. Seasonal investors enter the sector in late January, in order to take advantage of the increasing interest in the sector by other investors that takes place over the next two to three months.

The January retail bounce coincides with the "rosy" stock market analysts' forecasts that tend to occur at the beginning of the year. These forecasts generally rely on healthy consumer spending which makes up approximately 2/3 of the GDP. The retail sector benefits from the optimistic forecasts and tends to outperform the S&P 500.

From a seasonal basis, investors have been best served by exiting the retail sector in April and then returning to it later, at the end of October (see *Retail Shop Early* strategy).

 Retail SP GIC Sector # 2550: An index designed to represent a cross section of retail companies For more information on the retail sector, see www.standardandpoors.com.

Retail Performance

Retail Monthly Performance (1990-2017)

	Jan	Feb	Mar	Apr	May	Jun	Jul	Aug	Sep	Oct	Nov	Dec
Avg. % Gain	-0.2	2.0	3.4	0.8	1.7	-0.6	1.2	-0.6	-0.4	2.0	3.4	0.9
Med. % Gain	0.1	2.0	1.8	0.7	1.8	-0.5	1.3	-0.5	0.2	2.2	3.9	0.0
Fq %>0	50	68	75	61	64	43	61	50	50	68	82	50
Fq %>S&P 500	54	71	75	46	57	54	61	57	50	57	68	36

Retail 5 Year (2013-2017) % Gain

Retail Performance 2017-2018

Relative Strength, % gain vs. S&P 500

WEEK 06

Market Indices & Rates
Weekly Values**

Stock Markets	2017	2018
Dow	20,269	24,191
S&P500	2,316	2,620
Nasdaq	5,734	6,874
TSX	15,729	15,035
FTSE	7,259	7,092
DAX	11,667	12,107
Nikkei	19,379	21,383
Hang Seng	23,575	29,507

Commodities	2017	2018
Oil	53.86	59.20
Gold	1228.3	1314.1

Bond Yields	2017	2018
USA 5 Yr Treasury	1.89	2.52
USA 10 Yr T	2.41	2.83
USA 20 Yr T	2.75	3.02
Moody's Aaa	3.97	3.82
Moody's Baa	4.64	4.50
CAN 5 Yr T	1.09	2.08
CAN 10 Yr T	1.70	2.35

Money Market	2017	2018
USA Fed Funds	0.75	1.50
USA 3 Mo T-B	0.55	1.55
CAN tgt overnight rate	0.50	1.25
CAN 3 Mo T-B	0.46	1.17

Foreign Exchange	2017	2018
EUR/USD	1.06	1.23
GBP/USD	1.25	1.38
USD/CAD	1.31	1.26
USD/JPY	113.22	108.80

FEBRUARY

M	T	W	T	F	S	S
				1	2	3
4	5	6	7	8	9	10
11	12	13	14	15	16	17
18	19	20	21	22	23	24
25	26	27	28			

MARCH

M	T	W	T	F	S	S
				1	2	3
4	5	6	7	8	9	10
11	12	13	14	15	16	17
18	19	20	21	22	23	24
25	26	27	28	29	30	31

APRIL

M	T	W	T	F	S	S
1	2	3	4	5	6	7
8	9	10	11	12	13	14
15	16	17	18	19	20	21
22	23	24	25	26	27	28
29	30					

From 1990 to 2017, the two best months of the year on an average basis for the retail sector were March and November. November is the core part of the autumn retail seasonal trade and March is the core part of the spring retail seasonal trade. On average, over the last five years, the retail sector has followed its seasonal pattern as February, March, October and November have been strong months. These months are part of the spring seasonal trade or the autumn seasonal trade. July has been an exception to the seasonal trend as it has been a strong month outside of retail's strong seasonal periods. In 2018, the retail sector outperformed the S&P 500 in its spring seasonal period.

EASTMAN CHEMICAL COMPANY

EMN

①LONG (Jan28-May5)
②SELL SHORT (May30-Oct27)

In its positive seasonal period from January 28th to May 5th, Eastman Chemical during the period from 1994 to 2017, has produced an average 13.1% gain and has been positive 88% of the time.

In its short sell seasonal period from May 30th to October 27th, in the same yearly period, Eastman Chemical has produced an average loss of 5.4% and has been positive 38% of the time.

The short sell seasonal period has not been as successful as the long seasonal period, especially in recent years. Nevertheless, investors should still be aware of the weaker period for Eastman Chemical in the summer months.

19.3% growth & positive 71% of the time

Eastman Chemical, in its 10-K report filed with regulators in 2013, outlines the seasonal trends in its business. "The Company's earnings are typically greater in second and third quarters." This is a bit different than many other cyclical companies, that tend to have weaker earnings over the summer months.

The net result is for Eastman Chemical to outperform into May and then underperform at the tail end of Q2, and Q3, as investors anticipate a weaker Q4 earnings report. In Q4, Eastman tends to perform at market.

ⓘ *Eastman Chemical Company manufactures and sells chemicals, fibers, and plastics, globally. Its stock symbol is EMN. which trades on the NYSE, adjusted for splits.*

Eastman Chemical* vs. S&P 500 1994 to 2017

Positive Long [ ]   Negative Short [ ]

Year	Jan 28 to May 5 S&P 500	Jan 28 to May 5 EMN	May 30 to Oct 27 S&P 500	May 30 to Oct 27 EMN	Compound Growth S&P 500	Compound Growth EMN
1994	-5.4	7.8 %	1.9 %	8.7 %	-3.6 %	-1.6 %
1995	10.6	11.0	10.7	2.6	22.4	8.2
1996	3.2	7.1	4.9	-21.8	8.3	30.5
1997	8.5	-1.1	3.9	2.7	12.8	-3.8
1998	15.1	18.7	-2.3	-15.3	12.4	36.8
1999	8.4	32.1	-0.4	-24.5	8.0	64.4
2000	2.4	21.9	0.1	-19.3	2.6	45.3
2001	-6.5	22.7	-12.9	-33.1	-18.6	63.2
2002	-5.3	13.1	-15.9	-21.2	-20.4	37.0
2003	9.3	-11.4	8.6	-0.6	18.7	-10.9
2004	-2.0	16.4	0.4	-1.9	-1.6	18.6
2005	-0.2	10.5	-1.7	-15.7	-1.8	27.9
2006	3.3	17.3	7.6	5.5	11.1	10.9
2007	5.9	11.8	1.1	-0.1	7.1	11.9
2008	5.8	14.9	-39.3	-55.6	-35.8	78.8
2009	6.9	52.4	15.7	34.3	23.6	0.2
2010	6.2	12.4	8.5	33.0	15.3	-24.7
2011	2.7	9.2	-3.5	-23.1	-0.8	34.5
2012	4.0	0.6	6.0	21.6	10.2	-21.1
2013	7.4	-5.6	6.8	8.4	14.7	-13.5
2014	5.8	15.5	2.2	-15.6	8.1	33.4
2015	3.0	13.1	-2.0	-6.0	0.9	19.9
2016	8.9	21.5	1.6	-8.8	10.7	32.1
2017	4.6	2.5	6.8	16.4	11.7	-14.3
Avg.	4.3 %	13.1 %	0.4 %	-5.4 %	4.8 %	19.3 %
Fq>0	79 %	88 %	67 %	38 %	71 %	71 %

Eastman - Avg. Year 1994 to 2017

Eastman / S&P 500 Rel. Strength- Avg Yr. 1994-2017

Eastman Chemical Performance

EMN Monthly Performance (1994-2017)

	Jan	Feb	Mar	Apr	May	Jun	Jul	Aug	Sep	Oct	Nov	Dec
Avg. % Gain	-1.5	3.2	2.5	6.5	0.9	-2.1	0.5	-1.8	-2.1	1.4	2.3	0.7
Med. % Gain	-2.3	4.9	0.7	5.2	1.0	-2.6	-2.6	-0.3	-0.6	-0.2	1.5	0.0
Fq %>0	33	75	58	71	58	29	38	50	42	46	71	50
Fq %>S&P 500	29	67	58	67	46	29	46	54	33	42	63	42

EMN 5 Year (2013-2017) % Gain

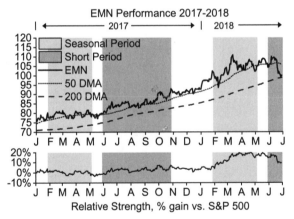

EMN Performance 2017-2018

Relative Strength, % gain vs. S&P 500

Market Indices & Rates
Weekly Values**

Stock Markets	2017	2018
Dow	20,624	25,219
S&P500	2,351	2,732
Nasdaq	5,839	7,239
TSX	15,839	15,453
FTSE	7,300	7,295
DAX	11,757	12,452
Nikkei	19,235	21,720
Hang Seng	24,034	31,115

Commodities	2017	2018
Oil	53.40	61.68
Gold	1242.0	1352.1

Bond Yields	2017	2018
USA 5 Yr Treasury	1.92	2.63
USA 10 Yr T	2.42	2.87
USA 20 Yr T	2.78	3.02
Moody's Aaa	3.95	3.87
Moody's Baa	4.63	4.53
CAN 5 Yr T	1.17	2.12
CAN 10 Yr T	1.71	2.32

Money Market	2017	2018
USA Fed Funds	0.75	1.50
USA 3 Mo T-B	0.53	1.62
CAN tgt overnight rate	0.50	1.25
CAN 3 Mo T-B	0.48	1.13

Foreign Exchange	2017	2018
EUR/USD	1.06	1.24
GBP/USD	1.24	1.40
USD/CAD	1.31	1.26
USD/JPY	112.84	106.21

FEBRUARY

M	T	W	T	F	S	S
			1	2	3	
4	5	6	7	8	9	10
11	12	13	14	15	16	17
18	19	20	21	22	23	24
25	26	27	28			

MARCH

M	T	W	T	F	S	S
			1	2	3	
4	5	6	7	8	9	10
11	12	13	14	15	16	17
18	19	20	21	22	23	24
25	26	27	28	29	30	31

APRIL

M	T	W	T	F	S	S
1	2	3	4	5	6	7
8	9	10	11	12	13	14
15	16	17	18	19	20	21
22	23	24	25	26	27	28
29	30					

From 1994 to 2017, two of the best performing months for Eastman Chemical have been February and April on an average, median and frequency basis. These months are the cornerstones of the long seasonal trade. On a median basis, the worst performing contiguous months were June through October, as all five months had negative medians. These months make up the bulk of the ideal time to short Eastman Chemical.

Over the last five years, Eastman Chemical has performed well in its seasonally strong period. In 2017 and 2018, both the long and short sell seasonal trades did not outperform the S&P 500.

AUTOMOTIVE & COMPONENTS
①LONG (Dec14-Jan7) ②LONG (Feb24-Apr24)
③SELL SHORT (Aug3-Oct3)

The automotive and components sector (auto sector) has its main seasonal period from February 24th to April 24. In this time period, from 1990 to 2017, the sector has produced an average gain of 7.7% and has been positive 71% of the time.

From 1989/90 to 2016/17, the total seasonal strategy of investing in the auto sector on December 14th, exiting on January 7th, reinvesting on February 24th, exiting on April 24th and shorting the sector from August 3rd to October 3rd, has produced an average gain of 18.5%.

18.5% gain & positive 75% of the time

The auto sector tends to rise in the spring, as investors look to benefit from being in this sector ahead of the peak in auto sales in May.

After the peak, auto sales generally decline from May until November (1975-2013, source: BEA). As a result, shorting the sector from August 3rd to October 3rd has proven to be profitable. The trend changes as auto sales increase in December, creating a positive seasonal period from December 14th to January 7th.

The SP GICS Automotive and Components Sector encompasses a wide range of automotive based companies. For more information, see www.standardandpoors.com

Automotive & Components* vs. S&P 500 1989/90 to 2016/17
Negative Short ☐   Positive Long ▨

Year	Dec 14 to Jan 7 S&P 500	Auto	Feb 24 to Apr 24 S&P 500	Auto	Aug 3 to Oct 3 S&P 500	Auto	Compound Growth S&P 500	Auto
1989/90	-0.2 %	-0.8 %	1.9 %	4.4 %	-11.4 %	-19.3 %	-9.8 %	23.6 %
1990/91	-4.2	-4.0	4.7	6.9	-0.7	-6.3	-0.4	9.1
1991/92	8.6	15.7	-0.6	9.1	-3.2	-16.4	4.4	46.8
1992/93	-0.7	3.6	0.5	11.2	2.5	-1.8	2.3	17.3
1993/94	0.9	1.5	-4.9	-11.1	0.3	-9.5	-3.8	-1.2
1994/95	2.3	10.9	5.3	2.7	4.2	-0.5	12.3	14.4
1995/96	-0.8	1.1	-1.4	11.4	4.6	-2.1	2.3	15.0
1996/97	3.4	4.3	-3.8	-4.0	1.9	6.9	1.3	-6.7
1997/98	1.1	0.1	6.7	10.4	-10.5	-23.0	-3.5	35.9
1998/99	8.9	10.0	6.7	5.8	-3.4	-2.8	12.2	19.5
1999/00	1.9	8.5	5.1	22.9	-0.9	1.8	6.1	31.0
2000/01	-4.5	8.7	-2.9	4.0	-12.2	-27.9	-18.6	44.7
2001/02	4.1	4.6	0.3	12.2	-5.2	-12.1	-1.1	31.6
2002/03	3.8	5.2	7.5	10.1	5.1	7.2	17.2	7.5
2003/04	4.9	12.8	0.0	7.0	2.3	-2.8	7.2	24.0
2004/05	-1.0	0.7	-3.3	-22.4	-1.4	-10.5	-5.6	-13.6
2005/06	1.4	0.8	1.6	-0.8	4.4	7.9	7.6	-7.9
2006/07	-0.3	5.1	2.0	-2.5	4.6	2.0	6.4	0.4
2007/08	-4.9	-9.6	2.6	6.1	-12.8	-15.1	-14.8	10.4
2008/09	3.1	1.0	16.5	102.4	3.8	-11.4	24.7	127.8
2009/10	3.2	16.3	11.2	21.3	1.8	-3.1	16.8	45.4
2010/11	2.5	9.8	2.3	2.7	-12.4	-24.0	-8.1	39.8
2011/12	4.3	10.3	0.6	-5.8	6.3	10.8	11.5	-7.3
2012/13	3.0	13.6	4.2	6.9	-1.8	-0.3	5.3	21.8
2013/14	3.5	-1.4	2.3	1.0	2.2	-6.8	8.3	6.3
2014/15	1.2	3.5	0.4	-1.7	-7.3	-4.2	-5.8	5.9
2015/16	-3.4	-9.5	8.9	12.6	0.2	3.9	5.3	-2.0
2016/17	0.2	-1.9	0.4	-5.8	2.3	15.0	3.0	-21.5
Avg.	1.5 %	4.3 %	2.7 %	7.7 %	-1.3 %	-5.1 %	3.0 %	18.5 %
Fq>0	68 %	79 %	75	71 %	54 %	29 %	64 %	75 %

Automotive Sector - Avg. Year 1990-2017

Automotive / S&P 500 Rel. Strength- Avg Yr. 1990-2017

- 23 -

Automotive Performance

Auto Monthly Performance (1990-2017)

	Jan	Feb	Mar	Apr	May	Jun	Jul	Aug	Sep	Oct	Nov	Dec
Avg. % Gain	0.6	0.8	1.5	5.6	0.2	-1.7	1.4	-3.2	-2.1	0.7	1.7	1.1
Med. % Gain	2.0	-0.2	0.7	1.7	-0.2	-0.2	0.7	-1.7	-1.5	1.9	2.7	1.4
Fq %>0	57	43	54	64	50	50	57	39	32	57	64	57
Fq %>S&P 500	50	46	54	50	25	46	50	36	39	43	54	36

Auto 5 Year (2013-2017) % Gain

Auto Performance 2017-2018

Relative Strength, % gain vs. S&P 500

Market Indices & Rates
Weekly Values**

Stock Markets	2017	2018
Dow	20,822	25,310
S&P500	2,367	2,747
Nasdaq	5,845	7,337
TSX	15,533	15,638
FTSE	7,244	7,244
DAX	11,804	12,484
Nikkei	19,284	21,893
Hang Seng	23,966	31,267

Commodities	2017	2018
Oil	53.49	63.48
Gold	1253.7	1328.0

Bond Yields	2017	2018
USA 5 Yr Treasury	1.80	2.62
USA 10 Yr T	2.31	2.88
USA 20 Yr T	2.69	3.04
Moody's Aaa	3.85	3.89
Moody's Baa	4.54	4.56
CAN 5 Yr T	1.09	2.05
CAN 10 Yr T	1.61	2.25

Money Market	2017	2018
USA Fed Funds	0.75	1.50
USA 3 Mo T-B	0.52	1.64
CAN tgt overnight rate	0.50	1.25
CAN 3 Mo T-B	0.48	1.15

Foreign Exchange	2017	2018
EUR/USD	1.06	1.23
GBP/USD	1.25	1.40
USD/CAD	1.31	1.26
USD/JPY	112.12	106.89

FEBRUARY

M	T	W	T	F	S	S
				1	2	3
4	5	6	7	8	9	10
11	12	13	14	15	16	17
18	19	20	21	22	23	24
25	26	27	28			

MARCH

M	T	W	T	F	S	S
				1	2	3
4	5	6	7	8	9	10
11	12	13	14	15	16	17
18	19	20	21	22	23	24
25	26	27	28	29	30	31

APRIL

M	T	W	T	F	S	S
1	2	3	4	5	6	7
8	9	10	11	12	13	14
15	16	17	18	19	20	21
22	23	24	25	26	27	28
29	30					

From 1990 to 2017, April has been the best month of the year for the auto sector on an average basis. April is the core of the spring seasonal strategy.

Over the last five years, the auto sector has generally followed its seasonal trend of weakness in the summer months and strength in the autumn months. October has been uncharacteristically strong, and January has been uncharacteristically weak. In 2017 and 2018, the combination of long and short trades produced a loss and underperformed the S&P 500.

OIL STOCKS – WINTER/SPRING STRATEGY
February 25th to May 9th

(Stocks)

The *Energy- Winter/Spring Strategy* is a strong seasonal performer over the long-term. From 1984 to 2018, for the two and half months starting on February 25th and ending May 9th, the energy sector (XOI) has outperformed the S&P 500 by an average 4.2%.

What is even more impressive are the positive returns, 29 out of 35 times, and the outperformance of the S&P 500, 77% of the time.

4.2% extra and 77% of the time better than the S&P 500, in just over two months

Oil Sector (XOI) - Avg. Year 1984 to 2017

XOI / S&P 500 Relative Strength - Avg Yr. 1984 - 2017

Feb 25 to May 9	S&P 500	positive XOI	Diff
1984	1.7 %	5.6 %	3.9 %
1985	1.4	4.9	3.5
1986	6.0	7.7	1.7
1987	3.7	25.5	21.8
1988	-3.0	5.6	8.6
1989	6.3	8.1	1.8
1990	5.8	-0.6	-6.3
1991	4.8	6.8	2.0
1992	0.9	5.8	4.9
1993	0.3	6.3	6.0
1994	-4.7	3.2	7.9
1995	7.3	10.3	3.1
1996	-2.1	2.2	4.3
1997	1.8	4.7	2.9
1998	7.5	9.8	2.3
1999	7.3	35.4	28.1
2000	4.3	22.2	17.9
2001	0.8	10.2	9.4
2002	-1.5	5.3	6.9
2003	12.1	5.7	-6.4
2004	-3.5	4.0	7.5
2005	-1.8	-1.0	0.8
2006	2.8	9.4	6.6
2007	4.2	10.1	5.8
2008	2.6	7.6	5.0
2009	20.2	15.8	-4.4
2010	0.5	-2.3	-2.8
2011	3.1	-0.6	-3.7
2012	-0.8	-13.4	-12.5
2013	7.3	3.8	-3.5
2014	1.7	9.1	7.4
2015	0.3	1.2	1.1
2016	6.7	11.1	4.4
2017	1.3	-4.0	-5.2
2018	-1.8	15.4	17.2
Avg	3.0 %	7.2 %	4.2 %
Fq > 0	77 %	83 %	77 %

XOI* vs S&P 500 1984 to 2018

A lot of investors assume that the time to buy oil stocks is just before the cold winter sets in. The rationale is that oil will climb in price as the temperature drops.

The results in the market have not supported this assumption. The price for a barrel of oil has more to do with oil inventory. Refineries have a choice: they can produce either gasoline or heating oil. As the winter progresses, refineries start to convert their operations from heating oil to gasoline.

In late winter and early spring, as refineries start coming off their conversion and winter maintenance programs, they increase their demand for oil, putting upward pressure on its price. In addition, later in the spring, in April and early May, investors increase their holdings in the oil sector before the driving season kicks off (Memorial Day in May), helping to drive up the price of oil stocks.

ⓘ *NYSE Arca Oil Index (XOI):* *An index designed to represent a cross section of widely held oil corporations involved in various phases of the oil industry.*

For more information on the XOI index, see www.cboe.com

NYSE Arca Oil Index (XOI) Performance

XOI Monthly Performance (1984-2017)

	Jan	Feb	Mar	Apr	May	Jun	Jul	Aug	Sep	Oct	Nov	Dec
Avg. % Gain	0.5	0.7	2.9	3.0	0.5	-0.8	0.4	0.6	0.1	0.3	-0.3	1.9
Med. % Gain	0.1	1.0	2.5	2.4	0.5	-1.6	1.7	0.4	0.5	0.5	0.9	1.1
Fq %>0	47	53	71	79	59	38	56	56	53	50	56	65
Fq %>S&P 500	32	53	65	62	38	35	50	62	59	50	35	56

XOI 5 Year (2013-2017) % Gain

XOI Performance 2017-2018

Relative Strength, % gain vs. S&P 500

Market Indices & Rates Weekly Values**

Stock Markets	2017	2018
Dow	21,006	24,538
S&P500	2,383	2,691
Nasdaq	5,871	7,258
TSX	15,609	15,385
FTSE	7,374	7,070
DAX	12,027	11,914
Nikkei	19,469	21,182
Hang Seng	23,553	30,583
Commodities	2017	2018
Oil	53.33	61.25
Gold	1226.5	1322.3
Bond Yields	2017	2018
USA 5 Yr Treasury	2.02	2.63
USA 10 Yr T	2.49	2.86
USA 20 Yr T	2.83	3.02
Moody's Aaa	3.95	3.90
Moody's Baa	4.65	4.58
CAN 5 Yr T	1.17	2.02
CAN 10 Yr T	1.70	2.20
Money Market	2017	2018
USA Fed Funds	0.75	1.50
USA 3 Mo T-B	0.71	1.65
CAN tgt overnight rate	0.50	1.25
CAN 3 Mo T-B	0.48	1.14
Foreign Exchange	2017	2018
EUR/USD	1.06	1.23
GBP/USD	1.23	1.38
USD/CAD	1.34	1.29
USD/JPY	114.04	105.75

FEBRUARY

M	T	W	T	F	S	S
				1	2	3
4	5	6	7	8	9	10
11	12	13	14	15	16	17
18	19	20	21	22	23	24
25	26	27	28			

MARCH

M	T	W	T	F	S	S
				1	2	3
4	5	6	7	8	9	10
11	12	13	14	15	16	17
18	19	20	21	22	23	24
25	26	27	28	29	30	31

APRIL

M	T	W	T	F	S	S
1	2	3	4	5	6	7
8	9	10	11	12	13	14
15	16	17	18	19	20	21
22	23	24	25	26	27	28
29	30					

From 1984 to 2017, March and April have been the best performing months for the energy sector on an average, median and frequency basis. Over the last five years, the energy sector has generally followed its seasonal pattern of positive performance in early winter and weaker performance in summer.

In 2017, the energy sector underperformed in its February to May seasonal period. In its 2018 winter/spring seasonal period, the energy sector was positive and outperformed the S&P 500 as it bounced off its February lows.

MARCH

	MONDAY	TUESDAY	WEDNESDAY
WEEK 09	25	26	27
WEEK 10	4 27	5 26	6 25
WEEK 11	11 20	12 19	13 18
WEEK 12	18 13	19 12	20 11
WEEK 13	25 6	26 5	27 4

THURSDAY		FRIDAY	
28		**1**	30
7	24	**8**	23
14	17	**15**	16
21	10	**22**	9
28	3	**29**	2

APRIL

M	T	W	T	F	S	S
1	2	3	4	5	6	7
8	9	10	11	12	13	14
15	16	17	18	19	20	21
22	23	24	25	26	27	28
29	30					

MAY

M	T	W	T	F	S	S
		1	2	3	4	5
6	7	8	9	10	11	12
13	14	15	16	17	18	19
20	21	22	23	24	25	26
27	28	29	30	31		

JUNE

M	T	W	T	F	S	S
					1	2
3	4	5	6	7	8	9
10	11	12	13	14	15	16
17	18	19	20	21	22	23
24	25	26	27	28	29	30

JULY

M	T	W	T	F	S	S
1	2	3	4	5	6	7
8	9	10	11	12	13	14
15	16	17	18	19	20	21
22	23	24	25	26	27	28
29	30	31				

MARCH
S U M M A R Y

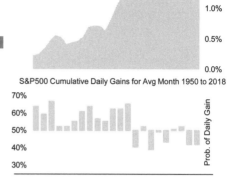

S&P500 Cumulative Daily Gains for Avg Month 1950 to 2018

	Dow Jones	S&P 500	Nasdaq	TSX Comp
Month Rank	5	4	7	3
# Up	44	44	29	20
# Down	24	24	17	13
% Pos	65	65	63	61
% Avg. Gain	1.1	1.2	0.8	1.1

Dow & S&P 1950-2017, Nasdaq 1972-2017, TSX 1985-2017

♦ March tends to be a strong month for stocks, but in 2018 the S&P 500 was negative as investors were concerned about stock market valuations. ♦ Typically, in March, it is the cyclicals that perform well and the defensive sectors that underperform. ♦ The energy sector is typically the best performing sector in March, which was the case in 2018. ♦ The financial sector typically performs well in March, but in 2018, the sector was negative as investors started to move away from the US banks as the US government bond yield curve flattened.

BEST / WORST MARCH BROAD MKTS. 2009-2018

BEST MARCH MARKETS
- ♦ Nasdaq (2009) 10.9%
- ♦ Nikkei 225 (2010) 9.5%
- ♦ Russell 2000 (2009) 8.7%

WORST MARCH MARKETS
- ♦ Nikkei 225 (2011) -8.2%
- ♦ Dow (2009) -3.7%
- ♦ FTSE 100 (2014) -3.1%

Index Values End of Month

	2009	2010	2011	2012	2013	2014	2015	2016	2017	2018
Dow	7,609	10,857	12,320	13,212	14,579	16,458	17,776	17,685	20,663	24,103
S&P 500	798	1,169	1,326	1,408	1,569	1,872	2,068	2,060	2,363	2,641
Nasdaq	1,529	2,398	2,781	3,092	3,268	4,199	4,901	4,870	5,912	7,063
TSX	8,720	12,038	14,116	12,392	12,750	14,335	14,902	13,494	15,548	15,367
Russell 1000	434	644	737	779	872	1,046	1,157	1,139	1,310	1,465
Russell 2000	423	679	844	830	952	1,173	1,253	1,114	1,386	1,529
FTSE 100	3,926	5,680	5,909	5,768	6,412	6,598	6,773	6,175	7,323	7,057
Nikkei 225	8,110	11,090	9,755	10,084	12,398	14,828	19,207	16,759	18,909	21,454

Percent Gain for March

	2009	2010	2011	2012	2013	2014	2015	2016	2017	2018
Dow	7.7	5.1	0.8	2.0	3.7	0.8	-2.0	7.1	-0.7	-3.7
S&P 500	8.5	5.9	-0.1	3.1	3.6	0.7	-1.7	6.6	0.0	-2.7
Nasdaq	10.9	7.1	0.0	4.2	3.4	-2.5	-1.3	6.8	1.5	-2.9
TSX	7.4	3.5	-0.1	-2.0	-0.6	0.9	-2.2	4.9	1.0	-0.5
Russell 1000	8.5	6.0	0.1	3.0	3.7	0.5	-1.4	6.8	-0.1	-2.4
Russell 2000	8.7	8.0	2.4	2.4	4.4	-0.8	1.6	7.8	-0.1	1.1
FTSE 100	2.5	6.1	-1.4	-1.8	0.8	-3.1	-2.5	1.3	0.8	-2.4
Nikkei 225	7.1	9.5	-8.2	3.7	7.3	-0.1	2.2	4.6	-1.1	-2.8

March Market Avg. Performance 2009 to 2018[1]

Dow	2.1%
S&P 500	2.4%
Nasdaq	2.7%
TSX Comp (CAN)	1.2%
Russell 1000 (Lg Cap)	2.5%
Russell 2000 (Sm Cap)	3.5%
FTSE 100	0.0%
Nikkei 225	2.2%

Interest Corner Mar[2]

	Fed Funds % [3]	3 Mo. T-Bill % [4]	10 Yr % [5]	20 Yr % [6]
2018	1.75	1.73	2.74	2.85
2017	1.00	0.76	2.40	2.76
2016	0.50	0.21	1.78	2.20
2015	0.25	0.03	1.94	2.31
2014	0.25	0.05	2.73	3.31

(1) Russell Data provided by Russell (2) Federal Reserve Bank of St. Louis- end of month values (3) Target rate set by FOMC (4)(5)(6) Constant yield maturities.

| S&P GIC | 2018 | 1990-2018[1] | |
Sectors	% Gain	GIC[2] % Avg Gain	Fq% Gain >S&P 500
Energy	1.6 %	2.3 %	59 %
Consumer Discretionary	-2.5	2.0	72
Financials	-4.5	1.8	59
Industrials	-2.8	1.8	62
Materials	-4.4	1.6	48
Telecom	-1.1	1.4	52
Utilities	3.4	1.2	52
Information Technology	-3.9	0.9	41
Consumer Staples	-1.3	0.7	48
Health Care	-3.2 %	0.3 %	31 %
S&P 500	-2.7 %	1.3 %	N/A %

Sector Commentary

♦ In March 2018, the S&P 500 was negative as investors were concerned that the economy was slowing, and that the rally in the stock market that started in early February after a correction in late January and early February was not sustainable. ♦ Generally, the defensive sectors of the stock market outperformed the cyclical sectors. ♦ The information technology sector had finished its seasonal period and corrected sharply in March. ♦ The financial sector also corrected sharply as interest rates declined, hurting the bank's net interest margins.

Sub-Sector Commentary

♦ In March 2018, the cyclical sub-sectors were generally underperformers. ♦ Banks were sharply negative for the month, producing a loss of 6.7%. ♦ Homebuilders bounced from a loss the previous month, producing a gain of 4.5%. ♦ The agriculture sector also produced a gain of 4.5% ♦ The biotech sector produced a large loss of 7.6% as rumors swirled about possible government action to mitigate rising pharmaceutical prices.

SELECTED SUB-SECTORS[3]			
Retail	-2.7 %	3.2 %	76 %
Steel	-6.6	2.4	59
Transportation	0.5	2.0	62
Chemicals	-4.6	1.9	52
Railroads	2.4	1.8	55
SOX (1995-2018)	-2.4	1.6	50
Silver	-1.0	1.6	48
Automotive & Components	-3.2	1.3	52
Homebuilders	4.5	1.3	52
Banks	-6.7	1.3	48
Metals & Mining	-3.5	0.9	41
Agriculture (1994-2018)	4.5	0.8	36
Pharma	-0.6	0.5	34
Biotech (1993-2018)	-7.6	-0.5	35
Gold	0.5	-1.0	34

NIKE – RUNS INTO EARNINGS
①Mar1-Mar20 ②Sep1-Sep25 ③Dec12-Dec24

Nike has had a strong run in the stock market since it went public in 1980. A lot of the gains in the stock price can be accounted for in the two to three week periods leading up to its first, second and third quarters earnings reports.

Nike Inc* Seasonal Gains 1990 to 2017

Positive ▢

Year %	Mar 1 to Mar 20	Sep 1 to Sep 25	Dec 12 to Dec 24	Compound Growth
1990	51.2 %	14.5 %	1.3 %	11.5 %	29.5 %
1991	79.8	-5.7	9.3	12.7	12.4
1992	14.7	-8.4	6.0	-2.9	-6.8
1993	-44.3	5.7	-13.5	0.6	-9.0
1994	61.4	10.4	-7.0	14.5	17.3
1995	86.6	5.3	18.8	10.7	34.4
1996	72.4	22.1	13.7	13.0	56.9
1997	-34.9	-6.1	0.9	-14.1	-18.6
1998	3.8	1.0	18.0	14.8	36.8
1999	22.2	15.6	15.1	18.2	57.3
2000	12.6	16.0	1.5	16.3	37.1
2001	0.8	-2.6	-8.7	3.7	-7.8
2002	-20.9	8.7	2.8	2.1	14.0
2003	53.9	14.0	6.0	4.4	26.1
2004	32.5	4.9	5.8	5.3	17.0
2005	-4.3	-1.8	3.0	1.3	2.5
2006	14.1	-1.5	7.1	2.6	8.3
2007	29.7	4.6	3.8	4.2	13.0
2008	-20.6	11.7	7.3	0.8	20.8
2009	29.5	8.4	5.9	2.2	17.3
2010	29.3	8.8	13.7	-2.0	21.2
2011	12.8	-12.9	2.3	-0.8	-11.6
2012	7.1	3.5	-2.3	6.2	7.4
2013	52.4	0.7	9.7	1.1	11.6
2014	22.3	1.2	1.5	-0.7	2.1
2015	30.0	5.0	11.9	0.1	17.5
2016	-18.7	2.3	-4.3	0.4	-1.8
2017	23.1	2.7	0.8	2.2	5.8
Avg.	21.4 %	4.6 %	4.7 %	4.6 %	15.0 %

NKE - Avg. Year 1990 to 2017

NKE / S&P 500 Relative Strength - Avg Yr. 1990 - 2017

Nike's year-end is May 31st, and although from year to year the actual report dates for Nike's earnings changes, generally speaking, Nike reports its earnings in the third or fourth week in the months of March, June, September and December.

It is interesting to note that Nike has strong seasonal runs at different times of the year. Stocks typically have similar seasonal patterns as the sector to which they belong. Nike belongs to the consumer discretionary sector and it would be expected that Nike would have a similar seasonal pattern.

There are large differences in Nike's pattern of seasonal strength compared with the seasonal pattern of the consumer discretionary sector. First, Nike has a period of seasonal strength that includes September, a month that is not favorable to consumer discretionary stocks. Second, Nike's outperformance is focused on very short periods in the weeks leading up to three of its earnings reports. In contrast, the consumer discretionary sector has a much longer seasonal period and has a more gradual transition from its favorable seasonal period to its unfavorable seasonal period and vice versa.

From 1990 to 2017, Nike produced an average annual gain of 21.4%. In comparison, its three short seasonal periods within the year have produced an average compound gain of 15.0%. The seasonal periods in total are approximately eight weeks and yet, they have produced most of the average annual gains of Nike. Investors have been well served investing in Nike in its seasonal periods and then running to another investment during its "off-season."

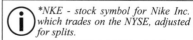

ⓘ *NKE - stock symbol for Nike Inc. which trades on the NYSE, adjusted for splits.*

Nike Performance

NKE Monthly Performance (1990-2017)

	Jan	Feb	Mar	Apr	May	Jun	Jul	Aug	Sep	Oct	Nov	Dec
Avg. % Gain	0.5	0.5	4.3	0.6	1.2	-0.7	2.5	-2.4	4.9	2.0	2.8	3.9
Med. % Gain	-0.5	3.6	2.9	1.4	1.5	1.4	0.4	-0.2	5.4	2.8	4.2	1.6
Fq %>0	46	68	68	57	54	61	61	46	64	64	68	64
Fq %>S&P 500	54	57	57	43	61	54	54	54	75	57	61	50

NKE 5 Year (2013-2017) % Gain

NKE Performance 2017-2018

Relative Strength, % gain vs. S&P 500

From 1990 to 2017, on average, the three best months for Nike were March, September and December, which are all part of the *Nike Runs Into Earnings* strategy. September has been the best month of the three as it has higher average and median values than the other two months. Performing well in September is particularly valuable as the S&P 500 tends not to perform well in this month. On average, over the last five years, Nike has performed extremely well in the month of September.

In 2017 and 2018, the Nike combination strategy was positive.

Market Indices & Rates
Weekly Values**

Stock Markets	2017	2018
Dow	20,903	25,336
S&P500	2,373	2,787
Nasdaq	5,862	7,561
TSX	15,507	15,578
FTSE	7,343	7,225
DAX	11,963	12,347
Nikkei	19,605	21,469
Hang Seng	23,569	30,996

Commodities	2017	2018
Oil	48.49	62.04
Gold	1202.7	1320.6

Bond Yields	2017	2018
USA 5 Yr Treasury	2.11	2.65
USA 10 Yr T	2.58	2.90
USA 20 Yr T	2.94	3.04
Moody's Aaa	4.11	3.90
Moody's Baa	4.76	4.67
CAN 5 Yr T	1.27	2.08
CAN 10 Yr T	1.81	2.27

Money Market	2017	2018
USA Fed Funds	0.75	1.50
USA 3 Mo T-B	0.75	1.67
CAN tgt overnight rate	0.50	1.25
CAN 3 Mo T-B	0.48	1.09

Foreign Exchange	2017	2018
EUR/USD	1.07	1.23
GBP/USD	1.22	1.39
USD/CAD	1.35	1.28
USD/JPY	114.79	106.82

MARCH

M	T	W	T	F	S	S
				1	2	3
4	5	6	7	8	9	10
11	12	13	14	15	16	17
18	19	20	21	22	23	24
25	26	27	28	29	30	31

APRIL

M	T	W	T	F	S	S
	2	3	4	5	6	7
8	9	10	11	12	13	14
15	16	17	18	19	20	21
22	23	24	25	26	27	28
29	30					

MAY

M	T	W	T	F	S	S
	1	2	3	4	5	
6	7	8	9	10	11	12
13	14	15	16	17	18	19
20	21	22	23	24	25	26
27	28	29	30	31		

CANADIAN TIRE – MORE THAN TIRES

CTC.A
①SELL SHORT (Jan1-Jan31)
②LONG (Feb11-Apr12) ③LONG (Oct28-Nov30)

Canadian Tire is an iconic Canadian store that has successfully developed a diversified portfolio of retail operations selling a wide range of products including clothing, home products, leisure products, sports equipment and auto repair parts.

16.4% gain & positive 86% of the time

Despite its diversified product approach, Canadian Tire is still a retail operation and generally follows the seasonal trends for the retail sector.

Although Canada does not have an "official" Black Friday, Canadian Tire's stock price tends to peak, relative to the TSX Composite Index at the end of November, after performing well starting in the last few days in October.

Canadian Tire also tends to perform well from February 11th to April 12th, which is similar to the retail sector's seasonal period.

Investors should note that Canadian Tire tends to perform poorly in the month of January, which also happens to be a weak month for the retail sector.

> ⓘ * *Canadian Tire is a diversified retail company that trades on the Toronto exchange under the symbol CTC.A. Data from TSX Exchange, includes stock splits only.*

Canadian Tire* vs. TSX Comp. 1996 to 2017
Negative Short ☐   Positive Long ☐

Year	Jan 1 to Jan 31 TSX Comp	CTC.A	Feb 11 to Apr 12 TSX Comp	CTC.A	Oct 28 to Nov 30 TSX Comp	CTC.A	Compound Growth TSX Comp	CTC.A
1996	5.4 %	-1.7 %	-0.3 %	9.5 %	8.4	16.8 %	13.9 %	30.1 %
1997	3.1	-6.2	-6.5	9.3	-1.3	0.2	-4.9	16.2
1998	0.0	3.4	10.7	9.7	5.8	8.5	17.2	14.9
1999	3.8	3.1	8.4	3.8	7.3	-4.9	20.7	-4.3
2000	0.8	-20.1	-2.9	14.0	-5.4	-2.8	-7.4	33.0
2001	4.4	12.6	-12.5	16.9	6.0	14.2	-3.2	16.6
2002	-0.5	-2.3	2.6	25.2	2.6	3.7	4.7	32.7
2003	-0.7	-9.4	-0.2	4.7	2.6	-0.5	1.7	13.9
2004	3.7	3.9	1.7	3.9	2.7	6.3	8.3	6.0
2005	-0.5	-8.1	1.4	7.7	5.7	12.8	6.6	31.3
2006	6.0	-4.9	4.4	-5.5	3.9	3.1	15.0	2.2
2007	1.0	-3.7	3.2	7.5	-4.3	-15.1	-0.2	-5.3
2008	-4.9	-13.1	5.3	8.1	8.6	7.1	8.8	31.0
2009	-3.3	-5.9	4.2	24.4	3.6	-3.7	4.4	26.8
2010	-5.6	-7.0	7.6	1.3	3.1	8.0	4.8	17.1
2011	0.8	-8.6	-0.3	-4.6	-2.1	7.2	-1.6	11.2
2012	4.2	-2.5	-1.4	5.1	-0.5	-8.2	2.2	-1.2
2013	2.0	0.1	-3.6	3.5	0.0	1.9	-1.7	5.4
2014	0.5	-4.4	3.4	11.6	1.9	3.3	5.9	20.5
2015	0.3	-4.5	1.8	14.1	-1.7	8.0	0.4	28.7
2016	-1.4	-3.4	11.5	17.9	1.7	6.4	11.7	29.6
2017	0.6	-0.6	-0.5	14.2	0.7	2.8	0.8	18.1
Avg.	0.9 %	-3.8 %	1.8 %	9.2 %	1.9 %	2.8 %	4.5 %	16.4 %
Fq>0	68 %	23 %	59	91 %	68 %	73 %	73 %	86 %

From 1996 to 2017, short selling in January and then investing from February 11th to April 12th and then once again investing from October 28th to November 30th, has produced an average gain of 16.4% and has been positive 86% of the time.

Canadian Tire- Avg. Year 1996 to 2017

Canadian Tire / TSX Comp Rel. Strength- Avg Yr. 1996-2017

Canadian Tire Performance

Canadian Tire Monthly Performance (1996-2017)

	Jan	Feb	Mar	Apr	May	Jun	Jul	Aug	Sep	Oct	Nov	Dec
Avg. % Gain	-3.8	1.9	4.1	2.8	2.7	0.4	-2.0	0.4	0.8	2.5	2.4	1.7
Med. % Gain	-4.1	1.1	4.1	1.2	3.1	-1.8	-2.7	0.8	2.2	2.5	3.0	1.7
Fq %>0	23	55	77	68	64	41	32	55	64	59	73	64
Fq %>TSX Comp	14	68	77	55	64	50	23	41	59	55	68	50

Canadian Tire 5 Year (2013-2017) % Gain

Canadian Tire Performance 2017-2018

Relative Strength, % gain vs. TSX Comp.

Market Indices & Rates
Weekly Values**

Stock Markets	2017	2018
Dow	20,915	24,947
S&P500	2,378	2,752
Nasdaq	5,901	7,482
TSX	15,490	15,711
FTSE	7,425	7,164
DAX	12,095	12,390
Nikkei	19,522	21,677
Hang Seng	24,310	31,502

Commodities	2017	2018
Oil	48.78	62.34
Gold	1229.6	1310.1

Bond Yields	2017	2018
USA 5 Yr Treasury	2.03	2.65
USA 10 Yr T	2.50	2.85
USA 20 Yr T	2.86	2.96
Moody's Aaa	4.06	3.87
Moody's Baa	4.72	4.64
CAN 5 Yr T	1.21	1.98
CAN 10 Yr T	1.76	2.14

Money Market	2017	2018
USA Fed Funds	1.00	1.50
USA 3 Mo T-B	0.73	1.78
CAN tgt overnight rate	0.50	1.25
CAN 3 Mo T-B	0.50	1.07

Foreign Exchange	2017	2018
EUR/USD	1.07	1.23
GBP/USD	1.24	1.39
USD/CAD	1.34	1.31
USD/JPY	112.70	106.01

MARCH

M	T	W	T	F	S	S
				1	2	3
4	5	6	7	8	9	10
11	12	13	14	15	16	17
18	19	20	21	22	23	24
25	26	27	28	29	30	31

APRIL

M	T	W	T	F	S	S
						1
2	3	4	5	6	7	
8	9	10	11	12	13	14
15	16	17	18	19	20	21
22	23	24	25	26	27	28
29	30					

MAY

M	T	W	T	F	S	S
	1	2	3	4	5	
6	7	8	9	10	11	12
13	14	15	16	17	18	19
20	21	22	23	24	25	26
27	28	29	30	31		

From 1996 to 2017, the worst month of the year for Canadian Tire has been January on a median, average and frequency basis. July has also been a poor performer. The best month of the year has been March, which is also a strong month of the year for retail stocks. Over the last five years, Canadian Tire has generally followed its seasonal trend with January being the worst month of the year and March and November being two of the strongest months. In its 2017 autumn seasonal period, overall the Canadian Tire strategies outperformed the TSX Composite. In 2018, the short sell trade did not work and the long trade was positive, but underperformed the TSX Composite.

NATURAL GAS – FIRES UP AND DOWN
①LONG (Mar22-Jun19) ②LONG (Sep5-Dec21)
③SELL SHORT (Dec22-Dec31)

There are two high consumption times for natural gas: winter and summer. The colder it gets in winter, the more natural gas is consumed to keep the furnaces going. The warmer it gets in summer, the more natural gas is used to produce power for air conditioners.

On the supply side, weather plays a large factor in determining price. During the hurricane season in the Gulf of Mexico, the price of natural gas is affected by the number and severity of hurricanes.

68% of the time. The price of natural gas also tends to rise between September 5th and December 21st, due to the demands of the heating season. In this period, from 1995 to 2017, natural gas has produced an average gain of 36.6% and has been positive 74% of the time.

Positive 83% of the time

Natural gas tends to fall in price from December 22nd to December 31st. Although this is a short time period, for the years from 1995 to 2017, natural gas has produced an average loss of 3.1% and has only been positive 43% of the time. Also, in this period, when gains did occur, they were relatively small. The poor performance of natural gas at this time is largely driven by southern U.S. refiners dumping inventory on the market to help mitigate year-end taxes on their inventory.

Applying a strategy of investing in natural gas from March 22nd to June 19th, reinvesting the proceeds from September 5th to December 21st, reinvesting the proceeds again to short natural gas from December 22nd to December 31st, has produced a compound average return of 61.0% and has been positive 83% of the time.

Using the natural gas compound strategy has produced returns that are over three times greater than the average annual gain in natural gas. By using the strategy, an investor would have caught most of the large gains and missed most of the large losses.

Natural Gas (Cash) Henry Hub LA*
Seasonal Gains 1995 to 2017

Year	%	Pos. Mar 22 to Jun 19	Pos. Sep 5 to Dec 21	Neg. (Short) Dec 22 to Dec 31	Pos. Compound Growth
1995	99.4	13.0 %	103.0 %	1.2 %	126.7 %
1996	-27.4	-6.6	170.4	-46.2	269.2
1997	-9.4	16.8	-13.1	-6.3	7.9
1998	-13.0	-2.6	20.9	-6.7	25.7
1999	18.6	28.9	5.3	-11.2	50.9
2000	356.5	57.1	121.9	0.7	246.3
2001	-74.3	-24.1	21.5	1.5	-9.2
2002	70.0	0.6	61.3	-9.1	77.1
2003	26.4	9.5	47.1	-16.3	87.4
2004	3.6	18.2	54.6	-11.6	103.9
2005	58.4	6.3	14.5	-29.6	57.7
2006	-42.2	-1.8	17.4	-9.5	26.3
2007	30.2	9.2	32.7	2.0	42.1
2008	-21.4	52.2	-21.4	-0.9	20.6
2009	3.6	1.5	208.0	0.7	210.4
2010	-27.4	28.6	10.4	2.4	38.6
2011	-29.6	10.0	-26.1	-1.7	-17.3
2012	15.4	18.7	21.7	0.6	43.7
2013	26.3	-1.4	18.2	-0.2	16.8
2014	-31.1	7.7	-11.8	-12.9	7.2
2015	-22.8	-0.5	-36.1	35.6	-59.0
2016	59.2	46.6	21.9	5.8	68.3
2017	-3.9	-6.6	-10.4	36.0	-46.4
Avg.	20.2 %	12.3 %	36.6 %	-3.1 %	61.0 %

Natural Gas (Henry Hub Spot)- Avg. Year 1995 to 2017

Natural gas prices tend to rise from mid-March to mid-June ahead of the cooling season demands in the summer. From 1995 to 2017, during the period of March 22nd to June 19th, the spot price of natural gas has on average increased 12.3% and has been positive

⚠ *Caution: The cash price for natural gas is extremely volatile and extreme caution should be used. Care must be taken to ensure that investments are within risk tolerances.*

ⓘ *Source: New York Mercantile Exchange. NYMX is an exchange provider of futures and options.*

Natural Gas Performance

NatGas Monthly Performance (1995-2017)

	Jan	Feb	Mar	Apr	May	Jun	Jul	Aug	Sep	Oct	Nov	Dec
Avg. % Gain	-1.6	-1.6	1.8	1.5	3.5	0.9	-2.0	-1.8	3.3	7.8	5.8	6.5
Med. % Gain	-3.2	-6.3	6.4	2.7	3.1	-1.6	-0.5	-3.2	1.2	-0.2	5.3	6.0
Fq %>0	39	39	70	65	65	43	39	43	52	48	65	57
Fq %>S&P 500	43	30	65	48	61	39	39	57	43	48	65	52

NatGas 5 Year (2013-2017) % Gain

NatGas Performance 2017-2018

WEEK 12

Market Indices & Rates
Weekly Values**

Stock Markets	2017	2018
Dow	20,597	23,533
S&P500	2,344	2,588
Nasdaq	5,829	6,993
TSX	15,443	15,224
FTSE	7,337	6,922
DAX	12,064	11,886
Nikkei	19,263	20,618
Hang Seng	24,358	30,309

Commodities	2017	2018
Oil	47.32	65.83
Gold	1247.5	1346.6

Bond Yields	2017	2018
USA 5 Yr Treasury	1.93	2.61
USA 10 Yr T	2.40	2.82
USA 20 Yr T	2.74	2.94
Moody's Aaa	3.94	3.88
Moody's Baa	4.62	4.69
CAN 5 Yr T	1.13	2.07
CAN 10 Yr T	1.64	2.19

Money Market	2017	2018
USA Fed Funds	1.00	1.75
USA 3 Mo T-B	0.78	1.74
CAN tgt overnight rate	0.50	1.25
CAN 3 Mo T-B	0.49	1.09

Foreign Exchange	2017	2018
EUR/USD	1.08	1.24
GBP/USD	1.25	1.41
USD/CAD	1.34	1.29
USD/JPY	111.34	104.74

MARCH

M	T	W	T	F	S	S
			1	2	3	
4	5	6	7	8	9	10
11	12	13	14	15	16	17
18	19	20	21	22	23	24
25	26	27	28	29	30	31

APRIL

M	T	W	T	F	S	S
						1
2	3	4	5	6	7	
8	9	10	11	12	13	14
15	16	17	18	19	20	21
22	23	24	25	26	27	28
29	30					

From 1995 to 2017, on average, September through to December has been the best cluster of positive months for natural gas. Natural gas is a very volatile commodity and as a result there is a large difference between the mean and median performances on a month to month basis.

April and May are also strong months and make up the core of the spring trade. In the last five years, natural gas has generally followed its seasonal trend, with a strong performance in March and April, a weak performance in summer and a strong performance in autumn. In 2017/2018, the overall return for the combination of natural gas trades was negative.

MAY

M	T	W	T	F	S	S
	1	2	3	4	5	
6	7	8	9	10	11	12
13	14	15	16	17	18	19
20	21	22	23	24	25	26
27	28	29	30	31		

![flag] CANADIANS GIVE 3 CHEERS FOR AMERICAN HOLIDAYS

When I used to work on the retail side of the investment business, I was always amazed at how often the Canadian stock market increased on U.S. holidays, when the U.S. stock market was closed.

The Canadian stock market on U.S. holidays always had light volume, tended not to have large increases or decreases, but usually ended the day with a gain.

1.0% average gain

How the trade works

For the three big holidays in the United States that do not exist in Canada (Memorial, Independence and U.S. Thanksgiving Days), buy at the end of the market day before the holiday (TSX Composite) and sell at the end of the U.S. holiday when the U.S markets are closed.

For U.S. investors to take advantage of this trade, they must have access to the TSX Composite. Unfortunately, SEC regulations do not allow most Americans to purchase foreign ETFs.

Generally, markets perform well around most major U.S. holidays, hence the trading strategies for U.S holidays included in this book. The typical U.S. holiday trade is to get into the stock market the day before the holiday and then exit the day after the holiday.

The main reason for the strong performance around these holidays is a lack of institutional involvement in the markets, allowing bullish retail investors to push up the markets.

On the actual American holidays, economic reports are not released in the U.S. and are very seldom released in Canada. During market hours on U.S. holidays, without any strong influences, the TSX Composite tends to float, as investors wait until the next day before making any significant moves. Despite this laxidasical action during the day, the TSX Composite tends to end the day on a gain. This is true for the three major U.S. holidays: Memorial Day, Independence Day and U.S. Thanksgiving.

From a theoretical perspective, a lot of the gain that is captured on the U.S. holidays in the Canadian stock market is realized the next day when the U.S stock market is open. This does not invalidate the *Canadians Give 3 Cheers* trade – it presents more alternatives for the astute investor.

For example, an investor can allocate a portion of money to a standard U.S. holiday trade and another portion to the *Canadian Give 3 Cheers* version. By spreading out the exit days, the overall risk in the trade is reduced.

S&P/TSX Comp
Gain 1977-2017   Positive ▢

	Memorial	Independence	Thanksgiving	Compound Growth
1977	0.10 %	-0.08 %	0.61 %	0.63 %
1978	-0.05	-0.16	0.57	0.36
1979	1.11	0.23	0.58	1.93
1980	1.64	0.76	0.89	3.32
1981	0.51	-0.15	1.03	1.40
1982	-0.18	-0.01	0.35	0.17
1983	0.29	0.53	0.15	0.97
1984	0.86	-0.11	0.73	1.48
1985	0.61	0.31	0.31	1.24
1986	0.23	-0.02	0.22	0.44
1987	-0.11	1.08	1.57	2.55
1988	0.44	0.08	0.58	1.11
1989	0.10	-0.12	-0.11	-0.13
1990	0.11	0.43	0.02	0.57
1991	0.02	0.18	-0.09	0.11
1992	-0.06	0.35	0.36	0.65
1993	0.42	-0.18	0.14	0.38
1994	-0.19	0.70	0.91	1.43
1995	0.14	0.25	0.29	0.68
1996	0.11	0.25	0.54	0.90
1997	1.08	-0.04	-0.85	0.18
1998	0.56	0.18	0.51	1.25
1999	0.57	1.63	1.14	3.39
2000	0.43	1.04	0.91	2.40
2001	-0.02	-0.23	0.70	0.45
2002	-0.01	0.08	0.38	0.45
2003	0.03	0.03	0.26	0.31
2004	0.84	-0.02	0.55	1.39
2005	0.56	0.39	1.48	2.45
2006	0.70	1.04	0.70	2.46
2007	0.35	-0.03	0.76	1.08
2008	0.24	-0.94	1.28	0.56
2009	0.76	0.36	-1.29	-0.18
2010	0.78	-0.92	0.34	0.19
2011	0.23	0.64	-0.75	0.12
2012	-0.09	0.55	0.44	0.90
2013	0.23	0.17	0.07	0.47
2014	0.05	0.05	-0.77	-0.67
2015	-0.09	0.30	0.16	0.38
2016	-0.13	1.48	-0.04	1.21
2017	0.03	-0.34	0.00	-0.30
Avg	0.32 %	0.24 %	0.38 %	0.94 %
Fq > 0	76 %	63 %	83 %	90 %

Canadians Give 3 Cheers Performance

Market Indices & Rates
Weekly Values**

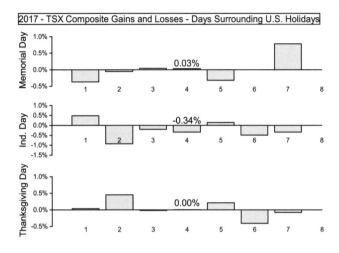

2017 - TSX Composite Gains and Losses - Days Surrounding U.S. Holidays

Stock Markets	2017	2018
Dow	20,663	24,103
S&P500	2,363	2,641
Nasdaq	5,912	7,063
TSX	15,548	15,367
FTSE	7,323	7,057
DAX	12,313	12,097
Nikkei	18,909	21,454
Hang Seng	24,112	30,093

Commodities	2017	2018
Oil	50.60	64.94
Gold	1244.9	1323.9

Bond Yields	2017	2018
USA 5 Yr Treasury	1.93	2.56
USA 10 Yr T	2.40	2.74
USA 20 Yr T	2.76	2.85
Moody's Aaa	3.94	3.77
Moody's Baa	4.64	4.59
CAN 5 Yr T	1.12	1.97
CAN 10 Yr T	1.63	2.09

Money Market	2017	2018
USA Fed Funds	1.00	1.75
USA 3 Mo T-B	0.76	1.73
CAN tgt overnight rate	0.50	1.25
CAN 3 Mo T-B	0.52	1.10

Foreign Exchange	2017	2018
EUR/USD	1.07	1.23
GBP/USD	1.26	1.40
USD/CAD	1.33	1.29
USD/JPY	111.39	106.28

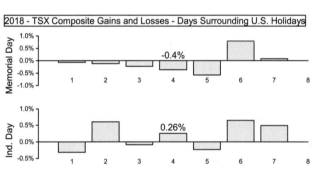

2018 - TSX Composite Gains and Losses - Days Surrounding U.S. Holidays

MARCH

M	T	W	T	F	S	S
				1	2	3
4	5	6	7	8	9	10
11	12	13	14	15	16	17
18	19	20	21	22	23	24
25	26	27	28	29	30	31

Canadians Give 3 Cheers Performance

In 2017, the TSX Composite produced a nominal gain on Memorial Day, a loss on Independence Day and was flat on Thanksgiving Day.

In 2018, the TSX Composite produced a loss on Memorial Day. On Independence Day, the TSX was positive, producing a gain of 0.26%. Both the Canadian and U.S. stock markets rallied strongly, shortly after the end of the "Canadian Independence Day" trade.

APRIL

M	T	W	T	F	S	S
	2	3	4	5	6	7
8	9	10	11	12	13	14
15	16	17	18	19	20	21
22	23	24	25	26	27	28
29	30					

MAY

M	T	W	T	F	S	S
	1	2	3	4	5	
6	7	8	9	10	11	12
13	14	15	16	17	18	19
20	21	22	23	24	25	26
27	28	29	30	31		

APRIL

	MONDAY	TUESDAY	WEDNESDAY
WEEK 14	**1** 29	**2** 28	**3** 27
WEEK 15	**8** 22	**9** 21	**10** 20
WEEK 16	**15** 15	**16** 14	**17** 13
WEEK 17	**22** 8	**23** 7	**24** 6
WEEK 18	**29** 1	**30**	1

THURSDAY		FRIDAY	
4	26	**5**	25
11	19	**12**	18
18	12	**19**	11
		USA Market Closed- Good Friday CAN Market Closed- Good Friday	
25	5	**26**	4
2		3	

MAY

M	T	W	T	F	S	S
		1	2	3	4	5
6	7	8	9	10	11	12
13	14	15	16	17	18	19
20	21	22	23	24	25	26
27	28	29	30	31		

JUNE

M	T	W	T	F	S	S
					1	2
3	4	5	6	7	8	9
10	11	12	13	14	15	16
17	18	19	20	21	22	23
24	25	26	27	28	29	30

JULY

M	T	W	T	F	S	S
1	2	3	4	5	6	7
8	9	10	11	12	13	14
15	16	17	18	19	20	21
22	23	24	25	26	27	28
29	30	31				

AUGUST

M	T	W	T	F	S	S
			1	2	3	4
5	6	7	8	9	10	11
12	13	14	15	16	17	18
19	20	21	22	23	24	25
26	27	28	29	30	31	

APRIL SUMMARY

S&P500 Cumulative Daily Gains for Avg Month 1950 to 2018

	Dow Jones	S&P 500	Nasdaq	TSX Comp
Month Rank	1	3	4	7
# Up	46	47	29	20
# Down	22	21	17	13
% Pos	68	69	63	61
% Avg. Gain	1.9	1.4	1.3	0.8

Dow & S&P 1950-2017, Nasdaq 1972-2017 TSX 1985-2017

♦ April, on average, from 1950 to 2017 has been the third strongest month for the S&P 500 with an average gain of 1.4% and a positive frequency of 69%. ♦ The first part of April tends to be the strongest (see *18 Day Earnings Month Effect strategy*). ♦ The last part of April tends to be "flat." ♦ Overall, April tends to be a volatile month with the cyclical sectors outperforming. ♦ When the defensive sectors outperform in April, it often indicates market weakness ahead.

BEST / WORST APRIL BROAD MKTS. 2009-2018

BEST APRIL MARKETS
- ♦ Russell 2000 (2009) 15.3%
- ♦ Nasdaq (2009) 12.3%
- ♦ Nikkei 225 (2013) 11.8%

WORST APRIL MARKETS
- ♦ Nikkei 225 (2012) -5.6%
- ♦ Russell 2000 (2014) -3.9%
- ♦ Nikkei 225 (2014) -3.5%

Index Values End of Month

	2009	2010	2011	2012	2013	2014	2015	2016	2017	2018
Dow	8,168	11,009	12,811	13,214	14,840	16,581	17,841	17,774	20,941	24,163
S&P 500	873	1,187	1,364	1,398	1,598	1,884	2,086	2,065	2,384	2,648
Nasdaq	1,717	2,461	2,874	3,046	3,329	4,115	4,941	4,775	6,048	7,066
TSX	9,325	12,211	13,945	12,293	12,457	14,652	15,225	13,951	15,586	15,608
Russell 1000	477	655	758	774	887	1,050	1,164	1,144	1,322	1,468
Russell 2000	488	717	865	817	947	1,127	1,220	1,131	1,400	1,542
FTSE 100	4,244	5,553	6,070	5,738	6,430	6,780	6,961	6,242	7,204	7,509
Nikkei 225	8,828	11,057	9,850	9,521	13,861	14,304	19,520	16,666	19,197	22,468

Percent Gain for April

	2009	2010	2011	2012	2013	2014	2015	2016	2017	2018
Dow	7.3	1.4	4.0	0.0	1.8	0.7	0.4	0.5	1.3	0.2
S&P 500	9.4	1.5	2.8	-0.7	1.8	0.6	0.9	0.3	0.9	0.3
Nasdaq	12.3	2.6	3.3	-1.5	1.9	-2.0	0.8	-1.9	2.3	0.0
TSX	6.9	1.4	-1.2	-0.8	-2.3	2.2	2.2	3.4	0.2	1.6
Russell 1000	10.0	1.8	2.9	-0.7	1.7	0.4	0.6	0.4	0.9	0.2
Russell 2000	15.3	5.6	2.6	-1.6	-0.4	-3.9	-2.6	1.5	1.0	0.8
FTSE 100	8.1	-2.2	2.7	-0.5	0.3	2.8	2.8	1.1	-1.6	6.4
Nikkei 225	8.9	-0.3	1.0	-5.6	11.8	-3.5	1.6	-0.6	1.5	4.7

April Market Avg. Performance 2009 to 2018[1]

Dow	1.8%
S&P 500	1.8%
Nasdaq	1.8%
TSX Comp (CAN)	1.4%
Russell 1000 (Lg Cap)	1.8%
Russell 2000 (Sm Cap)	1.8%
FTSE 100	2.0%
Nikkei 225	2.0%

Interest Corner Apr[2]

	Fed Funds %[3]	3 Mo. T-Bill %[4]	10 Yr %[5]	20 Yr %[6]
2018	1.75	1.87	2.95	3.01
2017	1.00	0.80	2.29	2.67
2016	0.50	0.22	1.83	2.26
2015	0.25	0.01	2.05	2.49
2014	0.25	0.03	2.67	3.22

(1) Russell Data provided by Russell (2) Federal Reserve Bank of St. Louis- end of month values (3) Target rate set by FOMC (4)(5)(6) Constant yield maturities.

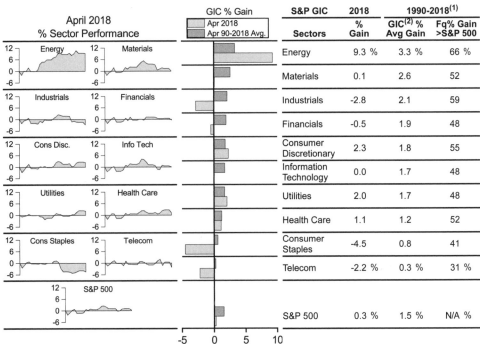

S&P GIC	2018	1990-2018[1]	
Sectors	**% Gain**	**GIC[2] % Avg Gain**	**Fq% Gain >S&P 500**
Energy	9.3 %	3.3 %	66 %
Materials	0.1	2.6	52
Industrials	-2.8	2.1	59
Financials	-0.5	1.9	48
Consumer Discretionary	2.3	1.8	55
Information Technology	0.0	1.7	48
Utilities	2.0	1.7	48
Health Care	1.1	1.2	52
Consumer Staples	-4.5	0.8	41
Telecom	-2.2 %	0.3 %	31 %
S&P 500	0.3 %	1.5 %	N/A %

Sector Commentary

♦ On average, April is one of the strongest months of the year for commodities, including oil. ♦ In 2018, the energy sector produced a large gain of 9.3%. ♦ The consumer discretionary sector also produced a strong gain of 2.3%. ♦ The technology sector was flat, not producing a gain, or a loss. ♦ The consumer staples sector produced a large loss of 4.5% as investors favored the cyclical sectors of the stock market.

Sub-Sector Commentary

♦ In April 2018, the agriculture sub-sector of the stock market produced a big gain of 4.6%. ♦ The agriculture sub-sector tends to be one of the weaker sectors at this time of the year. ♦ The homebuilders sub-sector produced a loss of 3.4% as rising interest rates continued to hurt the sector. ♦ The metals and mining sub-sector produced a large loss of 4.5% as increasing trade war hostilities continued to provide uncertainty in the sector.

SELECTED SUB-SECTORS[3]		
Automotive & Components	0.1 %	5.4 %	48 %
Railroads	2.2	3.5	62
Chemicals	1.3	3.0	72
SOX (1995-2018)	-6.4	2.7	46
Banks	-0.2	2.4	52
Transportation	0.9	2.1	59
Metals & Mining	-4.5	2.0	41
Steel	0.9	1.6	52
Pharma	-1.1	1.6	52
Retail	4.9	1.0	48
Homebuilders	-3.4	1.0	41
Agriculture (1994-2018)	4.6	0.6	56
Gold	-0.8	0.4	45
Biotech (1993-2018)	-1.4	0.2	38
Silver	0.6	0.1	41

(1) Sector data provided by Standard and Poors (2) GIC is short form for Global Industry Classification (3) Sub Sector data provided by Standard and Poors, except where marked by symbol.

18 DAY EARNINGS MONTH EFFECT
Markets Outperform 1st 18 Calendar Days of Earnings Months

Earnings season occurs the first month of every quarter. At this time, public companies report their financials for the previous quarter and give guidance on future expectations. As a result, investors tend to bid up stocks, anticipating good earnings. Earnings are a major driver of stock market prices as investors generally get in the stock market early, in anticipation of favorable results, which helps to run stock prices up in the first half of the month.

1st to 18th Day 1950-2017

Avg Gain 0.5%	Fq Pos 62%

The first month of the year generally has a good start. Investors and money managers generally push the market upward as they try to lock in their new positions for the year. The result is that the market tends to increase for the first eighteen days, pause, and then accelerate through the end of the month.

Avg Gain 1.3%	Fq Pos 68%

This month has a reputation of being a strong month. If you look at the graph, you can see that almost all of the gains have come in the first half of the month. It is interesting to note that the month returns tend to peak just after the last day to file tax returns.

Avg Gain 0.9%	Fq Pos 66%

This is the month in which the market can peak in strong bull markets. The returns in the first half of the month can be positive, but investors should be cautious, as the time period following in August and September has a tendency towards negative returns.

Avg Gain 0.9%	Fq Pos 65%

This is the month with a bad reputation. Once again, the first part of the month tends to do well. It is the middle segment, centered around the notorious Black Monday, that brings down the results. Toward the end of the month, investors realize that the world has not ended and start to buy stocks again, providing a strong finish to the month.

1st to 18th Day Gain S&P500

	JAN	APR	JUL	OCT
1950	0.36 %	4.28 %	-3.56 %	2.88 %
1951	4.75	3.41	4.39	1.76
1952	2.02	-3.57	-0.44	-1.39
1953	-2.07	-2.65	0.87	3.38
1954	2.50	3.71	2.91	-1.49
1955	-3.28	4.62	3.24	-4.63
1956	-2.88	-1.53	4.96	2.18
1957	-4.35	2.95	2.45	-4.93
1958	2.78	1.45	1.17	2.80
1959	1.09	4.47	1.23	0.79
1960	-3.34	2.26	-2.14	1.55
1961	2.70	1.75	-0.36	2.22
1962	-4.42	-1.84	2.65	0.12
1963	3.30	3.49	-1.27	2.26
1964	2.05	1.99	2.84	0.77
1965	2.05	2.31	1.87	1.91
1966	1.64	2.63	2.66	2.77
1967	6.80	1.84	3.16	-1.51
1968	-0.94	7.63	1.87	2.09
1969	-1.76	-0.27	-2.82	3.37
1970	-1.24	-4.42	6.83	-0.02
1971	1.37	3.17	0.42	-1.01
1972	1.92	2.40	-1.22	-2.13
1973	0.68	0.02	2.00	1.46
1974	-2.04	0.85	-2.58	13.76
1975	3.50	3.53	-2.09	5.95
1976	7.55	-2.04	0.38	-3.58
1977	-3.85	2.15	0.47	-3.18
1978	-4.77	4.73	1.40	-2.00
1979	3.76	0.11	-1.19	-5.22
1980	2.90	-1.51	6.83	4.83
1981	-0.73	-0.96	-0.34	2.59
1982	-4.35	4.33	1.33	13.54
1983	4.10	4.43	-2.20	1.05
1984	1.59	-0.80	-1.16	1.20
1985	2.44	0.10	1.32	2.72
1986	-1.35	1.46	-5.77	3.25
1987	9.96	-1.64	3.48	-12.16
1988	1.94	0.12	-1.09	2.75
1989	3.17	3.78	4.20	-2.12
1990	-4.30	0.23	1.73	-0.10
1991	0.61	3.53	3.83	1.20
1992	0.42	3.06	1.83	-1.45
1993	0.26	-0.60	-1.06	2.07
1994	1.67	-0.74	2.46	1.07
1995	2.27	0.93	2.52	0.52
1996	-1.25	-0.29	-4.04	3.42
1997	4.78	1.22	3.41	-0.33
1998	-0.92	1.90	4.67	3.88
1999	1.14	2.54	3.36	-2.23
2000	-0.96	-3.80	2.69	-6.57
2001	2.10	6.71	-1.36	2.66
2002	-1.79	-2.00	-10.94	8.48
2003	2.50	5.35	1.93	4.35
2004	2.51	0.75	-3.46	-0.05
2005	-1.32	-2.93	2.50	-4.12
2006	2.55	1.22	0.51	3.15
2007	1.41	4.33	-3.20	1.48
2008	-9.75	5.11	-1.51	-19.36
2009	-5.88	8.99	2.29	2.89
2010	1.88	1.94	3.32	3.81
2011	2.97	-1.56	-1.15	8.30
2012	4.01	-1.66	0.78	1.16
2013	4.2	-1.76	5.17	3.74
2014	-0.52	-0.4	0.92	-4.34
2015	-1.92	0.64	3.08	5.89
2016	-8.0	1.68	3.21	-1.32
2017	1.48	-0.87	1.54	1.66
Avg	52 %	1.34 %	0.91 %	0.85 %

Earnings Month Effect Performance

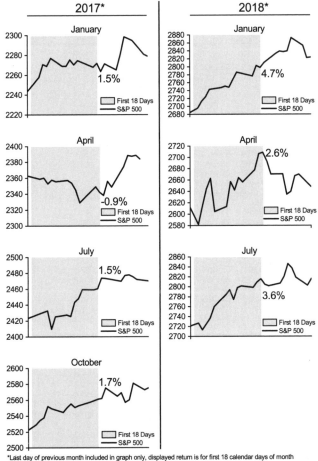

Market Indices & Rates
Weekly Values**

Stock Markets	2017	2018
Dow	20,656	23,933
S&P500	2,356	2,604
Nasdaq	5,878	6,915
TSX	15,667	15,207
FTSE	7,349	7,184
DAX	12,225	12,241
Nikkei	18,665	21,568
Hang Seng	24,267	29,845

Commodities	2017	2018
Oil	52.24	62.06
Gold	1266.5	1331.2

Bond Yields	2017	2018
USA 5 Yr Treasury	1.92	2.58
USA 10 Yr T	2.38	2.77
USA 20 Yr T	2.74	2.89
Moody's Aaa	3.93	3.78
Moody's Baa	4.62	4.61
CAN 5 Yr T	1.12	2.00
CAN 10 Yr T	1.60	2.14

Money Market	2017	2018
USA Fed Funds	1.00	1.75
USA 3 Mo T-B	0.82	1.73
CAN tgt overnight rate	0.50	1.25
CAN 3 Mo T-B	0.54	1.12

Foreign Exchange	2017	2018
EUR/USD	1.06	1.23
GBP/USD	1.24	1.41
USD/CAD	1.34	1.28
USD/JPY	111.09	106.93

*Last day of previous month included in graph only, displayed return is for first 18 calendar days of month

APRIL

M	T	W	T	F	S	S
	2	3	4	5	6	7
8	9	10	11	12	13	14
15	16	17	18	19	20	21
22	23	24	25	26	27	28
29	30					

MAY

M	T	W	T	F	S	S
	1	2	3	4	5	
6	7	8	9	10	11	12
13	14	15	16	17	18	19
20	21	22	23	24	25	26
27	28	29	30	31		

JUNE

M	T	W	T	F	S	S
					1	2
3	4	5	6	7	8	9
10	11	12	13	14	15	16
17	18	19	20	21	22	23
24	25	26	27	28	29	30

Earnings Month Effect Performance

In 2017, the first eighteen calendar days of the earnings months were positive three out of four times. The biggest gain occurred in October, as the S&P 500 benefited from an early transition into the stock market prior to the favorable six month period for stocks which starts on October 28th.

In 2018, the first eighteen calendar days for the earnings months' phenomenon started off on a positive note as January rallied strongly at the beginning of the month. The first eighteen calendar days in April were also positive as investors anticipated strong earnings from the tax reforms that had been put in place.

The first eighteen calendar days of July 2018 were strong as investors continued to expect strong earnings due to tax reforms.

CONSUMER SWITCH – SELL CONSUMBER DISCRETIONARY, BUY CONSUMER STAPLES
Consumer Staples Outperform Apr 23 to Oct 27

The *Consumer Switch* strategy has allowed investors to use a set portion of their account to switch between the two related consumer sectors. To use this strategy, investors take a position in the consumer discretionary sector from October 28th to April 22nd, and then use the proceeds to invest in the consumer staples sector from April 23rd to October 27th, and then repeat the cycle.

The end result has been outperformance compared with buying and holding both consumer sectors, or buying and holding the broad market.

4498% total aggregate gain

The basic premise of the strategy is that the consumer discretionary sector tends to outperform during the favorable six month period for stocks (October 28th to May 5th), when more money flows into the stock market, pushing up stock prices. On the other hand, the consumer staples sector tends to outperform when investors are looking for safety and stability of earnings in the other six months when the market tends to move into a defensive mode.

Consumer Staples & Discretionary Switch Strategy*

Investment Period	Buy @ Beginning of Period	% Gain @ End of Period	% Gain Cumulative
90 Apr23 - 90 Oct27	Staples	8.3%	8%
90 Oct28 - 91 Apr22	Discretionary	40.0	52
91 Apr23 - 91 Oct27	Staples	0.7	53
91 Oct28 - 92 Apr22	Discretionary	16.9	78
92 Apr23 - 92 Oct27	Staples	6.9	91
92 Oct28 - 93 Apr22	Discretionary	6.3	103
93 Apr23 - 93 Oct27	Staples	5.4	114
93 Oct28 - 94 Apr22	Discretionary	-4.8	103
94 Apr23 - 94 Oct27	Staples	11.2	126
94 Oct28 - 95 Apr22	Discretionary	4.1	136
95 Apr23 - 95 Oct27	Staples	16.2	174
95 Oct28 - 96 Apr22	Discretionary	16.5	219
96 Apr23 - 96 Oct27	Staples	13.3	261
96 Oct28 - 97 Apr22	Discretionary	4.2	277
97 Apr23 - 97 Oct27	Staples	1.0	281
97 Oct28 - 98 Apr22	Discretionary	36.9	421
98 Apr23 - 98 Oct27	Staples	-0.9	417
98 Oct28 - 99 Apr22	Discretionary	40.1	624
99 Apr23 - 99 Oct27	Staples	-10.3	550
99 Oct28 - 00 Apr22	Discretionary	11.6	625
00 Apr23 - 00 Oct27	Staples	18.8	762
00 Oct28 - 01 Apr22	Discretionary	10.9	855
01 Apr23 - 01 Oct27	Staples	5.3	906
01 Oct28 - 02 Apr22	Discretionary	12.1	1027
02 Apr23 - 02 Oct27	Staples	-11.8	894
02 Oct28 - 03 Apr22	Discretionary	0.5	899
03 Apr23 - 03 Oct27	Staples	8.4	982
03 Oct28 - 04 Apr22	Discretionary	9.9	1090
04 Apr23 - 04 Oct27	Staples	-7.3	1003
04 Oct28 - 05 Apr22	Discretionary	-2.9	971
05 Apr23 - 05 Oct27	Staples	0.3	975
05 Oct28 - 06 Apr22	Discretionary	9.5	1077
06 Apr23 - 06 Oct27	Staples	10.9	1205
06 Oct28 - 07 Apr22	Discretionary	6.6	1292
07 Apr23 - 07 Oct27	Staples	3.9	1346
07 Oct28 - 08 Apr22	Discretionary	-13.7	1147
08 Apr23 - 08 Oct27	Staples	-20.9	887
08 Oct28 - 09 Apr22	Discretionary	17.6	1061
09 Apr23 - 09 Oct27	Staples	20.4	1298
09 Oct28 - 10 Apr22	Discretionary	29.1	1704
10 Apr23 - 10 Oct27	Staples	2.3	1746
10 Oct28 - 11 Apr22	Discretionary	14.0	2004
11 Apr23 - 11 Oct27	Staples	1.8	2042
11 Oct28 - 12 Apr22	Discretionary	12.1	2301
12 Apr23 - 12 Oct27	Staples	3.0	2373
12 Oct28 - 13 Apr22	Discretionary	16.7	2786
13 Apr23 - 13 Oct27	Staples	1.8	2839
13 Oct28 - 14 Apr22	Discretionary	1.9	2897
14 Apr23 - 14 Oct27	Staples	5.8	3069
14 Oct28 - 15 Apr22	Discretionary	14.7	3535
15 Apr23 - 15 Oct27	Staples	2.6	3629
15 Oct28 - 16 Apr22	Discretionary	-0.4	3616
16 Apr23 - 16 Oct27	Staples	1.1	3657
16 Oct28 - 17 Apr22	Discretionary	13.1	4149
17 Apr23 - 17 Oct27	Staples	-3.1	4016
17 Oct28 - 18 Apr22	Discretionary	11.7	4498

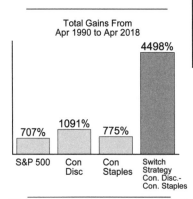

Total Gains From Apr 1990 to Apr 2018

S&P 500 — 707%
Con Disc — 1091%
Con Staples — 775%
Switch Strategy Con. Disc.-Con. Staples — 4498%

Consumer Discretionary / Consumer Staples Relative Strength Avg. Year 1990 - 2017

* If buy date lands on weekend or holiday, then next day is used

Consumer Switch Performance

2017

Legend:
- Seasonal Cons. Disc.
- Seasonal Cons. Staples
- S&P 500
- Cons. Disc.
- Cons. Staples

(Chart: 25%, 20%, 15%, 10%, 5%, 0%, -5% from Jan through Dec)

2018

Legend:
- Seasonal Cons. Disc.
- Seasonal Cons. Staples
- S&P 500
- Cons. Disc.
- Cons. Staples

(Chart: 20%, 15%, 10%, 5%, 0%, -5%, -10%, -15%, -20% from Jan through Dec)

Market Indices & Rates
Weekly Values**

Stock Markets	2017	2018
Dow	20,453	24,360
S&P500	2,329	2,656
Nasdaq	5,805	7,107
TSX	15,535	15,274
FTSE	7,328	7,265
DAX	12,109	12,442
Nikkei	18,336	21,779
Hang Seng	24,262	30,808

Commodities	2017	2018
Oil	53.18	67.39
Gold	1284.2	1343.7

Bond Yields	2017	2018
USA 5 Yr Treasury	1.77	2.67
USA 10 Yr T	2.24	2.82
USA 20 Yr T	2.62	2.91
Moody's Aaa	3.83	3.79
Moody's Baa	4.52	4.61
CAN 5 Yr T	1.04	2.10
CAN 10 Yr T	1.49	2.24

Money Market	2017	2018
USA Fed Funds	1.00	1.75
USA 3 Mo T-B	0.81	1.76
CAN tgt overnight rate	0.50	1.25
CAN 3 Mo T-B	0.51	1.16

Foreign Exchange	2017	2018
EUR/USD	1.06	1.23
GBP/USD	1.25	1.42
USD/CAD	1.33	1.26
USD/JPY	108.64	107.35

APRIL

M	T	W	T	F	S	S
	2	3	4	5	6	7
8	9	10	11	12	13	14
15	16	17	18	19	20	21
22	23	24	25	26	27	28
29	30					

In 2017, the consumer discretionary sector performed slightly better than the S&P 500 in its seasonal period, at the beginning of the year. It also outperformed in its seasonal period at the end of the year. In both instances, the S&P 500 was rallying sharply. The consumer staples sector underperformed both the S&P 500 and the consumer discretionary sector in its seasonal period.

So far in 2018, the consumer discretionary sector has outperformed the S&P 500 in its seasonal period and the consumer staples sector has underperformed the S&P 500 in the first half of its seasonal period.

MAY

M	T	W	T	F	S	S
	1	2	3	4	5	
6	7	8	9	10	11	12
13	14	15	16	17	18	19
20	21	22	23	24	25	26
27	28	29	30	31		

JUNE

M	T	W	T	F	S	S
					1	2
3	4	5	6	7	8	9
10	11	12	13	14	15	16
17	18	19	20	21	22	23
24	25	26	27	28	29	30

U.S. GOVERNMENT BONDS (7-10 YEARS)
May 6th to Oct 3rd

The following government bond seasonal period analysis has been broken down into two contiguous periods in order to demonstrate the relative strength of the first part of the trade compared with the second part. Although both the May 6th to August 8th and the August 9th to October 3rd periods provide value, the sweet spot to the government bond trade is in the latter period from August 9th to October 3rd.

Bonds outperform from late spring into autumn for three reasons. First, governments and companies tend to raise more money through bond issuance at the beginning of the year to meet their needs for the rest of the year. With more bonds competing in the market for money, bond prices tend to decrease. Less bonds tend to be issued in late spring and early summer during their seasonal period, helping to support bond prices.

> **4.0% gain &**
> **positive 80% of the time**

Second, optimistic forecasts at the beginning of the year for stronger GDP growth tend to increase inflation expectations and as a result interest rates respond by increasing. As economic growth expectations tend to decrease in the summer, interest rates respond by retreating.

Third, the stock market often peaks in May and investors rotate their money into bonds. As the demand for bonds increases, interest rates decrease and bonds increase in value. For seasonal investors looking to put their money to work in the unfavora-

ble six months of the year, buying bonds in the summer months fits perfectly.

In periods when the stock market rallies in the early summer months, positive bond performance can be delayed until later in the summer, typically early August, which coincides with the bond seasonal period sweet spot, from August 9th to October 3rd.

Investors should note that government bonds have a track record of appreciating in November and December, but despite their typical positive performance at this time, there are other investments, such as high yield bonds, corporate bonds and equities that have a better return profile.

U.S. Gov. Bonds* vs. S&P 500 1998 to 2017 Positive ☐

Year	May 6 to Aug 8 S&P 500	May 6 to Aug 8 Gov. Bonds	Aug 9 to Oct 3 S&P 500	Aug 9 to Oct 3 Gov. Bonds	Total Growth S&P 500	Total Growth Gov. Bonds
1998	-2.3 %	3.3 %	-8.0 %	8.3 %	-10.1 %	11.9 %
1999	-3.5	-3.0	-1.3	0.9	-4.8	-2.1
2000	3.5	5.8	-3.8	0.9	-0.4	6.7
2001	-6.6	2.6	-9.4	4.4	-15.3	7.1
2002	-15.7	6.5	-9.6	5.0	-23.7	11.9
2003	5.5	-1.3	5.4	1.3	11.2	0.0
2004	-5.1	3.6	6.4	0.8	0.9	4.4
2005	4.3	-0.9	0.3	0.7	4.6	-0.2
2006	-4.1	2.6	4.9	2.7	0.6	5.3
2007	-0.5	-0.3	2.8	3.3	2.3	3.0
2008	-7.9	0.9	-15.2	2.4	-21.9	3.4
2009	11.8	-4.0	1.5	5.4	13.4	1.1
2010	-3.8	7.1	2.2	2.6	-1.7	9.8
2011	-16.2	7.6	-1.8	4.6	-17.7	12.6
2012	2.4	2.3	3.5	0.9	6.0	3.3
2013	5.1	-5.2	-1.1	0.3	4.0	-4.9
2014	2.5	2.3	1.9	0.1	4.4	2.4
2015	-0.6	0.6	-6.1	2.1	-6.6	2.6
2016	6.4	1.6	-0.9	-0.1	5.4	1.6
2017	3.2	1.3	2.4	-0.1	5.6	1.2
Avg.	-1.1 %	1.7 %	-1.3 %	2.3 %	-2.2 %	4.0 %
Fq>0	45 %	70 %	50 %	90 %	55 %	80 %

ⓘ Source: Barclays Capital Inc.
The U.S. Treasury: 7-10 Year is a total return index, which includes both interest and capital appreciation. For more information on fixed income indices, see www.barcap.com.

U.S. Gov. Bonds- Avg. Year 1998 to 2017

U.S. Government Bond Performance

U.S Gov Bonds 7-10yr Monthly Performance (1998-2017)

	Jan	Feb	Mar	Apr	May	Jun	Jul	Aug	Sep	Oct	Nov	Dec
Avg. % Gain	0.7	0.3	0.1	0.1	0.4	0.3	0.6	1.5	1.0	-0.1	0.4	0.1
Med. % Gain	0.7	0.7	0.0	0.3	0.3	0.0	0.7	1.7	0.7	-0.1	-0.0	0.1
Fq %>0	70	60	50	60	55	50	75	80	75	35	50	55

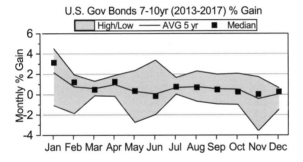

U.S. Gov Bonds 7-10yr (2013-2017) % Gain

U.S. Gov Bonds 7-10yr Performance 2017-2018

Relative Strength, % gain vs. S&P 500

Market Indices & Rates
Weekly Values**

Stock Markets	2017	2018
Dow	20,548	24,463
S&P500	2,349	2,670
Nasdaq	5,911	7,146
TSX	15,614	15,484
FTSE	7,115	7,368
DAX	12,049	12,541
Nikkei	18,621	22,162
Hang Seng	24,042	30,418

Commodities	2017	2018
Oil	49.27	68.38
Gold	1281.9	1336.8

Bond Yields	2017	2018
USA 5 Yr Treasury	1.77	2.80
USA 10 Yr T	2.24	2.96
USA 20 Yr T	2.61	3.04
Moody's Aaa	3.83	3.90
Moody's Baa	4.53	4.74
CAN 5 Yr T	1.01	2.17
CAN 10 Yr T	1.47	2.34

Money Market	2017	2018
USA Fed Funds	1.00	1.75
USA 3 Mo T-B	0.79	1.81
CAN tgt overnight rate	0.50	1.25
CAN 3 Mo T-B	0.53	1.19

Foreign Exchange	2017	2018
EUR/USD	1.07	1.23
GBP/USD	1.28	1.40
USD/CAD	1.35	1.28
USD/JPY	109.09	107.66

APRIL

M	T	W	T	F	S	S
	2	3	4	5	6	7
8	9	10	11	12	13	14
15	16	17	18	19	20	21
22	23	24	25	26	27	28
29	30					

MAY

M	T	W	T	F	S	S
		1	2	3	4	5
6	7	8	9	10	11	12
13	14	15	16	17	18	19
20	21	22	23	24	25	26
27	28	29	30	31		

JUNE

M	T	W	T	F	S	S
					1	2
3	4	5	6	7	8	9
10	11	12	13	14	15	16
17	18	19	20	21	22	23
24	25	26	27	28	29	30

From 1998 to 2017, U.S. government bonds have performed well from May until October, particularly in August and September which is the sweet spot for the seasonal *U.S. Government Bond Trade*. In the last five years, the magnitude of the relative gains in the seasonal period compared to the rest of the year have not been as strong as the long-term trend.

In 2017, U.S. government bonds were positive. In 2018, at the beginning of their seasonal period, U.S. government bonds have been positive.

CANADIAN DOLLAR – STRONG TWICE
①April ②Aug20-Sep25

All other things being equal, if oil increases in price, investors favor the Canadian dollar over the U.S. dollar. They do so with good reason, as Canada is a net exporter of oil and benefits from its rising price.

Oil tends to do well in the month of April, which is the core of the main energy seasonal strategy that lasts from February 25th to May 9th.

April has been a strong month for the Canadian dollar relative to the U.S. dollar. The largest losses have had a tendency to occur in years when the Federal Reserve has been aggressively hiking its target rate.

Since 1971, at some point during the years 1987, 2000, 2004 and 2005, the Federal Reserve increased their target rate by a total of at least 1% in each

CAD vs USD Avg. % Gain 1971 to 2017

year. Three of these years (1987, 2004 and 2005) were three of the biggest losers for the Canadian dollar in the month of April.

The Canadian dollar also has a second period of seasonality, August 20th to September 25th. It is not a coincidence that oil also has a second period of seasonal strength at this time. Although the August 20th to September 25th seasonal period is not as strong as the April seasonal period, it is still a trade worth considering.

CAD vs USD Apr & Aug 20 to Sep 25 % Gain (1971-2018) Source: Bloomberg   Positive

	Apr1-Apr30	Aug20-Sep25		Apr1-Apr30	Aug20-Sep25		Apr1-Apr30	Aug20-Sep25		Apr1-Apr30	Aug20-Sep25		Apr1-Apr30	Aug20-Sep25
1980	0.29%	-0.15%	1990	0.44%	-0.43%	2000	-1.89%	-0.96%	2010	0.44%	1.32%			
1971	-0.10%	0.46%	1981	-0.74	1.08	1991	0.65	0.86	2001	2.76	-1.76	2011	2.44	-4.20
1972	0.53	0.01	1982	0.89	0.78	1992	-0.48	-3.37	2002	1.77	-0.61	2012	1.05	1.16
1973	-0.41	-0.32	1983	0.64	0.17	1993	-1.02	-0.08	2003	2.50	3.95	2013	1.01	0.39
1974	1.27	-0.40	1984	-0.62	-1.01	1994	0.14	2.22	2004	-4.46	1.57	2014	0.88	-1.58
1975	-1.56	1.33	1985	0.04	-0.32	1995	2.91	0.96	2005	-3.77	3.75	2015	4.67	-1.18
1976	0.55	1.41	1986	1.69	0.35	1996	0.15	0.48	2006	4.17	0.64	2016	3.40	-2.29
1977	0.91	0.31	1987	-2.38	1.41	1997	-0.97	0.79	2007	4.17	6.30	2017	-2.45	1.73
1978	0.09	-3.22	1988	0.41	0.43	1998	-0.85	1.37	2008	1.81	2.59	2018	0.44	
1979	1.61	0.15	1989	0.60	0.55	1999	3.53	1.36	2009	5.59	0.46			
Avg.	0.32%	-0.03%		0.06%	0.38%		0.45%	0.51%		1.62%	1.88%		1.33%	-0.57%

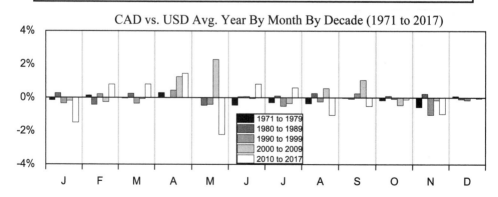

CAD vs. USD Avg. Year By Month By Decade (1971 to 2017)

Legend: 1971 to 1979, 1980 to 1989, 1990 to 1999, 2000 to 2009, 2010 to 2017

CAD/USD Performance

CAD/USD Monthly Performance (1971-2017)

	Jan	Feb	Mar	Apr	May	Jun	Jul	Aug	Sep	Oct	Nov	Dec
Avg. % Gain	-0.4	0.1	0.1	0.7	-0.1	0.0	-0.1	-0.2	0.2	-0.2	-0.5	-0.0
Med. % Gain	-0.4	0.4	-0.0	0.6	-0.3	0.2	-0.2	0.0	0.1	0.0	-0.4	-0.0
Fq %>0	34	64	49	70	34	53	40	49	55	53	34	49

CAD/USD 5 Year (2013-2017) % Gain

CAD/USD Performance 2017-2018

WEEK 17

Market Indices & Rates
Weekly Values**

Stock Markets	2017	2018
Dow	20,941	24,311
S&P500	2,384	2,670
Nasdaq	6,048	7,120
TSX	15,586	15,669
FTSE	7,204	7,502
DAX	12,438	12,581
Nikkei	19,197	22,468
Hang Seng	24,615	30,281

Commodities	2017	2018
Oil	49.33	68.10
Gold	1266.5	1321.5

Bond Yields	2017	2018
USA 5 Yr Treasury	1.81	2.80
USA 10 Yr T	2.29	2.96
USA 20 Yr T	2.67	3.03
Moody's Aaa	3.85	3.94
Moody's Baa	4.57	4.76
CAN 5 Yr T	1.01	2.13
CAN 10 Yr T	1.55	2.32

Money Market	2017	2018
USA Fed Funds	1.00	1.75
USA 3 Mo T-B	0.80	1.82
CAN tgt overnight rate	0.50	1.25
CAN 3 Mo T-B	0.52	1.19

Foreign Exchange	2017	2018
EUR/USD	1.09	1.21
GBP/USD	1.30	1.38
USD/CAD	1.37	1.28
USD/JPY	111.49	109.05

APRIL

M	T	W	T	F	S	S
	2	3	4	5	6	7
8	9	10	11	12	13	14
15	16	17	18	19	20	21
22	23	24	25	26	27	28
29	30					

MAY

M	T	W	T	F	S	S
		1	2	3	4	5
6	7	8	9	10	11	12
13	14	15	16	17	18	19
20	21	22	23	24	25	26
27	28	29	30	31		

JUNE

M	T	W	T	F	S	S
					1	2
3	4	5	6	7	8	9
10	11	12	13	14	15	16
17	18	19	20	21	22	23
24	25	26	27	28	29	30

Canadian Dollar Performance (CAD/USD)

From 1971 to 2017, April has been the strongest month of the year for CAD/USD on an average, median and frequency basis. On a median basis, February is the second strongest month. Over the last five years, May has been the worst performing month.

In 2017, the Canadian dollar started the year on a positive note and then turned negative at the beginning of March. The Canadian dollar was negative in its spring seasonal period. In its August-September seasonal period in 2017 and its 2018 spring seasonal period, the Canadian dollar was positive, despite an overall declining trend for the Canadian dollar that started in September 2017. In 2018, the Canadian dollar was positive in its spring seasonal period.

MAY

	MONDAY	TUESDAY	WEDNESDAY
WEEK 18	29	30	**1** 30
WEEK 19	**6** 25	**7** 24	**8** 23
WEEK 20	**13** 18	**14** 17	**15** 16
WEEK 21	**20** 11 CAN Market Closed- Victoria Day	**21** 10	**22** 9
WEEK 22	**27** 4 USA Market Closed- Memorial Day	**28** 3	**29** 2

THURSDAY		FRIDAY	
2	29	**3**	28
9	22	**10**	21
16	15	**17**	14
23	8	**24**	7
30	1	**31**	

JUNE

M	T	W	T	F	S	S
					1	2
3	4	5	6	7	8	9
10	11	12	13	14	15	16
17	18	19	20	21	22	23
24	25	26	27	28	29	30

JULY

M	T	W	T	F	S	S
1	2	3	4	5	6	7
8	9	10	11	12	13	14
15	16	17	18	19	20	21
20	23	24	25	26	27	28
29	30	31				

AUGUST

M	T	W	T	F	S	S
			1	2	3	4
5	6	7	8	9	10	11
12	13	14	15	16	17	18
19	20	21	22	23	24	25
26	27	28	29	30	31	

SEPTEMBER

M	T	W	T	F	S	S
						1
2	3	4	5	6	7	8
9	10	11	12	13	14	15
16	17	18	19	20	21	22
23	24	25	26	27	28	29
30						

MAY
S U M M A R Y

0.6%
0.4%
0.2%
0.0%
-0.2%
-0.4%

	Dow Jones	S&P 500	Nasdaq	TSX Comp
Month Rank	9	8	5	2
# Up	36	40	29	20
# Down	32	28	17	13
% Pos	53	59	63	61
% Avg. Gain	0.0	0.2	1.1	1.3

Dow & S&P 1950-2017, Nasdaq 1972-2017, TSX 1985-2017

70%
60%
50%
40%

Prob. of Daily Gain

♦ The S&P 500 often peaks in May, and as a result seasonal investors should start to be more cautious with their investments at this time. ♦ Defensive sectors often perform well in May. ♦ The first few days and the last few days in May tend to be strong and the period in between tends to be negative. ♦ A lot of the cyclical sectors finish their seasonal periods at the beginning of May. ♦ The month of May starts the six month unfavorable period for stocks, which has historically been the weaker six months of the year.

BEST / WORST MAY BROAD MKTS. 2009-2018

BEST MAY MARKETS
♦ TSX Comp. (2009) 11.2%
♦ Nikkei 225 (2009) 7.9%
♦ Russell 2000 (2018) 5.9%

WORST MAY MARKETS
♦ Nikkei 225 (2010) -11.7%
♦ Nikkei 225 (2012) -10.3%
♦ Nasdaq (2010) -8.3%

Index Values End of Month

	2009	2010	2011	2012	2013	2014	2015	2016	2017	2018
Dow	8,500	10,137	12,570	12,393	15,116	16,717	18,011	17,787	21,009	24,416
S&P 500	919	1,089	1,345	1,310	1,631	1,924	2,107	2,097	2,412	2,663
Nasdaq	1,774	2,257	2,835	2,827	3,456	4,243	5,070	4,948	6,199	7,442
TSX Comp.	10,370	11,763	13,803	11,513	12,650	14,604	15,014	14,066	15,350	16,062
Russell 1000	502	602	749	724	904	1,072	1,177	1,161	1,336	1,502
Russell 2000	502	662	848	762	984	1,135	1,247	1,155	1,370	1,634
FTSE 100	4,418	5,188	5,990	5,321	6,583	6,845	6,984	6,231	7,520	7,678
Nikkei 225	9,523	9,769	9,694	8,543	13,775	14,632	20,563	17,235	19,651	22,202

Percent Gain for May

	2009	2010	2011	2012	2013	2014	2015	2016	2017	2018
Dow	4.1	-7.9	-1.9	-6.2	1.9	0.8	1.0	0.1	0.3	1.0
S&P 500	5.3	-8.2	-1.4	-6.3	2.1	2.1	1.0	1.5	1.2	0.6
Nasdaq	3.3	-8.3	-1.3	-7.2	3.8	3.1	2.6	3.6	2.5	5.3
TSX Comp.	11.2	-3.7	-1.0	-6.3	1.6	-0.3	-1.4	0.8	-1.5	2.9
Russell 1000	5.3	-8.1	-1.3	-6.4	2.0	2.1	1.1	1.5	1.0	2.3
Russell 2000	2.9	-7.7	-2.0	-6.7	3.9	0.7	2.2	2.1	-2.2	5.9
FTSE 100	4.1	-6.6	-1.3	-7.3	2.4	1.0	0.3	-0.2	4.4	2.2
Nikkei 225	7.9	-11.7	-1.6	-10.3	-0.6	2.3	5.3	3.4	2.4	-1.2

May Market Avg. Performance 2009 to 2018[1]

Dow	-0.7%
S&P 500	-0.2%
Nasdaq	0.7%
TSX Comp (CAN)	0.2%
Russell 1000 (Lg Cap)	-0.1%
Russell 2000 (Sm Cap)	-0.1%
FTSE 100	-0.1%
Nikkei 225	-0.4%

-1.0%   -0.5%   0.0%   0.5%   1.0%

Interest Corner May[2]

	Fed Funds % [3]	3 Mo. T-Bill % [4]	10 Yr % [5]	20 Yr % [6]
2018	1.75	1.93	2.83	2.91
2017	1.00	0.98	2.21	2.60
2016	0.50	0.34	1.84	2.23
2015	0.25	0.01	2.12	2.63
2014	0.25	0.04	2.48	3.05

(1) Russell Data provided by Russell (2) Federal Reserve Bank of St. Louis- end of month values (3) Target rate set by FOMC (4)(5)(6) Constant yield maturities.

| S&P GIC | 2018 | 1990-2018[1] | |
Sectors	% Gain	GIC[2] % Avg Gain	Fq% Gain >S&P 500
Consumer Staples	-1.8 %	1.9 %	55 %
Information Technology	7.1	1.7	62
Health Care	0.0	1.6	52
Financials	-1.1	1.4	45
Consumer Discretionary	1.9	1.3	55
Industrials	2.7	1.0	38
Materials	1.8	0.8	31
Energy	2.5	0.5	34
Utilities	-1.7	0.4	41
Telecom	-2.3 %	0.3 %	45 %
S&P 500	2.2 %	1.1 %	N/A %

Sector Commentary

♦ In May 2018, the information technology sector produced a large 7.1% gain. ♦ The energy sector is typically one of the weaker performing sectors in May, but in 2018 the sector managed to outperform the S&P 500. ♦ The defensive sectors of the stock market were generally negative for the month. The telecom sector produced a loss of 2.3%. ♦ The utilities sector produced a loss of 1.7% and the consumer staples sector produced a loss of 1.8%.

Sub-Sector Commentary

♦ In May 2018, the automotive sub-sector produced a large gain of 8.8%. Some of this gain can be attributed to trade talks during the month progressing well, at least on a temporary basis. ♦ The semiconductor sub-sector produced a gain of 10.8%. ♦ Homebuilders produced a loss of 2.7% as rising interest rates dampened the expected demand for homes. ♦ Pharma stocks were also negative, as investors favored more cyclical sub-sectors in May.

SELECTED SUB-SECTORS[3]

Biotech (1993-2018)	-0.1 %	1.9 %	65 %
Agriculture (1994-2018)	8.8	1.9	52
Banks	-1.0	1.8	48
Retail	3.9	1.8	59
SOX (1995-2018)	10.8	1.5	58
Railroads	6.8	1.5	59
Pharma	-1.8	1.2	45
Chemicals	1.1	0.9	45
Transportation	3.9	0.7	52
Steel	4.2	0.6	48
Automotive & Components	8.8	0.5	28
Metals & Mining	4.8	0.4	45
Gold	-0.6	0.0	48
Silver	1.0	-0.5	41
Homebuilders	-2.7	-0.9	45

Although some children receive Disney stock as a gift to hold onto for life, using a seasonal investment approach to owning the stock has proven to be a better strategy. Disney's stock price has performed like a seasonal roller coaster: on average, up strongly in late autumn, into winter; and down in summer.

Gain of 28.1%

According to Disney's Form 10-K filed with the Securities and Exchange Commission for the year ended September 29, 2012: "Revenues in our Media Networks segment are subject to seasonal advertising patterns... these commitments are typically satisfied during the second half of the Company's fiscal year." The media segment is the biggest driver of revenue for Disney. In addition, their other business segments are skewed towards revenue generation in the summer.

Disney's year-end occurs at the end of September and it typically reports its results in the first week of November. Investors start to increase their positions at the beginning of October in anticipation of positive year-end news.

Investors are particularly attracted to Disney at this time of the year as Q4 tends to be a big revenue reporting quarter.

Do not "visit" the Disney stock from June 5th to September 30th. For the period from 1990 to 2017, Disney produced an average loss of 8.0% and only beat the S&P 500, 18% of the time.

> (i) DIS - stock symbol for Walt Disney Company which trades on the NYSE. is a diversified worldwide entertainment company. Price is adjusted for stock splits.

Disney vs. S&P 500 1990/91 to 2017/18

Negative Short | Positive Long

Year	Jun 5 to Sep 30 S&P 500	Jun 5 to Sep 30 Disney	Oct 1 to Feb 15 S&P 500	Oct 1 to Feb 15 Disney	Compound Growth S&P 500	Compound Growth Disney
1990/91	-16.7 %	-29.4 %	20.6 %	30.1 %	3.9 %	68.4 %
1991/92	0.0	-3.0	6.4	25.4	6.4	29.1
1992/93	1.1	-2.7	6.4	29.7	7.5	33.1
1993/94	2.0	-14.7	3.0	23.9	4.9	42.1
1994/95	0.6	-13.2	4.7	38.5	5.3	56.7
1995/96	9.8	2.7	11.5	11.3	21.2	8.3
1996/97	2.2	5.2	17.5	23.6	19.8	17.1
1997/98	12.8	0.9	7.7	38.2	20.5	36.9
1998/99	-7.1	-30.4	21.0	39.6	13.9	82.1
1999/00	-3.4	-15.1	9.3	41.9	5.9	63.3
2001/01	-2.8	-5.4	-7.7	-15.3	-10.4	-10.7
2001/02	-17.9	-41.1	6.1	28.4	-11.8	81.1
2002/03	-21.7	-31.9	2.4	10.5	-19.3	45.8
2003/04	1.0	-2.7	15.0	33.5	16.0	37.1
2004/05	-0.7	-6.3	8.6	31.2	7.9	39.4
2005/06	2.7	-11.7	4.2	11.4	6.9	24.4
2006/07	3.7	1.0	9.1	12.2	12.8	11.1
2007/08	-0.8	-3.7	-11.6	-5.5	-12.4	-2.1
2008/09	-15.3	-10.7	-29.1	-39.7	-44.4	-33.2
2009/10	12.2	9.2	1.7	9.5	13.9	0.6
2010/11	7.2	-1.8	16.4	30.2	23.5	32.5
2011/12	-13.0	-23.4	18.7	36.8	5.7	68.8
2012/13	12.7	17.7	5.5	6.4	18.2	-12.5
2013/14	3.1	0.2	9.3	22.9	12.4	22.6
2014/15	2.3	5.7	6.3	17.0	8.6	10.4
2015/16	-8.4	-7.3	-2.9	-10.8	-11.3	-4.3
2016/17	3.3	-6.0	8.4	18.7	11.6	25.7
2017/18	3.3	-8.0	8.4	6.7	11.7	15.3
Avg.	1.0 %	-8.0 %	6.3 %	18.1 %	5.3 %	28.1 %
Fq>0	61 %	29 %	86 %	86 %	79 %	79 %

Disney - Avg. Year 1990 to 2017

Disney / S&P 500 Rel. Strength- Avg Yr. 1990-2017

Disney - Performance

DIS Monthly Performance (1990-2017)

	Jan	Feb	Mar	Apr	May	Jun	Jul	Aug	Sep	Oct	Nov	Dec
Avg. % Gain	3.9	3.9	0.2	2.5	1.4	-2.6	-0.7	-3.4	-1.8	3.5	3.8	1.1
Med. % Gain	4.9	4.7	-0.0	1.8	1.4	-2.2	-0.5	-2.7	-1.7	2.1	4.7	1.9
Fq %>0	75	71	50	68	68	29	46	32	43	75	79	71
Fq %>S&P 500	68	71	32	50	50	36	43	36	39	68	75	46

DIS 5 Year (2013-2017) % Gain

DIS Performance 2017-2018

Relative Strength, % gain vs. S&P 500

WEEK 18

Market Indices & Rates
Weekly Values**

Stock Markets	2017	2018
Dow	21,007	24,263
S&P500	2,399	2,663
Nasdaq	6,101	7,210
TSX	15,582	15,729
FTSE	7,297	7,567
DAX	12,717	12,820
Nikkei	19,446	22,473
Hang Seng	24,476	29,927

Commodities	2017	2018
Oil	46.22	69.72
Gold	1228.1	1309.4

Bond Yields	2017	2018
USA 5 Yr Treasury	1.89	2.78
USA 10 Yr T	2.36	2.95
USA 20 Yr T	2.73	3.02
Moody's Aaa	3.90	4.01
Moody's Baa	4.60	4.81
CAN 5 Yr T	0.99	2.15
CAN 10 Yr T	1.54	2.33

Money Market	2017	2018
USA Fed Funds	1.00	1.75
USA 3 Mo T-B	0.90	1.84
CAN tgt overnight rate	0.50	1.25
CAN 3 Mo T-B	0.51	1.21

Foreign Exchange	2017	2018
EUR/USD	1.10	1.20
GBP/USD	1.30	1.35
USD/CAD	1.37	1.28
USD/JPY	112.71	109.12

MAY

M	T	W	T	F	S	S
	1	2	3	4	5
6	7	8	9	10	11	12
13	14	15	16	17	18	19
20	21	22	23	24	25	26
27	28	29	30	31		

JUNE

M	T	W	T	F	S	S
					1	2
3	4	5	6	7	8	9
10	11	12	13	14	15	16
17	18	19	20	21	22	23
24	25	26	27	28	29	30

JULY

M	T	W	T	F	S	S
1	2	3	4	5	6	7
8	9	10	11	12	13	14
15	16	17	18	19	20	21
22	23	24	25	26	27	28
29	30	31				

From 1990 to 2017, Disney has on average been negative from June to September and positive from October into February. The transition from the short sell period to the long period is best navigated with technical analysis. Over the last five years, Disney has generally followed its seasonal trend. October, November and February have been the strongest months (included in the long seasonal period). June and August have been two of the weakest months (included in the short sell seasonal period). In 2017, Disney was negative in its short sell seasonal period. In 2018, Disney was positive in its long seasonal period.

Several times in the last few years, the stock market has corrected sharply in spring, which has prompted many pundits to release reports in the media on "Sell in May and Go Away." But most pundits do not grasp the full value of the favorable six month period for stocks from October 28th to May 5th, compared with the other six months: the unfavorable six month period.

Not only does the favorable period on average have bigger gains more frequently and smaller losses, but also on a yearly basis, outperforms the unfavorable period 71% of the time (last column in the table with YES values). There is no question which six month period seasonal investors should favor.

$1,691,662 gain on $10,000

The accompanying table uses the S&P 500 to compare the returns made from Oct 28th to May 5th, to the returns made during the remainder of the year.

Starting with $10,000 and investing from October 28th to May 5th every year (October 28th, 1950, to May 5th, 2018) has produced a gain of $1,691,662. On the flip side, being invested from May 6th to October 27th, has actually lost money. An initial investment of $10,000 has lost $1,409 over the same time period.

S&P 500 Unfavorable 6 Month Avg. Gain vs Favorable 6 Month Avg. Gain (1950-2017)

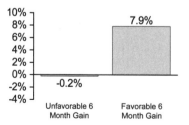

- Favorable 6 Month Gain: 7.9%
- Unfavorable 6 Month Gain: -0.2%

(i) *The above growth rates are geometric averages in order to represent the cumulative growth of a dollar investment over time. These figures differ from the arithmetic mean calculations used in the Six 'N' Six Take a Break Strategy, which are used to represent an average year.*

	S&P 500 % May 6 to Oct 27	$10,000 Start	S&P 500 % Oct 28 to May 5	$10,000 Start	Oct28-May5 > May6-Oct27
1950/51	8.5%	10,851	15.2%	11,517	YES
1951/52	0.2	10,870	3.7	11,947	YES
1952/53	1.8	11,067	3.9	12,413	YES
1953/54	-3.1	10,727	16.6	14,475	YES
1954/55	13.2	12,141	18.1	17,097	YES
1955/56	11.4	13,528	15.1	19,681	YES
1956/57	-4.6	12,903	0.2	19,711	YES
1957/58	-12.4	11,302	7.9	21,265	YES
1958/59	15.1	13,013	14.5	24,356	
1959/60	-0.6	12,939	-4.5	23,270	
1960/61	-2.3	12,647	24.1	28,869	YES
1961/62	2.7	12,993	-3.1	27,982	
1962/63	-17.7	10,698	28.4	35,929	YES
1963/64	5.7	11,306	9.3	39,264	YES
1964/65	5.1	11,882	5.5	41,440	YES
1965/66	3.1	12,253	-5.0	39,388	
1966/67	-8.8	11,180	17.7	46,364	YES
1967/68	0.6	11,241	3.9	48,171	YES
1968/69	5.6	11,872	0.2	48,249	
1969/70	-6.2	11,141	-19.7	38,722	
1970/71	5.8	11,782	24.9	48,346	YES
1971/72	-9.6	10,647	13.7	54,965	YES
1972/73	3.7	11,046	0.3	55,154	
1973/74	0.3	11,084	-18.0	45,205	
1974/75	-23.2	8,513	28.5	58,073	YES
1975/76	-0.4	8,480	12.4	65,290	YES
1976/77	0.9	8,554	-1.6	64,231	
1977/78	-7.8	7,890	4.5	67,146	YES
1978/79	-2.0	7,732	6.4	71,476	YES
1979/80	-0.1	7,723	5.8	75,605	YES
1980/81	20.2	9,283	1.9	77,047	
1981/82	-8.5	8,498	-1.4	76,001	YES
1982/83	15.0	9,769	21.4	92,293	YES
1983/84	0.3	9,803	-3.5	89,085	
1984/85	3.9	10,183	8.9	97,057	YES
1985/86	4.1	10,604	26.8	123,044	YES
1986/87	0.4	10,651	23.7	152,196	YES
1987/88	-21.0	8,409	11.0	168,904	YES
1988/89	7.1	9,010	10.9	187,380	YES
1989/90	8.9	9,814	1.0	189,242	
1990/91	-10.0	8,837	25.0	236,498	YES
1991/92	0.9	8,916	8.5	256,590	YES
1992/93	0.4	8,952	6.2	272,550	YES
1993/94	4.5	9,356	-2.8	264,789	
1994/95	3.2	9,656	11.6	295,636	YES
1995/96	11.5	10,762	10.7	327,219	
1996/97	9.2	11,757	18.5	387,591	YES
1997/98	5.6	12,419	27.2	493,003	YES
1998/99	-4.5	11,860	26.5	623,489	YES
1999/00	-3.8	11,415	10.5	688,842	YES
2000/01	-3.7	10,992	-8.2	632,435	
2001/02	-12.8	9,586	-2.8	614,583	YES
2002/03	-16.4	8,016	3.2	634,369	YES
2003/04	11.3	8,921	8.8	689,985	
2004/05	0.3	8,952	4.2	718,942	YES
2005/06	0.5	9,000	12.5	808,503	YES
2006/07	3.9	9,350	9.3	883,804	YES
2007/08	2.0	9,534	-8.3	810,240	
2008/09	-39.7	5,750	6.5	862,619	YES
2009/10	17.7	6,766	9.6	934,470	
2010/11	1.4	6,862	12.9	1,067,851	YES
2011/12	-3.8	6,602	6.6	1,138,103	YES
2012/13	3.1	6,809	14.3	1,301,313	YES
2013/14	9.0	7,422	7.1	1,393,667	
2014/15	4.1	7,725	6.5	1,484,478	YES
2015/16	-1.1	7,638	-0.7	1,473,513	YES
2016/17	4.0	7,985	12.5	1,649,048	YES
2017/18	7.6	8,591	3.2	1,701,662	
Total Gain (Loss)	**(1,409)**			**$1,691,662**	

6 'n' 6 Strategy Performance

S&P 500 - 5 Year (2013-2017) % Gain

Legend: High/Low — AVG 5 yr ■ Median

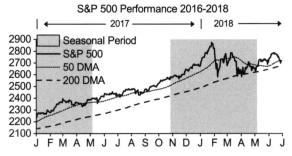

S&P 500 Performance 2016-2018

Legend: Seasonal Period, S&P 500, 50 DMA, 200 DMA

Market Indices & Rates
Weekly Values**

Stock Markets	2017	2018
Dow	20,897	24,831
S&P500	2,391	2,728
Nasdaq	6,121	7,403
TSX	15,538	15,983
FTSE	7,435	7,725
DAX	12,770	13,001
Nikkei	19,884	22,758
Hang Seng	25,156	31,122

Commodities	2017	2018
Oil	47.84	70.70
Gold	1231.3	1324.4

Bond Yields	2016	2017
USA 5 Yr Treasury	1.85	2.84
USA 10 Yr T	2.33	2.97
USA 20 Yr T	2.74	3.03
Moody's Aaa	3.86	3.98
Moody's Baa	4.58	4.79
CAN 5 Yr T	1.00	2.21
CAN 10 Yr T	1.57	2.38

Money Market	2017	2018
USA Fed Funds	1.00	1.75
USA 3 Mo T-B	0.88	1.92
CAN tgt overnight rate	0.50	1.25
CAN 3 Mo T-B	0.51	1.21

Foreign Exchange	2017	2018
EUR/USD	1.09	1.19
GBP/USD	1.29	1.35
USD/CAD	1.37	1.28
USD/JPY	113.38	109.39

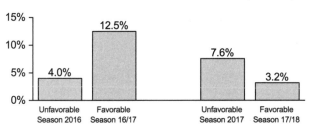

Favorable vs. Unfavorable Seasons 2016-2018 (S&P 500)

Unfavorable Season 2016: 4.0%
Favorable Season 16/17: 12.5%
Unfavorable Season 2017: 7.6%
Favorable Season 17/18: 3.2%

MAY

M	T	W	T	F	S	S
	1	2	3	4	5
6	7	8	9	10	11	12
13	14	15	16	17	18	19
20	21	22	23	24	25	26
27	28	29	30	31		

Over the last five years, the six month seasonal strategy for the stock market has generally followed its seasonal pattern. The months in the six month favorable seasonal period have generally been better than the other six months of the year. The exception to this has been the performance of January, which has been the worst month of the year on a median basis. July, although one of the better months of the year over the last five years, is part of *Summer Sizzler Trade*, when the stock market tends to perform well from the last few days in June and the beginning of July.

In 2016/17, the favorable six month period produced a large gain and outperformed the unfavorable six month period, which produced a much smaller gain. In 2017/18, the favorable six month period was positive, but underperformed the gains in unfavorable six month period.

JUNE

M	T	W	T	F	S	S
					1	2
3	4	5	6	7	8	9
10	11	12	13	14	15	16
17	18	19	20	21	22	23
24	25	26	27	28	29	30

JULY

M	T	W	T	F	S	S
1	2	3	4	5	6	7
8	9	10	11	12	13	14
15	16	17	18	19	20	21
22	23	24	25	26	27	28
29	30	31				

In analyzing long-term trends for the broad markets such as the S&P 500 or the TSX Composite, a large data set is preferable because it incorporates various economic cycles. The daily data set for the TSX Composite starts in 1977.

Over this time period, investors have been rewarded for following the six month cycle of investing from October 28th to May 5th, versus the other unfavorable six month period, May 6th to October 27th.

Starting with an investment of $10,000 in 1977, investing in the unfavorable six months has produced a loss of $3,165, versus investing in the favorable six month period which has produced a gain of $219,205.

$219,205 gain on $10,000 since 1977

The TSX Composite Average Year 1977 to 2017 graph (below), indicates that the market tended to peak in mid-July or the end of August. In our book *Time In Time Out, Outsmart the Stock Market Using Calendar Investment Strategies*, Bruce Lindsay and I analyzed a number of market trends and peaks over different decades.

What we found was that the markets tend to peak at the beginning of May or mid-July. The mid-July peak was usually the result of a strong bull market in place that had a lot of momentum.

The main reason that the TSX Composite data shows a peak occurring in July-August is that the data is primarily from the biggest bull market in history, starting in 1982.

TSX Composite % Gain Avg. Year 1977 to 2017

Does a later average peak in the stock market mean that the best six month cycle does not work? No. Dividing the year up into six month intervals, the period from October to May is far superior compared with the other half of the year. The table below illustrates the superiority of the best six months over the worst six months. Going down the table year by year, the period from October 28th to May 5th outperforms the period from May 6th to October 27th on a regular basis. In a strong bull market, investors always have the choice of using a stop loss or technical indicators to help extend the exit point past the May date.

	TSX Comp May 6 to Oct 27	$10,000 Start	TSX Comp Oct 28 to May 5	$10,000 Start
1977/78	-3.9 %	9,608	13.1 %	11,313
1978/79	12.1	10,775	21.3	13,728
1979/80	2.9	11,084	23.0	16,883
1980/81	22.5	13,579	-2.4	16,479
1981/82	-17.0	11,272	-18.2	13,488
1982/83	16.6	13,138	34.6	18,150
1983/84	-0.9	13,015	-1.9	17,811
1984/85	1.6	13,226	10.7	19,718
1985/86	0.5	13,299	16.5	22,978
1986/87	-1.9	13,045	24.8	28,666
1987/88	-23.4	9,992	15.3	33,050
1988/89	2.7	10,260	5.7	34,939
1989/90	7.9	11,072	-13.3	30,294
1990/91	-8.4	10,148	13.1	34,266
1991/92	-1.6	9,982	-2.0	33,571
1992/93	-2.3	9,750	15.3	38,704
1993/94	10.8	10,801	1.7	39,365
1994/95	-0.1	10,792	0.3	39,483
1995/96	1.3	10,936	18.2	46,671
1996/97	8.3	11,843	10.8	51,725
1997/98	7.3	12,707	17.0	60,510
1998/99	-22.3	9,870	17.1	70,871
1999/00	-0.2	9,853	36.9	97,009
2000/01	-2.9	9,570	-14.4	83,062
2001/02	-12.2	8,399	9.4	90,875
2002/03	-16.4	7,020	4.0	94,476
2003/04	15.1	8,079	10.3	104,252
2004/05	3.9	8,398	7.8	112,379
2005/06	8.1	9,080	19.8	134,587
2006/07	0.0	9,079	12.2	151,053
2007/08	3.8	9,426	-0.2	150,820
2008/09	-40.2	5,638	15.7	174,551
2009/10	11.9	6,307	7.4	187,526
2010/11	5.8	6,674	7.1	200,778
2011/12	-7.4	6,183	-4.8	191,207
2012/13	3.6	6,407	1.1	193,348
2013/14	7.7	6,902	9.7	212,072
2014/15	-1.6	6,795	4.9	222,404
2015/16	-9.7	6,135	-4.9	221,307
2016/17	8.8	6,676	5.0	232,470
2017/18	2.4	6,835	-1.4	229,205
Total Gain (Loss)	**($3,165)**		**$219,205**	

6n6 Canada Strategy Performance

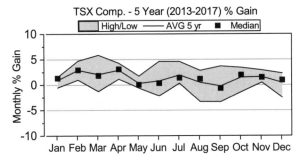

TSX Comp. - 5 Year (2013-2017) % Gain

High/Low — AVG 5 yr ■ Median

TSX Comp. Performance 2017-2018

| 2017 | 2018

- Seasonal Period
- TSX Comp.
- 50 DMA
- 200 DMA

Market Indices & Rates
Weekly Values**

Stock Markets	2017	2018
Dow	20,805	24,715
S&P500	2,382	2,713
Nasdaq	6,084	7,354
TSX	15,458	16,162
FTSE	7,471	7,779
DAX	12,639	13,078
Nikkei	19,591	22,930
Hang Seng	25,175	31,048

Commodities	2017	2018
Oil	50.33	71.28
Gold	1252.0	1288.3

Bond Yields	2017	2018
USA 5 Yr Treasury	1.79	2.90
USA 10 Yr T	2.23	3.06
USA 20 Yr T	2.63	3.14
Moody's Aaa	3.80	4.04
Moody's Baa	4.49	4.89
CAN 5 Yr T	0.95	2.30
CAN 10 Yr T	1.48	2.49

Money Market	2017	2018
USA Fed Funds	1.00	1.75
USA 3 Mo T-B	0.92	1.91
CAN tgt overnight rate	0.50	1.25
CAN 3 Mo T-B	0.51	1.26

Foreign Exchange	2017	2018
EUR/USD	1.12	1.18
GBP/USD	1.30	1.35
USD/CAD	1.35	1.29
USD/JPY	111.26	110.78

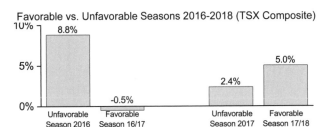

Favorable vs. Unfavorable Seasons 2016-2018 (TSX Composite)

- 8.8% — Unfavorable Season 2016
- -0.5% — Favorable Season 16/17
- 2.4% — Unfavorable Season 2017
- 5.0% — Favorable Season 17/18

MAY

M	T	W	T	F	S	S
	1	2	3	4	5
6	7	8	9	10	11	12
13	14	15	16	17	18	19
20	21	22	23	24	25	26
27	28	29	30	31		

JUNE

M	T	W	T	F	S	S
					1	2
3	4	5	6	7	8	9
10	11	12	13	14	15	16
17	18	19	20	21	22	23
24	25	26	27	28	29	30

JULY

M	T	W	T	F	S	S
1	2	3	4	5	6	7
8	9	10	11	12	13	14
15	16	17	18	19	20	21
22	23	24	25	26	27	28
29	30	31				

Over the last five years, the TSX Composite has generally followed its six month favorable/unfavorable cycle. The worst two months of the year on an average and median basis have been June and September, which are in the unfavorable six month period. The best months of the year have been February and April. February and April are in the favorable six month period.

In 2016, the unfavorable six month period produced a gain of 8.8% for the TSX Composite. The following six month favorable period produced a nominal loss of 0.5%. In 2017, the unfavorable period produced a gain of 2.4% for the TSX Composite, which was less than the gain in the 2017/18 favorable period of 5.0%.

COSTCO – BUY AT A DISCOUNT
①May26-Jun30 ②Oct4-Dec1

Shoppers are attracted to Costco because of its consistently low prices. They take comfort in the fact that although the prices may not always be the lowest, they are consistently in the lower range.

Costco performs well in late spring into early summer, and in autumn into early winter. These two periods are considered to be transition periods where the stock market is moving to and from its unfavorable and favorable seasons. Companies such as Costco that have stable earnings are desirable at these times.

There are two times when Costco is a seasonal bargain: May 26th to June 30th and October 4th to December 1st. From 1994 to 2017, during the period of May 26th to June 30th, Costco has averaged a gain of 4.4% and has been positive 67% of the time. From October 4th to December 1st, Costco has averaged a gain of 8.9% and has been positive 83% of the time.

13.7% gain & positive 96% of the time

Putting both seasonal periods together has produced a 96% positive success rate and an average gain of 13.7%. Although the earlier strong years in the 1990's skews the data to the high-side, Costco has still maintained its strong seasonal performances in both the May to June and the October to December time periods. When investors go shopping for stocks, Costco is one consumer staples company that should be on their list, at least in its favorable seasonal periods.

(i) *COST - stock symbol for Costco which trades on the Nasdaq exchange. Stock data adjusted for stock splits.

Costco* vs. S&P 500 1994 to 2017 Positive ☐

Year	May 26 to Jun 30 S&P 500	COST	Oct 4 to Dec 1 S&P 500	COST	Compound Growth S&P 500	COST
1994	-2.6 %	10.7 %	-2.8	-6.3 %	-5.3	3.7 %
1995	3.1	19.3	4.2	-2.2	7.4	16.7
1996	-1.2	9.5	9.3	15.5	8.0	26.5
1997	4.5	3.1	1.0	16.5	5.6	20.2
1998	2.1	17.6	17.2	41.1	19.7	66.0
1999	6.9	8.1	9.0	30.7	16.5	41.3
2000	5.3	10.0	-7.8	-3.6	-2.9	6.1
2001	-4.2	9.3	6.3	12.3	1.8	22.6
2002	-8.7	-0.8	14.3	4.6	4.4	3.8
2003	4.4	5.3	3.9	13.5	8.5	19.4
2004	2.5	10.3	5.3	17.4	7.9	29.4
2005	0.1	-1.5	3.1	13.9	3.2	12.2
2006	-0.2	5.0	4.7	6.0	4.5	11.3
2007	-0.8	3.8	-3.8	8.9	-4.6	12.9
2008	-7.0	-1.7	-25.8	-23.5	-30.9	-24.7
2009	3.6	-5.2	8.2	7.5	12.1	1.9
2010	-4.0	-3.0	5.2	5.0	1.0	1.9
2011	0.0	1.2	13.2	6.7	13.2	7.9
2012	3.4	12.5	-2.4	4.3	0.9	17.3
2013	-2.6	-3.3	7.6	9.6	4.7	6.0
2014	3.1	0.2	4.4	11.7	7.6	11.9
2015	-3.0	-6.0	7.8	10.6	4.6	3.9
2016	0.4	8.7	1.4	0.5	1.8	9.2
2017	0.4	-8.5	4.3	12.2	4.6	2.7
Avg.	0.2 %	4.4 %	3.7 %	8.9 %	3.9 %	13.7 %
Fq>0	58 %	67 %	79 %	83 %	83 %	96 %

Costco - Avg. Year 1994 to 2017

Costco / S&P 500 Rel. Strength- Avg Yr. 1994-2017

Costco Performance

COST Monthly Performance (1994-2017)

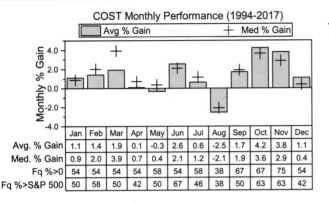

	Jan	Feb	Mar	Apr	May	Jun	Jul	Aug	Sep	Oct	Nov	Dec
Avg. % Gain	1.1	1.4	1.9	0.1	-0.3	2.6	0.6	-2.5	1.7	4.2	3.8	1.1
Med. % Gain	0.9	2.0	3.9	0.7	0.4	2.1	1.2	-2.1	1.9	3.6	2.9	0.4
Fq %>0	54	54	54	54	58	54	58	38	67	67	75	54
Fq %>S&P 500	50	58	50	42	50	67	46	38	50	63	63	42

COST 5 Year (2013-2017) % Gain

COST Performance 2017-2018

Relative Strength, % gain vs. S&P 500

Market Indices & Rates
Weekly Values**

Stock Markets	2017	2018
Dow	21,080	24,753
S&P500	2,416	2,721
Nasdaq	6,210	7,434
TSX	15,417	16,076
FTSE	7,548	7,730
DAX	12,602	12,938
Nikkei	19,687	22,451
Hang Seng	25,639	30,588

Commodities	2017	2018
Oil	49.80	67.91
Gold	1265.1	1303.5

Bond Yields	2017	2018
USA 5 Yr Treasury	1.79	2.76
USA 10 Yr T	2.25	2.93
USA 20 Yr T	2.65	3.01
Moody's Aaa	3.81	3.93
Moody's Baa	4.49	4.78
CAN 5 Yr T	0.97	2.19
CAN 10 Yr T	1.45	2.35

Money Market	2017	2018
USA Fed Funds	1.00	1.75
USA 3 Mo T-B	0.94	1.90
CAN tgt overnight rate	0.50	1.25
CAN 3 Mo T-B	0.52	1.28

Foreign Exchange	2017	2018
EUR/USD	1.12	1.17
GBP/USD	1.28	1.33
USD/CAD	1.34	1.30
USD/JPY	111.33	109.41

MAY

M	T	W	T	F	S	S
	1	2	3	4	5	
6	7	8	9	10	11	12
13	14	15	16	17	18	19
20	21	22	23	24	25	26
27	28	29	30	31		

JUNE

M	T	W	T	F	S	S
					1	2
3	4	5	6	7	8	9
10	11	12	13	14	15	16
17	18	19	20	21	22	23
24	25	26	27	28	29	30

JULY

M	T	W	T	F	S	S
						1
2	3	4	5	6	7	
8	9	10	11	12	13	14
15	16	17	18	19	20	21
22	23	24	25	26	27	28
29	30	31				

From 1994 to 2017, October and November have been the best two contiguous months for Costco on an average and frequency basis. This has been mainly driven by Costco releasing its year-end earnings at the end of September. The other strong month is June, which occurs right after Costco typically announces its Q3 results. Over the last five years, on average, July has been Costco's best month (not in seasonal period) juxtaposed with August, which has been one of its worst months.

In 2017, Costco outperformed the S&P 500 in its October 4th to December 1st seasonal period, and also more recently in its first seasonal period in 2018.

MID CAPS – THE FORGOTTEN SECTOR
①SELL SHORT (Jun3-Jun26) ②LONG (Nov23-Dec31)
③LONG (Jan9-Mar7)

The terms, large caps and small caps get bantered around in the media frequently. The part of the stock market between these two sectors is the mid-cap sector, and is often overlooked. The mid-cap sector of the stock market behaves differently than its "bookends" and it is an important sector to follow. Tracking the mid cap sector can help establish if the small caps or large caps are becoming favorable. In addition, the mid-cap sector has seasonal periods during the year when it tends to outperform the S&P 500.

8.0% gain & positive 85% of the time

From June 3rd to June 26th, mid caps tend to underperform large caps as investors have a preference for large caps in an often volatile market at this time of the year.

From November 23rd to December 31st, mid caps tend to outperform as investment managers try to reposition their portfolios with a higher beta for the start of the year.

From January 9th to March 7th, the mid cap sector tends to perform well as investment managers start the year on a positive note and try to get ahead of the broad index with the higher beta mid cap sector of the stock market.

ⓘ *The mid cap sector of the stock market is the middle capitalization sector of the stock market.*

Mid Caps* vs. S&P 500 1992 to 2017

Negative Short [ ]   Positive Long [▒]

Year	Jan 9 to Mar 7 S&P 500	Jan 9 to Mar 7 Mid Caps	Jun 3 to Jun 26 S&P 500	Jun 3 to Jun 26 Mid Caps	Nov 23 to Dec 31 S&P 500	Nov 23 to Dec 31 Mid Caps	Compound Growth S&P 500	Compound Growth Mid Caps
1992	-3.3 %	-1.5 %	-2.4 %	-6.2 %	2.1 %	4.8 %	-3.6 %	9.6 %
1993	4.0	3.2	-1.4	-1.2	1.6	6.1	4.2	10.8
1994	-0.6	2.0	-3.2	-5.9	2.0	2.0	-1.9	10.1
1995	4.7	4.5	2.2	2.8	2.9	2.4	10.1	4.0
1996	5.7	7.1	-0.7	-3.6	-1.1	0.2	3.8	11.2
1997	7.6	3.2	4.4	1.7	0.8	3.1	13.2	4.6
1998	10.4	10.0	3.7	0.6	5.6	11.0	20.9	21.3
1999	0.0	-6.7	1.6	1.9	3.4	3.7	5.1	-5.1
2000	-6.0	9.1	-1.5	-2.3	-0.2	5.9	-7.5	18.2
2001	-2.6	4.7	-3.5	-4.2	1.0	6.3	-5.1	16.0
2002	-0.3	3.9	-8.8	-9.2	-5.5	-3.4	-14.0	9.7
2003	-8.9	-8.5	2.0	1.4	7.4	5.1	-0.3	-5.3
2004	2.2	5.3	0.8	1.2	3.0	5.0	6.1	9.1
2005	3.3	7.5	-1.1	-0.3	-1.0	-0.2	1.2	7.6
2006	-0.7	0.1	-2.9	-4.5	0.9	-1.0	-2.8	3.5
2007	-1.5	2.9	-2.8	-3.7	3.6	4.2	-0.8	11.2
2008	-7.0	-4.5	-7.4	-5.5	12.9	21.9	-2.7	22.8
2009	-24.9	-25.2	-2.7	-3.7	2.2	5.7	-25.4	-18.0
2010	-0.6	2.5	-2.0	-2.2	5.0	6.0	2.4	11.0
2011	3.0	5.0	-3.4	-2.9	5.9	4.8	5.4	13.2
2012	5.9	8.1	3.3	1.0	2.5	4.3	12.1	11.6
2013	6.0	6.8	-1.7	-3.2	2.4	2.6	6.7	13.1
2014	2.2	3.8	1.7	2.7	-0.2	0.6	3.7	1.5
2015	0.4	2.3	-0.4	0.3	-2.2	-3.4	-2.1	-1.4
2016	4.2	7.4	-3.2	-3.3	1.6	2.0	2.4	13.1
2017	4.0	2.2	0.0	0.0	3.0	2.3	7.1	4.5
Avg.	0.3 %	2.1 %	-1.1 %	-1.9 %	2.3 %	3.9 %	1.5 %	8.0 %
Fq>0	58 %	81 %	31	35 %	77 %	85 %	58 %	85 %

Mid Caps - Avg. Year 1992-2017

Mid Caps / S&P 500 Rel. Strength- Avg Yr. 1992-2017

Mid Cap Strategy Performance

Mid Caps Monthly Performance (1992-2017)

	Jan	Feb	Mar	Apr	May	Jun	Jul	Aug	Sep	Oct	Nov	Dec
Avg. % Gain	0.0	1.1	1.7	2.0	1.0	-0.4	0.5	-0.2	-0.0	1.2	1.9	2.4
Med. % Gain	1.0	1.3	1.4	1.2	1.6	0.3	-0.0	0.4	0.8	2.2	3.2	2.0
Fq %>0	54	65	73	65	65	54	50	54	58	69	77	73
Fq %>S&P 500	50	69	50	42	58	46	46	54	46	38	54	69

Mid Caps 5 Year (2013-2017) % Gain

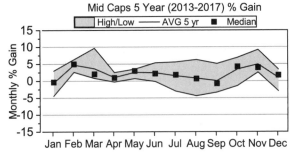

Mid Caps Performance 2017-2018

Relative Strength, % gain vs. S&P 500

Market Indices & Rates
Weekly Values**

Stock Markets	2017	2018
Dow	21,206	24,635
S&P500	2,439	2,735
Nasdaq	6,306	7,554
TSX	15,443	16,044
FTSE	7,548	7,702
DAX	12,823	12,724
Nikkei	20,177	22,171
Hang Seng	25,924	30,493

Commodities	2017	2018
Oil	47.66	65.81
Gold	1275.0	1294.6

Bond Yields	2017	2018
USA 5 Yr Treasury	1.71	2.74
USA 10 Yr T	2.15	2.89
USA 20 Yr T	2.53	2.96
Moody's Aaa	3.70	3.92
Moody's Baa	4.39	4.79
CAN 5 Yr T	0.93	2.12
CAN 10 Yr T	1.40	2.25

Money Market	2017	2018
USA Fed Funds	1.00	1.75
USA 3 Mo T-B	0.98	1.92
CAN tgt overnight rate	0.50	1.25
CAN 3 Mo T-B	0.51	1.26

Foreign Exchange	2017	2018
EUR/USD	1.13	1.17
GBP/USD	1.29	1.33
USD/CAD	1.35	1.30
USD/JPY	110.40	109.54

From 1992 to 2017, one of the strongest months of the year for mid caps has been November on an average basis. Both December and February have performed well and are the core of the strong seasonal periods. June tends to be a weaker month for the mid caps.

Over the last five years, mid caps have generally followed their seasonal trend with February and November being two of the better months.

In the autumn of 2017 and the beginning of 2018, mid caps were positive in their strong seasonal periods, but underperformed the S&P 500.

MAY

M	T	W	T	F	S	S
	1	2	3	4	5
6	7	8	9	10	11	12
13	14	15	16	17	18	19
20	21	22	23	24	25	26
27	28	29	30	31

JUNE

M	T	W	T	F	S	S
					1	2
3	4	5	6	7	8	9
10	11	12	13	14	15	16
17	18	19	20	21	22	23
24	25	26	27	28	29	30

JULY

M	T	W	T	F	S	S
1	2	3	4	5	6	7
8	9	10	11	12	13	14
15	16	17	18	19	20	21
22	23	24	25	26	27	28
29	30	31

JUNE

	MONDAY	TUESDAY	WEDNESDAY
WEEK 22	27	28	29
WEEK 23	**3** 27	**4** 26	**5** 25
WEEK 24	**10** 20	**11** 19	**12** 18
WEEK 25	**17** 13	**18** 12	**19** 11
WEEK 26	**24** 6	**25** 5	**26** 4

THURSDAY		FRIDAY	
30		31	
6	24	**7**	23
13	17	**14**	16
20	10	**21**	9
27	3	**28**	2

JULY

M	T	W	T	F	S	S
1	2	3	4	5	6	7
8	9	10	11	12	13	14
15	16	17	18	19	20	21
22	23	24	25	26	27	28
29	30	31				

AUGUST

M	T	W	T	F	S	S
			1	2	3	4
5	6	7	8	9	10	11
12	13	14	15	16	17	18
19	20	21	22	23	24	25
26	27	28	29	30	31	

SEPTEMBER

M	T	W	T	F	S	S
						1
2	3	4	5	6	7	8
9	10	11	12	13	14	15
16	17	18	19	20	21	22
23	24	25	26	27	28	29
30						

OCTOBER

M	T	W	T	F	S	S
	1	2	3	4	5	6
7	8	9	10	11	12	13
14	15	16	17	18	19	20
21	22	23	24	25	26	27
28	29	30	31			

JUNE
SUMMARY

	Dow Jones	S&P 500	Nasdaq	TSX Comp
Month Rank	11	10	9	11
# Up	32	36	25	14
# Down	36	32	21	19
% Pos	47	53	54	42
% Avg. Gain	-0.3	0.0	0.7	-0.4

Dow & S&P 1950-2017, Nasdaq 1972-2017, TSX 1985-2017

S&P500 Cumulative Daily Gains for Avg Month 1950 to 2018

♦ On average, June is not a strong month for the S&P 500. From 1950 to 2018, it was the third worst month of the year, producing a flat return of 0.0%. ♦ From year to year, different sectors of the market tend to lead in June as there is not a strong consistent outperforming major sector. ♦ On average, the bio-tech sector starts its seasonal run in late June. ♦ The last few days of June, the start of the successful *Summer Sizzler Trade,* tend to be positive.

BEST / WORST JUNE BROAD MKTS. 2009-2018

BEST JUNE MARKETS
♦ Nikkei 225 (2012) 5.4%
♦ Russell 2000 (2014) 5.2%
♦ Russell 2000 (2012) 4.8%

WORST JUNE MARKETS
♦ Nikkei 225 (2016) - 9.6%
♦ Russell 2000 (2010) -7.9%
♦ FTSE 100 (2015) - 6.6%

Index Values End of Month

	2009	2010	2011	2012	2013	2014	2015	2016	2017	2018
Dow	8,447	9,774	12,414	12,880	14,910	16,827	17,620	17,930	21,350	24,271
S&P 500	919	1,031	1,321	1,362	1,606	1,960	2,063	2,099	2,423	2,663
Nasdaq	1,835	2,109	2,774	2,935	3,403	4,408	4,987	4,843	6,140	7,510
TSX Comp.	10,375	11,294	13,301	11,597	12,129	15,146	14,553	14,065	15,182	16,278
Russell 1000	502	567	734	751	891	1,095	1,153	1,162	1,344	1,510
Russell 2000	508	609	827	798	977	1,193	1,254	1,152	1,415	1,643
FTSE 100	4,249	4,917	5,946	5,571	6,215	6,744	6,521	6,504	7,313	7,637
Nikkei 225	9,958	9,383	9,816	9,007	13,677	15,162	20,236	15,576	20,033	22,305

Percent Gain for June

	2009	2010	2011	2012	2013	2014	2015	2016	2017	2018
Dow	-0.6	-3.6	-1.2	3.9	-1.4	0.7	-2.2	0.8	1.6	-0.6
S&P 500	0.0	-5.4	-1.8	4.0	-1.5	1.9	-2.1	0.1	0.5	0.0
Nasdaq	3.4	-6.5	-2.2	3.8	-1.5	3.9	-1.6	-2.1	-0.9	0.9
TSX Comp.	0.0	-4.0	-3.6	0.7	-4.1	3.7	-3.1	0.0	-1.1	1.3
Russell 1000	0.1	-5.7	-1.9	3.7	-1.5	2.1	-2.0	0.1	0.5	0.5
Russell 2000	1.3	-7.9	-2.5	4.8	-0.7	5.2	0.6	-0.2	3.3	0.6
FTSE 100	-3.8	-5.2	-0.7	4.7	-5.6	-1.5	-6.6	4.4	-2.8	-0.5
Nikkei 225	4.6	-4.0	1.3	5.4	-0.7	3.6	-1.6	-9.6	1.9	0.5

June Market Avg. Performance 2009 to 2018[1]

Dow	-0.3%
S&P 500	-0.4%
Nasdaq	-0.3%
TSX Comp (CAN)	-1.0%
Russell 1000 (Lg Cap)	-0.4%
Russell 2000 (Sm Cap)	0.4%
FTSE 100	-1.8%
Nikkei 225	0.1%

-2.5% -2.0% -1.5% -1.0% -0.5% 0.0% 0.5% 1.0%

Interest Corner Jun[2]

	Fed Funds %[3]	3 Mo. T-Bill %[4]	10 Yr %[5]	20 Yr %[6]
2018	2.00	1.93	2.85	2.91
2017	1.25	1.03	2.31	2.61
2016	0.50	0.26	1.49	1.86
2015	0.25	0.01	2.35	2.83
2014	0.25	0.04	2.53	3.08

(1) Russell Data provided by Russell (2) Federal Reserve Bank of St. Louis- end of month values (3) Target rate set by FOMC (4)(5)(6) Constant yield maturities.

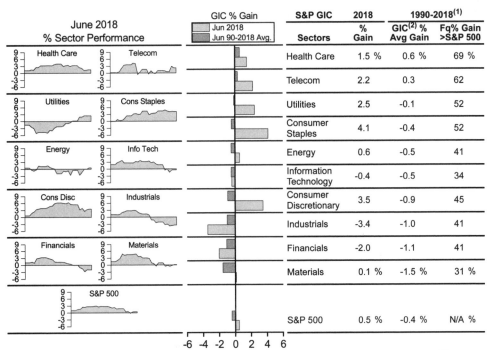

S&P GIC Sectors	2018 % Gain	1990-2018[1] GIC[2] % Avg Gain	1990-2018[1] Fq% Gain >S&P 500
Health Care	1.5 %	0.6 %	69 %
Telecom	2.2	0.3	62
Utilities	2.5	-0.1	52
Consumer Staples	4.1	-0.4	52
Energy	0.6	-0.5	41
Information Technology	-0.4	-0.5	34
Consumer Discretionary	3.5	-0.9	45
Industrials	-3.4	-1.0	41
Financials	-2.0	-1.1	41
Materials	0.1 %	-1.5 %	31 %
S&P 500	0.5 %	-0.4 %	N/A %

Sector Commentary

♦ In June 2018, the consumer staples sector was the top performing sector with a gain of 4.1%. ♦ The second best performing sector was the consumer discretionary sector with a gain 3.5%. ♦ Overall, investors favored the consumer sectors in June. ♦ Investors were also attracted to the defensive sectors with telecom producing a return of 2.2% and utilities 2.5%. ♦ The worst performing sector was the industrial sector with a loss of 3.4%. ♦ The industrial sector was largely negative as investors became increasingly concerned that the ongoing trade wars were going to have an impact on industrial companies.

Sub-Sector Commentary

♦ In June 2018, the agriculture sub-sector produced a strong gain of 4.8%. ♦ The retail sub-sector also produced a strong gain of 4.4%. ♦ Generally, the cyclical sub-sectors performed poorly. ♦ The auto sub-sector produced a loss of 6.0%. ♦ The transportation sub-sector produced a loss of 4.1% and the semi-conductor sub-sector produced a loss of 4.7%.

SELECTED SUB-SECTORS[3]

	2018 % Gain	GIC % Avg Gain	Fq% Gain >S&P 500
Pharma	1.4 %	0.7 %	69 %
Gold	-4.2	-0.3	48
Retail	4.4	-0.4	55
Biotech (1993-2018)	1.2	-0.6	50
Metals & Mining	-1.1	-0.8	52
Railroads	-0.9	-1.0	38
Homebuilders	-1.6	-1.0	45
Steel	-2.6	-1.2	41
SOX (1995-2018)	-4.7	-1.3	33
Transportation	-4.1	-1.3	31
Agriculture (1994-2018)	4.8	-1.3	36
Chemicals	0.8	-1.6	34
Automotive & Components	-6.0	-1.9	45
Silver	-3.1	-1.9	38
Banks	-1.5	-1.9	31

(1) Sector data provided by Standard and Poors (2) GIC is short form for Global Industry Classification (3) Sub Sector data provided by Standard and Poors, except where marked by symbol.

BIOTECH SUMMER SOLSTICE
June 23rd to September 13th

The *Biotech Summer Solstice* trade starts on June 23rd and lasts until September 13th. The trade is aptly named as its outperformance starts approximately when summer solstice starts– the longest day of the year.

There are two main drivers of the trade: biotech is a good substitute for technology stocks in the summer, and investors want to take a position in the biotech sector before the autumn conferences.

10.8% extra & 88% of the time better than the S&P 500

Biotech* vs. S&P 500 1992 to 2017

Jun 23 to Sep 13	S&P 500	Positive	
		Biotech	Diff
1992	4.0 %	17.9 %	13.8 %
1993	3.6	3.6	0.0
1994	3.2	24.2	21.0
1995	5.0	31.5	26.5
1996	2.1	7.0	4.9
1997	2.8	-18.9	-21.7
1998	-8.5	20.6	29.1
1999	0.6	64.3	63.7
2000	2.3	7.6	5.4
2001	-10.8	-3.6	7.2
2002	-10.0	8.1	18.2
2003	2.3	6.4	4.1
2004	-0.8	8.9	9.6
2005	1.4	26.0	24.5
2006	5.8	7.4	1.6
2007	-1.2	6.0	7.2
2008	-5.0	11.4	16.5
2009	16.8	7.7	-9.1
2010	2.4	2.8	0.4
2011	-8.9	-3.7	5.2
2012	9.4	15.6	6.2
2013	6.0	24.9	18.9
2014	1.2	14.8	13.6
2015	-7.6	-7.2	0.5
2016	2.0	7.3	5.3
2017	2.6	11.1	8.5
Avg	0.8 %	11.6 %	10.8 %
Fq>0	69 %	85 %	88 %

Biotech Sector - Avg. Year 1992 to 2017

Biotech / S&P 500 Relative Strength - Avg Yr. 1992 - 2017

As a result, in the summer months when investors tend to be more cautious, they are more willing to commit speculative money into the biotech sector, compared with the technology sector.

The biotech sector is one of the few sectors that starts its outperformance in June. This is in part because of the biotech conferences that occur in autumn and with the possibility of positive announcements, the price of biotech companies can increase dramatically. As a result, investors try to lock in positions early.

The biotechnology sector is often considered the cousin of the technology sector, a good place for speculative investments. The sectors are similar as both include concept companies (companies without a product but with good potential).

Despite their similarity, investors view the sectors differently. The technology sector is viewed as being much more dependent on the economy compared with the biotech sector. The end product of biotechnology companies is mainly medicine, which is not economically sensitive.

Biotech SP GIC Sector # 352010: Companies primarily engaged in the research, development, manufacturing and/or marketing of products based on genetic analysis and genetic engineering. This includes companies specializing in protein-based therapeutics to treat human diseases.

Biotech Performance

Biotech Monthly Performance (1992-2017)

	Jan	Feb	Mar	Apr	May	Jun	Jul	Aug	Sep	Oct	Nov	Dec
Avg. % Gain	1.5	-1.0	-0.3	-0.1	2.3	-0.6	6.7	0.4	1.4	1.4	2.3	3.4
Med. % Gain	2.7	0.9	-1.2	0.5	3.1	0.0	6.2	-0.7	0.5	3.1	3.0	0.6
Fq %>0	62	54	46	54	69	50	81	46	54	54	58	58
Fq %>S&P 500	54	50	35	38	69	50	85	58	62	46	46	46

Biotech 5 Year (2013-2017) % Gain

Biotech Performance 2017-2018

Relative Strength, % gain vs. S&P 500

Market Indices & Rates
Weekly Values**

Stock Markets	2017	2018
Dow	21,272	25,317
S&P500	2,432	2,779
Nasdaq	6,208	7,646
TSX	15,473	16,203
FTSE	7,527	7,681
DAX	12,816	12,767
Nikkei	20,013	22,695
Hang Seng	26,030	30,958

Commodities	2017	2018
Oil	45.83	65.74
Gold	1266.6	1298.3

Bond Yields	2017	2018
USA 5 Yr Treasury	1.77	2.77
USA 10 Yr T	2.21	2.93
USA 20 Yr T	2.59	3.00
Moody's Aaa	3.74	3.96
Moody's Baa	4.42	4.83
CAN 5 Yr T	0.96	2.17
CAN 10 Yr T	1.42	2.32

Money Market	2017	2018
USA Fed Funds	1.00	1.75
USA 3 Mo T-B	1.01	1.93
CAN tgt overnight rate	0.50	1.25
CAN 3 Mo T-B	0.51	1.23

Foreign Exchange	2017	2018
EUR/USD	1.12	1.18
GBP/USD	1.27	1.34
USD/CAD	1.35	1.29
USD/JPY	110.32	109.55

JUNE

M	T	W	T	F	S	S
					1	2
3	4	5	6	7	8	9
10	11	12	13	14	15	16
17	18	19	20	21	22	23
24	25	26	27	28	29	30

JULY

M	T	W	T	F	S	S
1	2	3	4	5	6	7
8	9	10	11	12	13	14
15	16	17	18	19	20	21
22	23	24	25	26	27	28
29	30	31				

From 1992 to 2017, the best month for the biotech sector has been July on an average, median and frequency basis. The start of the seasonal period for the sector is late June and runs into the middle of September. On the whole, June is a negative month, but the tail end of the month often provides a good buying opportunity. Although August has been positive on an average absolute basis, it can be a weaker month and investors should be prepared to exit the sector before the seasonal period finishes. Over the last five years, the sector has demonstrated superior performance in July. In 2017, the sector outperformed the S&P 500 during its seasonal period.

AUGUST

M	T	W	T	F	S	S
		1	2	3	4	
5	6	7	8	9	10	11
12	13	14	15	16	17	18
19	20	21	22	23	24	25
26	27	28	29	30	31	

CAMECO— CHARGES DOWN AND UP

①SELL SHORT (Jun5-Aug7)
②LONG (Oct4-Jan24)

Cameco is the world's largest publically traded uranium company. It trades on both the NYSE stock exchange (ticker: CCJ) and the Toronto Stock Exchange (ticker: CCO).

Cameco has a very narrow market for its product: countries that need uranium to power their nuclear reactors. Mining operations do not vary much throughout the year, so supply is fairly constant. In addition actual usage of uranium does not change much throughout the year as nuclear reactors are run most efficiently at one constant level over time. Yet, there is a seasonal tendency for Cameco to perform well from October 4th to January 24th. In this time period, from 1995 to 2018, Cameco has produced an average gain of 15.4%. Also, in the same yearly period, from June 5th to August 7th, Cameco has performed poorly, producing an average loss of 7.3%.

23.5% growth & positive 83% of the time

The seasonal trend for Cameco can be partly explained by the overall tendency of the stock market to perform well during Cameco's strong seasonal period, and poorly during Cameco's weak seasonal period.

The seasonal trend for Cameco can also be explained somewhat with buyer behavior. The World Nuclear Association (WNA) has an annual conference that takes place in the middle of September of each year. As a result of the conference, buyers tend to be reassured of the future demand of uranium, helping to give Cameco a boost starting in October.

ⓘ *Cameco Corporation is in the materials sector. Its stock symbol is CCO, which trades on the Toronto Stock Exchange, adjusted for splits.*

Cameco vs. TSX Composite Index - 1995/96 to 2017/18

Negative Short ☐   Positive Long ☐

Year	Jun 5 to Aug 7		Oct 4 to Jan 24		Compound Growth	
	TSX	CCO	TSX	CCO	TSX	CCO
1995/96	3.7 %	1.8 %	8.1	42.7 %	12.1 %	40.1 %
1996/97	-3.7	-6.1	12.2	-16.5	8.0	-11.5
1997/98	8.0	1.1	-8.5	-22.6	-1.1	-23.4
1998/99	-11.3	-23.2	19.5	44.4	6.0	77.9
1999/00	-0.9	-16.9	22.0	-24.8	21.0	-12.1
2000/01	8.4	-13.7	-11.0	25.0	-3.5	42.1
2001/02	-6.4	-20.3	10.9	14.6	3.9	37.9
2002/03	-14.3	-28.6	10.6	27.9	-5.2	64.5
2003/04	2.6	4.9	14.4	35.7	17.4	29.1
2004/05	-2.1	8.9	3.8	30.6	1.7	19.0
2005/06	9.1	5.7	5.5	38.3	15.1	30.4
2006/07	0.3	-9.1	12.9	18.6	13.2	29.4
2007/08	-4.1	-30.2	-7.9	-15.7	-11.8	9.8
2008/09	-8.9	-15.0	-20.1	-6.5	-27.2	7.5
2009/10	3.9	0.5	3.5	6.2	7.5	5.6
2010/11	2.0	11.2	8.0	35.6	10.1	20.4
2011/12	-10.0	-13.7	10.2	29.0	-0.9	45.0
2012/13	4.7	9.0	3.8	12.6	8.6	2.4
2013/14	-1.4	-10.3	7.7	29.6	6.2	42.9
2014/15	2.2	-3.1	-0.1	-8.9	2.1	-6.0
2015/16	-4.8	-6.2	-7.1	-0.9	-11.6	5.3
2016/17	3.0	-17.3	6.3	54.0	9.4	80.7
2017/18	-1.2	3.7	3.5	8.0	2.3	4.0
Avg.	-0.9 %	-7.3 %	4.7	15.4 %	3.6 %	23.5 %
Fq>0	48 %	39 %	74 %	70 %	83 %	83 %

Likewise, investors often have a low interest level in Cameco in the summer months ahead of the WNA conference in mid-September.

Cameco - Avg. Year 1996 to 2017

Cameco / TSX Comp. Rel. Strength- Avg Yr. 1996-2017

Cameco Performance

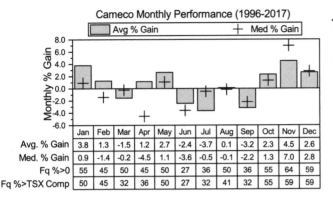

Cameco Monthly Performance (1996-2017)

Legend: Avg % Gain, Med % Gain

	Jan	Feb	Mar	Apr	May	Jun	Jul	Aug	Sep	Oct	Nov	Dec
Avg. % Gain	3.8	1.3	-1.5	1.2	2.7	-2.4	-3.7	0.1	-3.2	2.3	4.5	2.6
Med. % Gain	0.9	-1.4	-0.2	-4.5	1.1	-3.6	-0.5	-0.1	-2.2	1.3	7.0	2.8
Fq %>0	55	45	50	45	50	27	36	50	36	55	64	59
Fq %>TSX Comp	50	45	32	36	50	27	32	41	32	55	59	59

Cameco 5 Year (2013-2017) % Gain

Legend: High/Low, AVG 5 yr, Median

Cameco Performance 2017-2018

Legend: Seasonal Period, Short Period, CCO, 50 DMA, 200 DMA

Relative Strength, % gain vs. TSX Comp.

Market Indices & Rates
Weekly Values**

Stock Markets	2017	2018
Dow	21,384	25,090
S&P500	2,433	2,780
Nasdaq	6,152	7,746
TSX	15,193	16,314
FTSE	7,464	7,634
DAX	12,753	13,011
Nikkei	19,943	22,852
Hang Seng	25,626	30,309

Commodities	2017	2018
Oil	44.74	65.06
Gold	1255.4	1285.3

Bond Yields	2017	2018
USA 5 Yr Treasury	1.75	2.81
USA 10 Yr T	2.16	2.93
USA 20 Yr T	2.52	2.98
Moody's Aaa	3.67	3.91
Moody's Baa	4.35	4.80
CAN 5 Yr T	1.14	2.08
CAN 10 Yr T	1.52	2.22

Money Market	2017	2018
USA Fed Funds	1.25	2.00
USA 3 Mo T-B	1.03	1.94
CAN tgt overnight rate	0.50	1.25
CAN 3 Mo T-B	0.55	1.22

Foreign Exchange	2017	2018
EUR/USD	1.12	1.16
GBP/USD	1.28	1.33
USD/CAD	1.32	1.32
USD/JPY	110.88	110.66

From 1996 to 2017, October to January has been the strongest four month contiguous period for Cameco on an average basis.

Generally, over the last five years, Cameco has followed its seasonal pattern with November through February being strong months and June a weak month. July has been an anomaly, producing a positive return in a weak seasonal period.

In 2017 and 2018, Cameco was positive and outperformed the S&P 500 in its seasonal strong period.

JUNE

M	T	W	T	F	S	S
					1	2
3	4	5	6	7	8	9
10	11	12	13	14	15	16
17	18	19	20	21	22	23
24	25	26	27	28	29	30

JULY

M	T	W	T	F	S	S
1	2	3	4	5	6	7
8	9	10	11	12	13	14
15	16	17	18	19	20	21
22	23	24	25	26	27	28
29	30	31				

AUGUST

M	T	W	T	F	S	S
		1	2	3	4
5	6	7	8	9	10	11
12	13	14	15	16	17	18
19	20	21	22	23	24	25
26	27	28	29	30	31	

SUMMER SIZZLER– THE FULL TRADE
PROFIT BEFORE & AFTER FIREWORKS
Two Market Days Before June Month End
To 5 Market Days After Independence Day

The beginning of July is a time for celebration and the markets tend to agree.

Based on previous market data, the best way to take advantage of this trend is to be invested for the two market days prior to June month end and hold until five market days after Independence Day. This time period has produced above average returns on a fairly consistent basis.

Since 1950, 0.9% avg. gain & 72% of the time positive

S&P 500 Avg. Year 1950 to 2018

The typical strategy to take advantage of the tendency of positive performance around Independence Day has been to invest one or two days before the holiday and take profits one or two days after the holiday.

Although this strategy has produced profits, it has left a lot of money on the table. This strategy misses out on the positive days at the end of June and on the full slate of positive days after Independence Day.

The beginning part of the *Summer Sizzler Trade's* positive trend is driven by portfolio managers who "window dress" their portfolios, buying stocks at month end that have a favorable perception in the market in order to make their portfolios look good on month and quarter end statements. This is particularly true at quarter ends. The result is typically increased buying pressure that lifts the stock market.

Depending on market conditions at the time, investors should consider extending the exit date of the *Summer Sizzler Trade* until eighteen calendar days in July. With July being an earnings month, the market can continue to rally until mid-month (see *18 Day Earnings Month Strategy*).

S&P 500, 2 Market Days Before June Month End To 5 Market Days after Independence Day % Gain 1950 to 2018   Positive ☐

1950	-4.4 %	1960	-0.1 %	1970	1.5 %	1980	1.4 %	1990	1.7 %	2000	1.8 %	2010	0.4 %
1951	1.5	1961	1.7	1971	3.2	1981	-2.4	1991	1.4	2001	-2.6	2011	1.8
1952	0.9	1962	9.8	1972	0.3	1982	-0.6	1992	2.8	2002	-4.7	2012	0.7
1953	0.8	1963	0.5	1973	2.1	1983	1.5	1993	-0.6	2003	1.2	2013	4.5
1954	2.9	1964	2.3	1974	-8.8	1984	-0.7	1994	0.4	2004	-1.7	2014	0.5
1955	4.9	1965	5.0	1975	-0.2	1985	1.5	1995	1.8	2005	1.5	2015	-1.2
1956	3.4	1966	2.1	1976	2.4	1986	-2.6	1996	-2.8	2006	2.1	2016	5.0
1957	3.8	1967	1.3	1977	-0.6	1987	0.4	1997	3.7	2007	0.8	2017	0.2
1958	2.0	1968	2.3	1978	0.6	1988	-0.6	1998	2.7	2008	-3.4	2018	2.8
1959	3.3	1969	-1.5	1979	1.3	1989	0.9	1999	5.1	2009	-4.3		
Avg.	1.9 %		2.3 %		0.2 %		-0.1 %		1.8 %		-0.9 %		1.6 %

Summary Sizzler Strategy Performance

■ Summer Sizzler Trade

2016

5.0%

2017

0.2%

2018

2.8%

Market Indices & Rates
Weekly Values**

Stock Markets	2017	2018
Dow	21,395	24,581
S&P500	2,438	2,755
Nasdaq	6,265	7,693
TSX	15,320	16,450
FTSE	7,424	7,682
DAX	12,733	12,580
Nikkei	20,133	22,517
Hang Seng	25,670	29,339

Commodities	2016	2017
Oil	42.81	68.98
Gold	1255.7	1269.2

Bond Yields	2016	2017
USA 5 Yr Treasury	1.77	2.77
USA 10 Yr T	2.15	2.90
USA 20 Yr T	2.48	2.97
Moody's Aaa	3.60	3.99
Moody's Baa	4.30	4.87
CAN 5 Yr T	1.12	1.98
CAN 10 Yr T	1.48	2.13

Money Market	2016	2017
USA Fed Funds	1.25	2.00
USA 3 Mo T-B	0.97	1.93
CAN tgt overnight rate	0.50	1.25
CAN 3 Mo T-B	0.59	1.20

Foreign Exchange	2016	2017
EUR/USD	1.12	1.17
GBP/USD	1.27	1.33
USD/CAD	1.33	1.33
USD/JPY	111.28	109.97

JUNE

M	T	W	T	F	S	S
					1	2
3	4	5	6	7	8	9
10	11	12	13	14	15	16
17	18	19	20	21	22	23
24	25	26	27	28	29	30

JULY

M	T	W	T	F	S	S
1	2	3	4	5	6	7
8	9	10	11	12	13	14
15	16	17	18	19	20	21
22	23	24	25	26	27	28
29	30	31				

AUGUST

M	T	W	T	F	S	S
		1	2	3	4	
5	6	7	8	9	10	11
12	13	14	15	16	17	18
19	20	21	22	23	24	25
26	27	28	29	30	31	

In 2016, the S&P 500 benefited from the post Brexit rally. The rally started a few days before the end of June, but tapered off after the *Summer Sizzler Trade*.

In 2017, the S&P 500 produced a nominal return of 0.2% during the *Summer Sizzler Trade* period. After the *Summer Sizzler Trade* finished, the S&P 500 rallied sharply.

In 2018, the S&P 500 declined for most of June and rallied into the *Summer Sizzler Trade* to produce a gain of 2.8%.

SOUTHWEST AIRLINES– TAKES FLIGHT

①LONG (Jan25-Mar4) ②SELL SHORT (Aug1-Aug31)
③LONG (Sep1-Dec6)

Southwest Airlines is a domestically focused airline with some international travel. As a result, the airline includes a large number of short haul routes. Its business is largely funded by the discretionary spending of its clients and as such, is economically sensitive.

24.6% gain & positive 76% of the time

Southwest Airlines tends not to perform well in August as investors shy away from the stock with September on average being one of the lowest traffic months of the year for Southwest Airlines.

Despite September being a low traffic month for Southwest Airlines, investors front run the increase in passenger traffic in October and November, pushing up the price of the airline starting at the beginning of September.

Investors tend to lose interest in Southwest Airlines in early December, anticipating a reduction in traffic in January and February.

Despite February being one of the lowest traffic months for Southwest Airlines, investors tend to front run improving traffic flows and push up the stock price of Southwest Airlines from January 25th to March 4th.

*Southwest Airlines is in the consumer discretionary sector. It trades on the NYSE. Stock is adjusted for splits.

Southwest Airlines* vs. S&P 500 1990 to 2017

Negative Short ☐   Positive Long ▨

Year	Jan 25 to Mar 4 S&P 500	Jan 25 to Mar 4 LUV	Aug 1 to Aug 31 S&P 500	Aug 1 to Aug 31 LUV	Sep 1 to Dec 6 S&P 500	Sep 1 to Dec 6 LUV	Compound Growth S&P 500	Compound Growth LUV
1990	1.6 %	14.6 %	-9.4 %	-10.9 %	2.0 %	18.0 %	-6.1 %	50.0 %
1991	10.3	22.1	2.0	-9.7	-4.1	28.2	7.8	71.8
1992	-1.5	14.5	-2.4	-4.5	4.4	32.9	0.3	59.1
1993	2.6	26.3	3.4	6.8	0.6	-3.9	6.8	13.1
1994	-1.5	-7.8	3.8	-2.3	-4.7	-22.6	-2.6	-27.0
1995	4.2	-2.7	0.0	-10.0	10.4	0.0	15.0	7.0
1996	5.0	39.3	1.9	-8.1	13.4	8.8	21.3	63.8
1997	2.7	9.7	-5.7	-3.5	9.4	29.2	5.8	46.6
1998	9.4	12.0	-14.6	-18.9	22.9	24.2	14.8	65.4
1999	1.8	13.6	-0.6	-9.8	7.8	0.8	9.0	25.6
2000	0.6	19.4	6.1	-4.2	-11.0	39.3	-5.0	73.2
2001	-9.5	-5.6	-6.4	-10.6	3.0	8.1	-12.8	12.9
2002	1.9	14.4	0.5	2.9	-0.4	14.5	2.0	27.1
2003	-4.6	-5.3	1.8	4.1	5.3	-8.8	2.3	-17.2
2004	1.2	-8.3	0.2	2.4	7.8	7.0	9.3	-4.3
2005	5.0	7.1	-1.1	-6.1	3.6	24.0	7.5	41.0
2006	1.6	3.9	2.1	-3.7	8.4	-10.5	12.5	-3.5
2007	-3.7	-0.6	1.3	-3.5	2.3	-7.6	-0.2	-4.9
2008	-1.9	5.8	1.2	-2.3	-31.7	-42.0	-32.2	-37.3
2009	-14.3	-34.8	3.4	4.2	8.4	25.1	-4.0	-21.8
2010	2.9	7.9	-4.7	-8.3	16.6	17.7	14.2	37.6
2011	2.4	-7.5	-5.7	-13.5	3.3	-0.9	-0.3	3.9
2012	4.2	-2.2	2.0	-2.7	0.5	10.5	6.8	11.0
2013	2.0	5.2	-3.1	-7.4	10.5	42.9	9.3	61.4
2014	4.7	9.6	3.8	13.2	3.6	28.5	12.5	22.2
2015	2.3	-3.9	-6.3	1.4	6.1	34.6	1.7	27.6
2016	4.9	6.4	-0.1	-0.4	1.9	29.3	6.7	38.0
2017	4.5	18.6	0.1	-6.1	6.4	17.2	11.2	47.4
Avg.	1.4 %	6.1 %	-1.0 %	-4.0 %	3.8 %	12.3 %	4.1 %	24.6 %
Fq>0	75 %	64 %	54	25 %	82 %	71 %	71 %	75 %

LUV - Avg. Year 1990-2017

LUV / S&P 500 Rel. Strength- Avg Yr. 1990-2017

Southwest Airlines Performance

Southwest Monthly Performance (1990-2017)

	Jan	Feb	Mar	Apr	May	Jun	Jul	Aug	Sep	Oct	Nov	Dec
Avg. % Gain	1.4	3.8	2.7	1.8	0.3	-0.3	3.8	-4.0	1.2	4.0	5.3	0.2
Med. % Gain	-0.2	5.7	2.9	0.5	-1.0	-0.1	5.2	-3.9	0.3	5.1	5.2	0.4
Fq %>0	46	64	68	57	43	46	68	25	50	71	68	50
Fq %>S&P 500	50	64	57	57	46	50	57	29	61	61	61	39

Southwest 5 Year (2013-2017) % Gain

Southwest Performance 2017-2018

Relative Strength, % gain vs. S&P 500

Market Indices & Rates
Weekly Values**

Stock Markets	2017	2018
Dow	21,350	24,271
S&P500	2,423	2,718
Nasdaq	6,140	7,510
TSX	15,182	16,278
FTSE	7,313	7,637
DAX	12,325	12,306
Nikkei	20,033	22,305
Hang Seng	25,765	28,955
Commodities	**2017**	**2018**
Oil	46.04	74.15
Gold	1242.3	1250.5
Bond Yields	**2017**	**2018**
USA 5 Yr Treasury	1.89	2.73
USA 10 Yr T	2.31	2.85
USA 20 Yr T	2.61	2.91
Moody's Aaa	3.71	3.93
Moody's Baa	4.40	4.84
CAN 5 Yr T	1.39	2.07
CAN 10 Yr T	1.76	2.17
Money Market	**2017**	**2018**
USA Fed Funds	1.25	2.00
USA 3 Mo T-B	1.03	1.93
CAN tgt overnight rate	0.50	1.25
CAN 3 Mo T-B	0.71	1.26
Foreign Exchange	**2017**	**2018**
EUR/USD	1.14	1.17
GBP/USD	1.30	1.32
USD/CAD	1.30	1.31
USD/JPY	112.39	110.76

JUNE

M	T	W	T	F	S	S
					1	2
3	4	5	6	7	8	9
10	11	12	13	14	15	16
17	18	19	20	21	22	23
24	25	26	27	28	29	30

JULY

M	T	W	T	F	S	S
1	2	3	4	5	6	7
8	9	10	11	12	13	14
15	16	17	18	19	20	21
22	23	24	25	26	27	28
29	30	31				

AUGUST

M	T	W	T	F	S	S
		1	2	3	4
5	6	7	8	9	10	11
12	13	14	15	16	17	18
19	20	21	22	23	24	25
26	27	28	29	30	31	

From 1990 to 2017, February, October and November have been three of the strongest months of the year for Southwest Airlines on an average basis. February is the core part of the beginning of the year strong seasonal period and October and November are the core part of the autumn seasonal period. August has been the worst performing month for Southwest Airlines and has on average been the best time to short sell the stock. Over the last five years, Southwest Airlines has followed its general seasonal trend. In 2017, all of the seasonal trends worked for Southwest Airlines. In 2018, Southwest Airlines underperformed in its first seasonal period.

JULY

	MONDAY	TUESDAY	WEDNESDAY
WEEK 27	**1** CAN Market Closed- Canada Day	**2** 29	**3** 28
WEEK 28	**8** 23	**9** 22	**10** 21
WEEK 29	**15** 16	**16** 15	**17** 14
WEEK 30	**22** 9	**23** 8	**24** 7
WEEK 31	**29** 2	**30** 1	**31**

THURSDAY	FRIDAY
4 27	**5** 26
USA Market Closed - Independence Day	
11 20	**12** 19
18 13	**19** 12
25 6	**26** 5
1	2

AUGUST

M	T	W	T	F	S	S
			1	2	3	4
5	6	7	8	9	10	11
12	13	14	15	16	17	18
19	20	21	22	23	24	25
26	27	28	29	30	31	

SEPTEMBER

M	T	W	T	F	S	S
						1
2	3	4	5	6	7	8
9	10	11	12	13	14	15
16	17	18	19	20	21	22
23	24	25	26	27	28	29
30						

OCTOBER

M	T	W	T	F	S	S
	1	2	3	4	5	6
7	8	9	10	11	12	13
14	15	16	17	18	19	20
21	22	23	24	25	26	27
28	29	30	31			

NOVEMBER

M	T	W	T	F	S	S
				1	2	3
4	5	6	7	8	9	10
11	12	13	14	15	16	17
18	19	20	21	22	23	24
25	26	27	28	29	30	

JULY
S U M M A R Y

S&P500 Cumulative Daily Gains for Avg Month 1950 to 2017

	Dow Jones	S&P 500	Nasdaq	TSX Comp
Month Rank	4	5	10	6
# Up	43	38	25	21
# Down	25	30	21	12
% Pos	63	56	54	64
% Avg. Gain	1.2	1.0	0.5	0.9

Dow & S&P 1950-2017, Nasdaq 1972-2017, TSX 1985-2017

♦ When a summer rally occurs in the stock market, the gains are usually made in July. ♦ Typically, it is the first part of July that produces the gains as the market tends to rally before Independence Day and into the first eighteen calendar days (see the *18 Days Earnings Month Effect*). In 2017, July produced a strong gain of 1.5% during its first eighteen calendar days. ♦ On average, volatility starts to increase in July and continues this trend into October. ♦ August and September, the two months following July tend to be seasonally weak.

BEST / WORST JULY BROAD MKTS. 2008-2017

BEST JULY MARKETS
- ♦ Russell 2000 (2009) 9.5%
- ♦ Dow (2009) 8.6%
- ♦ FTSE 100 (2009) 8.5%

WORST JULY MARKETS
- ♦ Russell 2000 (2014) -6.1%
- ♦ TSX Comp (2008) -6.0%
- ♦ FTSE 100 (2008) -3.8%

Index Values End of Month

	2008	2009	2010	2011	2012	2013	2014	2015	2016	2017
Dow	11,378	9,172	10,466	12,143	13,009	15,500	16,563	17,690	18,432	21,891
S&P 500	1,267	987	1,102	1,292	1,379	1,686	1,931	2,104	2,174	2,470
Nasdaq	2,326	1,979	2,255	2,756	2,940	3,626	4,370	5,128	5,162	6,348
TSX Comp.	13,593	10,787	11,713	12,946	11,665	12,487	15,331	14,468	14,583	15,144
Russell 1000	694	540	606	718	759	937	1,076	1,174	1,204	1,369
Russell 2000	715	557	651	797	787	1,045	1,120	1,239	1,220	1,425
FTSE 100	5,412	4,608	5,258	5,815	5,635	6,621	6,730	6,696	6,724	7,372
Nikkei 225	13,377	10,357	9,537	9,833	8,695	13,668	15,621	20,585	16,569	19,925

Percent Gain for July

	2008	2009	2010	2011	2012	2013	2014	2015	2016	2017
Dow	0.2	8.6	7.1	-2.2	1.0	4.0	-1.6	0.4	2.8	2.5
S&P 500	-1.0	7.4	6.9	-2.1	1.3	4.9	-1.5	2.0	3.6	1.9
Nasdaq	1.4	7.8	6.9	-0.6	0.2	6.6	-0.9	2.8	6.6	3.4
TSX Comp.	-6.0	4.0	3.7	-2.7	0.6	2.9	1.2	-0.6	3.7	-0.3
Russell 1000	-1.3	7.5	6.8	-2.3	1.1	5.2	-1.7	1.8	3.7	1.9
Russell 2000	3.6	9.5	6.8	-3.7	-1.4	6.9	-6.1	-1.2	5.9	0.7
FTSE 100	-3.8	8.5	6.9	-2.2	1.2	6.5	-0.2	2.7	3.4	0.8
Nikkei 225	-0.8	4.0	1.6	0.2	-3.5	-0.1	3.0	1.7	6.4	-0.5

July Market Avg. Performance 2008 to 2017[1]

Dow	2.3%
S&P 500	2.3%
Nasdaq	3.4%
TSX Comp (CAN)	0.7%
Russell 1000 (Lg Cap)	2.3%
Russell 2000 (Sm Cap)	2.1%
FTSE 100	2.4%
Nikkei 225	1.2%

Interest Corner Jul[2]

	Fed Funds %[3]	3 Mo. T-Bill %[4]	10 Yr %[5]	20 Yr %[6]
2017	1.25	1.07	2.30	2.66
2016	0.50	0.28	1.46	1.78
2015	0.25	0.08	2.20	2.61
2014	0.25	0.03	2.58	3.07
2013	0.25	0.04	2.60	3.34

(1) Russell Data provided by Russell (2) Federal Reserve Bank of St. Louis- end of month values (3) Target rate set by FOMC (4)(5)(6) Constant yield maturities.

- 79 -

July 2017 % Sector Performance

S&P GIC	2017	1990-2017[1]		
Sectors	% Gain	GIC[2] % Avg Gain	Fq% Gain >S&P 500	
Financials	1.6 %	1.5 %	46 %	
Information Technology	4.3	1.4	54	
Materials	1.4	1.0	57	
Health Care	0.7	0.9	46	
Consumer Staples	0.4	0.8	54	
Energy	2.4	0.7	61	
Industrials	0.0	0.6	43	
Consumer Discretionary	1.8	0.5	54	
Utilities	2.4	0.1	46	
Telecom	5.1 %	-0.1 %	46 %	
S&P 500	1.9 %	0.9 %	N/A %	

Sector Commentary

♦ July is an earnings month and the S&P 500 performed positively into the start of the earnings season in July 2017. ♦ The information technology sector performed well as the "FAANG" stocks helped to propel the sector higher. ♦ The energy sector produced a strong gain of 2.4% as it started its summer seasonal period of strength early (seasonal period starts in late July). ♦ The industrial sector was the weakest performing sector as it was flat. The strongest performing sector was the telecom sector with a gain of 5.1%.

Sub-Sector Commentary

♦ In July 2017, the metals and mining sub-sector produced a large gain of 11.5%. ♦ The biotech sector, in its strongest seasonal month (July), produced a gain of 3.8%. ♦ The semi-conductor sub-sector produced a large gain of 4.9%. Semi-conductor stocks are typically not strong in July, but the increased demand for graphic chips to satisfy mining for cryptocurrencies helped to move the sub-sector higher. ♦ The transportation sub-sector produced a large loss of 5.2%.

SELECTED SUB-SECTORS[3]			
Biotech (1993-2017)	3.8 %	6.6 %	84 %
Railroads	-6.7	2.2	61
Silver	1.8	1.6	61
Banks	0.2	1.5	64
Automotive & Components	1.0	1.4	50
Chemicals	0.6	1.2	54
Retail	1.9	1.2	61
Transportation	-5.2	1.1	46
Homebuilders	0.6	0.8	46
SOX (1995-2017)	4.9	0.6	43
Metals & Mining	11.5	0.5	50
Pharma	0.4	0.4	50
Gold	2.0	0.3	50
Steel	-0.3	-0.2	46
Agriculture (1994-2017)	1.9	-0.7	46

(1) Sector data provided by Standard and Poors (2) GIC is short form for Global Industry Classification (3) Sub Sector data provided by Standard and Poors, except where marked by symbol.

GOLD SHINES
(Metal) ① Jul12-Oct9 ② Dec27-Jan26

There is very little seasonal change in the supply of gold. It tends to be constant throughout the year. The seasonal demand changes throughout the year tend to be a large driver in the price of gold.

Most of the gold produced each year is consumed in jewelery fabrication. The time of the year with the highest demand for gold is in the fourth quarter, particularly around Indian Diwali, the festival of lights. The demand for gold bullion takes place in previous months as gold fabricators purchase gold bullion to fashion into jewelery for Diwali.

5.7% gain & 67% of the time positive

The result is that gold bullion tends to rise from July 12th to October 9th. In this period, from 1984 to 2017, gold bullion has increased on average 3.4% and has been positive 70% of the time.

In more recent years, the Chinese have become large consumers of gold and have vied with India for the top gold consuming country. The Chinese consume most of their gold around the Chinese New Year, which takes place early in the calendar year.

In the yearly period from 1984 to 2018, from December 27th to January 26th, gold bullion has produced an average gain of 2.3% and has been positive 53%. Gains in this period have been more frequent in recent years as the Chinese population has increased its consumption of gold.

Source: Bank of England- London PM represents the close value of gold in afternoon trading in London.

Gold* vs. S&P 500 - 1984/85 to 2017/18   Positive [ ]

Year	Jul 12 to Oct 9 S&P 500	Gold	Dec 27 to Jan 26 S&P 500	Gold	Compound Growth S&P 500	Gold
1984/85	7.4 %	0.5 %	6.5 %	-3.9 %	14.4 %	-3.4 %
1985/86	-5.4	4.2	-0.4	9.0	-5.7	13.5
1986/87	-2.6	25.2	9.2	4.3	6.3	30.6
1987/88	0.9	3.9	-1.0	-2.4	-0.1	1.4
1988/89	2.8	-7.5	5.0	-2.6	7.9	-10.0
1989/90	9.4	-4.2	-6.1	1.3	2.8	-3.0
1990/91	-15.5	12.1	1.6	-2.5	-14.2	9.3
1991/92	-0.1	-2.9	2.6	-1.8	2.6	-4.6
1992/93	-2.9	0.4	0.0	-0.6	-2.8	-0.2
1993/94	2.7	-8.8	1.3	-0.5	4.0	-9.3
1994/95	1.6	1.6	1.9	-0.1	3.4	1.6
1995/96	4.3	-0.1	1.2	4.8	5.5	4.7
1996/97	7.9	-0.4	1.9	-4.4	10.0	-4.7
1997/98	5.9	4.4	2.2	3.5	8.2	8.0
1998/99	-15.5	2.8	2.1	0.5	-13.7	3.3
1999/00	-4.8	25.6	-3.7	-0.5	-8.3	25.0
2000/01	-5.3	-4.5	3.0	-3.5	-2.5	-7.9
2001/02	-10.5	8.4	-1.4	0.5	-11.7	9.0
2002/03	-16.2	1.7	-3.2	6.4	-18.9	8.2
2003/04	4.1	7.8	5.4	-0.3	9.7	7.5
2004/05	0.8	3.8	-3.0	-3.5	-2.2	0.1
2005/06	-1.9	11.4	0.4	11.3	-1.5	24.0
2006/07	6.1	-8.8		4.0	6.5	-5.1
2007/08	3.1	11.0	-11.2	13.3	-8.4	25.8
2008/09	-26.6	-8.2	-4.2	7.9	-29.6	-1.0
2009/10	21.9	15.2	-3.1	0.7	18.2	16.0
2010/11	8.1	11.0	3.2	-3.3	11.5	7.3
2011/12	-12.4	6.2	4.2	7.5	-8.8	14.2
2012/13	7.5	12.5	5.9	0.5	13.7	13.1
2013/14	-1.1	1.5	-2.8	5.7	-3.9	7.2
2014/15	-2.0	-8.1	-1.5	9.0	-3.5	0.1
2015/16	-3.0	-0.7	-7.6	4.3	-10.4	3.6
2016/17	0.8	-7.3	1.5	5.2	2.2	-2.5
2017/18	4.9	5.6	7.2	7.0	12.4	13.0
Avg.	-0.8 %	3.4 %	0.5 %	2.3 %	-0.2 %	5.7 %
Fq>0	53 %	70 %	63 %	53 %	50 %	67 %

Gold - Avg. Year 1984 to 2017

Gold / S&P 500 Rel. Strength- Avg Yr. 1984-2017

Gold Performance

Gold Monthly Performance (1984-2017)

	Jan	Feb	Mar	Apr	May	Jun	Jul	Aug	Sep	Oct	Nov	Dec
Avg. % Gain	1.3	0.7	-0.1	0.3	-0.0	-0.2	0.3	0.7	1.9	-0.9	1.2	-0.5
Med. % Gain	0.4	0.7	-0.9	-0.2	0.0	0.2	-0.4	0.7	2.1	-0.4	0.8	-0.3
Fq %>0	53	56	44	47	50	53	50	62	65	41	65	41
Fq %>S&P 500	53	44	35	44	47	44	50	50	65	26	53	29

Gold 5 Year (2013-2017) % Gain

Gold Performance 2017-2018

Relative Strength, % gain vs. S&P 500

Market Indices & Rates
Weekly Values**

Stock Markets	2016	2017
Dow	18,147	21,414
S&P500	2,130	2,425
Nasdaq	4,957	6,153
TSX	14,260	15,027
FTSE	6,591	7,351
DAX	9,630	12,389
Nikkei	15,107	19,929
Hang Seng	20,564	25,341

Commodities	2016	2017
Oil	45.41	44.23
Gold	1354.3	1215.7

Bond Yields	2016	2017
USA 5 Yr Treasury	0.95	1.95
USA 10 Yr T	1.37	2.39
USA 20 Yr T	1.69	2.71
Moody's Aaa	3.18	3.79
Moody's Baa	4.15	4.47
CAN 5 Yr T	0.52	1.47
CAN 10 Yr T	0.96	1.88

Money Market	2016	2017
USA Fed Funds	0.50	1.25
USA 3 Mo T-B	0.28	1.05
CAN tgt overnight rate	0.50	0.50
CAN 3 Mo T-B	0.46	0.75

Foreign Exchange	2016	2017
EUR/USD	1.11	1.14
GBP/USD	1.30	1.29
USD/CAD	1.30	1.29
USD/JPY	100.54	113.92

JULY

M	T	W	T	F	S	S
1	2	3	4	5	6	7
8	9	10	11	12	13	14
15	16	17	18	19	20	21
22	23	24	25	26	27	28
29	30	31				

AUGUST

M	T	W	T	F	S	S
				1	2	3	4
5	6	7	8	9	10	11
12	13	14	15	16	17	18
19	20	21	22	23	24	25
26	27	28	29	30	31	

SEPTEMBER

M	T	W	T	F	S	S
						1
2	3	4	5	6	7	8
9	10	11	12	13	14	15
16	17	18	19	20	21	22
23	24	25	26	27	28	29
30						

From 1984 to 2017, the best month for gold bullion on a average, median and frequency basis has been September. On average the worst month of the year has been October. With the juxtaposition of the best and worst months, investors have to be cautious. Over the last five years, gold has performed above average in July and August, and has performed poorly in September. It has also performed well in January.

In 2017/18, gold was positive in its seasonal periods, outperforming the S&P 500 in its July to October seasonal period and slightly underperforming in its early year seasonal period.

GOLD MINERS – DIG GAINS
(Stocks) ①Jul27-Sep25 ②Dec23-Feb14

The gold miners sector tends to perform well at approximately the same time in the year that gold bullion performs well. As gold bullion moves higher in price, gold miners benefit from their gold in the ground increasing in value.

Gold miners have their main seasonal period of strength from July 27th to September 25th. In this time period, from 1984 to 2017, gold miners have produced an average return of 5.0% and have been positive 60% of the time. Gold miners tend to perform well as gold bullion tends to increase at this time due to increased demand to make gold jewelery for fourth quarter consumption.

10.9% gain & 70% of the time positive

Gold miners also tend to perform well at the beginning of the year as Chinese New Year approaches. The Chinese buy a large amount of their gold in the period leading up to Chinese New Year. Over the years, this trend has become more predominant as the wealth of Chinese citizens has increased.

During the years 1984 to 2018, from December 23rd to February 14th, gold miners have produced an average gain of 6.2% and have been positive 53% of the time.

Combining the two gold seasonal trades together has proven to be beneficial as the frequency of gains for the combined trade increases to 70% and produces a average gain of 10.9%.

Year	Jul 27 to Sep 25 S&P 500	XAU	Dec 23 to Feb 14 S&P 500	XAU	Compound Growth S&P 500	XAU
1984/85	10.4 %	20.8 %	10.2 %	10.6 %	21.6 %	33.6 %
1985/86	-6.1	-5.5	4.2	-1.8	-2.2	-7.2
1986/87	-3.5	36.9	12.4	14.4	8.5	56.6
1987/88	3.5	23.0	3.1	-15.9	6.7	3.4
1988/89	1.7	-11.9	5.4	12.1	7.2	-1.3
1989/90	1.8	10.5	-4.4	6.8	-2.7	18.1
1990/91	-13.4	3.8	9.8	-0.8	-4.9	3.1
1991/92	1.6	-11.9	6.6	9.8	8.2	-3.3
1992/93	0.7	-3.8	1.0	8.9	1.6	4.8
1993/94	1.9	-7.3	0.6	-1.4	2.5	-8.6
1994/95	1.4	18.2	5.0	-4.4	6.4	13.0
1995/96	3.6	-1.0	7.1	20.8	11.0	19.6
1996/97	7.9	-1.0	8.0	-2.2	16.4	-3.2
1997/98	-0.1	8.7	7.0	6.9	6.9	16.2
1998/99	-8.4	12.0	2.2	8.8	-6.4	21.9
1999/00	-5.2	16.9	-3.2	-1.3	-8.3	15.3
2000/01	-0.9	-2.8	0.8	-12.5	-0.2	-15.0
2001/02	-15.9	3.2	-2.5	23.7	-17.9	27.6
2002/03	-1.6	29.8	-6.8	-3.7	-8.2	25.1
2003/04	0.5	11.0	4.8	-0.8	5.3	10.1
2004/05	2.4	16.5	-0.3	-3.8	2.1	12.1
2005/06	-1.3	20.6	0.6	10.0	-0.7	32.6
2006/07	4.6	-11.8	3.2	3.7	7.9	-8.5
2007/08	2.3	14.0	-9.1	5.3	-7.0	20.1
2008/09	-3.9	-18.5	-5.1	19.2	-8.8	-2.8
2009/10	6.7	6.0	-3.8	-3.8	2.6	2.0
2010/11	3.0	14.7	5.8	-5.0	9.0	8.9
2011/12	-14.7	-13.7	7.7	3.8	-8.1	-10.4
2012/13	6.0	24.0	6.4	-7.2	12.8	15.1
2013/14	0.1	-5.6	1.1	26.8	1.2	19.8
2014/15	-0.6	-16.4	0.9	18.0	0.3	-1.3
2015/16	-7.1	-2.6	-8.5	33.7	-15.1	30.2
2016/17	-0.2	-7.0	3.4	29.1	3.2	20.0
2017/18	0.8	1.5	0.6	1.8	1.3	3.3
Avg.	-0.7 %	5.0 %	2.2 %	6.2 %	1.5 %	10.9 %
Fq>0	60 %	60 %	73 %	53 %	60 %	70 %

XAU* vs. S&P 500 - 1984/85 to 2017/18   Positive ▭

XAU - Avg. Year 1984 to 2017

XAU / S&P 500 Rel. Strength- Avg Yr. 1984-2017

*XAU- PHLX Gold Silver Index consists of 12 precious metal mining companies.

Gold Miners Performance

XAU Monthly Performance (1984-2017)

	Jan	Feb	Mar	Apr	May	Jun	Jul	Aug	Sep	Oct	Nov	Dec
Avg. % Gain	1.0	2.7	0.3	-0.3	1.3	-0.9	-0.3	1.7	2.6	-4.6	0.9	1.2
Med. % Gain	0.3	3.3	-0.6	-2.7	2.1	-2.6	0.3	3.4	1.8	-3.1	1.4	-0.7
Fq %>0	59	56	47	41	59	47	53	68	65	41	53	47
Fq %>S&P 500	50	65	38	32	47	38	47	62	62	29	41	38

XAU 5 Year (2013-2017) % Gain

XAU Performance 2017-2018

Relative Strength, % gain vs. S&P 500

Market Indices & Rates
Weekly Values**

Stock Markets	2016	2017
Dow	18,517	21,638
S&P500	2,162	2,459
Nasdaq	5,030	6,312
TSX	14,482	15,175
FTSE	6,669	7,378
DAX	10,067	12,632
Nikkei	16,498	20,119
Hang Seng	21,659	26,389

Commodities	2016	2017
Oil	45.95	46.54
Gold	1327.0	1230.3

Bond Yields	2016	2017
USA 5 Yr Treasury	1.15	1.87
USA 10 Yr T	1.60	2.33
USA 20 Yr T	1.90	2.67
Moody's Aaa	3.33	3.71
Moody's Baa	4.26	4.42
CAN 5 Yr T	0.65	1.51
CAN 10 Yr T	1.08	1.90

Money Market	2016	2017
USA Fed Funds	0.50	1.25
USA 3 Mo T-B	0.32	1.04
CAN tgt overnight rate	0.50	0.75
CAN 3 Mo T-B	0.47	0.70

Foreign Exchange	2016	2017
EUR/USD	1.10	1.15
GBP/USD	1.32	1.31
USD/CAD	1.30	1.26
USD/JPY	104.88	112.53

From 1984 to 2017, gold miners have performed well in September on an average, median and frequency basis. The following month, October, has been the worst performing month for gold miners.

Over the last five years, gold miners have generally followed their seasonal trend with January, July and August being three of the strongest months of the year.

In 2017/18, gold miners were positive in their seasonal periods and outperformed the S&P 500.

JULY

M	T	W	T	F	S	S
1	2	3	4	5	6	7
8	9	10	11	12	13	14
15	16	17	18	19	20	21
22	23	24	25	26	27	28
29	30	31				

AUGUST

M	T	W	T	F	S	S
				1	2	3	4
5	6	7	8	9	10	11
12	13	14	15	16	17	18
19	20	21	22	23	24	25
26	27	28	29	30	31	

SEPTEMBER

M	T	W	T	F	S	S
						1
2	3	4	5	6	7	8
9	10	11	12	13	14	15
16	17	18	19	20	21	22
23	24	25	26	27	28	29
30						

VIX VOLATILITY INDEX
July 3rd to October 9th

The Chicago Board Options Exchange Market Volatility Index (VIX) is often referred to as a fear index as it measures investors' expectations of market volatility over the next thirty day period. The higher the VIX value, the greater the expectation of volatility and vice versa.

From 1990 to June 2017, the long-term average of the VIX is 19.3. In this time period, the VIX has bottomed at approximately 10 in the mid-90's, and the mid-2000's. In both cases, the VIX dropped below 10 for a few days.

VIX 1990 to June 2018

VIX - Avg. Year 1990 to 2017

S&P 500 Avg Yr. 1990 - 2017

	VIX* vs. S&P 500 1990 to 2017		
			Positive
July 3 to Oct 9		S&P 500	VIX %Gain
1990	-15.1%		88.9%
1991	-0.2		5.2
1992	-2.2		47.8
1993	3.3		6.3
1994	2.0		3.9
1995	6.2		30.5
1996	3.4		13.4
1997	7.4		13.3
1998	-14.1		138.8
1999	-4.0		9.8
2000	-3.6		22.9
2001	-14.6		85.7
2002	-18.1		45.5
2003	4.5		-1.1
2004	-0.3		-0.2
2005	0.1		28.0
2006	6.3		-10.7
2007	3.0		4.7
2008	-27.9		146.6
2009	19.5		-17.3
2010	13.9		-31.2
2011	-13.8		128.1
2012	5.6		-2.6
2013	2.6		19.2
2014	-2.4		73.4
2015	-2.9		1.7
2016	2.4		-8.7
2017	5.0		-7.6
Avg	-1.2%		29.8%
Fq > 0	54%		71%

October 9th, the VIX has increased 71% of the time. On average, the VIX tends to start increasing in July, particularly after the earnings season gets underway. After mid-July, without the expectation of strong earnings ahead, investors tend to focus on economic forecasts that often become more dire in the second half of the year.

In addition, stock market analysts tend to reduce their earnings forecasts at this time. Both of these effects tend to add volatility in the markets, increasing the VIX. The VIX tends to peak in October as the stock market often starts to establishing a rising trend at this time.

Levels below 15 are often associated with investor complacency, as investors are expecting very little volatility. Very often when a stock market correction occurs in this state, it can be sharp and severe. Knowing the trends of the VIX can be useful in adjusting the amount of risk in a portfolio.

From 1990 to 2017, during the period of July 3rd to

(i) * VIX - ticker symbol for the Chicago Board Options Exchange Market Volatility Index, measure implied volatility of S&P 500 index options

VIX Performance

Market Indices & Rates
Weekly Values

Stock Markets	2016	2017
Dow	18,571	21,580
S&P500	2,175	2,473
Nasdaq	5,100	6,388
TSX	14,601	15,183
FTSE	6,730	7,453
DAX	10,147	12,240
Nikkei	16,627	20,100
Hang Seng	21,964	26,706

Commodities	2015	2016
Oil	43.49	45.62
Gold	1320.8	1248.6

Bond Yields	2015	2016
USA 5 Yr Treasury	1.13	1.81
USA 10 Yr T	1.57	2.24
USA 20 Yr T	1.90	2.57
Moody's Aaa	3.34	3.61
Moody's Baa	4.23	4.29
CAN 5 Yr T	0.65	1.52
CAN 10 Yr T	1.10	1.89

Money Market	2015	2016
USA Fed Funds	0.50	1.25
USA 3 Mo T-B	0.33	1.16
CAN tgt overnight rate	0.50	0.75
CAN 3 Mo T-B	0.50	0.70

Foreign Exchange	2015	2016
EUR/USD	1.10	1.17
GBP/USD	1.31	1.30
USD/CAD	1.31	1.25
USD/JPY	106.13	111.13

JULY

M	T	W	T	F	S	S
1	2	3	4	5	6	7
8	9	10	11	12	13	14
15	16	17	18	19	20	21
22	23	24	25	26	27	28
29	30	31				

AUGUST

M	T	W	T	F	S	S
			1	2	3	4
5	6	7	8	9	10	11
12	13	14	15	16	17	18
19	20	21	22	23	24	25
26	27	28	29	30	31	

SEPTEMBER

M	T	W	T	F	S	S
						1
2	3	4	5	6	7	8
9	10	11	12	13	14	15
16	17	18	19	20	21	22
23	24	25	26	27	28	29
30						

An increase in volatility typically occurs at the beginning of July, just ahead of earnings season. Despite the pickup in volatility ahead of earnings, the S&P 500 tends to perform well for the first half of July.

In 2017, volatility maintained an overall downward trend for the first half of the year, and occasionally dropped below 10. It maintained low levels throughout the time of the year when it tends to increase.

In 2018, the VIX spiked in early February and then worked its way lower for the first half of the year.

July 24th to October 3rd
(Stocks)

Oil stocks tend to outperform the market from July 24th to October 3rd. Earlier in the year, there is another seasonal period of outperformance from late February to early May. Although the first seasonal period has had an incredible record of outperformance, the second seasonal period in July is still noteworthy.

While the seasonal period for oil stocks has more to do with oil inventories during the switch from producing heating oil to gasoline, the second seasonal period is more related to the conversion of production from gasoline to heating oil and the effects of the hurricane season.

1.6% extra

Oil (XOI) Sector - Avg. Year 1984 to 2017

Oil (XOI) / S&P 500 Relative Strength - Avg Yr. 1984 - 2017

XOI* vs. S&P 500 1984 to 2017			
Jul 24 to Oct 3	S&P 500	Positive XOI	Diff
1984	9.1 %	9.0 %	-0.1 %
1985	-4.3	6.7	11.0
1986	-2.1	15.7	17.7
1987	6.6	-1.2	-7.8
1988	3.0	-3.6	-6.6
1989	5.6	5.7	0.1
1990	-12.4	-0.5	11.8
1991	1.3	0.7	-0.7
1992	-0.4	2.9	3.3
1993	3.2	7.8	4.6
1994	1.9	-3.6	-5.5
1995	5.2	-2.2	-7.4
1996	10.5	7.7	-2.8
1997	3.0	8.9	5.9
1998	-12.0	1.4	13.5
1999	-5.5	-2.1	3.3
2000	-3.6	12.2	15.8
2001	-10.0	-5.1	4.8
2002	2.7	7.3	4.6
2003	4.2	5.5	1.4
2004	4.2	10.9	6.7
2005	-0.6	14.3	14.9
2006	7.6	-8.5	-16.9
2007	-0.1	-4.2	-4.1
2008	-14.3	-18.1	-3.8
2009	5.0	3.0	-2.0
2010	4.0	8.5	4.5
2011	-18.3	-26.0	-7.7
2012	7.4	6.1	-1.3
2013	-0.8	-0.8	0.0
2014	-1.0	-10.8	-9.8
2015	-7.2	-9.6	-2.4
2016	-0.6	2.2	2.8
2017	2.5	8.9	6.4
Avg	-0.2 %	1.5 %	1.6 %
Fq > 0	53 %	59 %	57 %

First, there is a large difference between how heating oil and gasoline are stored and consumed. For individuals and businesses, gasoline is consumed in an immediate fashion. It is stored by the local distributor and the supplies are drawn upon as needed. Heating oil, on the other hand, is largely inventoried by individuals, farms and business operations in rural areas.

The inventory process starts before the cold weather arrives. The production facilities have to start switching from gasoline to heating oil, dropping their inventory levels and boosting prices. Second, the hurricane season can play havoc with the production of oil and drive up prices substantially. The official duration of the hurricane season in the Gulf of Mexico is from June 1st to November 30th, but most major hurricanes occur in September and early October.

The threat of a strong hurricane can shut down the oil platforms temporarily, interrupting production. If a strong hurricane strikes the platforms, it can do significant damage and put the them out of commission for an extended period of time.

(i) *NYSE Arca Oil Index (XOI): An index designed to represent a cross section of widely held oil corporations involved in various phases of the oil industry. For more information on the XOI index, see www.cboe.com*

NYSE Arca Oil Index (XOI) Performance

XOI Monthly Performance (1984-2017)

	Jan	Feb	Mar	Apr	May	Jun	Jul	Aug	Sep	Oct	Nov	Dec
Avg. % Gain	0.5	0.7	2.9	3.0	0.5	-0.8	0.4	0.6	0.1	0.3	-0.3	1.9
Med. % Gain	0.1	1.0	2.5	2.4	0.5	-1.6	1.7	0.4	0.5	0.5	0.9	1.1
Fq %>0	47	53	71	79	59	38	56	56	53	50	56	65
Fq %>S&P 500	32	53	65	62	38	35	50	62	59	50	35	56

XOI 5 Year (2013-2017) % Gain

XOI Performance 2017-2018

Relative Strength, % gain vs. S&P 500

Market Indices & Rates
Weekly Values**

Stock Markets	2016	2017
Dow	18,432	21,830
S&P500	2,174	2,472
Nasdaq	5,162	6,375
TSX	14,583	15,129
FTSE	6,724	7,368
DAX	10,338	12,163
Nikkei	16,569	19,960
Hang Seng	21,891	26,979

Commodities	2016	2017
Oil	41.60	49.71
Gold	1342.0	1264.9

Bond Yields	2016	2017
USA 5 Yr Treasury	1.03	1.83
USA 10 Yr T	1.46	2.30
USA 20 Yr T	1.78	2.65
Moody's Aaa	3.25	3.68
Moody's Baa	4.17	4.35
CAN 5 Yr T	0.60	1.64
CAN 10 Yr T	1.03	2.03

Money Market	2016	2017
USA Fed Funds	0.50	1.25
USA 3 Mo T-B	0.28	1.08
CAN tgt overnight rate	0.50	0.75
CAN 3 Mo T-B	0.53	0.73

Foreign Exchange	2016	2017
EUR/USD	1.12	1.18
GBP/USD	1.32	1.31
USD/CAD	1.30	1.24
USD/JPY	102.06	110.68

JULY

M	T	W	T	F	S	S
1	2	3	4	5	6	7
8	9	10	11	12	13	14
15	16	17	18	19	20	21
22	23	24	25	26	27	28
29	30	31				

AUGUST

M	T	W	T	F	S	S
		1	2	3	4	
5	6	7	8	9	10	11
12	13	14	15	16	17	18
19	20	21	22	23	24	25
26	27	28	29	30	31	

SEPTEMBER

M	T	W	T	F	S	S
						1
2	3	4	5	6	7	8
9	10	11	12	13	14	15
16	17	18	19	20	21	22
23	24	25	26	27	28	29
30						

From 1984 to 2017, oil stocks have had a secondary seasonal period from late July to early October. The returns in this secondary seasonal period have largely been focused in August.

Over the last five years, the returns in the secondary seasonal period have produced mixed results.

In 2017, oil stocks advanced during their secondary seasonal period and continued to perform well into 2018.

Seasonal Investment Timeline[1]

[1] Holiday, End of Month, Witches' Hangover, - et al not included.

Investment	Season		2018 O N D	2019 J F M A M J J A S O N D
Core Positions				
S&P 500	Oct 28 - May 5			
TSX Composite	Oct 28 - May 5			
Cash	May 6 - Oct 27			
Primary Sectors				
[4]Consumer Staples	Jan 1 - Jan 22 (S)	Apr 23 - Oct 27		
Financials	Dec 15 - Apr 13			
Energy	Feb 25 - May 9	Jul 24 - Oct 3		
[2]Utilities	Jul 17 - Oct 3	Jan 1 - Mar 13 (S)		
Health Care	Aug 15 - Oct 18			
Information Tech	Oct 9 - Jan 17	Apr 16 - Apr 30		
Consumer Disc.	Oct 28 - Apr 22			
Industrials	Oct 28 - Dec 31	Jan 23- May 5		
Materials	Oct 28 - Jan 6	Jan 23 - May 5		
Small Cap	Dec 19 - Mar 7			
Secondary Sectors				
Silver Bullion	Dec 27- Feb 22			
[2]Platinum	Jan 1 - May 31			
Software Jan1 - Jan19	Jun 1 - Jun 30	Oct 10 - Dec 5		
[3]Semiconductors	Jan 1 - Mar 7	Oct 28 - Nov 6		
Canadian Dollar	Apr 1 - Apr 30	Aug 20 - Sep 25		
Biotech	Jun 23 - Sep 13			
Gold Bullion	Jul 12 - Oct 9	Dec 27 - Jan 26		
Gold Miners	Jul 27 - Sep 25	Dec 23 - Feb 14		
Agriculture	Sep 26 - Nov 11			
Transportation Jan23-Apr16	Aug 3 - Oct 9 (S)	Oct 10 - Nov 13		
Natural Gas Mar22 - Jun19	Sep 6 - Dec 21	Dec 22 - Dec 31(S)		
Airlines	Oct 3 - Nov 6	Aug 1- Aug 31 (S)		
Canadian Banks	Oct 10 - Dec 31	Jan 23 - Apr 13		
Retail	Oct 28 - Nov 29	Jan 21 - Apr 12		
Homebuilders	Oct 28 - Feb 3	Apr 27- Jun 13(S)		
Metals & Mining	Nov 19 - Jan 5	Jan 23 - May 5		
Emerging Markets	Nov 24 - April 18			
Aerospace & Defense	Dec 12 - May 5			
Automotive Dec14 - Jan7	Feb 24 - Apr 24	Aug 3- Oct 3 (S)		
Other Market / Sector Trades				
Nikkei 225	May 6 - Nov 19 (S)			
VIX (CBOE)	Jul 3 - Oct 9			
Canadian Snowbird Trade	Oct 28 - Dec 18			
Currency				
CAD / USD	Apr 1 - Apr 30	Aug 20 - Sep 25		
EUR / USD	Nov 17 - Dec 31			
USD / EUR	Jan 1 - Feb 7			
Fixed Income				
[3]U.S. Gov. Bonds	May 9 - Oct 3			
[3]U.S. High Yield	Nov 24 - Jan 8			

Long Investment ▓▓▓   Short Investment (S) ▭   [1] Holiday, End of Month, Witches' Hangover, - et al not included.

[2]Thackray's 2012 Investor's Guide [3]Thackray's 2013 Investor's Guide [4]Thackray's 2014 Investor's Guide [5]Thackray's 2015 Investor's Guide [6]Thackray's 2016 Investor's Guide [7]Thackray's 2017 Investor's Guide [8]Thackray's 2017 Investor's Guide

Seasonal Investment Timeline[1]

Investment	Season			2018	2019
Stocks				O N D	J F M A M J J A S O N D

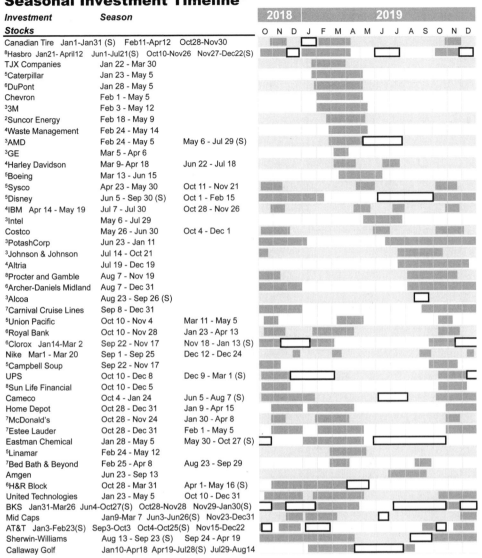

Investment	Season		
Canadian Tire Jan1-Jan31 (S)	Feb11-Apr12	Oct28-Nov30	
[8]Hasbro Jan21- April12	Jun1-Jul21(S)	Oct10-Nov26	Nov27-Dec22(S)
TJX Companies	Jan 22 - Mar 30		
[5]Caterpillar	Jan 23 - May 5		
[6]DuPont	Jan 28 - May 5		
Chevron	Feb 1 - May 5		
[3]3M	Feb 3 - May 12		
[2]Suncor Energy	Feb 18 - May 9		
[4]Waste Management	Feb 24 - May 14		
[3]AMD	Feb 24 - May 5	May 6 - Jul 29 (S)	
[3]GE	Mar 5 - Apr 6		
[4]Harley Davidson	Mar 9- Apr 18	Jun 22 - Jul 18	
[5]Boeing	Mar 13 - Jun 15		
[5]Sysco	Apr 23 - May 30	Oct 11 - Nov 21	
[5]Disney	Jun 5 - Sep 30 (S)	Oct 1 - Feb 15	
[4]IBM Apr 14 - May 19	Jul 7 - Jul 30	Oct 28 - Nov 26	
[3]Intel	May 6 - Jul 29		
Costco	May 26 - Jun 30	Oct 4 - Dec 1	
[3]PotashCorp	Jun 23 - Jan 11		
[3]Johnson & Johnson	Jul 14 - Oct 21		
[4]Altria	Jul 19 - Dec 19		
[8]Procter and Gamble	Aug 7 - Nov 19		
[6]Archer-Daniels Midland	Aug 7 - Dec 31		
[3]Alcoa	Aug 23 - Sep 26 (S)		
[7]Carnival Cruise Lines	Sep 8 - Dec 31		
[5]Union Pacific	Oct 10 - Nov 4	Mar 11 - May 5	
[6]Royal Bank	Oct 10 - Nov 28	Jan 23 - Apr 13	
[6]Clorox Jan14-Mar 2	Sep 22 - Nov 17	Nov 18 - Jan 13 (S)	
Nike Mar1 - Mar 20	Sep 1 - Sep 25	Dec 12 - Dec 24	
[5]Campbell Soup	Sep 22 - Nov 17		
UPS	Oct 10 - Dec 8	Dec 9 - Mar 1 (S)	
[8]Sun Life Financial	Oct 10 - Dec 5		
Cameco	Oct 4 - Jan 24	Jun 5 - Aug 7 (S)	
Home Depot	Oct 28 - Dec 31	Jan 9 - Apr 15	
[7]McDonald's	Oct 28 - Nov 24	Jan 30 - Apr 8	
[7]Estee Lauder	Oct 28 - Dec 31	Feb 1 - May 5	
Eastman Chemical	Jan 28 - May 5	May 30 - Oct 27 (S)	
[5]Linamar	Feb 24 - May 12		
[7]Bed Bath & Beyond	Feb 25 - Apr 8	Aug 23 - Sep 29	
Amgen	Jun 23 - Sep 13		
[6]H&R Block	Oct 28 - Mar 31	Apr 1- May 16 (S)	
United Technologies	Jan 23 - May 5	Oct 10 - Dec 31	
BKS Jan31-Mar26	Jun4-Oct27(S)	Oct28-Nov28	Nov29-Jan30(S)
Mid Caps	Jan9-Mar 7	Jun3-Jun26(S)	Nov23-Dec31
AT&T Jan3-Feb23(S)	Sep3-Oct3	Oct4-Oct25(S)	Nov15-Dec22
Sherwin-Williams	Aug 13 - Sep 23 (S)	Sep 24 - Apr 19	
Callaway Golf	Jan10-Apr18	Apr19-Jul28(S)	Jul29-Aug14

AUGUST

	MONDAY	TUESDAY	WEDNESDAY
WEEK 31	29	30	31
WEEK 32	**5** 26 CAN Market Closed- Civic Day	**6** 25	**7** 24
WEEK 33	**12** 19	**13** 18	**14** 17
WEEK 34	**19** 12	**20** 11	**21** 10
WEEK 35	**26** 5	**27** 4	**28** 3

THURSDAY		FRIDAY	
1 30		**2** 29	
8 23		**9** 22	
15 16		**16** 15	
22 9		**23** 8	
29 2		**30** 1	

SEPTEMBER

M	T	W	T	F	S	S
						1
2	3	4	5	6	7	8
6	7	11	12	13	14	15
16	17	18	19	20	21	22
23	24	25	26	27	28	29
30						

OCTOBER

M	T	W	T	F	S	S
	1	2	3	4	5	6
7	8	9	10	11	12	13
14	15	16	17	18	19	20
21	22	23	24	25	26	27
28	29	30	31			

NOVEMBER

M	T	W	T	F	S	S
				1	2	3
4	5	6	7	8	9	10
11	12	13	14	15	16	17
18	19	20	21	22	23	24
25	26	27	28	29	30	

DECEMBER

M	T	W	T	F	S	S
						1
2	3	4	5	6	7	8
9	10	11	12	13	14	15
16	17	18	19	20	21	22
23	24	25	26	27	28	29
30	31					

AUGUST
S U M M A R Y

	Dow Jones	S&P 500	Nasdaq	TSX Comp
Month Rank	10	11	11	10
# Up	38	37	25	19
# Down	30	31	21	14
% Pos	56	54	54	58
% Avg. Gain	-0.1	-0.1	0.1	-0.2

Dow & S&P 1950-2017, Nasdaq 1972-2017, TSX 1985-2017

0.3%
0.2%
0.1%
0.0%
-0.1%
-0.2%
-0.3%

S&P500 Cumulative Daily Gains for Avg Month 1950 to 2017

70%
60%
50%
40%

Prob. of Daily Gain

♦ August is typically a marginal month and has been the second worst month for the S&P 500 from 1950 to 2017. ♦ If there is a summer rally in July, it is often in jeopardy in August. ♦ In 2017, the S&P 500 rallied in July and then faded in August, producing a nominal gain of 0.1% in August. ♦ The TSX Composite is usually one of the better performing markets in August, but its strength is largely dependent on oil and gold stocks.

BEST / WORST AUGUST BROAD MKTS. 2008-2017

BEST AUGUST MARKETS
♦ FTSE 100 (2009) 6.5%
♦ Russell 2000 (2014) 4.8%
♦ Nasdaq (2014) 4.8%

WORST AUGUST MARKETS
♦ Nikkei 225 (2011) -8.9%
♦ Russell 2000 (2011) -8.8%
♦ Nikkei 225 (2015) - 8.2%

Index Values End of Month

	2008	2009	2010	2011	2012	2013	2014	2015	2016	2017
Dow	11,544	9,496	10,015	11,614	13,091	14,810	17,098	16,528	18,401	21,948
S&P 500	1,283	1,021	1,049	1,219	1,407	1,633	2,003	1,972	2,171	2,472
Nasdaq	2,368	2,009	2,114	2,579	3,067	3,590	4,580	4,777	5,213	6,429
TSX Comp.	13,771	10,868	11,914	12,769	11,949	12,654	15,626	13,859	14,598	15,212
Russell 1000	702	558	578	675	775	909	1,118	1,101	1,203	1,370
Russell 2000	740	572	602	727	812	1,011	1,174	1,159	1,240	1,405
FTSE 100	5,637	4,909	5,225	5,395	5,711	6,413	6,820	6,248	6,782	7,431
Nikkei 225	13,073	10,493	8,824	8,955	8,840	13,389	15,425	18,890	16,887	19,646

Percent Gain for August

	2008	2009	2010	2011	2012	2013	2014	2015	2016	2017
Dow	1.5	3.5	-4.3	-4.4	0.6	-4.4	3.2	-6.6	-0.2	0.3
S&P 500	1.2	3.4	-4.7	-5.7	2.0	-3.1	3.8	-6.3	-0.1	0.1
Nasdaq	1.8	1.5	-6.2	-6.4	4.3	-1.0	4.8	-6.9	1.0	1.3
TSX Comp.	1.3	0.8	1.7	-1.4	2.4	1.3	1.9	-4.2	0.1	0.4
Russell 1000	1.2	3.4	-4.7	-6.0	2.2	-3.0	3.9	-6.2	-0.1	0.1
Russell 2000	3.5	2.8	-7.5	-8.8	3.2	-3.3	4.8	-6.4	1.6	-1.4
FTSE 100	4.2	6.5	-0.6	-7.2	1.4	-3.1	1.3	-6.7	0.8	0.8
Nikkei 225	-2.3	1.3	-7.5	-8.9	1.7	-2.0	-1.3	-8.2	1.9	-1.4

August Market Avg. Performance 2008 to 2017[1]

Dow	-1.1%
S&P 500	-1.0%
Nasdaq	-0.6%
TSX Comp (CAN)	0.4%
Russell 1000 (Lg Cap)	-0.9%
Russell 2000 (Sm Cap)	-1.1%
FTSE 100	-0.3%
Nikkei 225	-2.7%

Interest Corner Aug[2]

	Fed Funds %[3]	3 Mo. T-Bill %[4]	10 Yr %[5]	20 Yr %[6]
2017	1.25	2.11	2.12	2.47
2016	0.50	0.33	1.58	1.90
2015	0.25	0.08	2.21	2.64
2014	0.25	0.03	2.35	2.83
2013	0.25	0.03	2.78	3.46

(1) Russell Data provided by Russell (2) Federal Reserve Bank of St. Louis- end of month values (3) Target rate set by FOMC (4)(5)(6) Constant yield maturities.

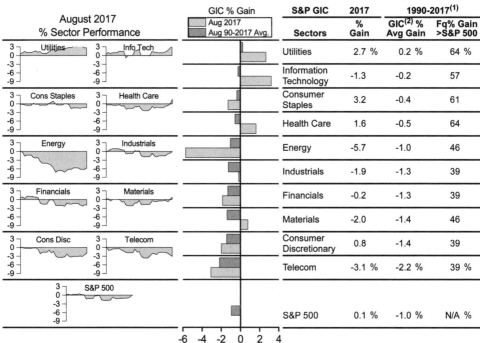

S&P GIC	2017	1990-2017[1]	
Sectors	% Gain	GIC[2] % Avg Gain	Fq% Gain >S&P 500
Utilities	2.7 %	0.2 %	64 %
Information Technology	-1.3	-0.2	57
Consumer Staples	3.2	-0.4	61
Health Care	1.6	-0.5	64
Energy	-5.7	-1.0	46
Industrials	-1.9	-1.3	39
Financials	-0.2	-1.3	39
Materials	-2.0	-1.4	46
Consumer Discretionary	0.8	-1.4	39
Telecom	-3.1 %	-2.2 %	39 %
S&P 500	0.1 %	-1.0 %	N/A %

Sector Commentary

♦ In August 2017, the S&P 500 produced a nominal gain of 0.1%. ♦ The defensive sectors generally performed well, with the consumer staples sector producing a gain of 3.2% and the utilities sector producing a return of 2.7%. ♦ The energy sector lost 5.7% as it faltered in its secondary seasonal period of strength. ♦ The industrial and materials sectors lost 1.9% and 2.0% respectively.

Sub-Sector Commentary

♦ In August 2017, the biotech sub-sector had a large gain of 5.7% in its strong seasonal period. ♦ The semi-conductor sector produced a gain of 2.7% as cryptocurrencies continued to drive demand for graphic chips. ♦ The railroad sector produced a large gain of 2.9%, after producing a loss in the previous month. ♦ Silver and gold both had strong months with gains of 3.5%. ♦ The steel sub-sector was a weak performer, producing a loss of 4.4%.

SELECTED SUB-SECTORS[3]			
Gold	3.5 %	0.7 %	50 %
Biotech (1993-2017)	5.3	0.6	60
Homebuilders	1.4	0.1	57
Agriculture (1994-2017)	-2.0	0.1	50
SOX (1995-2017)	2.7	-0.2	57
Silver	3.5	-0.5	50
Retail	-2.3	-0.6	57
Pharma	-0.2	-0.8	54
Banks	-2.4	-1.2	36
Chemicals	1.5	-1.4	46
Metals & Mining	0.0	-1.6	46
Railroads	2.9	-2.2	46
Transportation	0.2	-2.6	36
Automotive & Components	0.7	-3.2	36
Steel	-4.4	-3.6	46

(1) Sector data provided by Standard and Poors (2) GIC is short form for Global Industry Classification (3) Sub Sector data provided by Standard and Poors, except where marked by symbol.

AIRLINES – DESCEND IN AUGUST SOAR IN OCTOBER
①SELL SHORT (August) ②LONG (Oct3-Nov6)

Airline flights are seasonal based upon the time of year that flights are taken. Airline flights are often used in statistics classes to demonstrate time series seasonality. There are differences between the seasonality of different airlines depending on their business model. International charter airlines have somewhat different seasonality trends compared to domestic airlines.

Overall, airlines book most of their seats in the summer, particularly July and around the holidays.

11.9% growth

It is typically best to avoid the airline sector in August; although it is still considered part of the airlines "high season," it is at the back end of the season and any benefits have probably already been incorporated into the price of stocks in the sector. From 1990 to 2017, the airline sector in August has produced an average loss of 4.7% and has only been positive 29% of the time.

Historically, the best time for the sector has been from October 3rd to November 6th. Although this is a relatively short period, this is the sweet spot for airline sector performance. One factor driving performance at this time is that this period, on average, is one of the worst seasonal periods for oil prices. Oil is a large part of the cost of running airlines. Also, expectations for stronger economic growth in the next year, tend to surface at this time, helping to boost economically sensitive sectors, such as the airline sector.

From 1990 to 2017, short selling the airline sector for the month of August and then investing in the sector from October 3rd to November 6th has produced an average gain of 11.9%

Airlines vs. S&P 500 1990 to 2017

Positive Long ▢   Negative Short ▢

Year	Aug 1 to Aug 31		Oct 3 to Nov 6		Compound Growth	
	S&P 500	Airlines	S&P 500	Airlines	S&P 500	Airlines
1990	-9.4 %	-21.1 %	-1.1 %	0.0 %	-10.5 %	21.1 %
1991	2.0	-6.9	0.4	4.8	2.4	12.0
1992	-2.4	-11.6	1.7	14.4	-0.7	27.7
1993	3.4	3.0	-0.4	8.3	3.1	5.0
1994	3.8	2.1	-0.1	5.0	3.7	2.8
1995	0.0	-7.5	1.2	0.7	1.1	8.3
1996	1.9	0.4	4.4	5.6	6.4	5.2
1997	-5.7	-5.5	-2.3	9.3	-7.9	15.3
1998	-14.6	-20.7	13.8	16.4	-2.8	40.5
1999	-0.6	-11.4	6.8	12.6	6.1	25.4
2000	6.1	-5.4	-0.3	14.6	5.8	20.8
2001	-6.4	-11.4	6.4	3.9	-0.4	15.7
2002	0.5	2.8	11.6	31.4	12.1	27.7
2003	1.8	4.6	3.7	3.0	5.6	-1.7
2004	0.2	1.1	3.1	19.1	3.3	17.8
2005	-1.1	-7.8	-0.7	9.8	-1.8	18.3
2006	2.1	-3.7	3.6	-11.4	5.8	-8.1
2007	1.3	-3.5	-1.7	-8.8	-0.4	-5.6
2008	1.2	-2.3	-18.8	-17.2	-17.8	-15.3
2009	3.4	4.2	4.3	-6.0	7.8	-9.9
2010	-4.7	-8.3	7.0	9.7	1.9	18.8
2011	-5.7	-13.5	10.8	6.1	4.5	20.4
2012	2.0	-2.7	-1.2	1.9	0.8	4.7
2013	-3.1	-7.4	4.5	14.3	1.2	22.8
2014	3.8	8.5	4.4	19.6	8.3	9.4
2015	-6.3	-1.0	7.6	17.7	0.8	18.9
2016	-0.1	0.0	-3.8	7.4	-3.9	7.4
2017	0.1	-7.5	2.5	-0.9	2.5	6.6
Avg.	-1.0 %	-4.7 %	2.4 %	6.8 %	1.3 %	11.9 %
Fq>0	54 %	29 %	64 %	79 %	68 %	82 %

Airline Sector - Avg. Year 1990 to 2017

Airlines / S&P 500 Rel. Strength- Avg Yr. 1990-2017

ⓘ *The SP GICS Airlines Sector. For more information, see www.standardandpoors.com*

Airlines Performance

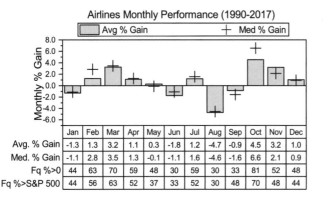

Airlines Monthly Performance (1990-2017)

	Jan	Feb	Mar	Apr	May	Jun	Jul	Aug	Sep	Oct	Nov	Dec
Avg. % Gain	-1.3	1.3	3.2	1.1	0.3	-1.8	1.2	-4.7	-0.9	4.5	3.2	1.0
Med. % Gain	-1.1	2.8	3.5	1.3	-0.1	-1.1	1.6	-4.6	-1.6	6.6	2.1	0.9
Fq %>0	44	63	70	59	48	30	59	30	33	81	52	48
Fq %>S&P 500	44	56	63	52	37	33	52	30	48	70	48	44

Airlines 5 Year (2013-2017) % Gain

Airlines Performance 2017-2018

Relative Strength, % gain vs. S&P 500

Market Indices & Rates
Weekly Values**

Stock Markets	2016	2017
Dow	18,544	22,093
S&P500	2,183	2,477
Nasdaq	5,221	6,352
TSX	14,649	15,258
FTSE	6,793	7,512
DAX	10,367	12,298
Nikkei	16,254	19,952
Hang Seng	22,146	27,563

Commodities	2016	2017
Oil	41.80	49.58
Gold	1340.4	1257.7

Bond Yields	2016	2017
USA 5 Yr Treasury	1.13	1.82
USA 10 Yr T	1.59	2.27
USA 20 Yr T	1.91	2.61
Moody's Aaa	3.42	3.65
Moody's Baa	4.32	4.32
CAN 5 Yr T	0.62	1.54
CAN 10 Yr T	1.07	1.92

Money Market	2016	2017
USA Fed Funds	0.50	1.25
USA 3 Mo T-B	0.28	1.08
CAN tgt overnight rate	0.50	0.75
CAN 3 Mo T-B	0.51	0.72

Foreign Exchange	2016	2017
EUR/USD	1.11	1.18
GBP/USD	1.31	1.30
USD/CAD	1.32	1.26
USD/JPY	101.82	110.69

AUGUST

M	T	W	T	F	S	S
		1	2	3	4
5	6	7	8	9	10	11
12	13	14	15	16	17	18
19	20	21	22	23	24	25
26	27	28	29	30	31

SEPTEMBER

M	T	W	T	F	S	S
						1
2	3	4	5	6	7	8
9	10	11	12	13	14	15
16	17	18	19	20	21	22
23	24	25	26	27	28	29
30

OCTOBER

M	T	W	T	F	S	S
	1	2	3	4	5	6
7	8	9	10	11	12	13
14	15	16	17	18	19	20
21	22	23	24	25	26	27
28	29	30	31

From 1990 to 2017, August has been the worst month of the year for the airline sector based upon average, median and frequency measurements. On the other hand, October has been the strongest month.

Over the last five years, the airline sector has generally followed its seasonal trend: October and November have been the two best months, August has been one of the weaker months of the year.

In 2017, the airline sector was negative in its weak seasonal period and its strong seasonal period.

TRANSPORTATION – ON A ROLL
①LONG (Jan23-Apr16) ②SELL SHORT (Aug1-Oct9)
③LONG (Oct10-Nov13)

The transportation sector can provide a "hilly" ride as the seasonal trends rise and fall throughout the year.

Activity in the transportation sub-sectors; railroads, airlines and freight, tends to bottom in February.

14.9% gain & positive 86% of the time

Increased transportation activity in the spring, coupled with a typically positive economic outlook in the first part of the year, creates a positive seasonal trend, starting January 23rd and lasting until April 16th.

The next seasonal period is a weak period, giving investors an opportunity to sell short the sector and profit from its decline. This negative seasonal period lasts from August 1st to October 9th and is largely the result of investors questioning economic growth at this time of the year.

The third seasonal period is positive and occurs from October 10th to November 13th. This trend is the result of a generally improved economic outlook at this time of the year and investors wanting to get into the sector ahead of earnings announcements.

The SP GICS Transportation Sector encompasses a wide range transportation based companies. For more information, see www.standardandpoors.com

Transportation Sector* vs. S&P 500 1990 to 2017

Negative Short ☐   Positive Long ▨

Year	Jan 23 to Apr 16 S&P 500	Jan 23 to Apr 16 Trans port	Aug 1 to Oct 9 S&P 500	Aug 1 to Oct 9 Trans port	Oct 10 to Nov 13 S&P 500	Oct 10 to Nov 13 Trans port	Compound Growth S&P 500	Compound Growth Trans port
1990	4.4 %	4.1 %	-14.3 %	-19.2 %	4.1 %	3.3 %	-6.9 %	28.1 %
1991	18.1	11.4	-2.8	0.5	5.5	9.6	21.0	21.5
1992	-0.5	3.7	-5.1	-9.1	4.9	14.1	-0.9	29.1
1993	2.9	9.1	2.7	-0.3	1.1	6.4	6.9	16.5
1994	-6.0	-10.7	-0.7	-9.3	1.6	0.8	-5.2	-1.6
1995	9.6	10.5	2.9	-1.3	2.4	5.0	15.5	17.6
1996	5.2	9.4	8.9	4.9	4.9	6.1	20.1	10.4
1997	-2.9	-2.0	1.7	0.9	-5.6	-5.4	-6.7	-8.2
1998	15.1	12.2	-12.2	-16.5	14.4	12.5	15.6	47.0
1999	7.7	17.7	0.6	-11.0	4.5	4.0	13.1	35.8
2000	-5.9	-2.7	-2.0	-6.0	-3.6	13.0	-11.1	16.6
2001	12.2	0.1	-12.8	-20.0	7.8	14.1	-17.4	37.0
2002	0.8	6.9	-14.8	-11.2	13.6	8.2	-2.4	28.6
2003	0.2	0.6	4.9	4.9	1.9	8.0	7.1	3.3
2004	-0.8	-2.9	1.9	6.6	5.5	11.1	6.6	0.7
2005	-2.2	-5.1	-3.1	-0.5	3.3	9.0	-2.1	3.9
2006	2.2	13.2	5.8	6.4	2.5	3.8	10.8	9.9
2007	3.2	4.8	7.6	-0.2	-5.4	-2.9	5.0	1.9
2008	4.1	19.1	-28.2	-23.5	0.2	4.0	-25.1	52.9
2009	4.6	7.2	8.5	6.7	2.1	5.9	15.8	5.9
2010	9.2	17.4	5.8	7.9	2.9	2.5	18.9	10.9
2011	2.8	2.2	-10.6	-11.8	9.4	11.4	0.6	26.9
2012	4.1	-2.0	4.5	-3.5	-4.6	-1.1	3.8	0.3
2013	5.5	3.5	-1.7	1.8	7.6	10.9	11.5	12.7
2014	1.0	1.7	-0.1	2.6	5.8	14.9	6.6	13.8
2015	2.0	-10.0	-4.2	-0.7	0.4	-2.0	-1.9	-11.2
2016	9.1	16.4	-0.9	4.3	0.5	6.4	8.7	18.6
2017	2.5	-4.0	3.0	6.5	1.6	-2.8	7.3	-12.7
Avg.	3.0 %	4.7 %	-2.0 %	-3.2 %	3.2 %	6.1 %	4.1 %	14.9 %
Fq>0	75 %	71 %	46 %	43 %	86 %	82 %	64 %	86 %

Transportation Sector - Avg. Year 1990 to 2017

Transportation / S&P 500 Rel. Strength- Avg Yr. 1990-2017

Transportation Performance

Transportation Monthly Performance (1990-2017)

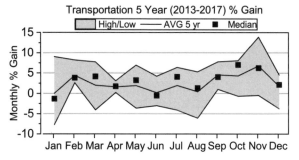

	Jan	Feb	Mar	Apr	May	Jun	Jul	Aug	Sep	Oct	Nov	Dec
Avg. % Gain	-0.2	0.7	2.0	2.2	0.5	-1.2	1.1	-2.6	-0.3	3.8	2.5	1.1
Med. % Gain	0.9	1.7	2.1	1.6	0.4	-1.1	0.0	-1.4	1.1	4.0	2.9	1.0
Fq %>0	54	61	64	75	54	32	50	39	54	79	71	71
Fq %>S&P 500	50	54	61	57	50	32	46	36	57	71	50	39

Transportation 5 Year (2013-2017) % Gain

Transportation Performance 2017-2018

Relative Strength, % gain vs. S&P 500

Market Indices & Rates
Weekly Values**

Stock Markets	2016	2017
Dow	18,576	21,858
S&P500	2,184	2,441
Nasdaq	5,233	6,257
TSX	14,747	15,033
FTSE	6,916	7,310
DAX	10,713	12,014
Nikkei	16,920	19,730
Hang Seng	22,767	26,884

Commodities	2016	2017
Oil	44.49	48.82
Gold	1352.2	1286.1

Bond Yields	2016	2017
USA 5 Yr Treasury	1.10	1.74
USA 10 Yr T	1.51	2.19
USA 20 Yr T	1.85	2.55
Moody's Aaa	3.28	3.63
Moody's Baa	4.22	4.31
CAN 5 Yr T	0.60	1.47
CAN 10 Yr T	1.01	1.85

Money Market	2016	2017
USA Fed Funds	0.50	1.25
USA 3 Mo T-B	0.29	1.03
CAN tgt overnight rate	0.50	0.75
CAN 3 Mo T-B	0.50	0.72

Foreign Exchange	2016	2017
EUR/USD	1.12	1.18
GBP/USD	1.29	1.30
USD/CAD	1.30	1.27
USD/JPY	101.30	109.19

AUGUST

M	T	W	T	F	S	S
		1	2	3	4	
5	6	7	8	9	10	11
12	13	14	15	16	17	18
19	20	21	22	23	24	25
26	27	28	29	30	31	

SEPTEMBER

M	T	W	T	F	S	S
						1
2	3	4	5	6	7	8
9	10	11	12	13	14	15
16	17	18	19	20	21	22
23	24	25	26	27	28	29
30						

OCTOBER

M	T	W	T	F	S	S
1	2	3	4	5	6	
7	8	9	10	11	12	13
14	15	16	17	18	19	20
21	22	23	24	25	26	27
28	29	30	31			

The transportation sector has a roller coaster seasonal trend. In the early part of the year it typically outperforms, and then under-derperforms in the summer, and then outperforms at the end of the year. From 1990 to 2017, October has been the best month for the transportation sector on an average, median and frequency basis. Over the last five years, on average, generally the transportation sector has followed its seasonal pattern throughout the year. In 2017, the transportation sector underperformed the S&P 500 during in its three seasonal periods. In 2018, the transportation sector was negative and underperformed the S&P 500 in its first seasonal period.

AGRICULTURE MOOOVES
September 26th to November 11th

The agriculture seasonal trade is the result of the major summer growing season in the northern hemisphere producing cash for growers and subsequently, increasing sales for farming suppliers typically in the fourth quarter of the year. The seasonal period for the agriculture sector occurs towards the beginning of the fourth quarter.

58% of the time
better than the S&P 500

Although this sector can represent a good opportunity, investors should be wary of the wide performance swings. Out of the twenty-four cycles from 1994 to 2017, during its seasonal period, the agriculture sector has had ten years of returns greater than +10%. In other words, this sector is very volatile.

Agriculture* vs. S&P 500 1994 to 2017

Sep 26 to Nov 11	S&P 500	Positive	
		Agri	Diff
1994	0.6 %	5.7 %	5.1 %
1995	1.9	12.0	10.2
1996	6.7	24.7	18.0
1997	-1.5	-6.9	-5.4
1998	7.3	-1.7	-9.0
1999	8.2	1.4	-6.8
2000	-5.1	35.3	40.4
2001	10.7	18.1	7.5
2002	4.4	13.7	9.3
2003	4.3	9.8	5.5
2004	5.7	25.0	19.2
2005	1.6	7.2	5.6
2006	4.1	-5.7	-9.9
2007	-4.2	12.6	16.8
2008	-25.7	2.3	28.0
2009	5.2	17.8	12.6
2010	5.7	-4.9	-10.6
2011	11.2	17.9	6.7
2012	-4.3	-8.2	-3.9
2013	4.7	12.2	7.5
2014	3.8	1.3	-2.5
2015	7.4	-4.7	-12.1
2016	0.0	-1.7	-1.7
2017	3.4	-8.4	-11.8
Avg.	2.3 %	7.3 %	4.9 %
Fq > 0	75 %	67 %	58 %

In the 2000's, after realizing that technology stocks were not going to grow to the sky, investors started to have an epiphany– that the world might be running out of food, and as a result interest in the agriculture sector started to pick up.

The world population is still increasing and imbalances in food supply and demand will continue to exist in the future, helping to support the agriculture seasonal trade.

Agriculture Sector - Avg. Year 1994 to 2017

Agriculture / S&P 500 Relative Strength - Avg Yr. 1994-2017

On a year by year basis, the agriculture sector has on average produced its biggest gains during its seasonally strong period. In 2000, the agriculture sector produced a gain of 35.3%. It is interesting to note that this is the same year that the technology sector's bubble burst.

*The SP GICS Agriculture Sector # 30202010
For more information on the agriculture sector, see www.standardandpoors.com

Agriculture Performance

Agriculture Monthly Performance (1994-2017)

	Jan	Feb	Mar	Apr	May	Jun	Jul	Aug	Sep	Oct	Nov	Dec
Avg. % Gain	-0.8	0.9	0.6	0.4	2.1	-1.6	-0.7	0.1	-0.3	5.6	2.8	2.2
Med. % Gain	-3.0	0.7	-0.2	2.7	3.1	-1.3	1.2	-1.1	1.1	5.4	1.3	1.5
Fq %>0	38	54	50	67	63	42	58	46	54	75	58	67
Fq %>S&P 500	38	50	33	54	54	33	46	50	54	75	42	54

Agriculture 5 Year (2013-2017) % Gain

Agriculture Performance 2017-2018

Relative Strength, % gain vs. S&P 500

Market Indices & Rates
Weekly Values**

Stock Markets	2016	2017
Dow	18,553	21,675
S&P500	2,184	2,426
Nasdaq	5,238	6,217
TSX	14,687	14,952
FTSE	6,859	7,324
DAX	10,544	12,165
Nikkei	16,546	19,470
Hang Seng	22,937	27,048

Commodities	2016	2017
Oil	48.52	48.51
Gold	1346.4	1295.8

Bond Yields	2016	2017
USA 5 Yr Treasury	1.17	1.77
USA 10 Yr T	1.58	2.19
USA 20 Yr T	1.93	2.54
Moody's Aaa	3.30	3.64
Moody's Baa	4.25	4.31
CAN 5 Yr T	0.68	1.49
CAN 10 Yr T	1.08	1.87

Money Market	2016	2017
USA Fed Funds	0.50	1.25
USA 3 Mo T-B	0.30	1.02
CAN tgt overnight rate	0.50	0.75
CAN 3 Mo T-B	0.50	0.72

Foreign Exchange	2016	2017
EUR/USD	1.13	1.18
GBP/USD	1.31	1.29
USD/CAD	1.29	1.26
USD/JPY	100.22	109.18

From 1994 to 2017, October has been the best month of the year on an average, median and frequency basis.

Over the last five years, on average, the general seasonal trend has not been profitable.

In 2017, the agriculture sector was negative in its seasonal period and underperformed the S&P 500.

AUGUST

M	T	W	T	F	S	S
		1	2	3	4	
5	6	7	8	9	10	11
12	13	14	15	16	17	18
19	20	21	22	23	24	25
26	27	28	29	30	31	

SEPTEMBER

M	T	W	T	F	S	S
						1
2	3	4	5	6	7	8
9	10	11	12	13	14	15
16	17	18	19	20	21	22
23	24	25	26	27	28	29
30						

OCTOBER

M	T	W	T	F	S	S
1	2	3	4	5	6
7	8	9	10	11	12	13
14	15	16	17	18	19	20
21	22	23	24	25	26	27
28	29	30	31			

AMGEN
June 23rd to September 13th

Biotech has a period of seasonal strength from June 23rd to September 13th (see *Biotech Summer Solstice* strategy). Amgen is considered one of the major biotech companies and has a similar seasonal trend. Amgen has an additional benefit during the biotech seasonal period, as it typically releases its second quarter earnings towards the end of July. This gives Amgen a seasonal boost as investors buy Amgen ahead of their earnings in anticipation of any possible good news.

Strong earnings are particularly welcome in the second quarter, as the first quarter tends to be the weakest quarter of the year for Amgen. The first quarter of the year tends to be weak due to slower sales and the effects of wholesale inventory over-stocking at the end of the previous year.

14.6% gain & positive 82% of the time

From 1990 to 2017, in its seasonal period, Amgen has produced an average gain of 14.6% and has been positive 82% of the time. During this same time period, it has beaten the S&P 500 by an average 14.2% and has outperformed it 86% of the time. This is a strong track record of outperformance, especially the percentage of times that Amgen has beaten the S&P 500.

AMGN* vs. S&P 500 - 1990 to 2017		Positive	
Jun 23 to Sep 13	S&P 500	AGMN	Diff
1990	-10.4 %	29.8 %	40.2 %
1991	1.6	42.0	40.5
1992	4.0	17.9	13.9
1993	3.6	3.6	-0.1
1994	3.2	24.2	21.0
1995	5.0	31.5	26.5
1996	2.1	7.0	4.9
1997	2.8	-18.9	-21.7
1998	-8.5	20.6	29.1
1999	0.6	64.3	63.7
2000	2.3	7.9	5.6
2001	-10.8	-1.6	9.3
2002	-10.0	12.9	23.0
2003	2.3	5.4	3.1
2004	-0.8	9.1	9.8
2005	1.4	36.0	34.5
2006	5.8	6.4	0.6
2007	-1.2	2.1	3.3
2008	-5.0	39.2	44.2
2009	16.8	14.8	-1.9
2010	2.4	-3.1	-5.5
2011	-8.9	-5.6	3.3
2012	9.4	15.1	5.7
2013	6.0	17.0	11.0
2014	1.2	14.0	12.8
2015	-7.6	-5.6	2.1
2016	2.0	13.0	11.0
2017	2.6	9.1	6.5
Avg	0.4 %	14.6 %	14.2 %
Fq > 0	68 %	82 %	86 %

AMGN - Avg. Year 1990 to 2017

AMGN / S&P 500 Relative Strength - Avg Yr. 1990 - 2017

place in the summer months when the stock market typically does not have strong results and the selection of seasonal long trades are limited.

The seasonal trade for Amgen focuses on the sweet spot of its best performance, producing an average large gain over a very short period of time. Like the biotech sector, on average the second half of the year for Amgen is much stronger than the first half of the year. From July 1st to December 31st, for the yearly period 1990 to 2017, Amgen has produced an average gain of 20.9% and has been positive 79% of the time. This compares to the weaker first half of the year, where the average gain over the same yearly period is 5.0% and the frequency of positive performance is 50%.

The Amgen seasonal trade is a valued trade not just because of its strong results, but also because of the time of year when the trade occurs. The trade takes

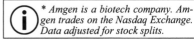

(i) *Amgen is a biotech company. Amgen trades on the Nasdaq Exchange. Data adjusted for stock splits.*

Amgen Performance

AMGN Monthly Performance (1990-2017)

	Jan	Feb	Mar	Apr	May	Jun	Jul	Aug	Sep	Oct	Nov	Dec
Avg. % Gain	1.5	0.5	1.0	-0.4	1.7	0.0	9.3	0.5	0.9	1.6	2.6	4.5
Med. % Gain	0.8	1.3	-0.2	-0.2	2.2	-1.1	7.7	0.9	0.1	2.7	1.9	1.3
Fq %>0	57	54	50	46	54	43	86	61	50	64	64	68
Fq %>S&P 500	54	50	32	32	57	54	79	54	54	50	46	50

AMGN 5 Year (2013-2017) % Gain

Market Indices & Rates Weekly Values**

Stock Markets	2016	2017
Dow	18,395	21,814
S&P500	2,169	2,443
Nasdaq	5,219	6,266
TSX	14,640	15,056
FTSE	6,838	7,401
DAX	10,588	12,168
Nikkei	16,361	19,453
Hang Seng	22,910	27,848

Commodities	2016	2017
Oil	47.64	47.62
Gold	1318.8	1285.3

Bond Yields	2016	2017
USA 5 Yr Treasury	1.23	1.77
USA 10 Yr T	1.62	2.17
USA 20 Yr T	1.96	2.51
Moody's Aaa	3.30	3.62
Moody's Baa	4.25	4.29
CAN 5 Yr T	0.73	1.54
CAN 10 Yr T	1.09	1.87

Money Market	2016	2017
USA Fed Funds	0.50	1.25
USA 3 Mo T-B	0.34	1.03
CAN tgt overnight rate	0.50	0.75
CAN 3 Mo T-B	0.52	0.72

Foreign Exchange	2016	2017
EUR/USD	1.12	1.19
GBP/USD	1.31	1.29
USD/CAD	1.30	1.25
USD/JPY	101.84	109.36

AMGN Performance 2017-2018

Relative Strength, % gain vs. S&P 500

From 1990 to 2017, the best month of the year for Amgen has been July on an average, median and frequency basis. The gains in July were substantially above the other months of the year.

Over the last five years, the seasonal trade has worked well, mainly with the strong support from July's results.

In 2017, Amgen outperformed the S&P 500 in its seasonal period. Shortly after its seasonal period started, Amgen started to underperform the S&P 500.

AUGUST

M	T	W	T	F	S	S
		1	2	3	4	
5	6	7	8	9	10	11
12	13	14	15	16	17	18
19	20	21	22	23	24	25
26	27	28	29	30	31	

SEPTEMBER

M	T	W	T	F	S	S
						1
2	3	4	5	6	7	8
9	10	11	12	13	14	15
16	17	18	19	20	21	22
23	24	25	26	27	28	29
30						

OCTOBER

M	T	W	T	F	S	S
	1	2	3	4	5	6
7	8	9	10	11	12	13
14	15	16	17	18	19	20
21	22	23	24	25	26	27
28	29	30	31			

HEALTH CARE – PRESCRIPTION RENEWAL
①LONG (May1-Aug2) ②SELL SHORT (Aug3-Aug11)
③LONG (Aug12-Oct24)

The seasonal period for the health care sector has been adjusted to start in May, when it provides strong absolute and relative performance compared to the S&P 500. It also includes a short sell period in early August when the sector tends to perform poorly.

Health care stocks have traditionally been classified as defensive stocks because of their stable earnings. Pharmaceutical and other health care companies typically still perform relatively well in an economic downturn. They also tend to outperform the S&P 500 in the unfavorable six month period from early May to late October.

6.8% gain & positive

The health care sector has on average been one of the top performing sectors in the month of May. Although the returns tend to be lower in June and July, there is value investing in the health care sector at this time. The sector does take a pause in early August, when the stock market tends to perform poorly.

The period from August 12th to October 24th tends to be positive for the health care sector as investor interest increases ahead of the many health care conferences that take place in autumn.

ⓘ *Health Care SP GIC Sector# 35: An index designed to represent a cross section of health care companies. For more information see www.standardandpoors.com.*

Health Care* vs. S&P 500 1990 to 2017
Negative Short ☐   Positive Long ▨

Year	May 1 to Aug 2 S&P 500	May 1 to Aug 2 Health Care	Aug 3 to Aug 11 S&P 500	Aug 3 to Aug 11 Health Care	Aug 12 to Oct 24 S&P 500	Aug 12 to Oct 24 Health Care	Compound Growth S&P 500	Compound Growth Health Care
1990	6.3 %	18.4 %	-4.5 %	-4.5 %	-6.8 %	2.8 %	-5.5 %	27.2 %
1991	3.2	7.9	0.0	-0.1	-0.5	1.8	2.6	9.9
1992	2.2	1.0	-1.3	-0.2	-1.2	-9.6	-0.2	-8.5
1993	2.3	-9.3	0.1	-4.2	2.8	12.2	5.2	6.0
1994	2.1	5.5	-0.4	3.6	0.4	7.4	2.2	9.2
1995	8.6	10.5	-0.7	-0.9	5.7	15.3	14.0	28.5
1996	1.3	4.7	-0.1	0.8	6.1	8.7	7.4	12.9
1997	18.2	16.3	-1.1	-3.9	0.5	6.1	17.5	28.0
1998	0.8	5.3	-4.6	-4.2	0.2	4.6	-3.7	14.8
1999	-0.5	-3.7	-2.0	-5.8	0.0	10.2	-2.5	12.2
2000	-1.0	13.0	2.3	-4.2	-5.0	7.1	-3.7	26.1
2001	-2.3	-0.1	-2.5	0.3	-8.8	0.9	-13.2	0.4
2002	-19.8	-16.1	5.1	4.8	-2.9	-1.1	-18.1	-20.9
2003	6.9	2.8	0.0	0.4	4.9	-2.3	12.2	0.0
2004	-0.1	-6.1	-2.8	-1.1	1.9	-5.5	-1.1	-10.3
2005	7.5	3.7	-0.5	-0.4	-3.1	-4.6	3.7	-0.7
2006	-2.5	3.8	-0.9	-1.8	8.7	7.3	5.1	13.2
2007	-0.7	-5.2	-1.3	-0.6	4.3	4.2	2.3	-0.6
2008	-0.7	0.7	3.6	5.2	-32.8	-23.4	-36.7	-26.9
2009	13.1	15.5	0.7	-0.5	8.6	3.4	23.7	20.0
2010	-5.1	-5.8	-3.2	-0.2	8.6	7.6	-0.3	1.6
2011	-8.0	-7.0	-6.5	-4.4	7.0	7.1	-8.0	4.0
2012	-2.4	1.4	3.0	1.8	0.2	3.7	0.8	3.3
2013	7.0	8.4	-1.1	-0.9	3.6	3.5	9.7	13.2
2014	2.2	4.6	0.6	-0.6	1.4	7.8	4.3	13.4
2015	0.9	6.7	-0.9	-1.7	-0.4	-8.0	-0.5	-0.1
2016	4.4	8.1	1.3	-0.6	-1.6	-7.1	4.2	1.0
2017	3.9	5.4	-1.5	-1.2	5.2	5.9	7.8	12.9
Avg.	1.4 %	3.2 %	-0.7 %	-0.9 %	0.2 %	2.4 %	1.0 %	6.8 %
Fq>0	61 %	71 %	32	25 %	61 %	71 %	57 %	71 %

Health Care Sector - Avg. Year 1990-2017

Health Care / S&P 500 Rel. Strength- Avg Yr. 1990-2017

Health Care Performance

Health Care Monthly Performance (1990-2017)

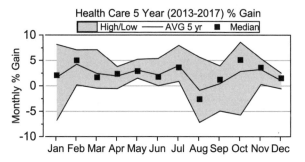

	Jan	Feb	Mar	Apr	May	Jun	Jul	Aug	Sep	Oct	Nov	Dec
Avg. % Gain	0.4	-0.2	0.4	1.2	1.7	0.6	0.9	-0.5	0.6	1.6	2.2	1.5
Med. % Gain	0.6	0.5	0.7	1.7	1.7	-0.2	1.3	0.6	0.6	1.7	2.0	1.6
Fq %>0	61	61	61	61	71	50	64	54	57	71	82	68
Fq %>S&P 500	61	39	32	50	54	68	46	64	61	43	57	46

Health Care 5 Year (2013-2017) % Gain

Health Care Performance 2017-2018

Relative Strength, % gain vs. S&P 500

From 1990 to 2017, three of the top performing months for the health care sector have been May, October and November. May and October are the start and end points of the seasonal period for the health care sector. The health care sector can perform well in November, but the seasonal benefits diminish at this time. Generally, over the last five years, the health care sector has followed its seasonal trend, except for its strong average performance in February and weak performance in August.

Overall, the health care sector was positive in its seasonal trades and outperformed the S&P 500 in 2017.

Market Indices & Rates
Weekly Values**

Stock Markets	2016	2017
Dow	18,492	21,988
S&P500	2,180	2,477
Nasdaq	5,250	6,435
TSX	14,796	15,192
FTSE	6,895	7,439
DAX	10,684	12,143
Nikkei	16,926	19,691
Hang Seng	23,267	27,953

Commodities	2016	2017
Oil	44.44	47.29
Gold	1324.7	1320.4

Bond Yields	2016	2017
USA 5 Yr Treasury	1.20	1.73
USA 10 Yr T	1.60	2.16
USA 20 Yr T	1.95	2.51
Moody's Aaa	3.28	3.64
Moody's Baa	4.23	4.31
CAN 5 Yr T	0.69	1.59
CAN 10 Yr T	1.06	1.91

Money Market	2016	2017
USA Fed Funds	0.50	1.25
USA 3 Mo T-B	0.33	1.02
CAN tgt overnight rate	0.50	0.75
CAN 3 Mo T-B	0.51	0.81

Foreign Exchange	2016	2017
EUR/USD	1.12	1.19
GBP/USD	1.33	1.30
USD/CAD	1.30	1.24
USD/JPY	103.92	110.25

AUGUST

M	T	W	T	F	S	S
			1	2	3	4
5	6	7	8	9	10	11
12	13	14	15	16	17	18
19	20	21	22	23	24	25
26	27	28	29	30	31	

SEPTEMBER

M	T	W	T	F	S	S
						1
2	3	4	5	6	7	8
9	10	11	12	13	14	15
16	17	18	19	20	21	22
23	24	25	26	27	28	29
30						

OCTOBER

M	T	W	T	F	S	S
	1	2	3	4	5	6
7	8	9	10	11	12	13
14	15	16	17	18	19	20
21	22	23	24	25	26	27
28	29	30	31			

SEPTEMBER

	MONDAY	TUESDAY	WEDNESDAY
WEEK 36	**2** 28 USA Market Closed- Labor Day CAN Market Closed- Labor Day	**3** 27	**4** 26
WEEK 37	**9** 21	**10** 20	**11** 19
WEEK 38	**16** 14	**17** 13	**18** 12
WEEK 39	**23** 7	**24** 6	**25** 5
WEEK 40	**30**	1	2

THURSDAY		FRIDAY	
5	25	**6**	24
12	18	**13**	17
19	11	**20**	10
26	4	**27**	3
3		4	

OCTOBER

M	T	W	T	F	S	S
	1	2	3	4	5	6
7	8	9	10	11	12	13
14	15	16	17	18	19	20
21	22	23	24	25	26	27
28	29	30	31			

NOVEMBER

M	T	W	T	F	S	S
				1	2	3
4	5	6	7	8	9	10
11	12	13	14	15	16	17
18	19	20	21	22	23	24
25	26	27	28	29	30	

DECEMBER

M	T	W	T	F	S	S
						1
2	3	4	5	6	7	8
9	10	11	12	13	14	15
16	17	18	19	20	21	22
23	24	25	26	27	28	29
30	31					

JANUARY

M	T	W	T	F	S	S
		1	2	3	4	5
6	7	8	9	10	11	12
13	14	15	16	17	18	19
20	21	22	23	24	25	26
27	28	29	30	31		

SEPTEMBER
S U M M A R Y

	Dow Jones	S&P 500	Nasdaq	TSX Comp
Month Rank	12	12	12	12
# Up	27	30	25	14
# Down	41	38	21	19
% Pos	40	44	54	42
% Avg. Gain	-0.7	-0.5	-0.5	-1.5

Dow & S&P 1950-2017, Nasdaq 1972-2017, TSX 1985-2017

S&P500 Cumulative Daily Gains for Avg Month 1950 to 2017

Prob. of Daily Gain

♦ September has the reputation of being the worst month of the year for the S&P 500. From 1950 to 2017, September has produced an average loss of 0.5% and has only been positive 44% of the time. ♦ In particular, the last part of September tends to be negative. ♦ The defensive sectors are typically the favored sectors in September as investors seek more stable earnings in a month that is often volatile ♦ The materials sector on average performs poorly in September and has outperformed the S&P 500 only 25% of the time from 1990 to 2017.

BEST / WORST SEPTEMBER BROAD MKTS. 2008-2017

BEST SEPTEMBER MARKETS
- ♦ Russell 2000 (2010) 12.3%
- ♦ Nasdaq (2010) 12.0%
- ♦ Russell 1000 (2010) 9.0%

WORST SEPTEMBER MARKETS
- ♦ TSX Comp. (2008) -14.7%
- ♦ Nikkei 225 (2008) -13.9%
- ♦ FTSE 100 (2008) -13.0%

Index Values End of Month

	2008	2009	2010	2011	2012	2013	2014	2015	2016	2017
Dow	10,851	9,712	10,788	10,913	13,437	15,130	17,043	16,285	18,308	22,405
S&P 500	1,166	1,057	1,141	1,131	1,441	1,682	1,972	1,920	2,168	2,519
Nasdaq	2,092	2,122	2,369	2,415	3,116	3,771	4,493	4,620	5,312	6,496
TSX Comp.	11,753	11,395	12,369	11,624	12,317	12,787	14,961	13,307	14,726	15,635
Russell 1000	633	580	630	623	794	940	1,096	1,068	1,202	1,397
Russell 2000	680	604	676	644	837	1,074	1,102	1,101	1,252	1,491
FTSE 100	4,902	5,134	5,549	5,128	5,742	6,462	6,623	6,062	6,899	7,373
Nikkei 225	11,260	10,133	9,369	8,700	8,870	14,456	16,174	17,388	16,450	20,356

Percent Gain for September

	2008	2009	2010	2011	2012	2013	2014	2015	2016	2017
Dow	-6.0	2.3	7.7	-6.0	2.6	2.2	-0.3	-1.5	-0.5	2.1
S&P 500	-9.1	3.6	8.8	-7.2	2.4	3.0	-1.6	-2.6	-0.1	1.9
Nasdaq	-11.6	5.6	12.0	-6.4	1.6	5.1	-1.9	-3.3	1.9	1.0
TSX Comp.	-14.7	4.8	3.8	-9.0	3.1	1.1	-4.3	-4.0	0.9	2.8
Russell 1000	-9.8	3.9	9.0	-7.6	2.4	3.3	-1.9	-2.9	-0.1	2.0
Russell 2000	-8.1	5.6	12.3	-11.4	3.1	6.2	-6.2	-5.1	0.9	6.1
FTSE 100	-13.0	4.6	6.2	-4.9	0.5	0.8	-2.9	-3.0	1.7	-0.8
Nikkei 225	-13.9	-3.4	6.2	-2.8	0.3	8.0	4.9	-8.0	-2.6	3.6

September Market Avg. Performance 2008 to 2017[1]

	Dow	0.3%
	S&P 500	-0.1%
	Nasdaq	0.4%
	TSX Comp (CAN)	-1.5%
	Russell 1000 (Lg Cap)	-0.2%
	Russell 2000 (Sm Cap)	0.4%
	FTSE 100	-1.1%
	Nikkei 225	-0.8%

Interest Corner Sep[2]

	Fed Funds %[3]	3 Mo. T-Bill %[4]	10 Yr %[5]	20 Yr %[6]
2017	1.25	1.01	2.33	2.63
2016	0.50	0.29	1.60	1.99
2015	0.25	0.00	2.06	2.51
2014	0.25	0.02	2.52	2.98
2013	0.25	0.02	2.64	3.41

(1) Russell Data provided by Russell (2) Federal Reserve Bank of St. Louis- end of month values (3) Target rate set by FOMC (4)(5)(6) Constant yield maturities.

September 2017 % Sector Performance

S&P GIC	2017	1990-2017[1]	
Sectors	% Gain	GIC[2] % Avg Gain	Fq% Gain >S&P 500
Telecom	3.5 %	1.0 %	61 %
Health Care	0.9	0.6	61
Energy	9.8	0.4	57
Utilities	-3.0	-0.1	36
Consumer Staples	-1.1	-0.1	54
Industrials	3.8	-0.4	50
Financials	5.1	-0.4	54
Information Technology	0.6	-0.7	64
Consumer Discretionary	0.8	-0.8	50
Materials	3.3 %	-2.0 %	25 %
S&P 500	1.9 %	-0.4 %	N/A %

Sector Commentary

♦ In September 2017, the financial sector produced a strong gain of 5.1%. Investors were attracted to the sector because of the perception that rising interest rates were going to increase profits of the banks due to better net interest margins. ♦ The energy sector produced a gain of 9.8% in its secondary seasonal period. ♦ The industrial and material sector both produced strong gains of 3.8% and 3.3% respectively. ♦ The defensive sectors, utilities and consumer staples both produced losses of 3.0% and 1.1% respectively.

Sub-Sector Commentary

♦ September is typically the month when precious metals tend to perform well. In September 2017, gold produced a loss of 2.2% and silver a loss of 2.8%. ♦ The transportation sub-sector typically starts its period of seasonal strength in October, but in 2017 it was positive in September, producing a gain of 6.6%. ♦ September tends to be a weak month for the chemicals sub-sector and in 2017, the sector went against its seasonal trend and produced a gain of 4.5%.

SELECTED SUB-SECTORS[3]

Gold	-2.2 %	2.3 %	64 %
Silver	-2.8	1.6	68
Biotech (1993-2017)	2.9	1.5	64
Pharma	0.7	0.7	57
Railroads	9.2	-0.2	43
Agriculture (1994-2017)	2.9	-0.3	54
Transportation	6.6	-0.3	57
Retail	3.4	-0.4	50
Banks	6.6	-0.8	54
Homebuilders	6.4	-0.8	57
Chemicals	4.5	-1.7	32
Metals & Mining	-2.0	-1.9	43
Automotive & Components	7.9	-2.1	39
SOX (1995-2017)	5.2	-2.2	48
Steel	1.7	-3.4	43

(1) Sector data provided by Standard and Poors (2) GIC is short form for Global Industry Classification (3) Sub Sector data provided by Standard and Poors, except where marked by symbol.

Sherwin-Williams is known for its paints, stains and other coatings. Approximately 70% of its business is derived from residential orders.

In the summer months, homebuilders tend to languish with poor stock performance. Sherwin-Williams follows the same trend and tends to underperform the S&P 500 from August 13th until September 23rd. In this time period, from 1990 to 2017, Sherwin-Williams has produced an average loss of 3.5% and has only been positive 36% of the time.

Gain of 25.4% and positive 86% of the time

On the other hand, Sherwin-Williams tends to outperform the S&P 500 from September 24th to April 19th, In this time period from 1990 to 2018, Sherwin-Williams has produced an average gain of 20.4% and has been positive 89% of the time. This performance tendency is very similar to the seasonal trend for the homebuilders sector which tends to outperform in approximately the same time period.

It is interesting to note the contrast of large gains and losses for Sherwin-Williams, comparing the seasonally strong period to the seasonally weak period. From August 13th to September 23rd, from 1990 to 2017, Sherwin-Williams has produced losses of 10% or greater, four times and gains of 10% or greater only once. In comparison, from September 24th to April 19th, Sherwin-Williams has produced losses of 10% or greater once and gains of 10% or greater twenty-two times.

ⓘ * The Sherwin-Williams Company is a consumer discretionary company. Data adjusted for stock splits.

SHW vs. S&P 500 1990/91 to 2017/18

Negative Short ☐   Positive Long ☐

Year	Aug 13 to Sep 23		Sep 24 to Apr 19		Compound Growth	
	S&P 500	SHW	S&P 500	SHW	S&P 500	SHW
1990/91	-7.2 %	-5.6 %	23.4 %	43.3 %	14.5 %	51.3 %
1991/92	-0.5	-5.1	7.8	24.5	7.2	30.8
1992/93	-0.1	-4.7	7.2	20.1	7.1	25.7
1993/94	2.0	8.9	-3.3	-9.2	-1.4	-17.3
1994/95	-0.5	-4.2	9.8	10.4	9.3	15.0
1995/96	4.8	-0.4	10.9	27.2	16.2	27.6
1996/97	3.1	-1.9	11.6	19.2	15.1	21.5
1997/98	2.7	-2.4	17.9	20.0	21.2	22.9
1998/99	-1.7	-31.6	21.0	54.5	18.9	103.3
1999/00	-1.4	-24.8	11.5	25.8	10.0	57.0
2001/01	-1.6	-9.0	-13.5	3.2	-14.8	12.4
2001/02	-18.9	-8.4	16.5	49.2	-5.5	61.7
2002/03	-7.8	-17.7	7.2	17.4	-1.1	38.1
2003/04	3.9	0.3	10.4	30.3	14.7	29.9
2004/05	4.2	10.1	4.0	7.7	8.4	-3.2
2005/06	-1.2	-6.9	7.8	20.0	6.5	28.2
2006/07	3.8	8.1	11.9	22.5	16.1	12.6
2007/08	5.0	-4.7	-8.9	-14.7	-4.4	-10.7
2008/09	-7.9	2.0	-26.8	-5.5	-32.6	-7.4
2009/10	5.5	-0.8	12.9	19.9	19.1	20.8
2010/11	3.8	7.3	16.7	14.3	21.1	6.0
2011/12	-3.6	-5.8	21.2	63.5	16.8	73.0
2012/13	3.9	6.1	6.5	19.3	10.6	12.0
2013/14	0.7	2.1	9.6	8.9	10.4	6.6
2014/15	2.5	3.7	5.0	29.1	7.6	24.3
2015/16	-7.1	-14.8	8.4	28.2	0.7	47.3
2016/17	-0.9	-4.3	8.0	10.1	7.0	14.8
2017/18	2.5	5.4	7.6	13.3	10.3	7.2
Avg.	-0.4 %	-3.5 %	7.9 %	20.4 %	7.5 %	25.4 %
Fq>0	50 %	36 %	86 %	89 %	79 %	86 %

SHW - Avg. Year 1990 to 2017

SHW / S&P 500 Rel. Strength- Avg Yr. 1990-2017

Sherwin-Williams Performance

SHW Monthly Performance (1990-2017)

	Jan	Feb	Mar	Apr	May	Jun	Jul	Aug	Sep	Oct	Nov	Dec
Avg. % Gain	0.1	0.9	3.7	3.8	0.7	-1.4	1.3	-1.8	-0.8	3.6	3.2	3.2
Med. % Gain	0.6	0.5	2.2	5.3	0.7	-1.1	0.8	-1.0	-1.0	3.4	4.0	1.5
Fq %>0	57	61	68	68	50	43	54	43	46	61	75	71
Fq %>S&P 500	57	50	68	68	46	46	50	43	50	57	64	61

SHW 5 Year (2013-2017) % Gain

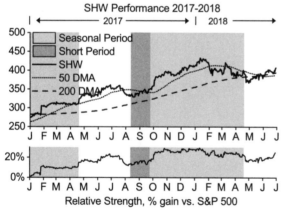

SHW Performance 2017-2018

Relative Strength, % gain vs. S&P 500

Market Indices & Rates Weekly Values**

Stock Markets	2016	2017
Dow	18,085	21,798
S&P500	2,128	2,461
Nasdaq	5,126	6,360
TSX	14,540	14,985
FTSE	6,777	7,378
DAX	10,573	12,304
Nikkei	16,966	19,275
Hang Seng	24,100	27,668

Commodities	2016	2017
Oil	45.88	47.48
Gold	1330.9	1346.3

Bond Yields	2016	2017
USA 5 Yr Treasury	1.23	1.64
USA 10 Yr T	1.67	2.06
USA 20 Yr T	2.05	2.41
Moody's Aaa	3.43	3.60
Moody's Baa	4.34	4.23
CAN 5 Yr T	0.71	1.72
CAN 10 Yr T	1.15	1.98

Money Market	2016	2017
USA Fed Funds	0.50	1.25
USA 3 Mo T-B	0.35	1.04
CAN tgt overnight rate	0.50	1.00
CAN 3 Mo T-B	0.48	0.94

Foreign Exchange	2016	2017
EUR/USD	1.12	1.20
GBP/USD	1.33	1.32
USD/CAD	1.30	1.22
USD/JPY	102.69	107.84

SEPTEMBER

M	T	W	T	F	S	S
						1
2	3	4	5	6	7	8
9	10	11	12	13	14	15
16	17	18	19	20	21	22
23	24	25	26	27	28	29
30						

OCTOBER

M	T	W	T	F	S	S
	1	2	3	4	5	6
7	8	9	10	11	12	13
14	15	16	17	18	19	20
21	22	23	24	25	26	27
28	29	30	31			

NOVEMBER

M	T	W	T	F	S	S
				1	2	3
4	5	6	7	8	9	10
11	12	13	14	15	16	17
18	19	20	21	22	23	24
25	26	27	28	29	30	

From 1990 to 2017, on average the best contiguous months of the year for Sherwin-Williams were October through to April. The worst two contiguous months were August and September.

Over the last five years, Sherwin-Williams has generally followed its seasonal pattern with October, November and February being the strongest months of the year and August and September being the weakest months of the year.

In late 2017, Sherwin-Williams was positive in its weak seasonal period. In 2018, Sherwin-Williams was positive in its strong seasonal period and outperformed the S&P 500.

CALLAWAY GOLF– TAKE YOUR BEST SHOT

①LONG (Jan10-Apr18) ②SELL SHORT (Apr19-Jul28) ③LONG (Jul29-Aug14)

According to Callaway Golf's form 10-K, filed with the Securities Exchange Commission, its revenues are greatly affected by seasonal trends. Callaway typically launches most of its new golf clubs and golf balls at the beginning of the year. Retailers stock up on the new inventory, driving up Callaway's sales. Second quarter sales tend to be strong. Although sales start to wane in the third quarter, Callaway typically introduces a secondary launch of new products in August to help boost sales. In the fourth quarter of the year, Callaway's sales decrease as retailers reduce their inventory for year-end.

24.2% gain

Investors tend to respond to the golf retail channel inventory cycle, buying Callaway's stock in the first few months of the year. Once the overall expected sales rate is embedded in the price of Callaway stock, it tends to suffer. The exception to this trend is the tendency of Callaway to perform well in August as investors anticipate a secondary launch of new products. For the remainder of the third and fourth quarters, investors tend to lose interest in Callaway stock.

(i) *Callaway is in the consumer discretionary sector. Its stock symbol is ELY. which trades on the NYSE, adjusted for splits.*

Callaway Golf* vs. S&P 500 1993 to 2017
Negative Short ☐   Positive Long ▨

Year	Jan 10 to Apr 18 S&P 500	ELY	Apr 19 to Jul 28 S&P 500	ELY	Jul 29 to Aug 14 S&P 500	ELY	Compound Growth S&P 500	ELY
1993	4.6 %	89.9 %	-0.4 %	31.6 %	0.7 %	27.5 %	4.9 %	65.6 %
1994	-5.8	27.8	2.7	3.0	1.7	1.8	-1.7	26.3
1995	9.7	-15.7	11.4	5.3	-0.6	-2.5	21.5	-22.2
1996	5.6	30.4	-1.2	13.8	4.1	6.7	8.6	19.9
1997	1.5	10.1	22.2	5.0	-1.3	1.3	22.5	6.0
1998	21.0	8.2	0.7	-53.6	-6.0	-8.4	14.6	52.2
1999	3.4	31.6	3.5	-5.4	-2.8	-17.2	4.1	14.8
2000	0.0	-7.6	-1.5	-18.4	5.1	12.6	3.5	23.2
2001	-4.8	42.8	-2.6	-36.2	-1.6	0.8	-8.8	96.1
2002	-2.7	13.6	-24.2	-29.3	7.8	0.4	-20.4	47.3
2003	-3.7	-4.5	11.5	17.1	-0.6	-0.5	6.8	-21.2
2004	1.1	8.9	-3.5	-43.5	-2.8	1.3	-5.1	58.2
2005	-3.4	-3.6	8.5	27.1	-1.1	-0.5	3.7	-30.0
2006	1.3	8.1	-2.2	-20.9	-0.8	2.7	-1.7	34.2
2007	4.3	29.1	-0.9	-10.7	-2.2	4.5	1.0	49.4
2008	-1.3	-7.4	-11.2	-9.6	4.7	6.6	-8.2	8.1
2009	-2.3	-15.3	12.7	-29.4	2.5	18.4	12.8	29.9
2010	4.1	21.1	-7.2	-32.4	-2.4	-2.6	-5.7	56.3
2011	2.7	-16.8	-0.3	-6.4	-9.4	-11.6	-7.3	-21.8
2012	8.2	18.4	0.1	-16.9	1.3	8.5	9.6	50.2
2013	5.5	-4.2	9.7	16.2	-0.4	-0.4	15.4	-20.0
2014	1.5	12.3	6.1	-17.4	-1.2	-1.8	6.4	29.5
2015	1.8	18.7	0.6	-13.7	-0.1	8.6	2.3	46.6
2016	9.0	3.1	3.6	11.9	0.6	11.9	13.6	1.6
2017	3.2	9.2	5.6	6.2	-0.3	2.6	8.7	5.1
Avg.	2.6 %	12.3 %	1.7 %	-8.3 %	-0.2 %	2.8 %	4.0 %	24.2 %
Fq>0	72 %	68 %	56 %	40 %	36 %	64 %	68 %	80 %

Callaway - Avg. Year 1993 to 2017

Callaway / S&P 500 Rel. Strength- Avg Yr. 1993-2017

Callaway Golf Performance

ELY Monthly Performance (1993-2017)

	Jan	Feb	Mar	Apr	May	Jun	Jul	Aug	Sep	Oct	Nov	Dec
Avg. % Gain	1.9	2.4	2.6	2.1	0.5	-4.4	-2.2	2.3	-0.6	2.4	5.4	0.5
Med. % Gain	0.9	3.1	3.2	1.6	1.2	-4.5	-1.4	1.7	1.7	3.0	2.8	-1.4
Fq %>0	52	64	60	60	52	36	36	60	56	56	64	48
Fq %>S&P 500	60	60	48	44	44	40	44	60	44	48	60	44

ELY 5 Year (2013-2017) % Gain

ELY Performance 2017-2018

Relative Strength, % gain vs. S&P 500

WEEK 37

Market Indices & Rates
Weekly Values**

Stock Markets	2016	2017
Dow	18,124	22,268
S&P500	2,139	2,500
Nasdaq	5,245	6,448
TSX	14,451	15,173
FTSE	6,710	7,215
DAX	10,276	12,519
Nikkei	16,519	19,910
Hang Seng	23,336	27,808

Commodities	2016	2017
Oil	43.03	49.89
Gold	1308.4	1322.9

Bond Yields	2016	2017
USA 5 Yr Treasury	1.21	1.81
USA 10 Yr T	1.70	2.20
USA 20 Yr T	2.10	2.52
Moody's Aaa	3.51	3.63
Moody's Baa	4.41	4.30
CAN 5 Yr T	0.74	1.81
CAN 10 Yr T	1.19	2.09

Money Market	2016	2017
USA Fed Funds	0.50	1.25
USA 3 Mo T-B	0.30	1.05
CAN tgt overnight rate	0.50	1.00
CAN 3 Mo T-B	0.49	1.00

Foreign Exchange	2016	2017
EUR/USD	1.12	1.19
GBP/USD	1.30	1.36
USD/CAD	1.32	1.22
USD/JPY	102.29	110.83

SEPTEMBER

M	T	W	T	F	S	S
						1
2	3	4	5	6	7	8
9	10	11	12	13	14	15
16	17	18	19	20	21	22
23	24	25	26	27	28	29
30						

OCTOBER

M	T	W	T	F	S	S
	1	2	3	4	5	6
7	8	9	10	11	12	13
14	15	16	17	18	19	20
21	22	23	24	25	26	27
28	29	30	31			

NOVEMBER

M	T	W	T	F	S	S
			1	2	3
4	5	6	7	8	9	10
11	12	13	14	15	16	17
18	19	20	21	22	23	24
25	26	27	28	29	30	

From 1993 to 2017, Callaway has generally performed well from early January to mid-April and then performed poorly in May through to July. August has on average been a strong month for Callaway.

Over the last five years, Callaway has followed its general seasonal trend with February and March being two of its strongest months and December being one of the weakest month of the year. In 2018, Callaway was positive in its strong seasonal period. Callaway continued its strong performance in April, into June when it is typically negative.

INFORMATION TECHNOLOGY
①Oct9-Dec5 ②Dec15-Jan17

Info Tech Interim Seasonal Period

The interim seasonal period (Dec 6th, to Dec 14th) is not part of the technology sector as it has produced an average loss of 1.7% and has only been positive 29% of the time from 1989 to 2017.

From 1989 to 2017, during its seasonal period of October 9th to December 5th, the information technology sector has produced an average gain of 7.3% and has been positive 72% of the time. From 1989/90 to 2017/18, during the second seasonal period of December 15th to January 17th, the information technology sector has produced an average gain of 3.4% and has been positive 72% of the time. The combined seasonal gains have been 11.2% and has been positive 72% of the time.

11.2% gain

Information technology stocks tend to get bid up at the end of the year for three reasons.

First, a lot of companies operate with year end budgets and if they do not spend the money in their budget, they lose it. In the last few months of the year, whatever money they have, they tend to spend. The number one purchase item for this budget flush is technology equipment. Second, consumers indirectly help push up technology stocks by purchasing electronic items during the holiday season.

Third, the "Conference Effect" helps maintain the momentum of the information technology sector in January. This phenomenon is the result of investors increasing positions in a sector ahead of major conferences in order to benefit from positive announcements. In the case of the information technology sector, investors increase their holdings ahead of the Las Vegas Consumer Electronics Conference that typically occurs in the second week of January.

Info Tech* vs. S&P 500 1989/90 to 2017/18   Positive ▢

	Oct 9 to Dec 5		Dec 15 to Jan 17		Compound Growth	
Year	S&P 500	IT	S&P 500	IT	S&P 500	IT
1989/90	-2.6%	-5.7%	-3.9%	3.8%	-6.3%	-2.1%
1990/91	5.2	11.2	0.4	5.5	5.6	17.3
1991/92	-0.9	-1.4	8.9	17.6	8.0	16.0
1992/93	6.0	6.8	1.0	7.4	7.0	14.7
1993/94	1.0	6.9	2.2	8.8	3.2	16.3
1994/95	-0.4	8.5	3.3	9.6	2.9	18.9
1995/96	6.0	3.2	-1.7	-8.0	4.2	-5.1
1996/97	6.2	14.4	6.5	7.3	13.2	22.8
1997/98	1.0	-8.1	0.9	4.0	1.9	-4.4
1998/99	22.7	46.8	8.9	18.7	33.6	74.2
1999/00	7.3	18.7	4.4	9.7	12.0	30.3
2000/01	-2.3	-12.8	-0.9	-3.3	-3.1	-15.7
2001/02	10.2	31.9	1.4	2.3	11.7	34.8
2002/03	13.5	37.2	1.4	-0.6	15.1	36.4
2003/04	2.7	2.3	6.1	11.1	9.0	13.6
2004/05	6.2	11.7	-1.6	-4.1	4.5	7.1
2005/06	5.5	8.4	0.8	1.5	6.4	10.0
2006/07	4.8	6.5	0.4	0.8	5.2	7.4
2007/08	-4.4	-2.6	-9.2	-12.7	-13.1	-14.9
2008/09	-11.1	-14.2	-3.4	-1.9	-14.0	-15.8
2009/10	3.8	6.3	2.0	2.7	5.8	9.2
2010/11	5.1	7.0	4.2	4.9	9.5	12.3
2011/12	8.8	7.6	6.8	4.9	16.1	12.8
2012/13	-3.2	-6.4	4.8	4.0	1.4	-2.6
2013/14	7.8	10.2	3.6	5.5	11.7	16.3
2014/15	5.4	6.8	0.9	-0.7	6.3	6.1
2015/16	3.9	8.2	-7.0	-9.4	-3.4	-1.9
2016/17	2.4	-1.5	0.7	1.5	3.0	0.0
2017/18	3.2	4.6	5.7	6.3	9.0	11.2
Avg.	3.9%	7.3%	1.6%	3.4%	5.7%	11.2%
Fq > 0	76%	72%	76%	72%	83%	72%

Info Tech Sector - Avg. Year 1990 to 2017

Info Tech / S&P 500 Rel. Strength - Avg Yr. 1990 - 2017

> **Y** *Alternate Strategy—* Investors can bridge the gap between the two positive seasonal trends for the information technology sector by holding from October 9th to January 17th. Longer term investors may prefer this strategy, shorter term investors can use technical tools to determine the appropriate strategy.

> **ⓘ** *The SP GICS Information Technology Sector. For more information on the information technology sector, see www.standardandpoors.com*

Information Technology Performance

Info Tech Monthly Performance (1990-2017)

	Jan	Feb	Mar	Apr	May	Jun	Jul	Aug	Sep	Oct	Nov	Dec
Avg. % Gain	2.5	0.3	1.0	1.8	1.5	-0.5	1.4	-0.2	-0.7	3.0	2.4	0.7
Med. % Gain	2.4	2.5	0.7	1.2	3.3	-1.7	2.0	0.8	0.3	3.2	2.0	0.7
Fq %>0	63	59	56	59	63	41	59	48	52	63	67	52
Fq %>S&P 500	74	52	41	48	59	37	52	56	67	56	63	33

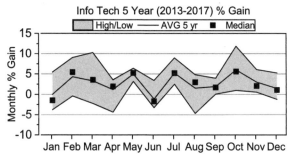

Info Tech 5 Year (2013-2017) % Gain

Info Tech Performance 2017-2018

Relative Strength, % gain vs. S&P 500

Market Indices & Rates
Weekly Values**

Stock Markets	2016	2017
Dow	18,261	22,350
S&P500	2,165	2,502
Nasdaq	5,306	6,427
TSX	14,698	15,454
FTSE	6,909	7,311
DAX	10,627	12,592
Nikkei	16,754	20,296
Hang Seng	23,686	27,881

Commodities	2016	2017
Oil	44.33	50.31
Gold	1338.7	1294.8

Bond Yields	2016	2017
USA 5 Yr Treasury	1.16	1.88
USA 10 Yr T	1.62	2.26
USA 20 Yr T	2.02	2.57
Moody's Aaa	3.44	3.62
Moody's Baa	4.30	4.31
CAN 5 Yr T	0.63	1.82
CAN 10 Yr T	1.04	2.11

Money Market	2016	2017
USA Fed Funds	0.50	1.25
USA 3 Mo T-B	0.18	1.03
CAN tgt overnight rate	0.50	1.00
CAN 3 Mo T-B	0.53	1.00

Foreign Exchange	2016	2017
EUR/USD	1.12	1.20
GBP/USD	1.30	1.35
USD/CAD	1.32	1.23
USD/JPY	101.02	111.99

SEPTEMBER

M	T	W	T	F	S	S
						1
2	3	4	5	6	7	8
9	10	11	12	13	14	15
16	17	18	19	20	21	22
23	24	25	26	27	28	29
30						

OCTOBER

M	T	W	T	F	S	S
	1	2	3	4	5	6
7	8	9	10	11	12	13
14	15	16	17	18	19	20
21	22	23	24	25	26	27
28	29	30	31			

NOVEMBER

M	T	W	T	F	S	S
			1	2	3
4	5	6	7	8	9	10
11	12	13	14	15	16	17
18	19	20	21	22	23	24
25	26	27	28	29	30	

From 1990 to 2017, on average, the technology sector has performed well from October to January.

Over the last five years, the technology sector has on average followed its seasonal trend. The largest anomaly has been the weak performance in January. February has been the strongest month, but has also had a wide dispersion of returns.

In its 2017/18 seasonal periods, the technology sector was positive and outperformed the S&P 500.

CANADIAN BANKS
①Oct10-Dec 31   ②Jan23-Apr13

Canadian banks have their year-end on October 31st. Why does this matter? In the past Canadian banks have announced most of their dividend increases and stock splits when they announce their typically optimistic full year fiscal reports at the end of November and beginning of December. This helps to push up the sector at this time.

10.6% gain & positive 79% of the time

The Canadian bank sector, from October 10th to December 31st for the years 1989 to 2017, has been positive 79% of the time and has produced an average gain of 5.3%. In the years from 1990 to 2018, from January 23rd to April 13th, the sector has been positive 69% of the time and has produced an average gain of 5.0%. On a compound basis, the strategy has been positive 79% of the time and produced an average gain of 10.6%.

Canadian bank returns in December have been separated out to show the impact of bank earnings on returns. In December, Canadian banks on average have provided gains 76% of the time, but they have underperformed the TSX Composite. If Canadian banks have performed well leading into their earnings, they often pause in December.

> ⓘ *Banks SP GIC Canadian Bank Sector Level 2 Represents a cross section of Canadian banking companies.*

Canadian Banks* vs. S&P 500 1989/90 to 2017/18
Positive ☐

Year	Oct 10 to Dec 31 TSX-Comp	Cdn. Banks	Jan 23 to Apr 13 TSX-Comp	Cdn. Banks	Compound Growth TSX-Comp	Cdn. Banks	1989 to 2017 Dec 1 Dec 31 TSX-Comp	Cdn. Banks
89/90	-1.7 %	-1.8 %	-6.3 %	-9.1 %	-7.9	-10.8 %	0.7 %	-1.4 %
90/91	3.7	8.9	9.8	14.6	13.9	24.8	3.4	5.5
91/92	5.2	10.2	-6.8	-11.6	-2.0	-2.6	1.9	4.6
92/93	4.1	2.5	10.7	14.4	15.2	17.3	2.1	1.8
93/94	6.3	6.8	-5.6	-13.3	0.3	-7.4	3.4	5.1
94/95	-1.8	3.4	5.0	10.0	3.1	13.8	2.9	0.9
95/96	4.9	3.5	3.6	-3.2	8.6	0.1	1.1	1.5
96/97	9.0	15.1	-6.2	0.7	2.3	15.9	-1.5	-1.9
97/98	-6.1	7.6	19.9	38.8	12.6	49.4	2.9	4.2
98/99	18.3	28.0	4.8	13.0	24.0	44.6	2.2	3.0
99/00	18.2	5.1	3.8	22.1	22.8	28.3	11.8	0.7
00/01	-14.4	1.7	-14.1	-6.7	-26.4	-5.1	1.3	9.6
01/02	11.9	6.5	2.3	8.2	14.5	15.1	3.5	3.4
02/03	16.1	21.3	-4.3	2.6	11.1	24.4	0.7	2.6
03/04	8.1	5.1	2.0	2.1	10.3	7.4	4.6	2.0
04/05	4.9	6.2	4.5	6.9	9.6	13.5	2.4	4.7
05/06	6.2	8.4	5.5	2.7	12.1	11.3	4.1	2.1
06/07	10.4	8.4	6.9	3.2	18.0	11.8	1.2	3.7
07/08	-3.0	-10.4	8.2	-3.5	5.0	-13.5	1.1	-7.7
08/09	-6.4	-14.8	9.4	24.4	2.4	6.1	-3.1	-11.2
09/10	2.7	2.4	6.7	15.2	9.6	18.0	2.6	0.1
10/11	7.2	-0.2	4.3	9.1	11.9	8.9	3.8	-0.5
11/12	3.2	3.1	-2.9	1.1	0.2	4.2	-2.0	2.7
12/13	1.3	4.4	-3.8	-2.0	-2.5	2.3	1.6	1.5
13/14	7.0	9.0	1.9	1.6	9.1	10.7	1.7	0.9
14/15	1.2	-0.9	4.2	4.4	5.4	3.5	-0.8	-4.3
15/16	-6.8	-1.5	10.4	11.0	2.8	9.4	-3.4	-3.6
16/17	5.0	11.8	-0.1	-1.5	4.9	10.2	1.4	4.3
17/18	3.1	4.4	-6.6	-8.8	-3.7	-4.8	0.9	1.1
Avg.	4.1 %	5.3 %	2.3 %	5.0 %	6.4 %	10.6 %	1.8 %	1.2 %
Fq>0	76 %	79 %	66 %	69 %	83 %	79 %	83 %	76 %

Canadian Banking Sector - Avg. Year 1990 to 2017

Cdn. Banking / TSX Comp Rel. Strength- Avg Yr. 1990-2017

Canadian Banks Performance

Canadian Banks Monthly Performance (1990-2017)

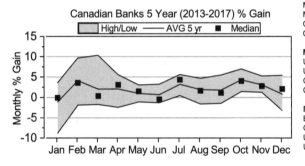

	Jan	Feb	Mar	Apr	May	Jun	Jul	Aug	Sep	Oct	Nov	Dec
Avg. % Gain	-0.8	1.8	1.3	0.9	1.4	-1.1	1.6	-0.2	0.2	2.6	1.6	1.3
Med. % Gain	-0.8	2.2	1.1	1.0	1.3	-1.0	2.3	1.0	0.6	2.3	1.3	1.9
Fq %>0	43	64	61	54	64	43	68	68	57	82	71	79
Fq %>TSX Comp	36	64	57	54	36	46	57	46	61	68	68	46

Canadian Banks 5 Year (2013-2017) % Gain

Canadian Banks Performance 2017-2018

Relative Strength, % gain vs. TSX Comp.

Market Indices & Rates
Weekly Values**

Stock Markets	2016	2017
Dow	18,308	22,405
S&P500	2,168	2,519
Nasdaq	5,312	6,496
TSX	14,726	15,635
FTSE	6,899	7,373
DAX	10,511	12,829
Nikkei	16,450	20,356
Hang Seng	23,297	27,554

Commodities	2016	2017
Oil	48.24	51.67
Gold	1322.5	1283.1

Bond Yields	2016	2017
USA 5 Yr Treasury	1.14	1.92
USA 10 Yr T	1.60	2.33
USA 20 Yr T	1.99	2.63
Moody's Aaa	3.44	3.62
Moody's Baa	4.29	4.33
CAN 5 Yr T	0.62	1.75
CAN 10 Yr T	1.00	2.10

Money Market	2016	2017
USA Fed Funds	0.50	1.25
USA 3 Mo T-B	0.29	1.06
CAN tgt overnight rate	0.50	1.00
CAN 3 Mo T-B	0.53	1.00

Foreign Exchange	2016	2017
EUR/USD	1.12	1.18
GBP/USD	1.30	1.34
USD/CAD	1.31	1.25
USD/JPY	101.35	112.51

SEPTEMBER

M	T	W	T	F	S	S
						1
2	3	4	5	6	7	8
9	10	11	12	13	14	15
16	17	18	19	20	21	22
23	24	25	26	27	28	29
30						

OCTOBER

M	T	W	T	F	S	S
1	2	3	4	5	6	
7	8	9	10	11	12	13
14	15	16	17	18	19	20
21	22	23	24	25	26	27
28	29	30	31			

NOVEMBER

M	T	W	T	F	S	S
			1	2	3	
4	5	6	7	8	9	10
11	12	13	14	15	16	17
18	19	20	21	22	23	24
25	26	27	28	29	30	

From 1990 to 2017, October has been the best month for Canadian banks on an average basis. September has been one of the weaker months of the year. This juxtaposition makes the timing of the transition into the seasonal period, that starts in October, important. The second seasonal period starts in late January. On average, January is a weak month making the timing of the transition critical. Over the last five years, February and July have been the best months of the year for Canadian banks on a median basis. In the late 2017 seasonal period, Canadian banks outperformed the TSX Composite. In their first seasonal period in 2018, Canadian banks underperformed the TSX Composite.

OCTOBER

	MONDAY	TUESDAY	WEDNESDAY
WEEK 40	30	**1** 30	**2** 29
WEEK 41	**7** 24	**8** 23	**9** 22

WEEK 42	**14** 17
	
	USA Bond Market Closed-
	       Columbus Day
	
	CAN Market Closed-
	       Thanksgiving Day
		15 16	**16** 15

WEEK 43	**21** 10	**22** 9	**23** 8
WEEK 44	**28** 3	**29** 2	**30** 1

THURSDAY	FRIDAY
3 28	**4** 27
10 21	**11** 20
17 14	**18** 13
24 7	**25** 6
31	1

NOVEMBER

M	T	W	T	F	S	S
				1	2	3
4	5	6	7	8	9	10
11	12	13	14	15	16	17
18	19	20	21	22	23	24
25	26	27	28	29	30	

DECEMBER

M	T	W	T	F	S	S
						1
2	3	4	5	6	7	8
9	10	11	12	13	14	15
16	17	18	19	20	21	22
23	24	25	26	27	28	29
30	31					

JANUARY

M	T	W	T	F	S	S
		1	2	3	4	5
6	7	8	9	10	11	12
13	14	15	16	17	18	19
20	21	22	23	24	25	26
27	28	29	30	31		

FEBRUARY

M	T	W	T	F	S	S
					1	2
3	4	5	6	7	8	9
10	11	12	13	14	15	16
17	18	19	20	21	22	23
24	25	26	27	28	29	

OCTOBER
S U M M A R Y

S&P500 Cumulative Daily Gains for Avg Month 1950 to 2017

	Dow Jones	S&P 500	Nasdaq	TSX Comp
Month Rank	7	7	6	9
# Up	41	41	26	22
# Down	27	27	20	11
% Pos	60	60	57	67
% Avg. Gain	0.7	0.9	0.9	0.2

Dow & S&P 1950-2017, Nasdaq 1972-2017, TSX 1985-2017

♦ October, on average, is the most volatile month of the year for the stock market and often provides opportunities for short-term traders. The first half of October tends to be positive. ♦ The second half of the month, leading up to the last four days, tends to be negative, and prone to large drops. ♦ Seasonal opportunities in mid-October include Canadian banks, technology and transportation. ♦ In late October, a lot of sectors start their seasonal period, including the materials, industrials, consumer discretionary and retail sectors.

BEST / WORST OCTOBER BROAD MKTS. 2008-2017

BEST OCTOBER MARKETS
♦ Russell 2000 (2011) 15.0%
♦ Nasdaq (2011) 11.1%
♦ Russell 1000 (2011) 11.1%

WORST OCTOBER MARKETS
♦ Nikkei 225 (2008) -23.8%
♦ Russell 2000 (2008) -20.9%
♦ Nasdaq (2008) -17.7%

Index Values End of Month

	2008	2009	2010	2011	2012	2013	2014	2015	2016	2017
Dow	9,325	9,713	11,118	11,955	13,096	15,546	17,391	17,664	18,142	23,377
S&P 500	969	1,036	1,183	1,253	1,412	1,757	2,018	2,079	2,126	2,575
Nasdaq	1,721	2,045	2,507	2,684	2,977	3,920	4,631	5,054	5,189	6,728
TSX Comp.	9,763	10,911	12,676	12,252	12,423	13,361	14,613	13,529	14,787	16,026
Russell 1000	522	567	654	692	779	980	1,122	1,154	1,177	1,427
Russell 2000	538	563	703	741	819	1,100	1,174	1,162	1,191	1,503
FTSE 100	4,377	5,045	5,675	5,544	5,783	6,731	6,546	6,361	6,954	7,493
Nikkei 225	8,577	10,035	9,202	8,988	8,928	14,328	16,414	19,083	17,425	22,012

Percent Gain for October

	2008	2009	2010	2011	2012	2013	2014	2015	2016	2017
Dow	-14.1	0.0	3.1	9.5	-2.5	2.8	2.0	8.5	-0.9	4.3
S&P 500	-16.9	-2.0	3.7	10.8	-2.0	4.5	2.3	8.3	-1.9	2.2
Nasdaq	-17.7	-3.6	5.9	11.1	-4.5	3.9	3.1	9.4	-2.3	3.6
TSX Comp.	-16.9	-4.2	2.5	5.4	0.9	4.5	-2.3	1.7	0.4	2.5
Russell 1000	-17.5	-2.3	3.8	11.1	-1.8	4.3	2.3	8.0	-2.1	2.2
Russell 2000	-20.9	-6.9	4.0	15.0	-2.2	2.5	6.5	5.6	-4.8	0.8
FTSE 100	-10.7	-1.7	2.3	8.1	0.7	4.2	-1.2	4.9	0.8	1.6
Nikkei 225	-23.8	-1.0	-1.8	3.3	0.7	-0.9	1.5	9.7	5.9	8.1

October Market Avg. Performance 2008 to 2017[1]

	Dow	1.3%
	S&P 500	0.9%
	Nasdaq	0.9%
	TSX Comp (CAN)	-0.6%
	Russell 1000 (Lg Cap)	0.8%
	Russell 2000 (Sm Cap)	-0.0%
	FTSE 100	0.9%
	Nikkei 225	0.2%

Interest Corner Oct[2]

	Fed Funds %[3]	3 Mo. T-Bill %[4]	10 Yr %[5]	20 Yr %[6]
2017	1.25	1.01	2.38	2.66
2016	0.50	0.34	1.84	2.25
2015	0.25	0.08	2.16	2.57
2014	0.25	0.01	2.35	2.81
2013	0.25	0.04	2.57	3.33

(1) Russell Data provided by Russell (2) Federal Reserve Bank of St. Louis- end of month values (3) Target rate set by FOMC (4)(5)(6) Constant yield maturities.

S&P GIC	2017	1990-2017[1]	
Sectors	**% Gain**	**GIC[2] % Avg Gain**	**Fq% Gain >S&P 500**
Information Technology	7.7 %	3.0 %	57 %
Consumer Staples	-1.6	2.5	57
Consumer Discretionary	2.0	1.8	50
Health Care	-0.8	1.6	43
Financials	2.8	1.5	46
Materials	3.8	1.4	46
Industrials	0.2	1.1	39
Telecom	-8.7	1.1	36
Utilities	3.9	0.9	43
Energy	-0.7 %	0.7 %	39 %
S&P 500	2.2 %	1.7 %	N/A %

Sector Commentary

♦ In October 2017, the information technology sector produced a 7.7% gain. The seasonal period for the technology sector starts in October (October 9th). ♦ The utilities sector produced a gain of 3.9%. ♦ The consumer staples sector is typically one of the best performing sectors, but in October 2017 it produced a loss of 1.6%.

Sub-Sector Commentary

♦ In October 2017, the semiconductor sub-sector produced a large gain of 8.9% largely as the result of investor interest in companies producing graphic chips to support cryptocurrency mining computers. ♦ Homebuliders started off their seasonal period on a strong note with a gain of 8.9%. ♦ Retail stocks produced a gain of 5.0% with most of the gain coming before the late-October start of its seasonal period. ♦ The biotech sub-sector finished its seasonal period in September, before it corrected 8.6% in October. ♦ The agriculture sub-sector produced a loss of 3.9%. Typically agriculture performs well in October.

SELECTED SUB-SECTORS[3]			
Agriculture (1994-2017)	-3.9 %	5.6 %	75 %
Transportation	-1.8	3.8	71
Railroads	-2.3	3.6	64
Steel	3.2	2.4	46
SOX (1995-2017)	8.9	2.4	48
Chemicals	4.3	2.2	57
Pharma	-1.6	2.0	54
Retail	5.0	2.0	57
Banks	3.6	1.2	39
Homebuilders	8.9	1.2	39
Biotech (1993-2017)	-8.6	1.2	44
Automotive & Components	2.8	0.7	43
Metals & Mining	-0.4	0.2	36
Gold	-1.0	-1.1	21
Silver	-0.2	-1.4	29

MCDONALD'S
①Oct 28-Nov 24   ②Jan 30-Apr 8

McDonald's is part of the consumer discretionary sector, but it has a slightly different seasonal pattern. Investors tend to push up the price of McDonald's stock price in autumn, but then lose interest once the holiday shopping season starts in November.

10.3% gain & 83% of the time positive

From 1989 to 2017, in the period from October 28th to November 24th, McDonald's has produced an average gain of 4.9% and has been positive 86% of the time.

McDonald's tends to underperform the S&P 500 in December and January, but once the holiday season ends and the worst month of the year for retail comes close to finishing (January), investors warm up to the idea of McDonald's once again.

McDonald's tends to perform well from January 30th to April 8th. In this period from 1990 to 2018, Mc-Donald's has produced an average gain of 5.1% and has been positive 66% of the time.

In the summer months, investors lose interest in McDonald's and it tends to underperform the S&P 500. The time period between July 19th to August 31st tends to be very weak for McDonald's. In this time period from 1990 to 2017, McDonald's has produced an average loss of 2.6% and has only been positive 36% of the time.

MCD* vs. S&P 500 - 1989/90 to 2017/18   Positive ☐

Year	Oct 28 to Nov 24 S&P 500	MCD	Jan 30 to Apr 8 S&P 500	MCD	Compound Growth S&P 500	MCD
1989/90	2.7 %	6.5 %	4.6 %	0.0 %	7.4 %	6.5 %
1990/91	3.4	12.8	12.8	32.2	16.6	49.2
1991/92	-2.1	-1.5	-3.9	-1.8	-5.9	-3.2
1992/93	2.2	6.8	0.7	3.9	2.9	11.0
1993/94	-0.5	2.9	-6.6	-5.8	-7.0	-3.1
1994/95	-3.4	0.9	7.7	8.1	4.0	9.1
1995/96	3.5	4.8	3.2	-5.0	6.8	-0.4
1996/97	6.8	7.3	-0.8	9.0	5.9	17.0
1997/98	8.0	11.2	11.8	27.2	20.7	41.5
1998/99	11.0	9.7	5.0	19.0	16.6	30.9
1999/00	9.3	14.9	11.5	0.7	21.8	15.7
2000/01	-2.7	13.2	-17.3	-11.1	-19.5	0.7
2001/02	4.1	-4.9	2.2	8.5	6.5	3.1
2002/03	3.7	0.8	1.6	10.2	5.3	11.0
2003/04	2.0	5.7	0.5	12.4	2.5	18.9
2004/05	5.0	4.2	0.8	-2.7	5.9	1.3
2005/06	7.4	6.9	0.9	-0.5	8.3	6.3
2006/07	1.7	1.0	1.6	5.9	3.4	6.9
2007/08	-6.2	-1.3	0.2	10.1	-5.9	8.7
2008/09	0.3	7.2	-2.4	-4.4	-2.0	2.5
2009/10	4.0	8.8	10.5	10.1	14.9	19.8
2010/11	1.3	2.6	4.1	3.8	5.5	6.4
2011/12	-9.6	-1.8	6.2	-0.1	-3.9	-1.8
2012/13	-0.2	0.4	3.7	6.9	3.5	7.3
2013/14	2.6	3.7	4.4	5.3	7.1	9.2
2014/15	5.5	5.6	3.0	3.8	8.7	9.7
2015/16	1.1	2.4	5.5	3.4	6.7	5.8
2016/17	3.4	7.2	2.7	5.8	6.1	13.4
2017/18	0.8	2.3	-8.7	-9.3	-8.0	-7.2
Avg.	2.2 %	4.9 %	2.3 %	5.1 %	4.6 %	10.3 %
Fq>0	76 %	86 %	79 %	66 %	76 %	83 %

MCD - Avg. Year 1990 to 2017

MCD / S&P 500 Rel. Strength- Avg Yr. 1990-2017

ⓘ *McDonald's Corporation is in the restaurant sector. For more information, see McDonalds.com*

- 121 -

McDonald's Performance

MCD Monthly Performance (1990-2017)

	Jan	Feb	Mar	Apr	May	Jun	Jul	Aug	Sep	Oct	Nov	Dec
Avg. % Gain	0.2	0.6	2.7	2.1	1.9	-0.9	0.3	-1.2	0.6	2.3	3.6	0.8
Med. % Gain	0.0	0.4	3.0	2.4	3.4	-1.3	0.3	-0.6	2.0	2.7	2.9	0.4
Fq %>0	50	57	71	64	61	36	50	43	68	61	89	54
Fq %>S&P 500	54	46	64	57	57	50	43	36	57	54	75	46

MCD 5 Year (2013-2017) % Gain

MCD Performance 2017-2018

Relative Strength, % gain vs. S&P 500

Stock Markets	2016	2017
Dow	18,240	22,774
S&P500	2,154	2,549
Nasdaq	5,292	6,590
TSX	14,566	15,728
FTSE	7,044	7,523
DAX	10,491	12,956
Nikkei	16,860	20,691
Hang Seng	23,852	28,458

Commodities	2016	2017
Oil	49.81	49.29
Gold	1258.8	1261.8

Bond Yields	2016	2017
USA 5 Yr Treasury	1.26	1.97
USA 10 Yr T	1.73	2.37
USA 20 Yr T	2.14	2.68
Moody's Aaa	3.50	3.63
Moody's Baa	4.36	4.35
CAN 5 Yr T	0.74	1.78
CAN 10 Yr T	1.17	2.13

Money Market	2016	2017
USA Fed Funds	0.50	1.25
USA 3 Mo T-B	0.33	1.07
CAN tgt overnight rate	0.50	1.00
CAN 3 Mo T-B	0.50	0.98

Foreign Exchange	2016	2017
EUR/USD	1.12	1.17
GBP/USD	1.24	1.31
USD/CAD	1.33	1.25
USD/JPY	102.98	112.65

OCTOBER

M	T	W	T	F	S	S
	1	2	3	4	5	6
7	8	9	10	11	12	13
14	15	16	17	18	19	20
21	22	23	24	25	26	27
28	29	30	31			

NOVEMBER

M	T	W	T	F	S	S
				1	2	3
4	5	6	7	8	9	10
11	12	13	14	15	16	17
18	19	20	21	22	23	24
25	26	27	28	29	30	

From 1990 to 2017, November and March have been two of the strongest months of the year for McDonald's on an average basis. Both months are the core months of the two strong seasonal periods for McDonald's.

Over the last five years, the average and median performance has oscillated in a tight range and has shown a relative seasonal trend. In its autumn 2017 seasonal period, McDonald's outperformed the S&P 500 in a very positive year for McDonald's. In its 2018 seasonal period, McDonald's was negative and underperformed the S&P 500.

DECEMBER

M	T	W	T	F	S	S
						1
2	3	4	5	6	7	8
9	10	11	12	13	14	15
16	17	18	19	20	21	22
23	24	25	26	27	28	29
30	31					

HOMEBUILDERS—
TIME TO BREAK & TIME TO BUILD
①SELL SHORT (Apr27-Jun13) ②LONG (Oct28-Feb3)

The homebuilders sector has been in the spotlight for the last few years: first when the mortgage meltdown occurred in 2007 and 2008, and more recently, as the housing market has bounced back giving the homebuilders sector a boost.

20.0% gain & positive 75% of the time

Historically, the best time to be in the homebuilders sector has been from October 28th to February 3rd. In this time period, during the years 1990/91 to 2017/18, the homebuilders sector has produced an average gain of 16.0% and have been positive 89% of the time.

Generally, the time period outside of the strong seasonal period for homebuilders should be avoided by investors, as not only has the average performance relative to the S&P 500 been negative, but the sector has produced both large gains and losses. In other words, the risk is substantially higher that a large drawdown will occur.

This is particularly true for the time period from April 27th to June 13th. In this time period, from 1990 to 2018, the homebuilders sector produced an average loss of 3.2% and has only been positive 32% of the time.

Homebuilders (HB)* vs. S&P 500 1990/91 to 2016/17
Negative Short☐   Positive Long☐

Year	SHORT Apr 27 to Jun 13		LONG Oct 28 to Feb 3		Compound Growth	
	S&P 500	HB.	S&P 500	HB.	S&P 500	HB.
1990/91	9.6 %	7.9 %	12.6 %	58.0 %	1.8 %	45.5 %
1991/92	-0.4	-4.8	6.6	41.2	7.0	48.0
1992/93	0.2	-11.5	6.9	26.7	6.7	41.2
1993/94	3.2	12.6	3.5	8.6	0.2	-5.1
1994/95	1.6	-4.0	2.8	-4.0	1.1	-0.2
1995/96	4.6	11.1	9.7	16.7	4.7	3.7
1996/97	2.2	10.6	12.2	6.3	9.8	-4.9
1997/98	16.7	22.6	14.7	24.8	-4.5	-3.4
1998/99	-0.8	-10.6	19.4	12.4	20.4	24.2
1999/00	-4.9	-7.1	9.9	-3.9	15.3	2.9
2000/01	0.6	-3.8	-2.2	18.6	-2.7	23.1
2001/02	0.6	-17.5	1.6	43.1	1.0	68.1
2002/03	-6.2	-5.3	-4.2	6.7	1.8	12.3
2003/04	10.0	31.5	10.2	7.6	-0.8	-26.3
2004/05	0.1	-2.6	5.7	23.7	5.6	26.9
2005/06	4.3	11.9	7.2	14.8	2.7	1.1
2006/07	-6.3	-27.1	5.2	16.8	11.7	48.4
2007/08	1.4	-7.9	-9.1	8.8	-10.4	17.4
2008/09	-2.7	-25.3	-1.2	27.7	1.4	60.0
2009/10	9.2	-25.1	3.2	15.5	-6.3	44.4
2010/11	-9.9	-22.9	10.5	12.9	21.5	38.7
2011/12	-5.6	-11.2	4.7	35.0	10.6	50.1
2012/13	-6.1	-9.3	7.2	13.7	13.7	24.3
2013/14	3.4	-7.2	-1.0	10.1	-4.4	18.1
2014/15	3.9	4.5	4.5	7.8	0.4	3.0
2015/16	-1.1	-0.8	-7.4	-15.3	-6.4	-14.6
2016/17	-0.6	-2.3	7.7	10.9	8.4	13.5
2017/18	2.2	4.6	7.0	4.2	4.6	-0.6
Avg.	1.0 %	-3.2 %	5.3 %	16.0 %	4.1 %	20.0 %
Fq>0	61 %	32 %	79 %	89 %	75 %	75 %

Homebuilders - Avg. Year 1990 to 2017

Homebuilders / S&P 500 Rel. Strength- Avg Yr. 1990-2017

ⓘ *Homebuilders: SP GIC Sector: An index designed to represent a cross section of homebuilding companies. For more information, see www.standarda-ndpoors.com.

Homebuilders Performance

Homebuilders Monthly Performance (1990-2017)

	Jan	Feb	Mar	Apr	May	Jun	Jul	Aug	Sep	Oct	Nov	Dec
Avg. % Gain	2.7	0.4	1.2	1.1	-0.8	-1.0	0.8	0.1	-0.8	1.2	3.1	7.0
Med. % Gain	3.0	1.4	0.4	-1.4	0.9	0.1	-0.5	-0.2	1.3	1.2	4.0	5.7
Fq %>0	68	54	50	46	57	50	46	50	57	61	64	71
Fq %>S&P 500	61	61	50	43	46	46	46	57	57	39	54	79

Homebuilders 5 Year (2013-2017) % Gain

Homebuilders Performance 2017-2018

Relative Strength, % gain vs. S&P 500

Market Indices & Rates
Weekly Values**

Stock Markets	2016	2017
Dow	18,138	22,872
S&P500	2,133	2,553
Nasdaq	5,214	6,606
TSX	14,585	15,807
FTSE	7,014	7,535
DAX	10,580	12,992
Nikkei	16,856	21,155
Hang Seng	23,233	28,476

Commodities	2016	2017
Oil	50.35	51.45
Gold	1251.8	1299.6

Bond Yields	2016	2017
USA 5 Yr Treasury	1.28	1.91
USA 10 Yr T	1.80	2.28
USA 20 Yr T	2.22	2.58
Moody's Aaa	3.56	3.54
Moody's Baa	4.43	4.25
CAN 5 Yr T	0.78	1.73
CAN 10 Yr T	1.25	2.04

Money Market	2016	2017
USA Fed Funds	0.50	1.25
USA 3 Mo T-B	0.32	1.09
CAN tgt overnight rate	0.50	1.00
CAN 3 Mo T-B	0.50	0.97

Foreign Exchange	2016	2017
EUR/USD	1.10	1.18
GBP/USD	1.22	1.33
USD/CAD	1.31	1.25
USD/JPY	104.18	111.82

OCTOBER

M	T	W	T	F	S	S
	1	2	3	4	5	6
7	8	9	10	11	12	13
14	15	16	17	18	19	20
21	22	23	24	25	26	27
28	29	30	31			

NOVEMBER

M	T	W	T	F	S	S
					1	2	3
4	5	6	7	8	9	10
11	12	13	14	15	16	17
18	19	20	21	22	23	24
25	26	27	28	29	30	

DECEMBER

M	T	W	T	F	S	S
						1
2	3	4	5	6	7	8
9	10	11	12	13	14	15
16	17	18	19	20	21	22
23	24	25	26	27	28	29
30	31					

From 1990 to 2017, the best month of the year for the homebuilders sector has been December on an average, median and frequency basis. May and June on average have produced a loss.

Over the last five years, on average, the homebuilders sector has followed its general seasonal trend, although December has been weaker than most other months of the year.

In 2017/18, the seasonal long position was positive but underperformed the S&P 500. In its 2018 seasonally weak period the homebuilders sector was positive.

UTX UNITED TECHNOLOGIES
①Jan23-May5 ②Oct10-Dec31

United Technologies is a conglomerate industrial company and as such has similar seasonal periods to the industrial sector. The difference is that United Technologies starts one of its seasonal periods earlier in October. The industrial sector starts its seasonal period on October 28th, whereas United Technologies starts its seasonal period on October 10th.

19.5% extra & positive 27 times out of 28

It is worthwhile to consider entering a position in United Technologies before the start of the industrial sector's seasonal period. When United Technologies outperforms in early October, it is often a precursor of what to expect for the broad market.

The combined trade of January 23rd to May 5th and October 10th to December 31st has produced a 19.5% gain and has been successful 96% of the time since 1990.

Investors should note that being positive 96% of the time in the past does not guarantee the success of the trade in the future. Nevertheless, it does indicate the strength of the seasonal trade.

Given that United Technologies produces 6% of its revenues from China (Reuters), investors should be looking to the strength of the Chinese economy in order to help determine the possible strength of the United Technologies seasonal trade.

*United Technologies Corporation is a multinational conglomerate in the industrial sector. For more information, see UTC.com

UTX* vs. S&P 500 - 1990 to 2017   Positive [ ]

Year	Jan 23 to May 5 S&P 500	UTX	Oct 10 to Dec 31 S&P 500	UTX	Compound Growth S&P 500	UTX
1990	2.4 %	10.2 %	8.2 %	5.2 %	10.8 %	15.9 %
1991	16.0	4.0	10.7	27.3	28.4	32.4
1992	-0.3	-0.9	8.2	4.1	7.9	3.1
1993	1.9	4.7	1.3	8.5	3.3	13.7
1994	-4.9	-0.4	0.9	1.2	-4.0	0.8
1995	11.9	15.0	6.5	12.0	19.2	28.8
1996	4.6	14.1	6.3	7.8	11.2	23.0
1997	5.6	15.9	0.0	-7.5	5.6	7.3
1998	15.8	31.5	24.9	41.7	44.6	86.3
1999	10.0	27.2	10.0	9.7	20.9	39.6
2000	-0.6	7.7	-5.8	12.2	-6.4	20.9
2001	-5.7	9.9	8.6	26.7	2.5	39.2
2002	-4.1	7.6	13.3	25.9	8.6	35.5
2003	5.5	-2.6	7.1	14.7	12.9	11.8
2004	-2.0	-9.6	8.0	11.8	5.9	1.1
2005	0.4	2.3	4.4	11.5	4.8	14.1
2006	5.1	18.0	5.0	-4.1	10.4	13.2
2007	5.8	6.1	-6.2	-5.7	-0.7	0.0
2008	7.4	11.0	-0.7	15.7	6.6	28.4
2009	9.2	5.9	4.1	11.7	13.7	18.2
2010	6.8	6.5	7.9	8.0	15.3	15.0
2011	4.0	10.4	8.8	2.3	13.2	12.9
2012	4.1	3.6	-1.1	6.1	3.0	9.9
2013	8.2	6.5	11.6	10.7	20.7	17.8
2014	2.2	0.6	6.8	15.1	9.1	15.8
2015	1.3	-4.5	1.4	0.7	2.7	-3.8
2016	7.5	16.1	4.0	9.0	11.8	26.6
2017	5.6	9.5	5.1	7.5	11.0	17.8
Avg.	4.4 %	8.1 %	5.7 %	10.4 %	10.5 %	19.5 %
Fq>0	79 %	82 %	82 %	89 %	89 %	96 %

UTX - Avg. Year 1990 to 2017

UTX / S&P 500 Rel. Strength- Avg Yr. 1990-2017

UTX Performance

UTX Monthly Performance (1990-2017)

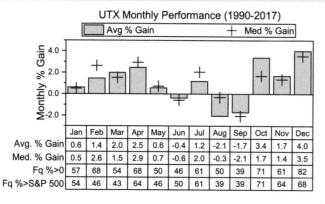

	Jan	Feb	Mar	Apr	May	Jun	Jul	Aug	Sep	Oct	Nov	Dec
Avg. % Gain	0.6	1.4	2.0	2.5	0.6	-0.4	1.2	-2.1	-1.7	3.4	1.7	4.0
Med. % Gain	0.5	2.6	1.5	2.9	0.7	-0.6	2.0	-0.3	-2.1	1.7	1.4	3.5
Fq %>0	57	68	54	68	50	46	61	50	39	71	61	82
Fq %>S&P 500	54	46	43	64	46	50	61	39	39	71	64	68

UTX 5 Year (2013-2017) % Gain

UTX Performance 2017-2018

Relative Strength, % gain vs. S&P 500

From 1990 to 2017, the best month for United Technologies has been December on an average, median and frequency basis.

Over the last five years, United Technologies has generally followed its seasonal trend with weaker summer months.

In 2017, United Technologies outperformed the S&P 500 in both seasonal periods and underperformed in its 2018 seasonal period.

WEEK 42

Market Indices & Rates
Weekly Values**

Stock Markets	2016	2017
Dow	18,146	23,329
S&P500	2,141	2,575
Nasdaq	5,257	6,629
TSX	14,939	15,857
FTSE	7,020	7,523
DAX	10,711	12,991
Nikkei	17,185	21,458
Hang Seng	23,374	28,487

Commodities	2016	2017
Oil	50.55	51.47
Gold	1266.1	1281.2

Bond Yields	2016	2017
USA 5 Yr Treasury	1.25	2.03
USA 10 Yr T	1.74	2.39
USA 20 Yr T	2.15	2.67
Moody's Aaa	3.45	3.60
Moody's Baa	4.34	4.33
CAN 5 Yr T	0.65	1.70
CAN 10 Yr T	1.13	2.03

Money Market	2016	2017
USA Fed Funds	0.50	1.25
USA 3 Mo T-B	0.34	1.11
CAN tgt overnight rate	0.50	1.00
CAN 3 Mo T-B	0.49	0.93

Foreign Exchange	2016	2017
EUR/USD	1.09	1.18
GBP/USD	1.22	1.32
USD/CAD	1.33	1.26
USD/JPY	103.80	113.52

OCTOBER

M	T	W	T	F	S	S
	1	2	3	4	5	6
7	8	9	10	11	12	13
14	15	16	17	18	19	20
21	22	23	24	25	26	27
28	29	30	31			

NOVEMBER

M	T	W	T	F	S	S
				1	2	3
4	5	6	7	8	9	10
11	12	13	14	15	16	17
18	19	20	21	22	23	24
25	26	27	28	29	30	

DECEMBER

M	T	W	T	F	S	S
						1
2	3	4	5	6	7	8
9	10	11	12	13	14	15
16	17	18	19	20	21	22
23	24	25	26	27	28	29
30	31					

RETAIL – SHOP EARLY
October 28th to November 29th

The *Retail – Shop Early* strategy is the second retail sector strategy of the year and it occurs before the biggest shopping season of the year – the Christmas holiday season.

2.9% extra & 79% of the time better than S&P 500

The time to go shopping for retail stocks is at the end of October, which is about one month before Thanksgiving. It is the time when two favorable influences happen at the same time.

Retail Sector - Avg. Year 1990 to 2017

Retail / S&P 500 Relative Strength - Avg Yr. 1990 - 2017

First, historically, November has been one of the stronger months of the year for the stock market, which helps support a higher beta sector, such as the retail sector.

Second, investors tend to buy retail stocks in anticipation of a strong holiday sales season. Seasonal investors position themselves ahead of the average investor that typically enters the retail sector in November.

Retail sales tend to be lower in the summer and a lot of investors view investing in retail stocks at this time as dead money. During the summertime, investors prefer not to invest in this sector until it comes back into favor towards the end of October.

The trick to investing is not to be too early, but early.

If an investor gets into a sector too early, they can suffer from the frustration of having dead money– an investment that goes nowhere, while the rest of the market increases.

If an investor moves into a sector too late, there is very little upside potential. In fact, this can be a dangerous strategy because if the sales or earnings numbers disappoint the analysts, the sector can severely correct.

For the *Retail – Shop Early* strategy, the time to enter is approximately one month before Black Friday.

Oct 28	Positive		
to Nov 29	S&P 500	Retail	Diff
1990	3.8 %	9.9 %	6.0 %
1991	-2.3	2.7	5.0
1992	2.8	5.5	2.8
1993	-0.6	6.3	6.9
1994	-2.3	0.4	2.7
1995	4.8	9.5	4.7
1996	8.0	0.4	-7.6
1997	8.9	16.9	7.9
1998	11.9	20.4	8.4
1999	8.6	14.1	5.5
2000	-2.7	9.9	12.6
2001	3.2	7.9	4.7
2002	4.3	-1.7	-6.0
2003	2.6	2.5	-0.1
2004	4.7	7.0	2.3
2005	6.7	9.9	3.2
2006	1.6	0.2	-1.4
2007	-4.3	-7.5	-3.2
2008	5.6	7.5	1.9
2009	2.6	3.6	1.0
2010	0.5	5.2	4.7
2011	-7.0	-4.5	2.5
2012	0.3	5.1	4.8
2013	2.6	5.0	2.4
2014	5.4	8.9	3.5
2015	1.2	3.9	2.7
2016	3.4	2.8	-0.6
2017	1.7	4.4	2.7
Avg.	2.7 %	5.6 %	2.9 %
Fq > 0	79 %	89 %	79 %

Retail Sector vs. S&P 500 1990 to 2017

(i) *Retail SP GIC Sector # 2550:*
An index designed to represent a cross section of retail companies
For more information on the retail sector, see www.standardandpoors.com.

Retail Performance

Retail Monthly Performance (1990-2017)

	Jan	Feb	Mar	Apr	May	Jun	Jul	Aug	Sep	Oct	Nov	Dec
Avg. % Gain	-0.2	2.0	3.4	0.8	1.7	-0.6	1.2	-0.6	-0.4	2.0	3.4	0.9
Med. % Gain	0.1	2.0	1.8	0.7	1.8	-0.5	1.3	-0.5	0.2	2.2	3.9	0.0
Fq %>0	50	68	75	61	64	43	61	50	50	68	82	50
Fq %>S&P 500	54	71	75	46	57	54	61	57	50	57	68	36

Retail 5 Year (2013-2017) % Gain

Retail Performance 2017-2018

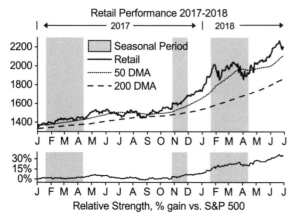

Relative Strength, % gain vs. S&P 500

Market Indices & Rates
Weekly Values**

Stock Markets	2016	2017
Dow	18,161	23,434
S&P500	2,126	2,581
Nasdaq	5,190	6,701
TSX	14,785	15,954
FTSE	6,996	7,505
DAX	10,696	13,218
Nikkei	17,446	22,008
Hang Seng	22,955	28,439

Commodities	2016	2017
Oil	48.70	53.90
Gold	1273.0	1266.5

Bond Yields	2016	2017
USA 5 Yr Treasury	1.33	2.03
USA 10 Yr T	1.86	2.42
USA 20 Yr T	2.27	2.71
Moody's Aaa	3.64	3.63
Moody's Baa	4.46	4.35
CAN 5 Yr T	0.72	1.66
CAN 10 Yr T	1.23	1.99

Money Market	2016	2017
USA Fed Funds	0.50	1.25
USA 3 Mo T-B	0.30	1.10
CAN tgt overnight rate	0.50	1.00
CAN 3 Mo T-B	0.47	0.93

Foreign Exchange	2016	2017
EUR/USD	1.10	1.16
GBP/USD	1.22	1.31
USD/CAD	1.34	1.28
USD/JPY	104.74	113.67

OCTOBER
M	T	W	T	F	S	S
	1	2	3	4	5	6
7	8	9	10	11	12	13
14	15	16	17	18	19	20
21	22	23	24	25	26	27
28	29	30	31			

NOVEMBER
M	T	W	T	F	S	S
			1	2	3	
4	5	6	7	8	9	10
11	12	13	14	15	16	17
18	19	20	21	22	23	24
25	26	27	28	29	30	

DECEMBER
M	T	W	T	F	S	S
						1
2	3	4	5	6	7	8
9	10	11	12	13	14	15
16	17	18	19	20	21	22
23	24	25	26	27	28	29
30	31					

From 1990 to 2017, March and November were two of the better months of the year on an average basis. November is the core part of the autumn retail seasonal trade and has the highest monthly median performance. Over the last five years, on average, the retail sector has followed its general seasonal pattern. The exception is the strong performance average performance in July.

In 2017, the retail sector underperformed the S&P 500 in its autumn seasonal period, and in 2018 it outperformed in its spring seasonal period.

INDUSTRIAL STRENGTH
①Oct28-Dec31 ②Jan23-May5

The industrial sector's seasonal trends are largely the same as the broad market, such as the S&P 500. Although the trends are similar, there still exists an opportunity to take advantage of the time period when the industrial sector tends to outperform.

11.4% gain & positive 90% of the time

Industrials tend to outperform in the favorable six months, but there is an opportunity to temporarily get out of the sector to avoid a time period when the sector has on average, decreased before turning positive again.

The overall strategy is to be invested in the industrial sector from October 28th to December 31st, sell at the end of the day on the 31st, and re-enter the sector to be invested from January 23rd to May 5th.

Using the complete *Industrial Strength* strategy from 1989/90 to 2017/18, the industrial sector has produced a total compound average annual gain of 11.4%.

In addition, the industrial sector has been positive 90% of the time and has outperformed the S&P 500, 72% of the time.

During the time period from January 1st to January 22nd, in the yearly period from 1990 to 2017, the industrial sector has on average lost 0.7% and has only been positive 52% of the time.

It should be noted that longer term investors may decide to be invested during the whole time period from October 28th to May 5th. Shorter term investors may decide to use technical analysis to determine, if and when, they should temporarily sell the industrials sector during its weak period from January 1st to January 22nd.

Industrials* vs. S&P 500 1989/90 to 2017/18   Positive☐

Year	Oct 28 to Dec 31 S&P 500	Ind.	Jan 23 to May 5 S&P 500	Ind.	Compound Growth S&P 500	Ind.
1989/90	5.5 %	6.9 %	2.4 %	5.5 %	8.0 %	12.7 %
1990/91	8.4	10.7	16.0	15.2	25.7	27.5
1991/92	8.6	7.2	-0.3	-1.0	8.2	6.1
1992/93	4.1	6.3	1.9	5.4	6.1	12.0
1993/94	0.4	5.1	-4.9	-6.7	-4.5	-2.0
1994/95	-1.4	-0.5	11.9	12.4	10.3	11.8
1995/96	6.3	10.7	4.6	7.6	11.1	19.1
1996/97	5.7	4.5	5.6	5.2	11.6	9.9
1997/98	10.7	10.5	15.8	11.5	28.2	23.2
1998/99	15.4	10.5	10.0	19.5	26.9	32.1
1999/00	13.3	10.8	-0.6	4.5	12.6	15.8
2000/01	-4.3	1.8	-5.7	4.7	-9.7	6.6
2001/02	3.9	8.1	-4.1	-5.3	-0.3	2.4
2002/03	-2.0	-1.3	5.5	8.6	3.4	7.1
2003/04	7.8	11.6	-2.0	-3.3	5.7	7.9
2004/05	7.7	8.7	0.4	0.2	8.1	8.9
2005/06	5.9	7.6	5.1	14.3	11.3	23.0
2006/07	3.0	3.1	5.8	6.8	9.0	10.1
2007/08	-4.4	-3.4	7.4	9.7	2.7	6.0
2008/09	6.4	7.1	9.2	6.1	16.2	13.7
2009/10	4.9	6.4	6.8	13.4	12.0	20.6
2010/11	6.4	8.1	4.0	4.9	10.6	13.5
2011/12	-2.1	-1.0	4.1	0.3	1.9	-0.7
2012/13	1.0	4.1	8.2	4.9	9.3	9.2
2013/14	5.0	7.3	2.2	1.6	7.3	9.0
2014/15	5.0	5.2	1.3	-1.0	6.3	4.1
2015/16	-1.1	-1.2	7.5	12.8	6.4	11.4
2016/17	5.0	9.7	5.6	5.0	10.9	15.2
2017/18	3.6	4.2	-6.0	-9.5	-2.6	-5.7
Avg.	4.4 %	5.8 %	4.1 %	5.3 %	8.7 %	11.4 %
Fq > 0	79 %	83 %	76 %	79 %	86 %	90 %

Industrials Sector - Avg. Year 1990 to 2017

Industrials / S&P 500 Rel. Strength - Avg Yr. 1990 - 2017

> **Ⓨ** *Alternate Strategy—*
> *Investors can bridge the gap between the two positive seasonal trends for the industrials sector by holding from October 28th to May 5th. Longer term investors may prefer this strategy, shorter term investors can use technical tools to determine the appropriate strategy.*

> **ⓘ** **The SP GICS Industrial Sector. For more information on the industrials sector, see www.standardandpoors.com*

Industrials Performance

Industrials Monthly Performance (1990-2017)

	Jan	Feb	Mar	Apr	May	Jun	Jul	Aug	Sep	Oct	Nov	Dec
Avg. % Gain	-0.5	0.7	1.9	2.3	0.9	-0.9	0.6	-1.3	-0.4	1.1	2.2	2.4
Med. % Gain	0.7	2.1	1.6	1.6	1.4	-0.6	0.8	-0.3	0.4	1.5	3.1	2.0
Fq %>0	54	64	75	64	68	43	64	43	50	68	79	82
Fq %>S&P 500	32	50	64	61	36	43	43	39	50	39	75	64

Industrials 5 Year (2013-2017) % Gain

Industrials Performance 2017-2018

Relative Strength, % gain vs. S&P 500

WEEK 44

Market Indices & Rates
Weekly Values**

Stock Markets	2016	2017
Dow	17,888	23,539
S&P500	2,085	2,588
Nasdaq	5,046	6,764
TSX	14,509	16,020
FTSE	6,693	7,560
DAX	10,259	13,479
Nikkei	16,905	22,539
Hang Seng	22,643	28,604

Commodities	2016	2017
Oil	44.07	55.64
Gold	1302.8	1267.2

Bond Yields	2016	2017
USA 5 Yr Treasury	1.24	1.99
USA 10 Yr T	1.79	2.34
USA 20 Yr T	2.22	2.59
Moody's Aaa	3.62	3.53
Moody's Baa	4.46	4.25
CAN 5 Yr T	0.67	1.66
CAN 10 Yr T	1.16	1.96

Money Market	2016	2017
USA Fed Funds	0.50	1.25
USA 3 Mo T-B	0.38	1.18
CAN tgt overnight rate	0.50	1.00
CAN 3 Mo T-B	0.44	0.87

Foreign Exchange	2016	2017
EUR/USD	1.11	1.16
GBP/USD	1.25	1.31
USD/CAD	1.34	1.28
USD/JPY	103.12	114.07

OCTOBER

M	T	W	T	F	S	S
	1	2	3	4	5	6
7	8	9	10	11	12	13
14	15	16	17	18	19	20
21	22	23	24	25	26	27
28	29	30	31			

NOVEMBER

M	T	W	T	F	S	S
				1	2	3
4	5	6	7	8	9	10
11	12	13	14	15	16	17
18	19	20	21	22	23	24
25	26	27	28	29	30	

DECEMBER

M	T	W	T	F	S	S
						1
2	3	4	5	6	7	8
9	10	11	12	13	14	15
16	17	18	19	20	21	22
23	24	25	26	27	28	29
30	31					

From 1990 to 2017, the sweet spot for the industrial sector trade, on average, has been November and December. The worst three months have been June, August and September.

Over the last five years, on average, the industrial sector has somewhat followed its seasonal trend, with its poorest performance in the summer months and its better performance in the autumn months. January has also been a very weak month.

In 2017, the industrial sector outperformed the S&P 500 in its autumn seasonal period and then underperformed in its 2018 spring seasonal period.

NOVEMBER

	MONDAY	TUESDAY	WEDNESDAY
WEEK 44	28	29	30
WEEK 45	**4** <div align="right">26</div>	**5** <div align="right">25</div>	**6** <div align="right">24</div>
WEEK 46	**11** <div align="right">19</div> USA Bond Market Closed- Veterans Day CAD Bond Market Closed- Remembrance Day	**12** <div align="right">18</div>	**13** <div align="right">17</div>
WEEK 47	**18** <div align="right">12</div>	**19** <div align="right">11</div>	**20** <div align="right">10</div>
WEEK 48	**25** <div align="right">5</div>	**26** <div align="right">4</div>	**27** <div align="right">3</div>

THURSDAY	FRIDAY
31	**1** 29
7 23	**8** 22
14 16	**15** 15
21 9	**22** 8
28 2	**29** 1
USA Market Closed- Thanksgiving Day	USA Early Market Close Thanksgiving

DECEMBER

M	T	W	T	F	S	S
						1
2	3	4	5	6	7	8
9	10	11	12	13	14	15
16	17	18	19	20	21	22
23	24	25	26	27	28	29
30	31					

JANUARY

M	T	W	T	F	S	S
		1	2	3	4	5
6	7	8	9	10	11	12
13	14	15	16	17	18	19
20	21	22	23	24	25	26
27	28	29	30	31		

FEBRUARY

M	T	W	T	F	S	S
					1	2
3	4	5	6	7	8	9
10	11	12	13	14	15	16
17	18	19	20	21	22	23
24	25	26	27	28	29	

MARCH

M	T	W	T	F	S	S
						1
2	3	4	5	6	7	8
9	10	11	12	13	14	15
16	17	18	19	20	21	22
23	24	25	26	27	28	29
30	31					

NOVEMBER
S U M M A R Y

	Dow Jones	S&P 500	Nasdaq	TSX Comp
Month Rank	3	2	2	8
# Up	47	46	32	20
# Down	21	22	14	13
% Pos	69	68	70	61
% Avg. Gain	1.6	1.6	1.7	0.6

Dow & S&P 1950-2017, Nasdaq 1972-2017, TSX 1985-2017

S&P500 Cumulative Daily Gains for Avg Month 1950 to 2017

Prob. of Daily Gain

♦ November, on average, is one of the better months of the year for the S&P 500. From 1950 to 2017, it has produced an average gain of 1.6% and has been positive 68% of the time. ♦ In November, the cyclical sectors tend to start increasing their relative performance to the S&P 500, with the metals and mining sector starting its period of seasonal strength on November 19th. ♦ For investors looking for a short-term investment, the day before and the day after Thanksgiving are on average the two strongest days of the year.

BEST / WORST NOVEMBER BROAD MKTS. 2008-2017

BEST NOVEMBER MARKETS
- ♦ Russell 2000 (2016) 11.0%
- ♦ Nikkei 225 (2013) 9.3%
- ♦ Nikkei 225 (2010) 8.0%

WORST NOVEMBER MARKETS
- ♦ Russell 2000 (2008) -12.0%
- ♦ Nasdaq (2008) -10.8%
- ♦ Russell 1000 (2008) -7.9%

Index Values End of Month

	2008	2009	2010	2011	2012	2013	2014	2015	2016	2017
Dow	8,829	10,345	11,006	12,046	13,026	16,086	17,828	17,720	19,124	24,272
S&P 500	896	1,096	1,181	1,247	1,416	1,806	2,068	2,080	2,199	2,648
Nasdaq	1,536	2,145	2,498	2,620	3,010	4,060	4,792	5,109	5,324	6,874
TSX Comp.	9,271	11,447	12,953	12,204	12,239	13,395	14,745	13,470	15,083	16,067
Russell 1000	481	598	654	689	783	1,005	1,149	1,155	1,221	1,467
Russell 2000	473	580	727	737	822	1,143	1,173	1,198	1,322	1,544
FTSE 100	4,288	5,191	5,528	5,505	5,867	6,651	6,723	6,356	6,784	7,327
Nikkei 225	8,512	9,346	9,937	8,435	9,446	15,662	17,460	19,747	18,308	22,725

Percent Gain for November

	2008	2009	2010	2011	2012	2013	2014	2015	2016	2017
Dow	-5.3	6.5	-1.0	0.8	-0.5	3.5	2.5	0.3	5.4	3.8
S&P 500	-7.5	5.7	-0.2	-0.5	0.3	2.8	2.5	0.1	3.4	2.8
Nasdaq	-10.8	4.9	-0.4	-2.4	1.1	3.6	3.5	1.1	2.6	2.2
TSX Comp.	-5.0	4.9	2.2	-0.4	-1.5	0.3	0.9	-0.4	2.0	0.3
Russell 1000	-7.9	5.6	0.1	-0.5	0.5	2.6	2.4	0.1	3.7	2.8
Russell 2000	-12.0	3.0	3.4	-0.5	0.4	3.9	0.0	3.1	11.0	2.8
FTSE 100	-2.0	2.9	-2.6	-0.7	1.5	-1.2	2.7	-0.1	-2.5	-2.2
Nikkei 225	-0.8	-6.9	8.0	-6.2	5.8	9.3	6.4	3.5	5.1	3.2

November Market Avg. Performance 2008 to 2017[1]

- Dow 1.6%
- S&P 500 0.9%
- Nasdaq 0.5%
- TSX Comp (CAN) 0.3%
- Russell 1000 (Lg Cap) 0.9%
- Russell 2000 (Sm Cap) 1.5%
- FTSE 100 0.4%
- Nikkei 225 2.7%

Interest Corner Nov[2]

	Fed Funds %[3]	3 Mo. T-Bill %[4]	10 Yr %[5]	20 Yr %[6]
2017	1.25	1.01	2.42	2.65
2016	0.50	0.48	2.37	2.73
2015	0.25	0.22	2.21	2.63
2014	0.25	0.02	2.18	2.62
2013	0.25	0.06	2.75	3.54

(1) Russell Data provided by Russell (2) Federal Reserve Bank of St. Louis- end of month values (3) Target rate set by FOMC (4)(5)(6) Constant yield maturities.

November 2017 % Sector Performance

S&P GIC Sectors	2017 % Gain	1990-2017[1] GIC[2] % Avg Gain	1990-2017[1] Fq% Gain >S&P 500
Consumer Discretionary	4.9 %	2.5 %	68 %
Information Technology	0.9	2.4	61
Industrials	3.5	2.2	75
Health Care	2.7	2.2	57
Materials	0.7	2.0	57
Consumer Staples	5.4	1.7	46
Financials	3.3	1.3	39
Telecom	5.9	1.2	39
Energy	1.2	0.1	29
Utilities	2.2 %	-0.5 %	29 %
S&P 500	2.8 %	1.5 %	N/A %

Sector Commentary

♦ In November 2017, the S&P 500 produced a gain of 2.8%. ♦ The telecom sector produced a gain of 5.9% and the consumer discretionary sector produced a gain of 4.9%. The consumer discretionary sector is on average one of the top performing sectors in November. ♦ The big surprise was the consumer staples sector which produced a gain of 5.4%. Typically, the consumer staples sector ranks in the middle of the performance spectrum in November. ♦ Utilities produced a gain of 2.2%. ♦ All of the major sectors of the stock market were positive as the stock market had a broad based rally.

Sub-Sector Commentary

♦ In November 2017, the homebuilders sub-sector produced a gain of 14.5% as the economy was on a solid growth track and interest rates were not rising at a rapid rate during the month. ♦ Railroads also had a strong month, producing a gain of 8.7%. ♦ On average, the retail sub-sector is one of the top performing groups in November. In November 2017, the sub-sector produced a strong gain of 5.5%. ♦ On the negative side, silver produced a loss of 1.5%.

SELECTED SUB-SECTORS[3]			
Steel	-0.6 %	3.5 %	50 %
Retail	5.5	3.4	68
SOX (1994-2017)	-0.2	3.3	57
Homebuilders	14.5	3.1	54
Agriculture (1994-2017)	-2.4	2.8	42
Transportation	6.9	2.5	50
Pharma	1.6	2.0	54
Chemicals	0.8	1.9	50
Biotech (1993-2017)	0.7	1.8	44
Railroads	8.7	1.8	57
Automotive & Components	2.6	1.7	54
Metals & Mining	0.5	1.5	50
Banks	2.7	1.5	46
Gold	0.8	1.1	50
Silver	-1.5	0.6	46

(1) Sector data provided by Standard and Poors (2) GIC is short form for Global Industry Classification (3) Sub Sector data provided by Standard and Poors, except where marked by symbol.

MATERIAL STOCKS — MATERIAL GAINS
①Oct28-Jan6 ②Jan23-May5

Materials Composition – CAUTION

The U.S. materials sector is substantially different from the Canadian materials sector. The U.S. sector has over a 60% weight in chemical companies, versus the Canadian sector which has over a 60% weight in gold companies.

The materials sector (U.S.) generally does well during the favorable six months of the year, from the end of October to the beginning of May. The sector is economically sensitive and is leveraged to economic forecasts. Generally, if the economy is expected to slow, the materials sector tends to decline and vice versa.

Positive 93% of the time

The materials sector has two seasonal periods. The first period is from October 28th to January 6th and the second period is from January 23rd to May 5th.

In the first seasonal period, the materials sector has produced an average gain of 6.6% in the years from 1990 to 2016 and has been positive 83% of the time.

The second seasonal period from January 23rd to May 5th, has produced an average gain of 7.0% and has been positive 76% of the time.

The time period in between the two seasonal periods, from January 7th to January 22nd, has had an average loss of 2.4% and only been positive 41% of the time (1990 to 2018). Investors may decide to bridge the gap between the two seasonal periods if the materials sector has strong momentum at the beginning of January.

The complete materials strategy is to be invested from October 28th to January 6th, out of the sector from January 7th to the 22nd, and back in from January 23rd to May 5th. This strategy has produced an average gain of 14.0% and has been positive 93% of the time.

Materials* vs. S&P 500 1989/90 to 2017/18   Positive ▢

Year	Oct 28 to Jan 6 S&P 500	Mat.	Jan 23 to May 5 S&P 500	Mat.	Compound Growth S&P 500	Mat.
1989/90	5.1 %	9.1 %	2.4 %	-3.1 %	7.7 %	5.7 %
1990/91	5.4	9.2	16.0	15.3	22.2	26.0
1991/92	8.8	1.5	-0.3	5.5	8.5	7.1
1992/93	3.8	5.6	1.9	4.3	5.8	10.2
1993/94	0.5	9.4	-4.9	-5.3	-4.4	3.6
1994/95	-1.1	-3.5	11.9	6.1	10.7	2.4
1995/96	6.4	7.6	4.6	11.1	11.3	19.5
1996/97	6.7	2.3	5.6	2.3	12.6	4.6
1997/98	10.2	1.4	15.8	20.9	27.7	22.6
1998/99	19.4	6.1	10.0	31.5	31.3	39.6
1999/00	8.2	15.7	-0.6	-7.1	7.6	7.5
2000/01	-5.9	19.2	-5.7	15.1	-11.2	37.2
2001/02	6.2	8.5	-4.1	14.9	1.8	24.7
2002/03	3.5	9.2	5.5	2.7	9.2	12.1
2003/04	9.0	16.6	-2.0	-3.0	6.8	13.1
2004/05	5.6	5.4	0.4	0.3	6.0	5.8
2005/06	9.0	16.3	5.1	14.7	14.6	33.5
2006/07	2.4	3.2	5.8	10.7	8.3	14.2
2007/08	-8.1	-5.1	7.4	16.7	-1.2	10.8
2008/09	10.1	12.0	9.2	23.3	20.3	38.1
2009/10	6.9	13.8	6.8	3.0	14.2	17.2
2010/11	7.7	11.7	4.0	4.2	12.1	16.4
2011/12	-0.5	-2.3	4.1	-2.7	3.5	-4.9
2012/13	3.9	7.2	8.2	0.0	12.3	7.2
2013/14	3.8	3.1	2.2	4.3	6.1	7.5
2014/15	2.1	-0.7	1.3	2.9	3.4	2.2
2015/16	-3.7	-6.2	7.5	18.3	3.6	11.0
2016/17	6.8	8.6	5.6	4.5	12.8	13.5
2017/18	6.3	6.4	-6.0	-8.6	-0.1	-2,8
Avg.	4.8 %	6.6 %	4.1 %	7.0 %	9.1 %	14.0 %
Fq > 0	83 %	83 %	76 %	76 %	86 %	93 %

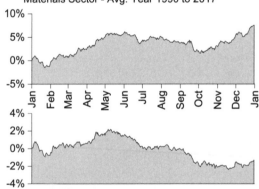

Materials Sector - Avg. Year 1990 to 2017

Materials / S&P 500 Rel. Strength - Avg Yr. 1990 - 2017

> **Ⓨ Alternate Strategy—**
> Investors can bridge the gap between the two positive seasonal trends for the materials sector by holding from October 28th to May 5th. Longer term investors may prefer this strategy. Shorter term investors can use technical tools to determine the appropriate strategy.

> **ⓘ** *The SP GICS Materials Sector encompasses a wide range of materials based companies.*
> *For more information on the materials sector, see www.standardandpoors.com*

Materials Performance

Materials Monthly Performance (1990-2017)

	Jan	Feb	Mar	Apr	May	Jun	Jul	Aug	Sep	Oct	Nov	Dec
Avg. % Gain	-0.9	1.6	1.8	2.7	0.8	-1.6	1.0	-1.4	-2.0	1.4	2.0	2.1
Med. % Gain	-1.3	1.9	1.1	2.0	1.7	-2.4	0.4	-0.7	-0.2	2.3	1.7	1.1
Fq %>0	43	71	68	75	57	29	57	39	46	64	75	61
Fq %>S&P 500	43	61	50	54	32	32	57	46	25	46	57	46

Materials 5 Year (2013-2017) % Gain

Materials Performance 2017-2018

Relative Strength, % gain vs. S&P 500

Market Indices & Rates
Weekly Values**

Stock Markets	2016	2017
Dow	18,848	23,422
S&P500	2,164	2,582
Nasdaq	5,237	6,751
TSX	14,555	16,039
FTSE	6,730	7,433
DAX	10,668	13,127
Nikkei	17,375	22,681
Hang Seng	22,531	29,121

Commodities	2016	2017
Oil	43.41	56.74
Gold	1236.5	1284.3

Bond Yields	2016	2017
USA 5 Yr Treasury	1.56	2.06
USA 10 Yr T	2.15	2.40
USA 20 Yr T	2.58	2.67
Moody's Aaa	3.87	3.60
Moody's Baa	4.75	4.26
CAN 5 Yr T	0.88	1.68
CAN 10 Yr T	1.43	1.97

Money Market	2016	2017
USA Fed Funds	0.50	1.25
USA 3 Mo T-B	0.48	1.23
CAN tgt overnight rate	0.50	1.00
CAN 3 Mo T-B	0.47	0.87

Foreign Exchange	2016	2017
EUR/USD	1.09	1.17
GBP/USD	1.26	1.32
USD/CAD	1.35	1.27
USD/JPY	106.65	113.53

NOVEMBER

M	T	W	T	F	S	S
				1	2	3
4	5	6	7	8	9	10
11	12	13	14	15	16	17
18	19	20	21	22	23	24
25	26	27	28	29	30	

DECEMBER

M	T	W	T	F	S	S
						1
2	3	4	5	6	7	8
9	10	11	12	13	14	15
16	17	18	19	20	21	22
23	24	25	26	27	28	29
30	31					

JANUARY

M	T	W	T	F	S	S
	1	2	3	4	5	
6	7	8	9	10	11	12
13	14	15	16	17	18	19
20	21	22	23	24	25	26
27	28	29	30	31		

From 1990 to 2017, on average, the six best months for the materials sector were February, March, April, October, November and December. February, March and April make up the core part of the spring seasonal trade, and October, November and December make up the core part of the winter seasonal trade. Over the last five years, the materials sector has on average, generally followed its seasonal trend with weaker performance in the summer months.

In 2017, the materials sector outperformed the S&P 500 in its winter seasonal period, and then underperformed in its 2018 spring seasonal period.

HOME DEPOT — BUILDING GAINS
①Oct28-Dec31 ②Jan9-Ap15

Home Depot is a consumer discretionary stock and as such, has a similar seasonal period. Both Home Depot and the consumer discretionary sector start their seasonal periods on October 28th. In the seasonal period from October 28th to December 31st (1989 to 2017), Home Depot has produced an average gain of 12.0% and has been positive 86% of the time.

20.2% gain & positive 86% of the time

Home Depot has a short period (January 1st to January 8th) at the beginning of January where it tends to underperform the S&P 500. In this time period, during the years 1990 to 2018, on average Home Depot has lost 1.8% and has only outperformed the S&P 500, 34% of the time.

Home Depot has a second seasonal period from January 9th to April 15th. In this period, Home Depot's strong seasonal period occurs at a similar time to the consumer discretionary and retail sectors' strong seasonal period. Home Depot, in this strong seasonal period, during the years 1990 to 2018 has on average produced a gain of 7.4% and has been positive 66% of the time.

Comparing the two seasonal periods, Home Depot has better performance in its October 28th to December 31st period compared to the January 9th to April 15th period. Over the last ten years, Home Depot has been positive and outperformed the S&P 500 every year in the October 31st to December 31st period.

In the same ten year period, from January 9th to April 15th, Home Depot has not had the same high frequency of success and has only been positive eight of ten times.

	Oct 28 to Dec 31		Jan 9 to Apr 15		Compound Growth	
Year	S&P 500	HD	S&P 500	HD	S&P 500	HD
1989/90	5.5%	9.3%	-2.7%	26.2%	2.7%	37.9%
1990/91	8.4	28.8	21.1	64.2	31.2	111.4
1991/92	8.6	23.3	-0.4	-0.2	8.1	23.1
1992/93	4.1	18.4	4.5	-9.6	8.8	7.0
1993/94	0.4	1.6	-5.1	8.1	-4.7	9.8
1994/95	-1.4	3.1	10.5	-3.4	9.0	-0.4
1995/96	6.3	29.5	3.9	4.3	10.4	35.0
1996/97	5.7	-9.3	0.8	10.7	6.6	0.5
1997/98	10.7	15.4	17.1	23.6	29.5	42.7
1998/99	15.4	49.7	3.8	8.4	19.7	62.2
1999/00	13.3	48.0	-5.9	-5.1	6.6	40.4
2000/01	-4.3	16.0	-8.7	-12.7	-12.6	1.3
2001/02	3.9	26.6	-5.0	-3.7	-1.3	21.9
2002/03	-2.0	-21.5	-2.1	28.4	-4.0	0.8
2003/04	7.8	-1.4	-0.3	0.7	7.5	-0.7
2004/05	7.7	4.8	-3.7	-12.8	3.7	-8.7
2005/06	5.9	2.8	0.3	1.8	6.2	4.7
2006/07	3.0	8.3	2.8	-4.1	5.9	4.0
2007/08	-4.4	-14.1	-4.0	12.9	-8.2	-3.0
2008/09	6.4	21.7	-6.3	5.3	-0.3	28.1
2009/10	4.9	11.3	5.8	21.3	11.0	34.9
2010/11	6.4	13.5	3.8	11.0	10.4	26.0
2011/12	-2.1	13.0	7.2	18.0	5.0	33.2
2012/13	1.0	3.0	6.5	14.3	7.6	17.7
2013/14	5.0	8.0	0.3	-7.4	5.3	0.0
2014/15	5.0	10.0	2.2	6.3	7.2	16.9
2015/16	-1.1	6.3	8.3	9.0	7.1	15.8
2016/17	5.0	9.7	2.3	9.3	7.4	19.8
2017/18	3.6	13.3	-3.3	-10.0	0.1	1.9
Avg.	4.4%	12.0%	1.9%	7.4%	6.4%	20.2%
Fq > 0	79%	86%	59%	66%	79%	86%

HD* vs. S&P 500 1989/90 to 2017/18   Positive ☐

Home Depot- Avg. Year 1990 to 2017

Home Depot / S&P 500 Rel. Str. - Avg Yr. 1990 - 2017

 Alternate Strategy—
Investors can bridge the gap between the two positive seasonal trends for Home Depot by holding from October 28th to April 15th. Longer term investors may prefer this strategy, shorter term investors can use technical tools to determine the appropriate strategy.

ⓘ ** Home Depot trades on the NYSE, adjusted for splits.*

Home Depot Performance

HD Monthly Performance (1990-2017)

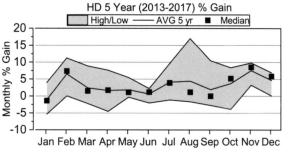

Avg % Gain		Med % Gain

	Jan	Feb	Mar	Apr	May	Jun	Jul	Aug	Sep	Oct	Nov	Dec
Avg. % Gain	-0.8	2.4	2.9	0.8	3.1	-1.2	0.9	1.0	-0.4	2.2	4.3	5.0
Med. % Gain	-1.2	2.4	1.6	1.3	2.4	-0.7	0.8	-0.8	-0.6	2.9	4.1	5.2
Fq %>0	39	61	64	61	57	39	54	46	46	64	75	64
Fq %>S&P 500	50	64	64	50	57	39	54	68	54	50	64	61

HD 5 Year (2013-2017) % Gain

High/Low — AVG 5 yr ■ Median

HD Performance 2017-2018

Seasonal Period
HD
50 DMA
200 DMA

Relative Strength, % gain vs. S&P 500

From 1990 to 2017, Home Depot has on average, performed well in the three contiguous months from October to December. February, March, April and May were also strong. Over the last five years, Home Depot has generally followed its seasonal trend.

In its autumn 2017 seasonal period, Home Depot was positive and outperformed the S&P 500. In its 2018 seasonal period, Home Depot was negative and underperformed the S&P 500.

Market Indices & Rates
Weekly Values**

Stock Markets	2016	2017
Dow	18,868	23,358
S&P500	2,182	2,579
Nasdaq	5,322	6,783
TSX	14,864	15,999
FTSE	6,776	7,381
DAX	10,665	12,994
Nikkei	17,967	22,397
Hang Seng	22,344	29,199

Commodities	2016	2017
Oil	45.69	56.55
Gold	1211.0	1284.4

Bond Yields	2016	2017
USA 5 Yr Treasury	1.80	2.06
USA 10 Yr T	2.34	2.35
USA 20 Yr T	2.70	2.59
Moody's Aaa	3.99	3.61
Moody's Baa	4.86	4.28
CAN 5 Yr T	0.99	1.66
CAN 10 Yr T	1.58	1.94

Money Market	2016	2017
USA Fed Funds	0.50	1.25
USA 3 Mo T-B	0.44	1.29
CAN tgt overnight rate	0.50	1.00
CAN 3 Mo T-B	0.50	0.87

Foreign Exchange	2016	2017
EUR/USD	1.06	1.18
GBP/USD	1.23	1.32
USD/CAD	1.35	1.28
USD/JPY	110.91	112.10

NOVEMBER

M	T	W	T	F	S	S
				1	2	3
4	5	6	7	8	9	10
11	12	13	14	15	16	17
18	19	20	21	22	23	24
25	26	27	28	29	30	

DECEMBER

M	T	W	T	F	S	S
						1
2	3	4	5	6	7	8
9	10	11	12	13	14	15
16	17	18	19	20	21	22
23	24	25	26	27	28	29
30	31					

JANUARY

M	T	W	T	F	S	S
		1	2	3	4	5
6	7	8	9	10	11	12
13	14	15	16	17	18	19
20	21	22	23	24	25	26
27	28	29	30	31		

At the macro level, the metals and mining (M&M) sector is driven by future economic growth expectations. When worldwide growth expectations are increasing, there is a greater need for raw materials, and vice versa.

Within the macro trend, the M&M sector has traditionally followed the overall market cycle of performing well from autumn until spring. This is the time of year that investors have a positive outlook on the economy and as a result, the cyclical sectors tend to outperform, including the metals and mining sector.

13.6% gain and positive 69% of the time

The metals and mining sector has two seasonal "sweet spots" – the first from November 19th to January 5th and the second from January 23rd to May 5th.

Investors have the option to hold and "bridge the gap" across the two sweet spots, but over the long-term, nimble traders have been able to capture extra value by being out of the sector from January 6th to the 22nd. During this period, from 1990 to 2017, the metals and mining sector has produced an average loss of 3.0% and has only been positive 52% of the time.

From a portfolio perspective, it is important to consider reducing exposure at the beginning of May. The danger of holding on too long is that the sector tends not to perform well in the late summer, particularly in September.

For more information on the metals and mining sector, see www.standardandpoors.com

Metals & Mining* vs. S&P 500
1989/90 to 2017/18   Positive

Year	Nov 19 to Jan 5 S&P 500	Nov 19 to Jan 5 M&M	Jan 23 to May 5 S&P 500	Jan 23 to May 5 M&M	Compound Growth S&P 500	Compound Growth M&M
1989/90	3.1 %	6.3 %	2.4 %	-4.6 %	5.6 %	1.4 %
1990/91	1.2	6.4	16.0	7.1	17.4	13.9
1991/92	8.9	1.0	-0.3	-1.7	8.5	-0.7
1992/93	2.7	12.5	1.9	3.2	4.7	16.1
1993/94	0.9	9.0	-4.9	-11.1	-4.1	-3.1
1994/95	-0.2	-1.2	11.9	-3.0	11.6	-4.1
1995/96	2.8	8.3	4.6	5.8	7.5	14.6
1996/97	1.5	-1.9	5.6	-1.2	7.2	-3.0
1997/98	4.1	-4.5	15.8	19.3	20.6	13.9
1998/99	8.8	-7.9	10.0	31.0	19.6	20.6
1999/00	-1.6	21.7	-0.6	-10.4	-2.2	9.1
2000/01	-5.1	17.0	-5.7	19.6	-10.5	40.0
2001/02	3.0	5.5	-4.1	12.8	-1.3	19.0
2002/03	0.9	9.3	5.5	3.2	6.4	12.8
2003/04	8.5	18.2	-2.0	-12.1	6.4	3.9
2004/05	0.0	-8.4	0.4	-4.0	0.4	-12.0
2005/06	2.0	17.3	5.1	27.3	7.2	49.4
2006/07	0.6	3.0	5.8	17.2	6.5	20.8
2007/08	-3.2	0.9	7.4	27.4	3.9	28.5
2008/09	8.0	43.8	9.2	30.6	17.9	87.8
2009/10	2.4	6.3	6.8	4.8	9.4	11.3
2010/11	6.7	15.0	4.0	-1.6	11.0	13.1
2011/12	5.4	1.2	4.1	-16.0	9.7	-15.0
2012/13	7.8	3.9	8.2	-16.8	16.6	-13.6
2013/14	2.2	1.2	2.2	2.6	4.4	3.8
2014/15	-1.5	-14.2	1.3	5.3	-0.3	-9.7
2015/16	-3.2	-3.4	7.5	76.3	4.1	70.2
2016/17	4.0	7.2	5.6	-10.8	9.8	-4.4
2017/18	6.4	24.3	-6.0	-11.5	0.0	9.9
Avg.	2.7 %	6.8 %	4.1 %	6.5 %	6.8 %	13.6 %
Fq > 0	79 %	76 %	76 %	55 %	83 %	69 %

Metals & Mining - Avg. Year 1990 to 2017

Metals & Mining / S&P 500 Rel. Strength- Avg Yr. 1990-2017

Metals & Mining Performance

Metals and Mining Monthly Performance (1990-2017)

	Jan	Feb	Mar	Apr	May	Jun	Jul	Aug	Sep	Oct	Nov	Dec
Avg. % Gain	-1.1	1.9	1.1	2.3	0.3	-0.8	0.5	-1.6	-1.9	0.2	1.5	3.0
Med. % Gain	0.2	1.4	1.4	0.2	1.9	-1.2	1.5	-0.2	-1.8	0.1	0.6	2.7
Fq %>0	54	64	57	54	54	36	61	50	43	54	57	54
Fq %>S&P 500	43	54	43	43	43	54	50	46	43	36	50	54

Metals and Mining 5 Year (2013-2017) % Gain

Metals and Mining Performance 2017-2018

Relative Strength, % gain vs. S&P 500

Market Indices & Rates
Weekly Values**

Stock Markets	2016	2017
Dow	19,152	23,558
S&P500	2,213	2,602
Nasdaq	5,399	6,889
TSX	15,075	16,108
FTSE	6,841	7,410
DAX	10,699	13,060
Nikkei	18,381	22,551
Hang Seng	22,723	29,866

Commodities	2016	2017
Oil	44.76	58.85
Gold	1187.7	1290.5

Bond Yields	2016	2017
USA 5 Yr Treasury	1.83	2.07
USA 10 Yr T	2.36	2.34
USA 20 Yr T	2.71	2.58
Moody's Aaa	4.02	3.53
Moody's Baa	4.84	4.24
CAN 5 Yr T	0.99	1.63
CAN 10 Yr T	1.56	1.89

Money Market	2016	2017
USA Fed Funds	0.50	1.25
USA 3 Mo T-B	0.49	1.29
CAN tgt overnight rate	0.50	1.00
CAN 3 Mo T-B	0.51	0.87

Foreign Exchange	2016	2017
EUR/USD	1.06	1.19
GBP/USD	1.25	1.33
USD/CAD	1.35	1.27
USD/JPY	113.22	111.53

NOVEMBER

M	T	W	T	F	S	S
				1	2	3
4	5	6	7	8	9	10
11	12	13	14	15	16	17
18	19	20	21	22	23	24
25	26	27	28	29	30	

DECEMBER

M	T	W	T	F	S	S
						1
2	3	4	5	6	7	8
9	10	11	12	13	14	15
16	17	18	19	20	21	22
23	24	25	26	27	28	29
30	31					

JANUARY

M	T	W	T	F	S	S
	1	2	3	4	5	
6	7	8	9	10	11	12
13	14	15	16	17	18	19
20	21	22	23	24	25	26
27	28	29	30	31		

From 1990 to 2017, one of the strongest months for the metals and mining sector was December on an average basis. Overall, the metals and mining sector does not have a strong track record of positive performance and outperforming the S&P 500 in any month. Nevertheless, the seasonal trend provides value, particularly in a strong commodity cycle. Over the last five years, on average, the metals and mining sector's monthly performance has somewhat followed its seasonal trend with the first few months of the year performing well (except January). The seasonal period starting in January 2018 underperformed the S&P 500.

UPS — DELIVERING RETURNS

UPS ①LONG (Oct10-Dec8)
②SELL SHORT (Dec9-Mar1)

In recent years, Amazon has shown an increasing interest in delivering its own packages, rather than using package delivery companies. Although this trend is expected to continue, consideration should still be given to investing in UPS in its seasonal period before Christmas, as this is when UPS would still be expected to outperform the S&P 500.

Investors look for an activity that could drive a stock price higher. In UPS' case investors typically become more interested in the stock just before the holiday season. The logic is that a busy time of year will help increase earnings, which should raise the stock price.

13.4% growth & positive 94% of the time

The best time to get into UPS is before most investors become excited about the stock. When maximum investor interest for the stock occurs, it has been best to exit.

"Get in before everyone else and exit once everyone is in." In other words, the seasonal trend takes advantage of human behavioral tendencies. From October 10th to December 8th, in the period from 2000 to 2017, UPS has produced an average gain of 7.5% and has been positive 89% of the time. Impressively, UPS has outperformed the S&P 500 during this time period, 78% of time.

Investors typically do not want to invest in UPS at the times of the year when its stock price lacks a near-term catalyst. January and February are low activity months for UPS. As a result, investors tend to reduce their

(i) *UPS which trades on the NYSE, adjusted for splits.*

UPS* vs. S&P 500 2000/01 to 2017/18

Positive Long ▭   Negative Short ▭

Year	Oct 10 to Dec 8 S&P 500	UPS	Dec 9 to Mar 1 S&P 500	UPS	Compound Growth S&P 500	UPS
2000/01	-2.3 %	12.0 %	-9.4 %	-12.1 %	-11.5 %	25.5 %
2001/02	9.6	12.1	-2.3	3.3	7.1	8.5
2002/03	17.4	6.5	-7.8	-10.2	8.3	17.4
2003/04	2.9	11.1	8.1	-4.9	11.3	16.5
2004/05	5.4	14.5	2.3	-11.0	7.9	27.1
2005/06	5.0	9.6	2.8	0.4	8.0	9.2
2006/07	4.4	5.6	-0.5	-10.2	3.9	16.3
2007/08	-3.9	-3.5	-11.6	-5.3	-15.0	1.6
2008/09	0.0	10.6	-19.2	-29.8	-19.2	43.5
2009/10	1.9	3.2	2.2	1.9	4.1	1.2
2010/11	5.4	6.6	6.4	0.5	12.1	6.1
2011/12	6.8	8.7	11.3	6.8	18.9	1.3
2012/13	-1.6	0.2	7.1	13.3	5.3	-13.1
2013/14	9.0	15.5	3.0	-6.5	12.3	23.0
2014/15	6.9	14.2	2.1	-7.7	9.1	22.9
2015/16	2.4	-2.4	-4.1	-2.8	-1.8	0.3
2016/17	4.3	9.4	6.7	-10.2	11.2	20.5
2017/18	4.2	2.1	1.0	-11.0	5.2	13.3
Avg.	4.3 %	7.5 %	-0.1 %	-5.3 %	4.3 %	13.4 %
Fq>0	78 %	89 %	61 %	33 %	78 %	94 %

buying of package delivery companies at the end of the year and into the beginning of March.

From December 9th to March 1st, UPS has on average produced a loss of 5.3% and has only been positive 33% of the time. Collectively, the long and short sell trades have produced an average gain of 13.4% and have been positive 94% of the time.

UPS - Avg. Year 2000 to 2017

UPS / S&P 500 Rel. Strength- Avg Yr. 2000-2017

UPS Strategy Performance

UPS Monthly Performance (2000-2017)

	Jan	Feb	Mar	Apr	May	Jun	Jul	Aug	Sep	Oct	Nov	Dec
Avg. % Gain	-3.6	-0.7	3.7	1.7	-0.9	-0.7	0.4	-1.0	0.6	2.1	4.0	-1.0
Med. % Gain	-3.4	0.2	2.4	0.7	-1.0	-0.0	0.1	-1.0	1.0	3.3	4.2	-0.8
Fq %>0	33	50	72	67	44	50	50	39	61	61	78	39
Fq %>S&P 500	33	33	72	50	39	56	44	50	78	61	78	28

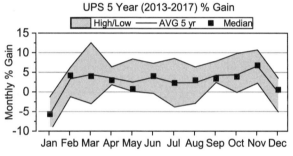

UPS 5 Year (2013-2017) % Gain

UPS Performance 2016-2017

Relative Strength, % gain vs. S&P 500

Market Indices & Rates
Weekly Values**

Stock Markets	2016	2017
Dow	19,170	24,232
S&P500	2,192	2,642
Nasdaq	5,256	6,848
TSX	15,053	16,039
FTSE	6,731	7,300
DAX	10,513	12,861
Nikkei	18,426	22,819
Hang Seng	22,565	29,074

Commodities	2016	2017
Oil	51.68	58.36
Gold	1173.5	1275.5

Bond Yields	2016	2017
USA 5 Yr Treasury	1.84	2.13
USA 10 Yr T	2.40	2.37
USA 20 Yr T	2.78	2.58
Moody's Aaa	4.03	3.52
Moody's Baa	4.82	4.24
CAN 5 Yr T	1.03	1.69
CAN 10 Yr T	1.62	1.91

Money Market	2016	2017
USA Fed Funds	0.50	1.25
USA 3 Mo T-B	0.49	1.27
CAN tgt overnight rate	0.50	1.00
CAN 3 Mo T-B	0.48	0.88

Foreign Exchange	2016	2017
EUR/USD	1.07	1.19
GBP/USD	1.27	1.35
USD/CAD	1.33	1.27
USD/JPY	113.51	112.17

NOVEMBER

M	T	W	T	F	S	S
				1	2	3
4	5	6	7	8	9	10
11	12	13	14	15	16	17
18	19	20	21	22	23	24
25	26	27	28	29	30	

DECEMBER

M	T	W	T	F	S	S
						1
2	3	4	5	6	7	8
9	10	11	12	13	14	15
16	17	18	19	20	21	22
23	24	25	26	27	28	29
30	31					

From 2000 to 2017, October and November have been the strongest months for UPS on a median basis. December has been negative on an average and median basis. The first/second week of December is the pivot point between the long and short sell periods of the trade. January has been the worst month on an average, median and frequency basis.

In the last five years, UPS has generally followed its seasonal trend with October and November being the best months of the year and January the worst month of the year. The long 2017 trade and the short sell 2018 trade, were both successful.

JANUARY

M	T	W	T	F	S	S
	1	2	3	4	5	
6	7	8	9	10	11	12
13	14	15	16	17	18	19
20	21	22	23	24	25	26
27	28	29	30	31		

DECEMBER

	MONDAY	TUESDAY	WEDNESDAY
WEEK 49	**2** ₂₉	**3** ₂₈	**4** ₂₇
WEEK 50	**9** ₂₂	**10** ₂₁	**11** ₂₀
WEEK 51	**16** ₁₅	**17** ₁₄	**18** ₁₃
WEEK 52	**23** ₈	**24** ₇	**25** ₆ — CAN Market Closed- Christmas Day / USA Market Closed- Christmas Day
WEEK 53	**30** ₁	**31**	1

THURSDAY		FRIDAY	
5	26	**6**	25
12	19	**13**	18
19	12	**20**	11
26	5	**27**	4
CAN Market Closed- Boxing Day			
2		3	

JANUARY

M	T	W	T	F	S	S
		1	2	3	4	5
6	7	8	9	10	11	12
13	14	15	16	17	18	19
20	21	22	23	24	25	26
27	28	29	30	31		

FEBRUARY

M	T	W	T	F	S	S
					1	2
3	4	5	6	7	8	9
10	11	12	13	14	15	16
17	18	19	20	21	22	23
24	25	26	27	28	29	

MARCH

M	T	W	T	F	S	S
						1
2	3	4	5	6	7	8
9	10	11	12	13	14	15
16	17	18	19	20	21	22
23	24	25	26	27	28	29
30	31					

APRIL

M	T	W	T	F	S	S
		1	2	3	4	5
6	7	8	9	10	11	12
13	14	15	16	17	18	19
20	21	22	23	24	25	26
27	28	29	30			

DECEMBER
S U M M A R Y

	Dow Jones	S&P 500	Nasdaq	TSX Comp
Month Rank	2	1	3	1
# Up	48	51	27	28
# Down	20	17	19	5
% Pos	71	75	59	85
% Avg. Gain	1.7	1.6	1.6	1.9

Dow & S&P 1950-2017, Nasdaq 1972-2017 TSX 1985-2017

S&P500 Cumulative Daily Gains for Avg Month 1950 to 2017

Prob. of Daily Gain

♦ December is typically one of the strongest months of the year for the S&P 500. From 1950 to 2017, the S&P 500 produced an average gain of 1.6% and was positive 75% of the time. ♦ Most of the gains for the S&P 500 tend to occur in the second half of the month. ♦ The Nasdaq tends to outperform the S&P 500 starting mid-December. ♦ The small cap sector typically starts to outperform the S&P 500 mid-month.

BEST / WORST DECEMBER BROAD MKTS. 2008-2017

BEST DECEMBER MARKETS
- Nikkei 225 (2009) 12.8%
- Nikkei 225 (2012) 10.0%
- Russell 2000 (2009) 7.9%

WORST DECEMBER MARKETS
- Russell 2000 (2015) -5.2%
- Nikkei 225 (2015) -3.6%
- TSX Comp (2015) - 3.4%

Index Values End of Month

	2008	2009	2010	2011	2012	2013	2014	2015	2016	2017
Dow	8,776	10,428	11,578	12,218	13,104	16,577	17,823	17,425	19,763	24,719
S&P 500	903	1,115	1,258	1,258	1,426	1,848	2,059	2,044	2,239	2,674
Nasdaq	1,577	2,269	2,653	2,605	3,020	4,177	4,736	5,007	5,383	6,903
TSX Comp.	8,988	11,746	13,443	11,955	12,434	13,622	14,632	13,010	15,288	16,209
Russell 1000	488	612	697	693	790	1,030	1,144	1,132	1,242	1,482
Russell 2000	499	625	784	741	849	1,164	1,205	1,136	1,357	1,536
FTSE 100	4,434	5,413	5,900	5,572	5,898	6,749	6,566	6,242	7,143	7,688
Nikkei 225	8,860	10,546	10,229	8,455	10,395	16,291	17,451	19,034	19,114	22,765

Percent Gain for December

	2008	2009	2010	2011	2012	2013	2014	2015	2016	2017
Dow	-0.6	0.8	5.2	1.4	0.6	3.0	0.0	-1.7	3.3	1.8
S&P 500	0.8	1.8	6.5	0.9	0.7	2.4	-0.4	-1.8	1.8	1.0
Nasdaq	2.7	5.8	6.2	-0.6	0.3	2.9	-1.2	-2.0	1.1	0.4
TSX Comp.	-3.1	2.6	3.8	-2.0	1.6	1.7	-0.8	-3.4	1.4	0.9
Russell 1000	1.3	2.3	6.5	0.7	0.8	2.5	-0.4	-2.0	1.7	1.0
Russell 2000	5.6	7.9	7.8	0.5	3.3	1.8	2.7	-5.2	2.6	-0.6
FTSE 100	3.4	4.3	6.7	1.2	0.5	1.5	-2.3	-1.8	5.3	4.9
Nikkei 225	4.1	12.8	2.9	0.2	10.0	4.0	-0.1	-3.6	4.4	0.2

December Market Avg. Performance 2008 to 2017[1]

Dow	1.4%
S&P 500	1.4%
Nasdaq	1.6%
TSX Comp (CAN)	0.3%
Russell 1000 (Lg Cap)	1.4%
Russell 2000 (Sm Cap)	2.6%
FTSE 100	2.4%
Nikkei 225	3.5%

Interest Corner Dec[2]

	Fed Funds % [3]	3 Mo. T-Bill % [4]	10 Yr % [5]	20 Yr % [6]
2017	1.50	1.01	2.40	2.58
2016	0.75	0.51	2.45	2.79
2015	0.50	0.16	2.27	2.67
2014	0.25	0.04	2.17	2.47
2013	0.25	0.07	3.04	3.72

(1) Russell Data provided by Russell (2) Federal Reserve Bank of St. Louis- end of month values (3) Target rate set by FOMC (4)(5)(6) Constant yield maturities.

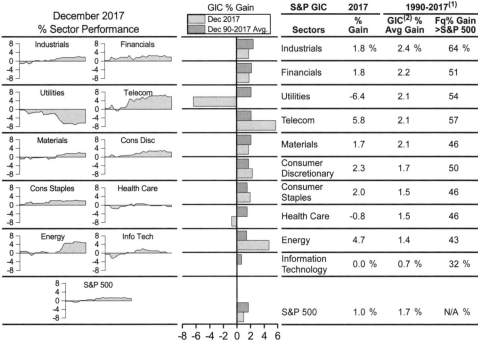

S&P GIC	2017	1990-2017[1]	
Sectors	% Gain	GIC[2] % Avg Gain	Fq% Gain >S&P 500
Industrials	1.8 %	2.4 %	64 %
Financials	1.8	2.2	51
Utilities	-6.4	2.1	54
Telecom	5.8	2.1	57
Materials	1.7	2.1	46
Consumer Discretionary	2.3	1.7	50
Consumer Staples	2.0	1.5	46
Health Care	-0.8	1.5	46
Energy	4.7	1.4	43
Information Technology	0.0 %	0.7 %	32 %
S&P 500	1.0 %	1.7 %	N/A %

Sector Commentary

♦ In December 2017, the S&P 500 produced a gain of 1.0%. ♦ The cyclical sectors performed well, with the industrial sector producing a gain of 1.8% and the materials sector producing a gain of 1.7%. ♦ The energy sector, which is usually one of the weaker sectors, produced a gain of 4.7%. ♦ The utilities sector was the worst performing sector as it produced a loss of 6.4% caused mainly by rising interest rates.

Sub-Sector Commentary

♦ The metals and mining sub-sector produced a gain of 15.9% as strong economic growth boosted optimism for future growth. ♦ Banks produced a gain of 2.9% as investors looked favorably on the sub-sector with the rising interest rates potentially increasing net interest margins. ♦ The retail sub-sector continued its positive trend from the previous month and posted a gain of 2.7%.

SELECTED SUB-SECTORS[3]			
Home builders	-0.3 %	7.0 %	79 %
Steel	10.6	4.7	64
Biotech (1993-2017)	0.0	3.8	48
Metals & Mining	15.9	3.0	54
Agriculture (1994-2017)	0.5	2.2	54
Banks	2.9	2.1	61
Chemicals	0.2	1.8	54
Railroads	3.2	1.5	50
Pharma	0.0	1.2	43
Automotive & Components	-2.5	1.1	36
Transportation	3.4	1.1	39
Silver	1.8	1.0	46
SOX (1994-2017)	-1.5	1.0	43
Retail	2.7	0.9	36
Gold	0.8	-0.1	32

EMERGING MARKETS (USD)– TRUNCATED SIX MONTH SEASONAL
November 24th to April 18th

Emerging markets become popular periodically, mainly after they have had a strong run, or if they have suffered a major correction and investors perceive them as having a lot of value.

Markets around the world tend to have the same broad seasonal trends, including emerging markets. Emerging markets outperform the S&P 500 more often, when the S&P 500 is increasing, and underperform when the S&P 500 is decreasing. Given that the S&P 500 has a higher probability of increasing in the favorable six-month period for stocks, from October 27th to May 5th, emerging markets will have a higher probability of outperforming the S&P 500 sometime within the six-month favorable for stocks.

9.9% gain & positive 86% of the time positive

Seasonal investors have benefited from concentrating their emerging market exposure in a truncated, or shorter time period within the favorable six month seasonal period.

Emerging Markets (USD)* vs. S&P 500
1989/90 to 2017/18

Nov 24 to Apr 18	S&P 500	Positive Em. Mkts.	Diff
1989/90	-0.4%	4.5	4.9%
1990/91	23.8	33.8%	10.5
1991/92	10.6	37.5	26.8
1992/93	5.6	11.8	6.2
1993/94	-4.0	3.7	7.8
1994/95	12.3	-16.4	-28.7
1995/96	7.6	14.7	7.1
1996/97	2.4	7.1	4.7
1997/98	16.6	6.7	-9.9
1998/99	11.0	18.1	7.1
1999/00	2.6	3.5	0.8
2000/01	-6.4	-4.6	1.8
2001/02	-2.3	22.3	24.5
2002/03	-4.0	0.0	4.0
2003/04	9.6	19.5	9.9
2004/05	-2.6	4.3	7.0
2005/06	3.3	24.7	21.4
2006/07	4.7	13.2	8.5
2007/08	-3.5	-0.9	2.6
2008/09	8.7	37.6	28.9
2009/10	7.8	5.6	-2.2
2010/11	10.5	6.6	-3.9
2011/12	19.2	15.6	-3.6
2012/13	9.4	0.1	-9.3
2013/14	3.3	0.3	-3.1
2014/15	0.9	3.8	3.0
2015/16	0.4	0.3	-0.1
2016/17	6.2	11.9	5.7
2017/18	4.3	2.1	-2.2
Avg	5.4%	9.9%	4.5%
Fq > 0	76%	86%	69%

Emerging Mkts. (USD)- Avg. Year 1990 to 2017

Emerg. Mkts. (USD)/S&P 500 Rel. Str. - Avg Yr. 1990-2017

When the world grappled with the sub-prime crisis and then the EU crisis, investors sought the safety of the U.S. markets, and as a result emerging markets underperformed. In 2017, the trend changed as global growth improved and the U.S. dollar fell relative to worldwide currencies. As a result, emerging markets rallied.

In 2018, the U.S. dollar rallied strongly due to strong economic growth. As a result, emerging markets corrected sharply.

The seasonally strong period for the emerging markets sector is from November 24th to April 18th. In this time period, from 1990/91 to 2017/18, the emerging markets sector (USD) produced an average rate of return of 9.9% and has been positive 86% of the time.

(i) *Emerging Markets (USD)-*
For more information on the emerging markets, see www.standardandpoors.com

Emerging Markets Performance

Emerging Markets Monthly Performance (1990-2017)

	Jan	Feb	Mar	Apr	May	Jun	Jul	Aug	Sep	Oct	Nov	Dec
Avg. % Gain	0.9	1.9	1.0	2.3	-0.1	-0.5	1.3	-1.8	-1.0	1.2	0.3	3.2
Med. % Gain	0.5	1.4	0.8	1.4	0.1	0.2	1.5	-0.1	0.6	2.5	-1.1	3.4
Fq %>0	61	61	64	71	50	54	68	50	57	68	46	71
Fq %>S&P 500	57	64	54	54	46	54	68	50	43	54	39	75

Emerging Markets 5 Year (2013-2017) % Gain

Emerging Markets Performance 2017-2018

Relative Strength, % gain vs. S&P 500

Market Indices & Rates Weekly Values**

Stock Markets	2016	2017
Dow	19,757	24,329
S&P500	2,260	2,652
Nasdaq	5,444	6,840
TSX	15,312	16,096
FTSE	6,954	7,394
DAX	11,204	13,154
Nikkei	18,996	22,811
Hang Seng	22,761	28,640

Commodities	2016	2017
Oil	51.50	57.36
Gold	1163.6	1250.7

Bond Yields	2016	2017
USA 5 Yr Treasury	1.89	2.14
USA 10 Yr T	2.47	2.38
USA 20 Yr T	2.87	2.59
Moody's Aaa	4.12	3.54
Moody's Baa	4.90	4.25
CAN 5 Yr T	1.09	1.67
CAN 10 Yr T	1.73	1.86

Money Market	2016	2017
USA Fed Funds	0.50	1.25
USA 3 Mo T-B	0.54	1.28
CAN tgt overnight rate	0.50	1.00
CAN 3 Mo T-B	0.48	0.89

Foreign Exchange	2016	2017
EUR/USD	1.06	1.18
GBP/USD	1.26	1.34
USD/CAD	1.32	1.28
USD/JPY	115.32	113.48

DECEMBER

M	T	W	T	F	S	S
						1
2	3	4	5	6	7	8
9	10	11	12	13	14	15
16	17	18	19	20	21	22
23	24	25	26	27	28	29
30	31					

JANUARY

M	T	W	T	F	S	S
	1	2	3	4	5
6	7	8	9	10	11	12
13	14	15	16	17	18	19
20	21	22	23	24	25	26
27	28	29	30	31		

FEBRUARY

M	T	W	T	F	S	S
					1	2
3	4	5	6	7	8	9
10	11	12	13	14	15	16
17	18	19	20	21	22	23
24	25	26	27	28	29	

From 1990 to 2017, December has been the strongest month of the year for emerging markets on an average, median and frequency basis. Although November tends to have a negative median, the last part of the month tends to be a good launching point into the seasonal period for emerging markets.

Over the last five years, on average emerging markets did not display a distinct seasonal pattern.

In its 2017/2018 seasonal period, the emerging markets sector was positive, but underperformed the S&P 500.

AEROSPACE & DEFENSE – FLYING HIGH
December 12th to May 5th

The aerospace and defense sector is highly dependent on government purchases and as a result is subject not only to economic cycles, but also the political environment. Despite the fact that outside variables have a large impact on aerospace and defense orders, the sector has a seasonal trend.

The aerospace and defense sector has a seasonal trend that is similar to the overall broad market's seasonal trend. The big difference is that aerospace and defense has a track record of strongly outperforming the S&P 500 from mid-December until the beginning of May.

9.5% gain & positive 90% of the time

The difference in the sector's seasonal trend compared with the S&P 500's trend is largely the result of the U.S. governments procurement cycle, which has a year-end of September 30th. The first quarter of the government's fiscal year (October, November and December) tends to be the weakest for orders. Government procurement tends to pick up at the start of the new calendar year, helping to boost aerospace and defense stocks up until the beginning of May.

Aerospace & Defense* vs. S&P 500 1989/90 to 2017/18			
Dec 12 to May 5	S&P 500	Aero & Def.	Positive Diff
1989/90	-2.9%	6.1%	9.0%
1990/91	16.7	11.6	-5.1
1991/92	10.4	10.1	-0.3
1992/93	2.5	14.3	11.9
1993/94	-2.7	2.7	5.4
1994/95	16.4	26.0	9.7
1995/96	3.6	11.6	8.0
1996/97	12.1	8.0	-4.1
1997/98	16.8	11.5	-5.3
1998/99	15.5	29.1	13.6
1999/00	1.1	3.6	2.5
2000/01	-8.2	-0.9	7.4
2001/02	-5.6	23.3	28.9
2002/03	2.4	-7.4	-9.8
2003/04	4.7	5.6	0.9
2004/05	-1.3	4.1	5.4
2005/06	5.3	21.0	15.8
2006/07	6.6	9.0	2.5
2007/08	-4.8	-2.5	2.3
2008/09	3.5	8.5	5.1
2009/10	5.4	12.8	7.4
2010/11	7.6	13.0	5.4
2011/12	9.1	7.4	-1.7
2012/13	13.1	14.7	1.7
2013/14	5.8	8.9	3.1
2014/15	2.7	3.0	0.3
2015/16	1.9	5.5	3.6
2016/17	6.2	10.3	4.1
2017/18	0.1	5.1	5.0
Avg	5.0%	9.5%	4.6%
Fq > 0	79%	90%	79%

500, it has produced an extra 4.6% and outperformed it 79% of the time.

In the other seven months of the year, from May 6th to December 11th, the aerospace and defense sector has only had an average gain of 3.2% and has only outperformed the S&P 500, 46% of the time. In this unfavorable period, there have been nine years of gains greater than 10% and five years of losses greater than 10%. In other words, the results in the unfavorable period for the sector tend to be volatile and on average not as strong as the favorable period.

Aerospace and Defense- Avg. Year 1990 to 2017

Aerospace & Def./ S&P 500 Rel. Str. - Avg Yr. 1990 - 2017

From 1989/90 to 2017/18, during its seasonal period, December 12th to May 5th, the aerospace and defense sector has produced an average gain of 9.5% and has been positive 90% of the time. Compared to the S&P

* For more information on the aerospace and defense sector, see www.standardandpoors.com

Aerospace & Defense Performance

Aerospace Monthly Performance (1990-2017)

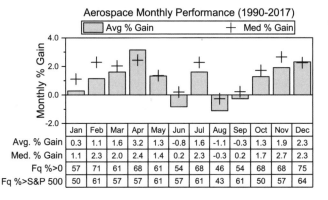

	Jan	Feb	Mar	Apr	May	Jun	Jul	Aug	Sep	Oct	Nov	Dec
Avg. % Gain	0.3	1.1	1.6	3.2	1.3	-0.8	1.6	-1.1	-0.3	1.3	1.9	2.3
Med. % Gain	1.1	2.3	2.0	2.4	1.4	0.2	2.3	-0.3	0.2	1.7	2.7	2.3
Fq %>0	57	71	61	68	61	54	68	46	54	68	68	75
Fq %>S&P 500	50	61	57	57	61	57	61	43	61	50	57	64

Aerospace 5 Year (2013-2017) % Gain

Aerospace Performance 2017-2018

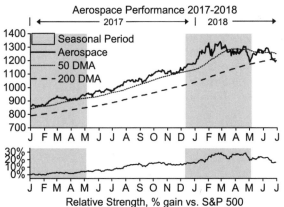

Relative Strength, % gain vs. S&P 500

Market Indices & Rates
Weekly Values**

Stock Markets	2016	2017
Dow	19,843	24,652
S&P500	2,258	2,676
Nasdaq	5,437	6,937
TSX	15,252	16,042
FTSE	7,012	7,491
DAX	11,404	13,104
Nikkei	19,401	22,553
Hang Seng	22,021	28,848

Commodities	2016	2017
Oil	51.90	57.30
Gold	1131.6	1254.6

Bond Yields	2016	2017
USA 5 Yr Treasury	2.07	2.16
USA 10 Yr T	2.60	2.35
USA 20 Yr T	2.91	2.52
Moody's Aaa	4.11	3.43
Moody's Baa	4.88	4.15
CAN 5 Yr T	1.22	1.68
CAN 10 Yr T	1.83	1.84

Money Market	2016	2017
USA Fed Funds	0.75	1.50
USA 3 Mo T-B	0.51	1.31
CAN tgt overnight rate	0.50	1.00
CAN 3 Mo T-B	0.48	0.94

Foreign Exchange	2016	2017
EUR/USD	1.05	1.17
GBP/USD	1.25	1.33
USD/CAD	1.33	1.29
USD/JPY	117.93	112.60

DECEMBER

M	T	W	T	F	S	S
						1
2	3	4	5	6	7	8
9	10	11	12	13	14	15
16	17	18	19	20	21	22
23	24	25	26	27	28	29
30	31					

JANUARY

M	T	W	T	F	S	S
	1	2	3	4	5	
6	7	8	9	10	11	12
13	14	15	16	17	18	19
20	21	22	23	24	25	26
27	28	29	30	31		

FEBRUARY

M	T	W	T	F	S	S
					1	2
3	4	5	6	7	8	9
10	11	12	13	14	15	16
17	18	19	20	21	22	23
24	25	26	27	28	29	

From 1990 to 2017, the aerospace and defense sector has increased its gains on a monthly basis from January to April, with April being the best month. The summer months have tended to be the weaker months, with August being the weakest.

Over the last five years, on average, the first few months of the year have been stronger than the average month for the rest of the year. August has been the worst month.

In the December 2017 to May 2018 seasonal period, the aerospace and defense sector was positive and outperformed the S&P 500.

DO THE "NAZ" WITH SANTA
Nasdaq Gives More at Christmas – Dec 15th to Jan 23rd

One of the best times to invest in the major stock markets is the period around Christmas. The markets are generally positive at this time of the year as investors reposition their portfolios for the start of the new year. A lot of investors are familiar with the *Small Cap Effect* opportunity that starts approximately at this time of the year, where small caps tend to outperform from mid-December until the beginning of March (*see Small Cap Effect*), but few investors know that the last half of December and the first half of January is also a seasonally strong period for the Nasdaq.

81% of time better than S&P 500

The Nasdaq tends to perform well in the last two weeks of December, as investors typically increase their investment allocation to higher beta investments, including the Nasdaq, to finish the year.

In addition, the major sector drivers of the Nasdaq (biotech and technology), tend to perform well in the second half of December and the first half of January. Biotech tends to perform well in the last half of December, and technology tends to perform well in the first half of January. The end result is a Nasdaq Christmas trade that lasts from December 15th to January 23rd. In this time period, for the years 1971/72 to 2017/18, the Nasdaq has outperformed the S&P 500 by an average 2.1% per year. This rate of return is considered to be very high given that the length of the favorable period is just over one month. Even more impressive is the 81% frequency that the Nasdaq outperforms the S&P 500.

Nasdaq vs. S&P 500 Dec 15th to Jan 23rd 1971/72 To 2017/18		Positive	
Dec 15 to Jan 23	S&P 500	Nasdaq	Diff
1971/72	6.1 %	7.5 %	1.3 %
1972/73	0.0	-0.7	-0.7
1973/74	4.1	6.8	2.8
1974/75	7.5	8.9	1.4
1975/76	13.0	13.8	0.9
1976/77	-1.7	2.8	4.5
1977/78	-5.1	-3.5	1.6
1978/79	4.7	6.2	1.4
1979/80	4.1	5.6	1.5
1980/81	0.8	3.3	2.5
1981/82	-6.0	-5.0	1.0
1982/83	4.7	5.5	0.8
1983/84	0.9	1.4	0.4
1984/85	9.0	13.3	4.3
1985/86	-2.7	0.8	3.5
1986/87	9.2	10.2	1.0
1987/88	1.8	9.1	7.3
1988/89	3.3	4.6	1.3
1989/90	-5.5	-3.8	1.7
1990/91	1.0	4.1	3.1
1991/92	7.9	15.2	7.2
1992/93	0.8	7.2	6.4
1993/94	2.5	5.7	3.2
1994/95	2.4	4.7	2.3
1995/96	-0.7	-1.0	-0.3
1996/97	6.7	7.3	0.6
1997/98	0.4	2.6	2.1
1998/99	7.4	18.9	11.6
1999/00	2.7	18.6	15.9
2000/01	1.5	4.1	2.6
2001/02	0.5	-1.6	-2.0
2002/03	-0.2	1.9	2.1
2003/04	6.3	9.0	2.7
2004/05	-3.0	-5.8	-2.9
2005/06	-0.7	-0.6	0.1
2006/07	0.2	-0.9	-1.1
2007/08	-8.8	-12.1	-3.3
2008/09	-5.4	-4.1	1.3
2009/10	-2.0	-0.3	1.7
2010/11	3.4	2.4	-1.0
2011/12	8.6	9.6	1.1
2012/13	5.8	6.1	0.4
2013/14	3.0	5.5	2.5
2014/15	2.5	2.2	-0.2
2015/16	-5.7	-7.3	-1.6
2016/17	0.5	2.1	1.6
2017/18	7.1	8.8	1.8
Avg	2.0 %	4.0 %	2.1 %
Fq > 0	70 %	72 %	81 %

Nasdaq - Avg. Year 1972 to 2017

Nasdaq / SP 500 Relative Strength - Avg Yr. 1972 - 2017

(Y) *Alternate Strategy — For those investors who favor the Nasdaq, an alternative strategy is to invest in the Nasdaq at an earlier date: October 28th. Historically, on average the Nasdaq has started its outperformance at this time. The "Do the Naz with Santa" strategy focuses on the sweet spot of the Nasdaq's outper-*

(i) *Nasdaq is a market that has a focused on biotech and technology and is typically more volatile than the S&P 500.*

Nasdaq Performance

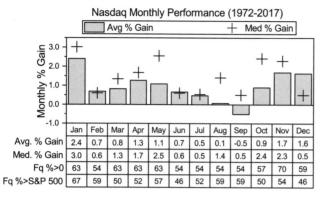

Nasdaq Monthly Performance (1972-2017)

Legend: ☐ Avg % Gain   + Med % Gain

	Jan	Feb	Mar	Apr	May	Jun	Jul	Aug	Sep	Oct	Nov	Dec
Avg. % Gain	2.4	0.7	0.8	1.3	1.1	0.7	0.5	0.1	-0.5	0.9	1.7	1.6
Med. % Gain	3.0	0.6	1.3	1.7	2.5	0.6	0.5	1.4	0.5	2.4	2.3	0.5
Fq %>0	63	54	63	63	63	54	54	54	54	57	70	59
Fq %>S&P 500	67	59	50	52	57	46	52	59	59	50	54	46

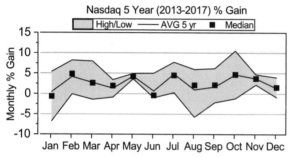

Nasdaq 5 Year (2013-2017) % Gain

Legend: ☐ High/Low — AVG 5 yr ■ Median

Nasdaq Performance 2017-2018

Relative Strength, % gain vs. S&P 500

DECEMBER

M	T	W	T	F	S	S
						1
2	3	4	5	6	7	8
9	10	11	12	13	14	15
16	17	18	19	20	21	22
23	24	25	26	27	28	29
30	31					

JANUARY

M	T	W	T	F	S	S
	1	2	3	4	5	
6	7	8	9	10	11	12
13	14	15	16	17	18	19
20	21	22	23	24	25	26
27	28	29	30	31		

FEBRUARY

M	T	W	T	F	S	S
					1	2
3	4	5	6	7	8	9
10	11	12	13	14	15	16
17	18	19	20	21	22	23
24	25	26	27	28	29	

From 1972 to 2017, the best month of the year for the Nasdaq has been January on an average and median basis. January is the core part of the Nasdaq trade. December is also a positive month, but on a median basis, it is weaker than most other months. It is the first part of December that tends to be weaker for the Nasdaq, leading to a mid-month entry into the Nasdaq trade. Over the last five years, the strongest month of the year for the Nasdaq has been February.

The 2017/18 Nasdaq trade was positive and outperformed the S&P 500.

SMALL CAP (SMALL COMPANY) EFFECT
Small Companies Outperform - Dec 19th to Mar 7th

At different stages of the business cycle, small capitalization companies (small caps represented by Russell 2000), perform better than large capitalization companies (large caps represented by Russell 1000).

Evidence shows that the small caps relative outperformance also has a seasonal component as they typically outperform large caps from December 19th to March 7th.

2.7% extra and positive 77% of the time

Russell 2000 - Avg. Year 1979 to 2017

Russell 2000 / Russell 1000 - Avg Yr. 1979 - 2017

Russell 2000 vs. Russell 1000* % Gains
Dec 19th to Mar 7th 1979/80 to 2017/18
Positive ▢

Dec 19 - Mar7	Russell 1000	Russell 2000	Diff
1979/80	-1.3 %	-0.4 %	0.9 %
1980/81	-2.8	4.0	6.8
1981/82	-12.4	-12.1	0.3
1982/83	11.8	19.8	8.0
1983/84	-6.4	-7.5	-1.1
1984/85	7.7	17.1	9.4
1985/86	8.2	11.7	3.5
1986/87	17.2	21.3	4.1
1987/88	8.3	16.4	8.0
1988/89	6.9	9.1	2.5
1989/90	-2.0	-1.9	0.2
1990/91	14.6	29.0	14.4
1991/92	6.0	16.8	10.8
1992/93	1.4	5.0	3.5
1993/94	0.5	5.7	5.3
1994/95	5.3	5.5	0.2
1995/96	8.3	7.8	-0.5
1996/97	9.5	3.5	-6.0
1997/98	10.2	10.3	0.1
1998/99	7.3	0.2	-7.2
1999/00	-1.7	27.7	29.4
2000/01	-5.2	4.7	9.8
2001/02	1.6	1.9	0.4
2002/03	-6.7	-7.8	-1.0
2003/04	6.4	9.6	3.3
2004/05	2.8	0.3	-2.5
2005/06	0.8	5.6	4.7
2006/07	-1.6	-0.8	0.9
2007/08	-10.9	-12.5	-1.5
2008/09	-22.2	-26.7	-4.5
2009/10	3.6	9.1	5.5
2010/11	5.5	4.2	-1.3
2011/12	11.3	10.2	-1.1
2012/13	7.1	10.3	3.1
2013/14	4.2	6.1	2.0
2014/15	1.0	2.1	1.1
2015/16	-0.3	-2.4	-2.1
2016/17	4.8	0.8	-4.1
2017/18	1.5	1.7	0.2
Avg.	2.6 %	5.3 %	2.7 %
Fq > 0	69 %	77 %	67 %

The core part of the small cap seasonal strategy occurs in January and includes what has been described as the January Effect (Wachtel 1942, 184).

This well documented anomaly of superior performance of stocks in the month of January is based upon the tenet that investors sell stocks in December for tax loss reasons, artificially driving down prices, and creating a great opportunity for astute investors.

In recent times, the January Effect start date has shifted to mid-December and is more pronounced for small caps as their prices are more volatile than large caps. At the beginning of the year, small cap stocks benefit from a phenomenon that I have coined, "beta out of the gate, and coast." If small cap stocks are outperforming at the beginning of the year, money managers will gravitate to the sector in order to produce

returns that are above their index benchmark. Once above average returns have been "locked in," the managers then rotate from their small cap overweight positions back to index large cap positions and coast for the rest of the year with above average returns. The overall process boosts small cap stocks at the beginning of the year.

ⓘ *Russell 2000 (small cap index): The 2000 smallest companies in the Russell 3000 stock index (a broad market index). Russell 1000 (large cap index): The 1000 largest companies in the Russell 3000 stock index*

For more information on the Russell indexes, see www.Russell.com

Wachtel, S.B. 1942. Certain observations on seasonal movements in stock prices. The Journal of Business and Economics (Winter): 184.

Small Caps Performance

Russell 2000 Monthly Performance (1979-2017)

Legend: Avg % Gain, + Med % Gain

	Jan	Feb	Mar	Apr	May	Jun	Jul	Aug	Sep	Oct	Nov	Dec
Avg. % Gain	1.4	1.2	1.4	1.5	1.3	0.6	-0.3	0.2	-0.3	-0.3	2.1	2.5
Med. % Gain	1.3	1.0	1.9	1.0	2.1	0.6	-1.1	2.2	0.6	1.9	3.1	2.5
Fq %>0	54	59	72	62	64	62	49	56	56	56	67	77
Fq %> Russ1000	49	56	59	38	59	62	36	51	59	36	49	59

Russell 2000 5 Year (2013-2017) % Gain

Legend: High/Low, AVG 5 yr, ■ Median

Russell 2000 Performance 2017-2018

Legend: Seasonal Period, Russell 2000, 50 DMA, 200 DMA

Relative Strength. % gain vs. Russell 1000

From 1979 to 2017, December through to February have been strong months for small cap stocks. Other months have performed well, but they have not provided the same risk-reward benefits. Over the last five years, the small cap sector has generally followed its seasonal trend with December and February being strong months. January has been the exception, with its poor performance. This data is largely skewed by the dramatic decline in the stock markets in January 2016.

In early 2017, the small cap sector underperformed in its seasonal period. In late 2017/18 the small cap sector outperformed the S&P 500.

Market Indices & Rates
Weekly Values**

Stock Markets	2016	2017
Dow	19,763	24,719
S&P500	2,239	2,674
Nasdaq	5,383	6,903
TSX	15,288	16,209
FTSE	7,143	7,688
DAX	11,481	12,918
Nikkei	19,114	22,765
Hang Seng	22,001	29,919

Commodities	2016	2017
Oil	53.72	60.42
Gold	1145.9	1291.0

Bond Yields	2016	2017
USA 5 Yr Treasury	1.93	2.20
USA 10 Yr T	2.45	2.40
USA 20 Yr T	2.79	2.58
Moody's Aaa	3.98	3.45
Moody's Baa	4.73	4.17
CAN 5 Yr T	1.11	1.87
CAN 10 Yr T	1.72	2.05

Money Market	2016	2017
USA Fed Funds	0.75	1.50
USA 3 Mo T-B	0.51	1.39
CAN tgt overnight rate	0.50	1.00
CAN 3 Mo T-B	0.46	1.06

Foreign Exchange	2016	2017
EUR/USD	1.05	1.20
GBP/USD	1.23	1.35
USD/CAD	1.34	1.26
USD/JPY	116.96	112.69

DECEMBER

M	T	W	T	F	S	S
						1
2	3	4	5	6	7	8
9	10	11	12	13	14	15
16	17	18	19	20	21	22
23	24	25	26	27	28	29
30	31					

JANUARY

M	T	W	T	F	S	S
	1	2	3	4	5	
6	7	8	9	10	11	12
13	14	15	16	17	18	19
20	21	22	23	24	25	26
27	28	29	30	31		

FEBRUARY

M	T	W	T	F	S	S
					1	2
3	4	5	6	7	8	9
10	11	12	13	14	15	16
17	18	19	20	21	22	23
24	25	26	27	28	29	

FINANCIALS (U.S.) YEAR END CLEAN UP
December 15th to April 13th

The main driver for the strong seasonal performance of the financial sector has been the year-end earnings of the banks that start to report in mid-January. A strong performance from mid-December has been the result of investors getting into the market early to take advantage of positive year-end earnings.

Extra 1.6% &
59% of the time better than the S&P 500

In 2014, 2015 and most of 2016, the U.S. financial sector performed "at market," producing approximately the same gain as the S&P 500. The sector strongly outperformed the stock market after Trump was elected, as investors expected to Trump to remove cumbersome financial regulations.

Dec 15 to Apr 13	S&P 500	Positive Financials	Diff
1989/90	-1.9 %	-9.9 %	-8.0 %
1990/91	16.4	29.2	12.8
1991/92	5.6	9.2	3.5
1992/93	3.8	17.9	14.1
1993/94	-3.6	-0.4	3.2
1994/95	11.9	14.0	2.1
1995/96	3.2	5.5	2.3
1996/97	1.2	4.7	3.4
19/9798	16.4	19.7	3.3
1998/99	18.3	24.9	6.6
1999/00	2.7	4.0	1.3
2000/01	-11.7	-4.8	6.9
2001/02	-1.1	6.5	7.6
2002/03	-2.4	-1.8	0.6
2003/04	5.2	6.7	1.5
2004/05	-2.5	-6.2	-3.7
2005/06	1.3	1.1	-0.2
2006/07	1.9	-2.2	-4.1
2007/08	-9.2	-14.1	-4.9
2008/09	-2.4	-7.0	-4.6
2009/10	7.5	15.2	7.8
2010/11	5.9	4.6	-1.3
2011/12	13.1	20.7	7.7
2012/13	12.4	16.0	3.6
2013/14	2.3	1.0	-1.3
2014/15	4.5	1.1	-3.4
2015/16	3.0	-2.0	-5.0
2016/17	3.4	-2.0	-5.4
2017/18	0.2	-0.6	-0.7
Avg.	3.6 %	5.2 %	1.6 %
Fq > 0	72 %	62 %	59 %

Financials* vs. S&P 500, 1989/90 to 2017/18

Financials Sector - Avg. Year 1990 to 2017

Financials / S&P 500 Relative Strength - Avg Yr. 1990-2017

Nevertheless, seasonal investors would be wise to consider concentrating their financial investments during the sector's strong seasonal period that lasts from mid-December to mid-April.

It should be noted that Canadian banks have their year-ends at the end of October (reporting in November) and as such, their seasonally strong period starts in October.

Overall, in 2017 and 2018, the financial sector underperformed the stock market, as US banks have been suffering from diminishing returns from rising interest rates. Generally, higher interest rates increase the banks net interest margin. On the other hand, as higher interest rates tend to slow the economy down, bank profitability erodes.

As banks have underperformed over the last two years, the financial sector has not performed well in its seasonal period.

Financial SP GIC Sector # 40: For more information on the financial sector, see www.standardandpoors.com

Financials Performance

Financials Monthly Performance (1990-2017)

	Jan	Feb	Mar	Apr	May	Jun	Jul	Aug	Sep	Oct	Nov	Dec
Avg. % Gain	-0.6	0.2	2.0	2.0	1.4	-1.0	1.5	-1.3	-0.4	1.5	1.3	2.2
Med. % Gain	-0.2	1.9	0.1	1.2	1.8	-0.3	2.0	-0.2	1.2	2.0	2.4	1.9
Fq %>0	50	64	54	61	64	46	64	50	57	68	61	75
Fq %>S&P 500	57	64	61	50	46	43	46	39	54	46	39	61

Financials 5 Year (2013-2017) % Gain

Financials Performance 2017-2018

Relative Strength, % gain vs. S&P 500

From 1990 to 2017, the months December through April, the core of the seasonal time period for the financial sector, have been the only months (other than September) that have outperformed the S&P 500 at least half of the time.

Over the last five years, January has been the weakest month of the year on an average and median basis.

The financial sector underperformed the S&P 500 in both its 2016/17 and 2017/18 seasonal periods.

JANUARY

M	T	W	T	F	S	S
		1	2	3	4	5
6	7	8	9	10	11	12
13	14	15	16	17	18	19
20	21	22	23	24	25	26
27	28	29	30	31		

FEBRUARY

M	T	W	T	F	S	S
					1	2
3	4	5	6	7	8	9
10	11	12	13	14	15	16
17	18	19	20	21	22	23
24	25	26	27	28	29	

MARCH

M	T	W	T	F	S	S
						1
2	3	4	5	6	7	8
9	10	11	12	13	14	15
16	17	18	19	20	21	22
23	24	25	26	27	28	29
30	31					

APRIL

M	T	W	T	F	S	S
		1	2	3	4	5
6	7	8	9	10	11	12
13	14	15	16	17	18	19
20	21	22	23	24	25	26
27	28	29	30			

MAY

M	T	W	T	F	S	S
				1	2	3
4	5	6	7	8	9	10
11	12	13	14	15	16	17
18	19	20	21	22	23	24
25	26	27	28	29	30	31

JUNE

M	T	W	T	F	S	S
1	2	3	4	5	6	7
8	9	10	11	12	13	14
15	16	17	18	19	20	21
22	23	24	25	26	27	28
29	30					

APPENDIX

STOCK MARKET RETURNS

S&P 500 PERCENT CHANGES

	JAN	FEB	MAR	APR	MAY	JUN
1950	1.5 %	1.0 %	0.4 %	4.5 %	3.9 %	— 5.8 %
1951	6.1	0.6	— 1.8	4.8	— 4.1	— 2.6
1952	1.6	— 3.6	4.8	— 4.3	2.3	4.6
1953	— 0.7	— 1.8	— 2.4	— 2.6	— 0.3	— 1.6
1954	5.1	0.3	3.0	4.9	3.3	0.1
1955	1.8	0.4	— 0.5	3.8	— 0.1	8.2
1956	— 3.6	3.5	6.9	— 0.2	— 6.6	3.9
1957	— 4.2	— 3.3	2.0	3.7	3.7	— 0.1
1958	4.3	2.1	3.1	3.2	1.5	2.6
1959	0.4	— 0.1	0.1	3.9	1.9	— 0.4
1960	— 7.1	0.9	— 1.4	— 1.8	2.7	2.0
1961	6.3	2.7	2.6	0.4	1.9	— 2.9
1962	— 3.8	1.6	— 0.6	— 6.2	— 8.6	— 8.2
1963	4.9	— 2.9	3.5	4.9	1.4	— 2.0
1964	2.7	1.0	1.5	0.6	1.1	1.6
1965	3.3	— 0.1	— 1.5	3.4	— 0.8	— 4.9
1966	0.5	— 1.8	— 2.2	2.1	— 5.4	— 1.6
1967	7.8	0.2	3.9	4.2	— 5.2	1.8
1968	— 4.4	— 3.1	0.9	8.0	1.3	0.9
1969	— 0.8	— 4.7	3.4	2.1	— 0.2	— 5.6
1970	— 7.6	5.3	0.1	— 9.0	— 6.1	— 5.0
1971	4.0	0.9	3.7	3.6	— 4.2	— 0.9
1972	1.8	2.5	0.6	0.4	1.7	— 2.2
1973	— 1.7	— 3.7	— 0.1	— 4.1	— 1.9	— 0.7
1974	— 1.0	— 0.4	— 2.3	— 3.9	— 3.4	— 1.5
1975	12.3	6.0	2.2	4.7	4.4	4.4
1976	11.8	— 1.1	3.1	— 1.1	— 1.4	4.1
1977	— 5.1	— 2.2	— 1.4	0.0	— 2.4	4.5
1978	— 6.2	— 2.5	2.5	8.5	0.4	— 1.8
1979	4.0	— 3.7	5.5	0.2	— 2.6	3.9
1980	5.8	— 0.4	— 10.2	4.1	4.7	2.7
1981	— 4.6	1.3	3.6	— 2.3	— 0.2	— 1.0
1982	— 1.8	— 6.1	— 1.0	4.0	— 3.9	— 2.0
1983	3.3	1.9	3.3	7.5	— 1.2	3.2
1984	— 0.9	— 3.9	1.3	0.5	— 5.9	1.7
1985	7.4	0.9	— 0.3	— 0.5	5.4	1.2
1986	0.2	7.1	5.3	— 1.4	5.0	1.4
1987	13.2	3.7	2.6	— 1.1	0.6	4.8
1988	4.0	4.2	— 3.3	0.9	0.3	4.3
1989	7.1	— 2.9	2.1	5.0	3.5	— 0.8
1990	— 6.9	0.9	2.4	— 2.7	9.2	— 0.9
1991	4.2	6.7	2.2	0.0	3.9	— 4.8
1992	— 2.0	1.0	— 2.2	2.8	0.1	— 1.7
1993	0.7	1.0	1.9	— 2.5	2.3	0.1
1994	3.3	— 3.0	— 4.6	1.2	1.2	— 2.7
1995	2.4	3.6	2.7	2.8	3.6	2.1
1996	3.3	0.7	0.8	1.3	2.3	0.2
1997	6.1	0.6	— 4.3	5.8	5.9	4.3
1998	1.0	7.0	5.0	0.9	— 1.9	3.9
1999	4.1	— 3.2	3.9	3.8	— 2.5	5.4
2000	— 5.1	— 2.0	9.7	— 3.1	— 2.2	2.4
2001	3.5	— 9.2	— 6.4	7.7	0.5	— 2.5
2002	— 1.6	— 2.1	3.7	— 6.1	— 0.9	— 7.2
2003	— 2.7	— 1.7	0.8	8.1	5.1	1.1
2004	1.7	1.2	— 1.6	— 1.7	1.2	1.8
2005	— 2.5	1.9	— 1.9	— 2.0	3.0	0.0
2006	2.5	0.0	1.1	1.2	— 3.1	0.0
2007	1.4	— 2.2	1.0	4.3	3.3	— 1.8
2008	— 6.1	— 3.5	— 0.6	4.8	1.1	— 8.6
2009	— 8.6	— 11.0	8.5	9.4	5.3	0.0
2010	— 3.7	2.9	5.9	1.5	— 8.2	— 5.4
2011	2.3	3.2	— 0.1	2.8	— 1.4	— 1.8
2012	4.4	4.1	3.1	— 0.7	— 6.3	4.0
2013	5.0	1.1	3.6	1.8	2.1	— 1.5
2014	— 3.6	4.3	0.7	0.6	2.1	1.9
2015	— 3.1	5.5	— 1.7	0.9	1.0	— 2.1
2016	— 5.1	— 0.4	6.6	0.3	1.5	0.1
2017	1.8	3.7	0.0	0.9	1.2	0.5
FQ POS*	41/68	38/68	44/68	47/68	40/68	36/68
% FQ POS*	60 %	56 %	65 %	69 %	59 %	53 %
AVG GAIN*	0.9 %	0.1 %	1.2 %	1.4 %	0.2 %	0.0 %
RANK GAIN*	6	9	4	3	8	10

JUL	AUG	SEP	OCT	NOV	DEC		YEAR
0.8 %	3.3 %	5.6 %	0.4 %	— 0.1 %	4.6 %	**1950**	21.7 %
6.9	3.9	— 0.1	— 1.4	— 0.3	3.9	**1951**	16.5
1.8	— 1.5	— 2.0	— 0.1	4.6	3.5	**1952**	11.8
2.5	— 5.8	0.1	5.1	0.9	0.2	**1953**	— 6.6
5.7	— 3.4	8.3	— 1.9	8.1	5.1	**1954**	45.0
6.1	— 0.8	1.1	— 3.0	7.5	— 0.1	**1955**	26.4
5.2	— 3.8	— 4.5	0.5	— 1.1	3.5	**1956**	2.6
1.1	— 5.6	— 6.2	— 3.2	1.6	— 4.1	**1957**	— 14.3
4.3	1.2	4.8	2.5	2.2	5.2	**1958**	38.1
3.5	— 1.5	— 4.6	1.1	1.3	2.8	**1959**	8.5
— 2.5	2.6	— 6.0	— 0.2	4.0	4.6	**1960**	— 3.0
3.3	2.0	— 2.0	2.8	3.9	0.3	**1961**	23.1
6.4	1.5	— 4.8	0.4	10.2	1.3	**1962**	— 11.8
0.3	4.9	— 1.1	3.2	— 1.1	2.4	**1963**	18.9
1.8	— 1.6	2.9	0.8	— 0.5	0.4	**1964**	13.0
1.3	2.3	3.2	2.7	— 0.9	0.9	**1965**	9.1
— 1.3	— 7.8	— 0.7	4.8	0.3	— 0.1	**1966**	— 13.1
4.5	— 1.2	3.3	— 3.5	0.8	2.6	**1967**	20.1
— 1.8	1.1	3.9	0.7	4.8	— 4.2	**1968**	7.7
— 6.0	4.0	— 2.5	4.3	— 3.4	— 1.9	**1969**	— 11.4
7.3	4.4	3.4	— 1.2	4.7	5.7	**1970**	0.1
— 3.2	3.6	— 0.7	— 4.2	— 0.3	8.6	**1971**	10.8
0.2	3.4	— 0.5	0.9	4.6	1.2	**1972**	15.6
3.8	— 3.7	4.0	— 0.1	— 11.4	1.7	**1973**	— 17.4
— 7.8	— 9.0	— 11.9	16.3	— 5.3	— 2.0	**1974**	— 29.7
— 6.8	— 2.1	— 3.5	6.2	2.5	— 1.2	**1975**	31.5
— 0.8	— 0.5	2.3	— 2.2	— 0.8	5.2	**1976**	19.1
— 1.6	— 2.1	— 0.2	— 4.3	2.7	0.3	**1977**	— 11.5
5.4	2.6	— 0.7	— 9.2	1.7	1.5	**1978**	1.1
0.9	5.3	0.0	— 6.9	4.3	1.7	**1979**	12.3
6.5	0.6	2.5	1.6	10.2	— 3.4	**1980**	25.8
— 0.2	— 6.2	— 5.4	4.9	3.7	— 3.0	**1981**	— 9.7
— 2.3	11.6	0.8	11.0	3.6	1.5	**1982**	14.8
— 3.0	1.1	1.0	— 1.5	1.7	— 0.9	**1983**	17.3
— 1.6	10.6	— 0.3	0.0	— 1.5	2.2	**1984**	1.4
— 0.5	— 1.2	— 3.5	4.3	6.5	4.5	**1985**	26.3
— 5.9	7.1	— 8.5	5.5	2.1	— 2.8	**1986**	14.6
4.8	3.5	— 2.4	— 21.8	— 8.5	7.3	**1987**	2.0
— 0.5	— 3.9	4.0	2.6	— 1.9	1.5	**1988**	12.4
8.8	1.6	— 0.7	— 2.5	1.7	2.1	**1989**	27.3
— 0.5	— 9.4	— 5.1	— 0.7	6.0	2.5	**1990**	— 6.6
4.5	2.0	— 1.9	1.2	— 4.4	11.2	**1991**	26.3
3.9	— 2.4	0.9	0.2	3.0	1.0	**1992**	4.5
— 0.5	3.4	— 1.0	1.9	— 1.3	1.0	**1993**	7.1
3.1	3.8	— 2.7	2.1	— 4.0	1.2	**1994**	— 1.5
3.2	0.0	4.0	— 0.5	4.1	1.7	**1995**	34.1
— 4.6	1.9	5.4	2.6	7.3	— 2.2	**1996**	20.3
7.8	— 5.7	5.3	— 3.4	4.5	1.6	**1997**	31.0
— 1.2	— 14.6	6.2	8.0	5.9	5.6	**1998**	26.7
— 3.2	— 0.6	— 2.9	6.3	1.9	5.8	**1999**	19.5
— 1.6	6.1	— 5.3	— 0.5	— 8.0	0.4	**2000**	— 10.1
— 1.1	— 6.4	— 8.2	1.8	7.5	0.8	**2001**	— 13.0
— 7.9	0.5	— 11.0	8.6	5.7	— 6.0	**2002**	— 23.4
1.6	1.8	— 1.2	5.5	0.7	5.1	**2003**	26.4
-3.4	0.2	0.9	1.4	3.9	3.2	**2004**	9.0
3.6	— 1.1	0.7	— 1.8	3.5	— 0.1	**2005**	3.0
0.5	2.1	2.5	3.2	1.6	1.3	**2006**	13.6
— 3.2	1.3	3.6	1.5	— 4.4	— 0.9	**2007**	3.5
— 1.0	1.2	— 9.1	— 16.9	— 7.5	0.8	**2008**	-38.5
7.4	3.4	3.6	— 2.0	5.7	1.8	**2009**	23.5
6.9	— 4.7	8.8	3.7	— 0.2	6.5	**2010**	12.8
— 2.1	— 5.7	7.2	10.8	— 0.5	0.9	**2011**	0.0
1.3	2.0	2.4	— 2.0	0.3	0.7	**2012**	13.4
4.9	— 3.1	3.0	4.5	2.8	2.4	**2013**	29.6
— 1.5	3.8	— 1.6	2.3	2.5	— 0.4	**2014**	11.4
2.0	— 6.3	— 2.6	8.3	0.1	— 1.8	**2015**	— 0.7
3.6	— 0.1	— 0.1	— 1.9	3.4	1.8	**2016**	9.5
1.9	0.1	1.9	2.2	2.8	1.0	**2017**	19.4
38/68	37/68	30/68	41/68	46/68	51/68		50/68
56 %	54 %	44 %	60 %	68 %	75 %		74 %
1.0 %	— 0.1 %	— 0.5 %	0.9 %	1.6 %	1.6 %		9.1 %
5	11	12	7	2	1		

S&P 500 MONTH CLOSING VALUES

	JAN	FEB	MAR	APR	MAY	JUN
1950	17	17	17	18	19	18
1951	22	22	21	22	22	21
1952	24	23	24	23	24	25
1953	26	26	25	25	25	24
1954	26	26	27	28	29	29
1955	37	37	37	38	38	41
1956	44	45	48	48	45	47
1957	45	43	44	46	47	47
1958	42	41	42	43	44	45
1959	55	55	55	58	59	58
1960	56	56	55	54	56	57
1961	62	63	65	65	67	65
1962	69	70	70	65	60	55
1963	66	64	67	70	71	69
1964	77	78	79	79	80	82
1965	88	87	86	89	88	84
1966	93	91	89	91	86	85
1967	87	87	90	94	89	91
1968	92	89	90	97	99	100
1969	103	98	102	104	103	98
1970	85	90	90	82	77	73
1971	96	97	100	104	100	99
1972	104	107	107	108	110	107
1973	116	112	112	107	105	104
1974	97	96	94	90	87	86
1975	77	82	83	87	91	95
1976	101	100	103	102	100	104
1977	102	100	98	98	96	100
1978	89	87	89	97	97	96
1979	100	96	102	102	99	103
1980	114	114	102	106	111	114
1981	130	131	136	133	133	131
1982	120	113	112	116	112	110
1983	145	148	153	164	162	168
1984	163	157	159	160	151	153
1985	180	181	181	180	190	192
1986	212	227	239	236	247	251
1987	274	284	292	288	290	304
1988	257	268	259	261	262	274
1989	297	289	295	310	321	318
1990	329	332	340	331	361	358
1991	344	367	375	375	390	371
1992	409	413	404	415	415	408
1993	439	443	452	440	450	451
1994	482	467	446	451	457	444
1995	470	487	501	515	533	545
1996	636	640	646	654	669	671
1997	786	791	757	801	848	885
1998	980	1049	1102	1112	1091	1134
1999	1280	1238	1286	1335	1302	1373
2000	1394	1366	1499	1452	1421	1455
2001	1366	1240	1160	1249	1256	1224
2002	1130	1107	1147	1077	1067	990
2003	856	841	848	917	964	975
2004	1131	1145	1126	1107	1121	1141
2005	1181	1204	1181	1157	1192	1191
2006	1280	1281	1295	1311	1270	1270
2007	1438	1407	1421	1482	1531	1503
2008	1379	1331	1323	1386	1400	1280
2009	826	735	798	873	919	919
2010	1074	1104	1169	1187	1089	1031
2011	1286	1327	1326	1364	1345	1321
2012	1312	1366	1408	1398	1310	1362
2013	1498	1515	1569	1598	1631	1606
2014	1783	1869	1872	1884	1924	1960
2015	1995	2105	2068	2086	2107	2063
2016	1940	1932	2060	2065	2097	2099
2017	2279	2364	2363	2384	2412	2423

S&P 500 MONTH CLOSING VALUES

JUL	AUG	SEP	OCT	NOV	DEC	
18	18	19	20	20	20	1950
22	23	23	23	23	24	1951
25	25	25	25	26	27	1952
25	23	23	25	25	25	1953
31	30	32	32	34	36	1954
44	43	44	42	46	45	1955
49	48	45	46	45	47	1956
48	45	42	41	42	40	1957
47	48	50	51	52	55	1958
61	60	57	58	58	60	1959
56	57	54	53	56	58	1960
67	68	67	69	71	72	1961
58	59	56	57	62	63	1962
69	73	72	74	73	75	1963
83	82	84	85	84	85	1964
85	87	90	92	92	92	1965
84	77	77	80	80	80	1966
95	94	97	93	94	96	1967
98	99	103	103	108	104	1968
92	96	93	97	94	92	1969
78	82	84	83	87	92	1970
96	99	98	94	94	102	1971
107	111	111	112	117	118	1972
108	104	108	108	96	98	1973
79	72	64	74	70	69	1974
89	87	84	89	91	90	1975
103	103	105	103	102	107	1976
99	97	97	92	95	95	1977
101	103	103	93	95	96	1978
104	109	109	102	106	108	1979
122	122	125	127	141	136	1980
131	123	116	122	126	123	1981
107	120	120	134	139	141	1982
163	164	166	164	166	165	1983
151	167	166	166	164	167	1984
191	189	182	190	202	211	1985
236	253	231	244	249	242	1986
319	330	322	252	230	247	1987
272	262	272	279	274	278	1988
346	351	349	340	346	353	1989
356	323	306	304	322	330	1990
388	395	388	392	375	417	1991
424	414	418	419	431	436	1992
448	464	459	468	462	466	1993
458	475	463	472	454	459	1994
562	562	584	582	605	616	1995
640	652	687	705	757	741	1996
954	899	947	915	955	970	1997
1121	957	1017	1099	1164	1229	1998
1329	1320	1283	1363	1389	1469	1999
1431	1518	1437	1429	1315	1320	2000
1211	1134	1041	1060	1139	1148	2001
912	916	815	886	936	880	2002
990	1008	996	1051	1058	1112	2003
1102	1104	1115	1130	1174	1212	2004
1234	1220	1229	1207	1249	1248	2005
1277	1304	1336	1378	1401	1418	2006
1455	1474	1527	1549	1481	1468	2007
1267	1283	1165	969	896	903	2008
987	1021	1057	1036	1096	1115	2009
1102	1049	1141	1183	1181	1258	2010
1292	1219	1131	1253	1247	1258	2011
1379	1407	1441	1412	1416	1426	2012
1686	1633	1682	1757	1806	1848	2013
1931	2003	1972	2018	2068	2059	2014
2104	1972	1920	2079	2080	2044	2015
2174	2171	2168	2126	2199	2239	2016
2470	2472	2519	2575	2648	2674	2017

DOW JONES PERCENT MONTH CHANGES

	JAN	FEB	MAR	APR	MAY	JUN
1950	0.8 %	0.8 %	1.3 %	4.0 %	4.2 %	— 6.4 %
1951	5.7	1.3	— 1.7	4.5	— 3.6	— 2.8
1952	0.6	— 3.9	3.6	— 4.4	2.1	4.3
1953	— 0.7	— 2.0	— 1.5	— 1.8	— 0.9	— 1.5
1954	4.1	0.7	3.1	5.2	2.6	1.8
1955	1.1	0.8	— 0.5	3.9	— 0.2	6.2
1956	— 3.6	2.8	5.8	0.8	— 7.4	3.1
1957	— 4.1	— 3.0	2.2	4.1	2.1	— 0.3
1958	3.3	— 2.2	1.6	2.0	1.5	3.3
1959	1.8	1.6	— 0.3	3.7	3.2	0.0
1960	— 8.4	1.2	— 2.1	— 2.4	4.0	2.4
1961	5.2	2.1	2.2	0.3	2.7	— 1.8
1962	— 4.3	1.2	— 0.2	— 5.9	— 7.8	— 8.5
1963	4.7	— 2.9	3.0	5.2	1.3	— 2.8
1964	2.9	1.9	1.6	— 0.3	1.2	1.3
1965	3.3	0.1	— 1.6	3.7	— 0.5	— 5.4
1966	1.5	— 3.2	— 2.8	1.0	— 5.3	— 1.6
1967	8.2	— 1.2	3.2	3.6	— 5.0	0.9
1968	— 5.5	— 1.8	0.0	8.5	— 1.4	— 0.1
1969	0.2	— 4.3	3.3	1.6	— 1.3	— 6.9
1970	— 7.0	4.5	1.0	— 6.3	— 4.8	— 2.4
1971	3.5	1.2	2.9	4.1	— 3.6	— 1.8
1972	1.3	2.9	1.4	1.4	0.7	— 3.3
1973	— 2.1	— 4.4	— 0.4	— 3.1	— 2.2	— 1.1
1974	0.6	0.6	— 1.6	— 1.2	— 4.1	0.0
1975	14.2	5.0	3.9	6.9	1.3	5.6
1976	14.4	— 0.3	2.8	— 0.3	— 2.2	2.8
1977	— 5.0	— 1.9	— 1.8	0.8	— 3.0	2.0
1978	— 7.4	— 3.6	2.1	10.5	0.4	— 2.6
1979	4.2	— 3.6	6.6	— 0.8	— 3.8	2.4
1980	4.4	— 1.5	— 9.0	4.0	4.1	2.0
1981	— 1.7	2.9	3.0	— 0.6	— 0.6	— 1.5
1982	— 0.4	— 5.4	— 0.2	3.1	— 3.4	— 0.9
1983	2.8	3.4	1.6	8.5	— 2.1	1.8
1984	— 3.0	— 5.4	0.9	0.5	— 5.6	2.5
1985	6.2	— 0.2	— 1.3	— 0.7	4.6	1.5
1986	1.6	8.8	6.4	— 1.9	5.2	0.9
1987	13.8	3.1	3.6	— 0.8	0.2	5.5
1988	1.0	5.8	— 4.0	2.2	— 0.1	5.4
1989	8.0	— 3.6	1.6	5.5	2.5	— 1.6
1990	— 5.9	1.4	3.0	— 1.9	8.3	0.1
1991	3.9	5.3	1.1	— 0.9	4.8	— 4.0
1992	1.7	1.4	— 1.0	3.8	1.1	— 2.3
1993	0.3	1.8	1.9	— 0.2	2.9	— 0.3
1994	6.0	— 3.7	— 5.1	1.3	2.1	— 3.5
1995	0.2	4.3	3.7	3.9	3.3	2.0
1996	5.4	1.7	1.9	— 0.3	1.3	0.2
1997	5.7	0.9	— 4.3	6.5	4.6	4.7
1998	0.0	8.1	3.0	3.0	— 1.8	0.6
1999	1.9	— 0.6	5.2	10.2	— 2.1	3.9
2000	— 4.5	— 7.4	7.8	— 1.7	— 2.0	— 0.7
2001	0.9	— 3.6	— 5.9	8.7	1.6	— 3.8
2002	— 1.0	1.9	2.9	— 4.4	— 0.2	— 6.9
2003	— 3.5	— 2.0	1.3	6.1	4.4	1.5
2004	0.3	0.9	— 2.1	— 1.3	— 0.4	2.4
2005	— 2.7	2.6	— 2.4	— 3.0	2.7	— 1.8
2006	1.4	1.2	1.1	2.3	— 1.7	— 0.2
2007	1.3	— 2.8	0.7	5.7	4.3	— 1.6
2008	— 4.6	— 3.0	0.0	4.5	— 1.4	— 10.2
2009	— 8.8	— 11.7	7.7	7.3	4.1	— 0.6
2010	— 3.5	2.6	5.1	1.4	— 7.9	— 3.6
2011	2.7	2.8	0.8	4.0	— 1.9	— 1.2
2012	3.4	3.8	2.0	0.0	— 6.2	3.9
2013	5.8	4.8	3.7	1.8	1.9	— 1.4
2014	— 5.3	5.8	0.8	0.7	0.8	0.7
2015	— 3.7	6.8	— 2.0	0.4	1.0	— 2.2
2016	— 5.5	0.3	7.1	0.5	0.1	0.8
2017	0.5	4.8	— 0.7	1.3	0.3	1.6
FQ POS	43/68	40/68	44/68	46/68	36/68	32/68
% FQ POS	63 %	59 %	65 %	67 %	53 %	47 %
AVG GAIN	0.9 %	0.4 %	1.1 %	1.9 %	0.0 %	— 0.3 %
RANK GAIN	6	8	5	1	9	11

DOW JONES PERCENT MONTH CHANGES 　STOCK MKT

JUL	AUG	SEP	OCT	NOV	DEC		YEAR
0.1 %	3.6 %	4.4 %	— 0.6 %	1.2 %	3.4 %	**1950**	17.6 %
6.3	4.8	0.3	— 3.2	— 0.4	3.0	**1951**	14.4
1.9	— 1.6	— 1.6	— 0.5	5.4	2.9	**1952**	8.4
2.6	— 5.2	1.1	4.5	2.0	— 0.2	**1953**	— 3.8
4.3	— 3.5	7.4	— 2.3	9.9	4.6	**1954**	44.0
3.2	0.5	— 0.3	— 2.5	6.2	1.1	**1955**	20.8
5.1	— 3.1	— 5.3	1.0	— 1.5	5.6	**1956**	2.3
1.0	— 4.7	— 5.8	— 3.4	2.0	— 3.2	**1957**	— 12.8
5.2	1.1	4.6	2.1	2.6	4.7	**1958**	34.0
4.9	— 1.6	— 4.9	2.4	1.9	3.1	**1959**	16.4
— 3.7	1.5	— 7.3	0.1	2.9	3.1	**1960**	— 9.3
3.1	2.1	— 2.6	0.4	2.5	1.3	**1961**	18.7
6.5	1.9	— 5.0	1.9	10.1	0.4	**1962**	— 10.8
— 1.6	4.9	0.5	3.1	— 0.6	1.7	**1963**	17.0
1.2	— 0.3	4.4	— 0.3	0.3	— 0.1	**1964**	14.6
1.6	1.3	4.2	3.2	— 1.5	2.4	**1965**	10.9
— 2.6	— 7.0	— 1.8	4.2	— 1.9	— 0.7	**1966**	— 18.9
5.1	— 0.3	2.8	— 5.1	— 0.4	3.3	**1967**	15.2
— 1.6	1.5	4.4	1.8	3.4	— 4.2	**1968**	4.3
— 6.6	2.6	— 2.8	5.3	— 5.1	— 1.5	**1969**	— 15.2
7.4	4.2	— 0.5	— 0.7	5.1	5.6	**1970**	4.8
— 3.7	4.6	— 1.2	— 5.4	— 0.9	7.1	**1971**	6.1
— 0.5	4.2	— 1.1	0.2	6.6	0.2	**1972**	14.6
3.9	— 4.2	6.7	1.0	— 14.0	3.5	**1973**	— 16.6
— 5.6	— 10.4	— 10.4	9.5	— 7.0	— 0.4	**1974**	— 27.6
— 5.4	0.5	— 5.0	5.3	3.0	— 1.0	**1975**	38.3
— 1.8	— 1.1	1.7	— 2.6	— 1.8	6.1	**1976**	17.9
— 2.9	— 3.2	— 1.7	— 3.4	1.4	0.2	**1977**	— 17.3
5.3	1.7	— 1.3	— 8.5	0.8	0.8	**1978**	— 3.2
0.5	4.9	— 1.0	— 7.2	0.8	2.0	**1979**	4.2
7.8	— 0.3	0.0	— 0.8	7.4	— 2.9	**1980**	14.9
— 2.5	— 7.4	— 3.6	0.3	4.3	— 1.6	**1981**	— 9.2
— 0.4	11.5	— 0.6	10.6	4.8	0.7	**1982**	19.6
— 1.9	1.4	1.4	— 0.6	4.1	— 1.4	**1983**	20.3
— 1.5	9.8	— 1.4	0.1	— 1.5	1.9	**1984**	3.7
0.9	— 1.0	— 0.4	3.4	7.1	5.1	**1985**	27.7
— 6.2	6.9	— 6.9	6.2	1.9	— 1.0	**1986**	22.6
6.4	3.5	— 2.5	— 23.2	— 8.0	5.7	**1987**	2.3
— 0.6	— 4.6	4.0	1.7	— 1.6	2.6	**1988**	11.9
9.0	2.9	— 1.6	— 1.8	2.3	1.7	**1989**	27.0
0.9	— 10.0	— 6.2	— 0.4	4.8	2.9	**1990**	— 4.3
4.1	0.6	— 0.9	1.7	— 5.7	9.5	**1991**	20.3
2.3	— 4.0	0.4	— 1.4	2.4	— 0.1	**1992**	4.2
0.7	3.2	— 2.6	3.5	0.1	1.9	**1993**	13.7
3.8	4.0	— 1.8	1.7	— 4.3	2.5	**1994**	2.1
3.3	— 2.1	3.9	— 0.7	6.7	0.8	**1995**	33.5
— 2.2	1.6	4.7	2.5	8.2	— 1.1	**1996**	26.0
7.2	— 7.3	4.2	— 6.3	5.1	1.1	**1997**	22.6
— 0.8	— 15.1	4.0	9.6	6.1	0.7	**1998**	16.1
— 2.9	1.6	— 4.5	3.8	1.4	5.3	**1999**	24.7
0.7	6.6	— 5.0	3.0	— 5.1	3.6	**2000**	— 5.8
0.2	— 5.4	— 11.1	2.6	8.6	1.7	**2001**	— 7.1
— 5.5	— 0.8	— 12.4	10.6	5.9	— 6.2	**2002**	— 16.8
2.8	2.0	— 1.5	5.7	— 0.2	6.9	**2003**	25.3
— 2.8	0.3	— 0.9	— 0.5	4.0	3.4	**2004**	3.1
3.6	— 1.5	0.8	— 1.2	3.5	— 0.8	**2005**	— 0.6
0.3	1.7	2.6	3.4	1.2	2.0	**2006**	16.3
— 1.5	1.1	4.0	0.2	— 4.0	— 0.8	**2007**	6.4
0.2	1.5	— 6.0	— 14.1	— 5.3	— 0.6	**2008**	— 33.8
8.6	3.5	2.3	0.0	6.5	0.8	**2009**	18.8
7.1	— 4.3	7.7	3.1	— 1.0	5.2	**2010**	11.0
— 2.2	— 4.4	— 6.0	9.5	0.8	1.4	**2011**	5.5
1.0	0.6	2.6	— 2.5	— 0.5	0.6	**2012**	7.3
4.0	— 4.4	2.2	2.8	3.5	3.0	**2013**	26.5
— 1.6	3.2	— 0.3	2.0	2.5	0.0	**2014**	7.5
0.4	— 6.6	— 1.5	8.5	0.3	— 2.2	**2015**	— 2.2
2.8	— 0.2	— 0.5	— 0.9	5.4	3.3	**2016**	13.4
2.5	0.3	2.1	4.3	3.8	1.8	**2017**	25.1
43/68	38/68	27/68	41/68	47/68	48/68		49/68
63 %	56 %	40 %	60 %	69 %	71 %		72 %
1.2 %	— 0.1 %	— 0.7 %	0.7 %	1.6 %	1.7 %		8.3 %
4	10	12	7	3	2		

DOW JONES
MONTH CLOSING VALUES

	JAN	FEB	MAR	APR	MAY	JUN
1950	202	203	206	214	223	209
1951	249	252	248	259	250	243
1952	271	260	270	258	263	274
1953	290	284	280	275	272	268
1954	292	295	304	319	328	334
1955	409	412	410	426	425	451
1956	471	484	512	516	478	493
1957	479	465	475	494	505	503
1958	450	440	447	456	463	478
1959	594	604	602	624	644	644
1960	623	630	617	602	626	641
1961	648	662	677	679	697	684
1962	700	708	707	665	613	561
1963	683	663	683	718	727	707
1964	785	800	813	811	821	832
1965	903	904	889	922	918	868
1966	984	952	925	934	884	870
1967	850	839	866	897	853	860
1968	856	841	841	912	899	898
1969	946	905	936	950	938	873
1970	744	778	786	736	700	684
1971	869	879	904	942	908	891
1972	902	928	941	954	961	929
1973	999	955	951	921	901	892
1974	856	861	847	837	802	802
1975	704	739	768	821	832	879
1976	975	973	1000	997	975	1003
1977	954	936	919	927	899	916
1978	770	742	757	837	841	819
1979	839	809	862	855	822	842
1980	876	863	786	817	851	868
1981	947	975	1004	998	992	977
1982	871	824	823	848	820	812
1983	1076	1113	1130	1226	1200	1222
1984	1221	1155	1165	1171	1105	1132
1985	1287	1284	1267	1258	1315	1336
1986	1571	1709	1819	1784	1877	1893
1987	2158	2224	2305	2286	2292	2419
1988	1958	2072	1988	2032	2031	2142
1989	2342	2258	2294	2419	2480	2440
1990	2591	2627	2707	2657	2877	2881
1991	2736	2882	2914	2888	3028	2907
1992	3223	3268	3236	3359	3397	3319
1993	3310	3371	3435	3428	3527	3516
1994	3978	3832	3636	3682	3758	3625
1995	3844	4011	4158	4321	4465	4556
1996	5395	5486	5587	5569	5643	5655
1997	6813	6878	6584	7009	7331	7673
1998	7907	8546	8800	9063	8900	8952
1999	9359	9307	9786	10789	10560	10971
2000	10941	10128	10922	10734	10522	10448
2001	10887	10495	9879	10735	10912	10502
2002	9920	10106	10404	9946	9925	9243
2003	8054	7891	7992	8480	8850	8985
2004	10488	10584	10358	10226	10188	10435
2005	10490	10766	10504	10193	10467	10275
2006	10865	10993	11109	11367	11168	11150
2007	12622	12269	12354	13063	13628	13409
2008	12650	12266	12263	12820	12638	11350
2009	8001	7063	7609	8168	8500	8447
2010	10067	10325	10857	11009	10137	9774
2011	11892	12226	12320	12811	12570	12414
2012	12633	12952	13212	13214	12393	12880
2013	13861	14054	14579	14840	15116	14910
2014	15699	16322	16458	16581	16717	16827
2015	17165	18133	17776	17841	18011	17620
2016	16466	16517	17685	17774	17787	17930
2017	19864	20812	20663	20941	21009	21350

DOW JONES
MONTH CLOSING VALUES

STOCK MKT

JUL	AUG	SEP	OCT	NOV	DEC	
209	217	226	225	228	235	**1950**
258	270	271	262	261	269	**1951**
280	275	271	269	284	292	**1952**
275	261	264	276	281	281	**1953**
348	336	361	352	387	404	**1954**
466	468	467	455	483	488	**1955**
518	502	475	480	473	500	**1956**
509	484	456	441	450	436	**1957**
503	509	532	543	558	584	**1958**
675	664	632	647	659	679	**1959**
617	626	580	580	597	616	**1960**
705	720	701	704	722	731	**1961**
598	609	579	590	649	652	**1962**
695	729	733	755	751	763	**1963**
841	839	875	873	875	874	**1964**
882	893	931	961	947	969	**1965**
847	788	774	807	792	786	**1966**
904	901	927	880	876	905	**1967**
883	896	936	952	985	944	**1968**
816	837	813	856	812	800	**1969**
734	765	761	756	794	839	**1970**
858	898	887	839	831	890	**1971**
925	964	953	956	1018	1020	**1972**
926	888	947	957	822	851	**1973**
757	679	608	666	619	616	**1974**
832	835	794	836	861	852	**1975**
985	974	990	965	947	1005	**1976**
890	862	847	818	830	831	**1977**
862	877	866	793	799	805	**1978**
846	888	879	816	822	839	**1979**
935	933	932	925	993	964	**1980**
952	882	850	853	889	875	**1981**
809	901	896	992	1039	1047	**1982**
1199	1216	1233	1225	1276	1259	**1983**
1115	1224	1207	1207	1189	1212	**1984**
1348	1334	1329	1374	1472	1547	**1985**
1775	1898	1768	1878	1914	1896	**1986**
2572	2663	2596	1994	1834	1939	**1987**
2129	2032	2113	2149	2115	2169	**1988**
2661	2737	2693	2645	2706	2753	**1989**
2905	2614	2453	2442	2560	2634	**1990**
3025	3044	3017	3069	2895	3169	**1991**
3394	3257	3272	3226	3305	3301	**1992**
3540	3651	3555	3681	3684	3754	**1993**
3765	3913	3843	3908	3739	3834	**1994**
4709	4611	4789	4756	5075	5117	**1995**
5529	5616	5882	6029	6522	6448	**1996**
8223	7622	7945	7442	7823	7908	**1997**
8883	7539	7843	8592	9117	9181	**1998**
10655	10829	10337	10730	10878	11453	**1999**
10522	11215	10651	10971	10415	10788	**2000**
10523	9950	8848	9075	9852	10022	**2001**
8737	8664	7592	8397	8896	8342	**2002**
9234	9416	9275	9801	9782	10454	**2003**
10140	10174	10080	10027	10428	10783	**2004**
10641	10482	10569	10440	10806	10718	**2005**
11186	11381	11679	12801	12222	12463	**2006**
13212	13358	13896	13930	13372	13265	**2007**
11378	11544	10851	9325	8829	8776	**2008**
9172	9496	9712	9713	10345	10428	**2009**
10466	10015	10788	11118	11006	11578	**2010**
12143	11614	10913	11955	12046	12218	**2011**
13009	13091	13437	13096	13026	13104	**2012**
15500	14810	15130	15546	16086	16577	**2013**
16563	17098	17043	17391	17828	17823	**2014**
17690	16528	16285	17664	17720	17425	**2015**
18432	18401	18308	18142	19124	19763	**2016**
21891	21948	22405	23377	24272	24719	**2017**

NASDAQ PERCENT MONTH CHANGES

	JAN	FEB	MAR	APR	MAY	JUN
1972	4.2	5.5	2.2	2.5	0.9	− 1.8
1973	− 4.0	− 6.2	− 2.4	− 8.2	− 4.8	− 1.6
1974	3.0	− 0.6	− 2.2	− 5.9	− 7.7	− 5.3
1975	16.6	4.6	3.6	3.8	5.8	4.7
1976	12.1	3.7	0.4	− 0.6	− 2.3	2.6
1977	− 2.4	− 1.0	− 0.5	1.4	0.1	4.3
1978	− 4.0	0.6	4.7	8.5	4.4	0.0
1979	6.6	− 2.6	7.5	1.6	− 1.8	5.1
1980	7.0	− 2.3	−17.1	6.9	7.5	4.9
1981	− 2.2	0.1	6.1	3.1	3.1	− 3.5
1982	− 3.8	− 4.8	− 2.1	5.2	− 3.3	− 4.1
1983	6.9	5.0	3.9	8.2	5.3	3.2
1984	− 3.7	− 5.9	− 0.7	− 1.3	− 5.9	2.9
1985	12.8	2.0	− 1.8	0.5	3.6	1.9
1986	3.4	7.1	4.2	2.3	4.4	1.3
1987	12.4	8.4	1.2	− 2.9	− 0.3	2.0
1988	4.3	6.5	2.1	1.2	− 2.3	6.6
1989	5.2	− 0.4	1.8	5.1	4.3	− 2.4
1990	− 8.6	2.4	2.3	− 3.5	9.3	0.7
1991	10.8	9.4	6.4	0.5	4.4	− 6.0
1992	5.8	2.1	− 4.7	− 4.2	1.1	− 3.7
1993	2.9	− 3.7	2.9	− 4.2	5.9	0.5
1994	3.0	− 1.0	− 6.2	− 1.3	0.2	− 4.0
1995	0.4	5.1	3.0	3.3	2.4	8.0
1996	0.7	3.8	0.1	8.1	4.4	− 4.7
1997	6.9	− 5.1	− 6.7	3.2	11.1	3.0
1998	3.1	9.3	3.7	1.8	− 4.8	6.5
1999	14.3	− 8.7	7.6	3.3	− 2.8	8.7
2000	− 3.2	19.2	− 2.6	−15.6	−11.9	16.6
2001	12.2	−22.4	−14.5	15.0	− 0.3	2.4
2002	− 0.8	−10.5	6.6	− 8.5	− 4.3	− 9.4
2003	− 1.1	1.3	0.3	9.2	9.0	1.7
2004	3.1	− 1.8	− 1.8	− 3.7	3.5	3.1
2005	− 5.2	− 0.5	− 2.6	− 3.9	7.6	− 0.5
2006	4.6	− 1.1	2.6	− 0.7	− 6.2	− 0.3
2007	2.0	− 1.9	0.2	4.3	3.1	0.0
2008	− 9.9	− 5.0	0.3	5.9	4.6	− 9.1
2009	− 6.4	− 6.7	10.9	12.3	3.3	3.4
2010	− 5.4	4.2	7.1	2.6	− 8.3	− 6.5
2011	1.8	3.0	0.0	3.3	− 1.3	− 2.2
2012	8.0	5.4	4.2	− 1.5	− 7.2	3.8
2013	4.1	0.6	3.4	1.9	3.8	− 1.5
2014	− 1.7	5.0	− 2.5	− 2.0	3.1	3.9
2015	− 2.1	7.1	− 1.3	0.8	2.6	− 1.6
2016	− 7.9	− 1.2	6.8	− 1.9	3.6	− 2.1
2017	4.3	3.8	1.5	2.3	2.5	− 0.9
FQ POS	29/46	25/46	29/46	29/46	29/46	25/46
% FQ POS	63 %	54 %	63 %	63 %	63 %	54 %
AVG GAIN	2.4 %	0.7 %	0.8 %	1.3 %	1.1 %	0.7 %
RANK GAIN	1	8	7	4	5	9

NASDAQ PERCENT MONTH CHANGES

STOCK MKT

JUL	AUG	SEP	OCT	NOV	DEC		YEAR
— 1.8	1.7	— 0.3	0.5	2.1	0.6	**1972**	17.2
7.6	— 3.5	6.0	— 0.9	— 15.1	— 1.4	**1973**	— 31.1
— 7.9	— 10.9	— 10.7	17.2	— 3.5	— 5.0	**1974**	— 35.1
— 4.4	— 5.0	— 5.9	3.6	2.4	— 1.5	**1975**	29.8
1.1	— 1.7	1.7	— 1.0	0.9	7.4	**1976**	26.1
0.9	— 0.5	0.7	— 3.3	5.8	1.8	**1977**	7.3
5.0	6.9	— 1.6	— 16.4	3.2	2.9	**1978**	12.3
2.3	6.4	— 0.3	— 9.6	6.4	4.8	**1979**	28.1
8.9	5.7	3.4	2.7	8.0	— 2.8	**1980**	33.9
— 1.9	— 7.5	— 8.0	8.4	3.1	— 2.7	**1981**	— 3.2
— 2.3	6.2	5.6	13.3	9.3	0.0	**1982**	18.7
— 4.6	— 3.8	1.4	— 7.4	4.1	— 2.5	**1983**	19.9
— 4.2	10.9	— 1.8	— 1.2	— 1.9	1.9	**1984**	— 11.3
1.7	— 1.2	— 5.8	4.4	7.4	3.5	**1985**	31.5
— 8.4	3.1	— 8.4	2.9	— 0.3	— 3.0	**1986**	7.4
2.4	4.6	— 2.4	— 27.2	— 5.6	8.3	**1987**	— 5.2
— 1.9	— 2.8	2.9	— 1.3	— 2.9	2.7	**1988**	15.4
4.2	3.4	0.8	— 3.7	0.1	— 0.3	**1989**	19.2
— 5.2	— 13.0	— 9.6	— 4.3	8.9	4.1	**1990**	— 17.8
5.5	4.7	0.2	3.1	— 3.5	11.9	**1991**	56.9
3.1	— 3.0	3.6	3.8	7.9	3.7	**1992**	15.5
0.1	5.4	2.7	2.2	— 3.2	3.0	**1993**	14.7
2.3	6.0	— 0.2	1.7	— 3.5	0.2	**1994**	— 3.2
7.3	1.9	2.3	— 0.7	2.2	— 0.7	**1995**	39.9
— 8.8	5.6	7.5	— 0.4	5.8	— 0.1	**1996**	22.7
10.5	— 0.4	6.2	— 5.5	0.4	— 1.9	**1997**	21.6
— 1.2	— 19.9	13.0	4.6	10.1	12.5	**1998**	39.6
— 1.8	3.8	0.2	8.0	12.5	22.0	**1999**	85.6
— 5.0	11.7	— 12.7	— 8.3	— 22.9	— 4.9	**2000**	— 39.3
— 6.2	— 10.9	— 17.0	12.8	14.2	1.0	**2001**	— 21.1
— 9.2	— 1.0	— 10.9	13.5	11.2	— 9.7	**2002**	— 31.5
6.9	4.3	— 1.3	8.1	1.5	2.2	**2003**	50.0
— 7.8	— 2.6	3.2	4.1	6.2	3.7	**2004**	8.6
6.2	— 1.5	0.0	— 1.5	5.3	— 1.2	**2005**	1.4
— 3.7	4.4	3.4	4.8	2.7	— 0.7	**2006**	9.5
— 2.2	2.0	4.0	5.8	— 6.9	— 0.3	**2007**	9.8
1.4	1.8	— 11.6	— 17.7	— 10.8	2.7	**2008**	— 40.5
7.8	1.5	5.6	— 3.6	4.9	5.8	**2009**	43.9
6.9	— 6.2	12.0	5.9	— 0.4	6.2	**2010**	16.9
— 0.6	— 6.4	— 6.4	11.1	— 2.4	— 0.6	**2011**	— 1.8
0.2	4.3	1.6	— 4.5	1.1	0.3	**2012**	15.9
6.6	— 1.0	5.1	3.9	3.6	2.9	**2013**	38.3
— 0.9	4.8	— 1.9	3.1	3.5	— 1.2	**2014**	13.4
2.8	— 6.9	— 3.3	9.4	1.1	— 2.0	**2015**	5.7
6.6	1.0	1.9	— 2.3	2.6	1.1	**2016**	7.5
3.4	1.3	1.0	3.6	2.2	0.4	**2017**	28.2
25/46	25/46	25/46	26/46	32/46	27/46		34/46
54 %	54 %	54 %	57 %	70 %	59 %		74 %
0.5 %	0.1 %	— 0.5 %	0.9 %	1.7 %	1.6 %		12.4 %
10	11	12	6	2	3		

NASDAQ MONTH
CLOSING VALUES

	JAN	FEB	MAR	APR	MAY	JUN
1972	119	125	128	131	133	130
1973	128	120	117	108	103	101
1974	95	94	92	87	80	76
1975	70	73	76	79	83	87
1976	87	90	91	90	88	90
1977	96	95	94	95	96	100
1978	101	101	106	115	120	120
1979	126	123	132	134	131	138
1980	162	158	131	140	150	158
1981	198	198	210	217	223	216
1982	188	179	176	185	179	171
1983	248	261	271	293	309	319
1984	268	253	251	247	233	240
1985	279	284	279	281	291	296
1986	336	360	375	383	400	406
1987	392	425	430	418	417	425
1988	345	367	375	379	370	395
1989	401	400	407	428	446	435
1990	416	426	436	420	459	462
1991	414	453	482	485	506	476
1992	620	633	604	579	585	564
1993	696	671	690	661	701	704
1994	800	793	743	734	735	706
1995	755	794	817	844	865	933
1996	1060	1100	1101	1191	1243	1185
1997	1380	1309	1222	1261	1400	1442
1998	1619	1771	1836	1868	1779	1895
1999	2506	2288	2461	2543	2471	2686
2000	3940	4697	4573	3861	3401	3966
2001	2773	2152	1840	2116	2110	2161
2002	1934	1731	1845	1688	1616	1463
2003	1321	1338	1341	1464	1596	1623
2004	2066	2030	1994	1920	1987	2048
2005	2062	2052	1999	1922	2068	2057
2006	2306	2281	2340	2323	2179	2172
2007	2464	2416	2422	2525	2605	2603
2008	2390	2271	2279	2413	2523	2293
2009	1476	1378	1529	1717	1774	1835
2010	2147	2238	2398	2461	2257	2109
2011	2700	2782	2781	2874	2835	2774
2012	2814	2967	3092	3046	2827	2935
2013	3142	3160	3268	3329	3456	3403
2014	4104	4308	4199	4115	4243	4408
2015	4635	4964	4901	4941	5070	4987
2016	4614	4558	4870	4775	4948	4843
2017	5615	5825	5912	6048	6199	6140

NASDAQ MONTH CLOSING VALUES 🇺🇸 STOCK MKT

JUL	AUG	SEP	OCT	NOV	DEC	
128	130	130	130	133	134	**1972**
109	105	111	110	94	92	**1973**
70	62	56	65	63	60	**1974**
83	79	74	77	79	78	**1975**
91	90	91	90	91	98	**1976**
101	100	101	98	103	105	**1977**
126	135	133	111	115	118	**1978**
141	150	150	136	144	151	**1979**
172	182	188	193	208	202	**1980**
212	196	180	195	201	196	**1981**
167	178	188	213	232	232	**1982**
304	292	297	275	286	279	**1983**
230	255	250	247	242	247	**1984**
301	298	280	293	314	325	**1985**
371	383	351	361	360	349	**1986**
435	455	444	323	305	331	**1987**
387	377	388	383	372	381	**1988**
454	469	473	456	456	455	**1989**
438	381	345	330	359	374	**1990**
502	526	527	543	524	586	**1991**
581	563	583	605	653	677	**1992**
705	743	763	779	754	777	**1993**
722	766	764	777	750	752	**1994**
1001	1020	1044	1036	1059	1052	**1995**
1081	1142	1227	1222	1293	1291	**1996**
1594	1587	1686	1594	1601	1570	**1997**
1872	1499	1694	1771	1950	2193	**1998**
2638	2739	2746	2966	3336	4069	**1999**
3767	4206	3673	3370	2598	2471	**2000**
2027	1805	1499	1690	1931	1950	**2001**
1328	1315	1172	1330	1479	1336	**2002**
1735	1810	1787	1932	1960	2003	**2003**
1887	1838	1897	1975	2097	2175	**2004**
2185	2152	2152	2120	2233	2205	**2005**
2091	2184	2258	2367	2432	2415	**2006**
2546	2596	2702	2859	2661	2652	**2007**
2326	2368	2092	1721	1536	1577	**2008**
1979	2009	2122	2045	2145	2269	**2009**
2255	2114	2369	2507	2498	2653	**2010**
2756	2579	2415	2684	2620	2605	**2011**
2940	3067	3116	2977	3010	3020	**2012**
3626	3590	3771	3920	4060	4177	**2013**
4370	4580	4493	4631	4792	4736	**2014**
5128	4777	4620	5054	5109	5007	**2015**
5162	5213	5312	5189	5324	5383	**2016**
6348	6429	6496	6728	6874	6903	**2017**

S&P/TSX MONTH PERCENT CHANGES

	JAN	FEB	MAR	APR	MAY	JUN
1985	8.1	0.0	0.7	0.8	3.8	— 0.8
1986	— 1.7	0.5	6.7	1.1	1.4	— 1.2
1987	9.2	4.5	6.9	— 0.6	— 0.9	1.5
1988	— 3.3	4.8	3.4	0.8	— 2.7	5.9
1989	6.7	— 1.2	0.2	1.4	2.2	1.5
1990	— 6.7	— 0.5	— 1.3	— 8.2	6.7	— 0.6
1991	0.5	5.8	1.0	-0.8	2.2	— 2.3
1992	2.4	— 0.4	— 4.7	— 1.7	1.0	0.0
1993	— 1.3	4.4	4.4	5.2	2.5	2.2
1994	5.4	— 2.9	— 2.1	— 1.4	1.4	— 7.0
1995	— 4.7	2.7	4.6	— -0.8	4.0	1.8
1996	5.4	— 0.7	0.8	3.5	1.9	— 3.9
1997	3.1	0.8	— 5.0	2.2	6.8	0.9
1998	0.0	5.9	6.6	1.4	— 1.0	— 2.9
1999	3.8	— 6.2	4.5	6.3	— 2.5	2.5
2000	0.8	7.6	3.7	— 1.2	— 1.0	10.2
2001	4.3	— 13.3	— 5.8	4.5	2.7	— 5.2
2002	— 0.5	— 0.1	2.8	— 2.4	— 0.1	— 6.7
2003	— 0.7	— 0.2	— 3.2	3.8	4.2	1.8
2004	3.7	3.1	— 2.3	— 4.0	2.1	1.5
2005	— 0.5	5.0	— 0.6	— 3.5	3.6	3.1
2006	6.0	— 2.2	3.6	0.8	— 3.8	— 1.1
2007	1.0	0.1	0.9	1.9	4.8	— 1.1
2008	— 4.9	3.3	— 1.7	4.4	5.6	— 1.7
2009	— 3.3	— 6.6	7.4	6.9	11.2	0.0
2010	— 5.5	4.8	3.5	1.4	— 3.7	— 4.0
2011	0.8	4.3	— 0.1	— 1.2	— 1.0	— 3.6
2012	4.2	1.5	— 2.0	— 0.8	— 6.3	0.7
2013	2.0	1.1	— 0.6	— 2.3	1.6	— 4.1
2014	0.5	3.8	0.9	2.2	— 0.3	3.7
2015	0.3	3.8	— 2.2	2.2	— 1.4	— 3.1
2016	— 1.4	0.3	4.9	3.4	0.8	0.0
2017	0.6	0.1	1.0	0.2	— 1.5	— 1.1
FQ POS	21/33	21/33	20/33	20/33	20/33	14/33
% FQ POS	64 %	64 %	61 %	61 %	61 %	42 %
AVG GAIN	1.0 %	1.0 %	1.1 %	0.8 %	1.3 %	-0.4 %
RANK GAIN	4	5	3	7	2	11

S&P/TSX MONTH PERCENT CHANGES

STOCK MKT

JUL	AUG	SEP	OCT	NOV	DEC		YEAR
2.4	1.5	— 6.7	1.6	6.8	1.3	**1985**	20.5
— 4.9	3.2	— 1.6	1.6	0.7	0.6	**1986**	6.0
7.8	— 0.9	— 2.3	— 22.6	— 1.4	6.1	**1987**	3.1
— 1.9	— 2.7	— 0.1	3.4	— 3.0	2.9	**1988**	7.3
5.6	1.0	— 1.7	— 0.6	0.6	0.7	**1989**	17.1
0.5	— 6.0	— 5.6	— 2.5	2.3	3.4	**1990**	— 18.0
2.1	— 0.6	— 3.7	3.8	— 1.9	1.9	**1991**	7.8
1.6	— 1.2	— 3.1	1.2	— 1.6	2.1	**1992**	— 4.6
0.0	4.3	— 3.6	6.6	— 1.8	3.4	**1993**	29.0
3.8	4.1	0.1	— 1.4	— 4.6	2.9	**1994**	— 2.5
1.9	— 2.1	0.3	— 1.6	4.5	1.1	**1995**	11.9
— 2.3	4.3	2.9	5.8	7.5	— 1.5	**1996**	25.7
6.8	— 3.9	6.5	— 2.8	— 4.8	2.9	**1997**	13.0
— 5.9	— 20.2	1.5	10.6	2.2	2.2	**1998**	— 3.2
1.0	— 1.6	— 0.2	4.3	3.6	11.9	**1999**	29.7
2.1	8.1	— 7.7	— 7.1	— 8.5	1.3	**2000**	6.2
— 0.6	— 3.8	— 7.6	0.7	7.8	3.5	**2001**	— 13.9
— 7.6	0.1	— 6.5	1.1	5.1	0.7	**2002**	— 14.0
3.9	3.6	— 1.3	4.7	1.1	4.6	**2003**	24.3
— 1.0	— 1.0	3.5	2.3	1.8	2.4	**2004**	12.5
5.3	2.4	3.2	— 5.7	4.2	4.1	**2005**	21.9
1.9	2.1	— 2.6	5.0	3.3	1.2	**2006**	14.5
— 0.3	— 1.5	3.2	3.7	— 6.4	1.1	**2007**	7.2
— 6.0	1.3	— 14.7	— 16.9	— 5.0	— 3.1	**2008**	— 35.0
4.0	0.8	4.8	— 4.2	4.9	2.6	**2009**	30.7
3.7	1.7	3.8	2.5	2.2	3.8	**2010**	14.4
— 2.7	— 1.4	— 9.0	5.4	— 0.4	— 2.0	**2011**	— 11.1
0.6	2.4	3.1	0.9	— 1.5	1.6	**2012**	4.0
2.9	1.3	1.1	4.5	0.3	1.7	**2013**	9.6
1.2	1.9	— 4.3	— 2.3	0.9	— 0.8	**2014**	7.4
— 0.6	— 4.2	— 4.0	1.7	— 0.4	— 3.4	**2015**	— 11.1
3.7	0.1	0.9	0.4	2.0	1.4	**2016**	17.5
— 0.3	0.4	2.8	2.5	0.3	0.9	**2017**	6.0
21/33	19/33	14/33	22/33	20/33	28/33		24/33
64 %	58 %	42 %	67 %	61 %	85 %		73 %
0.9 %	— 0.2 %	— 1.5 %	0.2 %	0.6 %	1.9 %		7.1 %
6	10	12	9	8	1		

S&P/TSX MONTH CLOSING VALUES

	JAN	FEB	MAR	APR	MAY	JUN
1985	2595	2595	2613	2635	2736	2713
1986	2843	2856	3047	3079	3122	3086
1987	3349	3499	3739	3717	3685	3740
1988	3057	3205	3314	3340	3249	3441
1989	3617	3572	3578	3628	3707	3761
1990	3704	3687	3640	3341	3565	3544
1991	3273	3462	3496	3469	3546	3466
1992	3596	3582	3412	3356	3388	3388
1993	3305	3452	3602	3789	3883	3966
1994	4555	4424	4330	4267	4327	4025
1995	4018	4125	4314	4280	4449	4527
1996	4968	4934	4971	5147	5246	5044
1997	6110	6158	5850	5977	6382	6438
1998	6700	7093	7559	7665	7590	7367
1999	6730	6313	6598	7015	6842	7010
2000	8481	9129	9462	9348	9252	10196
2001	9322	8079	7608	7947	8162	7736
2002	7649	7638	7852	7663	7656	7146
2003	6570	6555	6343	6586	6860	6983
2004	8521	8789	8586	8244	8417	8546
2005	9204	9668	9612	9275	9607	9903
2006	11946	11688	12111	12204	11745	11613
2007	13034	13045	13166	13417	14057	13907
2008	13155	13583	13350	13937	14715	14467
2009	8695	8123	8720	9325	10370	10375
2010	11094	11630	12038	12211	11763	11294
2011	13552	14137	14116	13945	13803	13301
2012	12452	12644	12392	12293	11513	11597
2013	12685	12822	12750	12457	12650	12129
2014	13695	14210	14335	14652	14604	15146
2015	14674	15234	14902	15225	15014	14553
2016	12822	12860	13494	13951	14066	14065
2017	15386	15399	15548	15586	15350	15182

S&P/TSX PERCENT CLOSING VALUES 🍁 STOCK MKT

JUL	AUG	SEP	OCT	NOV	DEC	
2779	2820	2632	2675	2857	2893	**1985**
2935	3028	2979	3027	3047	3066	**1986**
4030	3994	3902	3019	2978	3160	**1987**
3377	3286	3284	3396	3295	3390	**1988**
3971	4010	3943	3919	3943	3970	**1989**
3561	3346	3159	3081	3151	3257	**1990**
3540	3518	3388	3516	3449	3512	**1991**
3443	3403	3298	3336	3283	3350	**1992**
3967	4138	3991	4256	4180	4321	**1993**
4179	4350	4354	4292	4093	4214	**1994**
4615	4517	4530	4459	4661	4714	**1995**
4929	5143	5291	5599	6017	5927	**1996**
6878	6612	7040	6842	6513	6699	**1997**
6931	5531	5614	6208	6344	6486	**1998**
7081	6971	6958	7256	7520	8414	**1999**
10406	11248	10378	9640	8820	8934	**2000**
7690	7399	6839	6886	7426	7688	**2001**
6605	6612	6180	6249	6570	6615	**2002**
7258	7517	7421	7773	7859	8221	**2003**
8458	8377	8668	8871	9030	9247	**2004**
10423	10669	11012	10383	10824	11272	**2005**
11831	12074	11761	12345	12752	12908	**2006**
13869	13660	14099	14625	13689	13833	**2007**
13593	13771	11753	9763	9271	8988	**2008**
10787	10868	11935	10911	11447	11746	**2009**
11713	11914	12369	12676	12953	13443	**2010**
12946	12769	11624	12252	12204	11955	**2011**
11665	11949	12317	12423	12239	12434	**2012**
12487	12654	12787	13361	13395	13622	**2013**
15331	15626	14961	14613	14745	14632	**2014**
14468	13859	13307	13529	13470	13010	**2015**
14583	14598	14726	14787	15083	15288	**2016**
15144	15212	15635	16026	16067	16209	**2017**

S&P 500 1950 - 2017
BEST - WORST

10 BEST

YEARS

	Close	Change	Change
1954	36	11 pt	45.0 %
1958	55	15	38.1
1995	616	157	34.1
1975	90	22	31.5
1997	970	230	31.0
2013	1848	422	29.6
1989	353	76	27.3
1998	1229	259	26.7
1955	45	10	26.4
2003	1112	232	26.4

MONTHS

	Close	Change	Change
Oct 1974	74	10 pt	16.3 %
Aug 1982	120	12	11.6
Dec 1991	417	42	11.2
Oct 1982	134	13	11.0
Oct 2011	1253	122	10.8
Aug 1984	167	16	10.6
Nov 1980	141	13	10.2
Nov 1962	62	6	10.2
Mar 2000	1499	132	9.7
Apr 2009	798	75	9.4

DAYS

		Close	Change	Change
Mon	2008 Oct 13	1003	104 pt	11.6 %
Tue	2008 Oct 28	941	92	10.8
Wed	1987 Oct 21	258	22	9.1
Mon	2009 Mar 23	883	54	7.1
Thu	2008 Nov 13	911	59	6.9
Mon	2008 Nov 24	852	52	6.5
Tues	2009 Mar 10	720	43	6.4
Fri	2008 Nov 21	800	48	6.3
Wed	2002 Jul 24	843	46	5.7
Tue	2008 Sep 30	1166	60	5.4

10 WORST

YEARS

	Close	Change	Change
2008	903	− 566 pt	− 38.5 %
1974	69	− 29	− 29.7
2002	880	− 268	− 23.4
1973	98	− 21	− 17.4
1957	40	− 7	− 14.3
1966	80	− 12	− 13.1
2001	1148	− 172	− 13.0
1962	63	− 8	− 11.8
1977	95	− 12	− 11.5
1969	92	− 12	− 11.4

MONTHS

	Close	Change	Change
Oct 1987	252	− 70 pt	− 21.8 %
Oct 2008	969	− 196	− 16.8
Aug 1998	957	− 163	− 14.6
Sep 1974	64	− 9	− 11.9
Nov 1973	96	− 12	− 11.4
Sep 2002	815	− 101	− 11.0
Feb 2009	735	− 91	− 11.0
Mar 1980	102	− 12	− 10.2
Aug 1990	323	− 34	− 9.4
Feb 2001	1240	− 126	− 9.2

DAYS

		Close	Change	Change
Mon	1987 Oct 19	225	− 58 pt	− 20.5 %
Wed	2008 Oct 15	908	− 90	− 9.0
Mon	2008 Dec 01	816	− 80	− 8.9
Mon	2008 Sep 29	1106	− 107	− 8.8
Mon	1987 Oct 26	228	− 21	− 8.3
Thu	2008 Oct 09	910	− 75	− 7.6
Mon	1997 Oct 27	877	− 65	− 6.9
Mon	1998 Aug 31	957	− 70	− 6.8
Fri	1988 Jan 8	243	− 18	− 6.8
Thu	2008 Nov 20	752	− 54	− 6.7

10 BEST

10 WORST

YEARS

	Close	Change	Change
1954	404	124 pt	44.0 %
1975	852	236	38.3
1958	584	148	34.0
1995	5117	1283	33.5
1985	1547	335	27.7
1989	2753	585	27.0
2013	16577	3473	26.5
1996	6448	1331	26.0
2003	10454	2112	25.3
1999	11453	2272	25.2

YEARS

	Close	Change	Change
2008	8776	− 4488 pt	− 33.8 %
1974	616	− 235	− 27.6
1966	786	− 184	− 18.9
1977	831	− 174	− 17.3
2002	8342	− 1680	− 16.8
1973	851	− 169	− 16.6
1969	800	− 143	− 15.2
1957	436	− 64	− 12.8
1962	652	− 79	− 10.8
1960	616	− 64	− 9.3

MONTHS

	Close	Change	Change
Aug 1982	901	93 pt	11.5 %
Oct 1982	992	95	10.6
Oct 2002	8397	805	10.6
Apr 1978	837	80	10.5
Apr 1999	10789	1003	10.2
Nov 1962	649	60	10.1
Nov 1954	387	35	9.9
Aug 1984	1224	109	9.8
Oct 1998	8592	750	9.6
Oct 2011	11955	1042	9.5

MONTHS

	Close	Change	Change
Oct 1987	1994	− 603 pt	− 23.2 %
Aug 1998	7539	− 1344	− 15.1
Oct 2008	9325	− 1526	− 14.1
Nov 1973	822	− 134	− 14.0
Sep 2002	7592	− 1072	− 12.4
Feb 2009	7063	− 938	− 11.7
Sep 2001	8848	− 1102	− 11.1
Sep 1974	608	− 71	− 10.4
Aug 1974	679	− 79	− 10.4
Jun 2008	11350	− 1288	− 10.2

DAYS

		Close	Change	Change
Mon	2008 Oct 13	9388	936 pt	11.1 %
Tue	2008 Oct 28	9065	889	10.9
Wed	1987 Oct 21	2028	187	10.2
Mon	2009 Mar 23	7776	497	6.8
Thu	2008 Nov 13	8835	553	6.7
Fri	2008 Nov 21	8046	494	6.5
Wed	2002 Jul 24	8191	489	6.3
Tue	1987 Oct 20	1841	102	5.9
Tue	2009 Mar 10	6926	379	5.8
Mon	2002 Jul 29	8712	448	5.4

DAYS

		Close	Change	Change
Mon	1987 Oct 19	1739	− 508 pt	− 22.6 %
Mon	1987 Oct 26	1794	− 157	− 8.0
Wed	2008 Oct 15	8578	− 733	− 7.9
Mon	2008 Dec 01	8149	− 680	− 7.7
Thu	2008 Oct 09	8579	− 679	− 7.3
Mon	1997 Oct 27	8366	− 554	− 7.2
Mon	2001 Sep 17	8921	− 685	− 7.1
Mon	2008 Sep 29	10365	− 778	− 7.0
Fri	1989 Oct 13	2569	− 191	− 6.9
Fri	1988 Jan 8	1911	− 141	− 6.9

10 BEST

10 WORST

YEARS

	Close	Change	Change
1999	4069	1877 pt	85.6 %
1991	586	213	56.9
2003	2003	668	50.0
2009	2269	692	43.9
1995	1052	300	39.9
1998	2193	622	39.6
2013	4161	1157	38.3
1980	202	51	33.9
1985	325	78	31.5
1975	78	18	29.8

YEARS

	Close	Change	Change
2008	1577	– 1075 pt	– 40.5 %
2000	2471	– 1599	– 39.3
1974	60	– 32	– 35.1
2002	1336	– 615	– 31.5
1973	92	– 42	– 31.1
2001	1950	– 520	– 21.1
1990	374	– 81	– 17.8
1984	247	– 32	– 11.3
1987	331	– 18	– 5.2
1981	196	– 7	– 3.2

MONTHS

	Close	Change	Change
Dec 1999	4069	733 pt	22.0 %
Feb 2000	4697	756	19.2
Oct 1974	65	10	17.2
Jun 2000	3966	565	16.6
Apr 2001	2116	276	15.0
Nov 2001	1931	240	14.2
Oct 2002	1330	158	13.5
Oct 1982	1771	25	13.3
Sep 1998	1694	195	13.0
Oct 2001	1690	191	12.8

MONTHS

	Close	Change	Change
Oct 1987	323	– 121 pt	– 27.2 %
Nov 2000	2598	– 772	– 22.9
Feb 2001	2152	– 621	– 22.4
Aug 1998	1499	– 373	– 19.9
Oct 2008	1721	– 371	– 17.7
Mar 1980	131	– 27	– 17.1
Sep 2001	1499	– 307	– 17.0
Oct 1978	111	– 22	– 16.4
Apr 2000	3861	– 712	– 15.6
Nov 1973	94	– 17	– 15.1

DAYS

		Close	Change	Change
Wed	2001 Jan 3	2617	325 pt	14.2 %
Mon	2008 Oct 13	1844	195	11.8
Tue	2000 Dec 5	2890	274	10.5
Tue	2008 Oct 28	1649	144	9.5
Thu	2001 Apr 5	1785	146	8.9
Wed	2001 Apr 18	2079	156	8.1
Tue	2000 May 30	3459	254	7.9
Fri	2000 Oct 13	3317	242	7.9
Thu	2000 Oct 19	3419	247	7.8
Wed	2002 May 8	1696	122	7.8

DAYS

		Close	Change	Change
Mon	1987 Oct 19	360	– 46 pt	– 11.3 %
Fri	2000 Apr 14	3321	– 355	– 9.7
Mon	2008 Sep 29	1984	– 200	– 9.1
Mon	1987 Oct 26	299	– 30	– 9.0
Tue	1987 Oct 20	328	– 32	– 9.0
Mon	2008 Dec 01	1398	– 138	– 9.0
Mon	1998 Aug 31	1499	– 140	– 8.6
Wed	2008 Oct 15	1628	– 151	– 8.5
Mon	2000 Apr 03	4224	– 349	– 7.6
Tue	2001 Jan 02	2292	– 179	– 7.2

10 BEST

10 WORST

YEARS

	Close	Change	Change
2009	8414	2758 pt	30.7 %
1999	4321	1928	29.7
1993	5927	971	29.0
1996	8221	1213	25.7
2003	11272	1606	24.3
2005	2893	2026	21.9
1985	3970	500	20.8
1989	12908	580	17.1
2006	6699	1636	14.5
2010	13433	1697	14.4

YEARS

	Close	Change	Change
2008	8988	– 4845 pt	– 35.0 %
1990	3257	– 713	– 18.0
2002	6615	– 1074	– 14.0
2001	7688	– 1245	– 13.9
2015	13010	– 1622	– 11.9
2011	11955	– 1488	– 11.7
1992	3350	– 162	– 4.6
1998	6486	– 214	– 3.2
1994	4214	– 108	– 2.5
1987	3160	94	3.1

MONTHS

	Close	Change	Change
Dec 1999	8414	891 pt	11.8 %
May 2009	8500	1045	11.2
Oct 1998	6208	594	10.6
Jun 2000	10196	943	10.2
Jan 1985	2595	195	8.1
Aug 2000	11248	842	8.1
Nov 2001	7426	540	7.8
Jul 1987	4030	290	7.8
Feb 2000	9129	648	7.6
Nov 1996	6017	418	7.5

MONTHS

	Close	Change	Change
Oct 1987	3019	– 883 pt	– 22.6 %
Aug 1998	5531	– 1401	– 20.2
Oct 2008	9763	– 1990	– 16.9
Sep 2008	11753	– 2018	– 14.7
Feb 2001	8079	– 1243	– 13.3
Sep 2011	11624	– 1145	– 9.0
Nov 2000	8820	– 820	– 8.5
Apr 1990	3341	– 299	– 8.2
Sep 2000	10378	– 870	– 7.7
Sep 2001	6839	– 561	– 7.6

DAYS

		Close	Change	Change
Tue	2008 Oct 14	9956	891 pt	9.8 %
Wed	1987 Oct 21	3246	269	9.0
Mon	2008 Oct 20	10251	689	7.2
Tue	2008 Oct 28	9152	614	7.2
Fri	2008 Sep 19	12913	848	7.0
Fri	2008 Nov 28	9271	517	5.9
Fri	2008 Nov 21	8155	431	5.6
Mon	2008 Dec 08	8567	450	5.5
Mon	2009 Mar 23	8959	452	5.3
Fri	1987 Oct 30	3019	147	5.1

DAYS

		Close	Change	Change
Mon	1987 Oct 19	3192	– 407 pt	– 11.3 %
Mon	2008 Dec 01	8406	– 864	– 9.3
Thu	2008 Nov 20	7725	– 766	– 9.0
Mon	2008 Oct 27	8537	– 757	– 8.1
Wed	2000 Oct 25	9512	– 840	– 8.1
Mon	1987 Oct 26	2846	– 233	– 7.6
Thu	2008 Oct 02	10901	– 814	– 6.9
Mon	2008 Sep 29	11285	– 841	– 6.9
Tue	1987 Oct 20	2977	– 215	– 6.7
Fri	2001 Feb 16	8393	– 574	– 6.4

BOND YIELDS

	JAN	FEB	MAR	APR	MAY	JUN
1954	2.48	2.47	2.37	2.29	2.37	2.38
1955	2.61	2.65	2.68	2.75	2.76	2.78
1956	2.9	2.84	2.96	3.18	3.07	3
1957	3.46	3.34	3.41	3.48	3.6	3.8
1958	3.09	3.05	2.98	2.88	2.92	2.97
1959	4.02	3.96	3.99	4.12	4.31	4.34
1960	4.72	4.49	4.25	4.28	4.35	4.15
1961	3.84	3.78	3.74	3.78	3.71	3.88
1962	4.08	4.04	3.93	3.84	3.87	3.91
1963	3.83	3.92	3.93	3.97	3.93	3.99
1964	4.17	4.15	4.22	4.23	4.2	4.17
1965	4.19	4.21	4.21	4.2	4.21	4.21
1966	4.61	4.83	4.87	4.75	4.78	4.81
1967	4.58	4.63	4.54	4.59	4.85	5.02
1968	5.53	5.56	5.74	5.64	5.87	5.72
1969	6.04	6.19	6.3	6.17	6.32	6.57
1970	7.79	7.24	7.07	7.39	7.91	7.84
1971	6.24	6.11	5.7	5.83	6.39	6.52
1972	5.95	6.08	6.07	6.19	6.13	6.11
1973	6.46	6.64	6.71	6.67	6.85	6.9
1974	6.99	6.96	7.21	7.51	7.58	7.54
1975	7.5	7.39	7.73	8.23	8.06	7.86
1976	7.74	7.79	7.73	7.56	7.9	7.86
1977	7.21	7.39	7.46	7.37	7.46	7.28
1978	7.96	8.03	8.04	8.15	8.35	8.46
1979	9.1	9.1	9.12	9.18	9.25	8.91
1980	10.8	12.41	12.75	11.47	10.18	9.78
1981	12.57	13.19	13.12	13.68	14.1	13.47
1982	14.59	14.43	13.86	13.87	13.62	14.3
1983	10.46	10.72	10.51	10.4	10.38	10.85
1984	11.67	11.84	12.32	12.63	13.41	13.56
1985	11.38	11.51	11.86	11.43	10.85	10.16
1986	9.19	8.7	7.78	7.3	7.71	7.8
1987	7.08	7.25	7.25	8.02	8.61	8.4
1988	8.67	8.21	8.37	8.72	9.09	8.92
1989	9.09	9.17	9.36	9.18	8.86	8.28
1990	8.21	8.47	8.59	8.79	8.76	8.48
1991	8.09	7.85	8.11	8.04	8.07	8.28
1992	7.03	7.34	7.54	7.48	7.39	7.26
1993	6.6	6.26	5.98	5.97	6.04	5.96
1994	5.75	5.97	6.48	6.97	7.18	7.1
1995	7.78	7.47	7.2	7.06	6.63	6.17
1996	5.65	5.81	6.27	6.51	6.74	6.91
1997	6.58	6.42	6.69	6.89	6.71	6.49
1998	5.54	5.57	5.65	5.64	5.65	5.5
1999	4.72	5	5.23	5.18	5.54	5.9
2000	6.66	6.52	6.26	5.99	6.44	6.1
2001	5.16	5.1	4.89	5.14	5.39	5.28
2002	5.04	4.91	5.28	5.21	5.16	4.93
2003	4.05	3.9	3.81	3.96	3.57	3.33
2004	4.15	4.08	3.83	4.35	4.72	4.73
2005	4.22	4.17	4.5	4.34	4.14	4.00
2006	4.42	4.57	4.72	4.99	5.11	5.11
2007	4.76	4.72	4.56	4.69	4.75	5.10
2008	3.74	3.74	3.51	3.68	3.88	4.10
2009	2.52	2.87	2.82	2.93	3.29	3.72
2010	3.73	3.69	3.73	3.85	3.42	3.20
2011	3.39	3.58	3.41	3.46	3.17	3.00
2012	1.97	1.97	2.17	2.05	1.80	1.62
2013	1.91	1.98	1.96	1.76	1.93	2.30
2014	2.86	2.71	2.72	2.71	2.56	2.60
2015	1.88	1.98	2.04	1.94	2.20	2.36
2016	2.09	1.78	1.89	1.81	1.81	1.64
2017	2.43	2.42	2.48	2.30	2.30	2.19

* Source: Federal Reserve Bank of St. Louis, monthly data calculated as average of business days

10 YEAR TREASURY BOND YIELDS

JUL	AUG	SEP	OCT	NOV	DEC	
2.3	2.36	2.38	2.43	2.48	2.51	**1954**
2.9	2.97	2.97	2.88	2.89	2.96	**1955**
3.11	3.33	3.38	3.34	3.49	3.59	**1956**
3.93	3.93	3.92	3.97	3.72	3.21	**1957**
3.2	3.54	3.76	3.8	3.74	3.86	**1958**
4.4	4.43	4.68	4.53	4.53	4.69	**1959**
3.9	3.8	3.8	3.89	3.93	3.84	**1960**
3.92	4.04	3.98	3.92	3.94	4.06	**1961**
4.01	3.98	3.98	3.93	3.92	3.86	**1962**
4.02	4	4.08	4.11	4.12	4.13	**1963**
4.19	4.19	4.2	4.19	4.15	4.18	**1964**
4.2	4.25	4.29	4.35	4.45	4.62	**1965**
5.02	5.22	5.18	5.01	5.16	4.84	**1966**
5.16	5.28	5.3	5.48	5.75	5.7	**1967**
5.5	5.42	5.46	5.58	5.7	6.03	**1968**
6.72	6.69	7.16	7.1	7.14	7.65	**1969**
7.46	7.53	7.39	7.33	6.84	6.39	**1970**
6.73	6.58	6.14	5.93	5.81	5.93	**1971**
6.11	6.21	6.55	6.48	6.28	6.36	**1972**
7.13	7.4	7.09	6.79	6.73	6.74	**1973**
7.81	8.04	8.04	7.9	7.68	7.43	**1974**
8.06	8.4	8.43	8.14	8.05	8	**1975**
7.83	7.77	7.59	7.41	7.29	6.87	**1976**
7.33	7.4	7.34	7.52	7.58	7.69	**1977**
8.64	8.41	8.42	8.64	8.81	9.01	**1978**
8.95	9.03	9.33	10.3	10.65	10.39	**1979**
10.25	11.1	11.51	11.75	12.68	12.84	**1980**
14.28	14.94	15.32	15.15	13.39	13.72	**1981**
13.95	13.06	12.34	10.91	10.55	10.54	**1982**
11.38	11.85	11.65	11.54	11.69	11.83	**1983**
13.36	12.72	12.52	12.16	11.57	11.5	**1984**
10.31	10.33	10.37	10.24	9.78	9.26	**1985**
7.3	7.17	7.45	7.43	7.25	7.11	**1986**
8.45	8.76	9.42	9.52	8.86	8.99	**1987**
9.06	9.26	8.98	8.8	8.96	9.11	**1988**
8.02	8.11	8.19	8.01	7.87	7.84	**1989**
8.47	8.75	8.89	8.72	8.39	8.08	**1990**
8.27	7.9	7.65	7.53	7.42	7.09	**1991**
6.84	6.59	6.42	6.59	6.87	6.77	**1992**
5.81	5.68	5.36	5.33	5.72	5.77	**1993**
7.3	7.24	7.46	7.74	7.96	7.81	**1994**
6.28	6.49	6.2	6.04	5.93	5.71	**1995**
6.87	6.64	6.83	6.53	6.2	6.3	**1996**
6.22	6.3	6.21	6.03	5.88	5.81	**1997**
5.46	5.34	4.81	4.53	4.83	4.65	**1998**
5.79	5.94	5.92	6.11	6.03	6.28	**1999**
6.05	5.83	5.8	5.74	5.72	5.24	**2000**
5.24	4.97	4.73	4.57	4.65	5.09	**2001**
4.65	4.26	3.87	3.94	4.05	4.03	**2002**
3.98	4.45	4.27	4.29	4.3	4.27	**2003**
4.5	4.28	4.13	4.1	4.19	4.23	**2004**
4.18	4.26	4.20	4.46	4.54	4.47	**2005**
5.09	4.88	4.72	4.73	4.60	4.56	**2006**
5.00	4.67	4.52	4.53	4.15	4.10	**2007**
4.01	3.89	3.69	3.81	3.53	2.42	**2008**
3.56	3.59	3.40	3.39	3.40	3.59	**2009**
3.01	2.70	2.65	2.54	2.76	3.29	**2010**
3.00	2.30	1.98	2.15	2.01	1.98	**2011**
1.53	1.68	1.72	1.75	1.65	1.72	**2012**
2.58	2.74	2.81	2.62	2.72	2.90	**2013**
2.54	2.42	2.53	2.30	2.33	2.21	**2014**
2.32	2.17	2.17	2.07	2.26	2.24	**2015**
1.50	1.56	1.63	1.76	2.14	2.49	**2016**
2.32	2.21	2.20	2.36	2.35	2.40	**2017**

BOND YIELDS ≡≡ 5 YEAR TREASURY*

	JAN	FEB	MAR	APR	MAY	JUN
1954	2.17	2.04	1.93	1.87	1.92	1.92
1955	2.32	2.38	2.48	2.55	2.56	2.59
1956	2.84	2.74	2.93	3.20	3.08	2.97
1957	3.47	3.39	3.46	3.53	3.64	3.83
1958	2.88	2.78	2.64	2.46	2.41	2.46
1959	4.01	3.96	3.99	4.12	4.35	4.50
1960	4.92	4.69	4.31	4.29	4.49	4.12
1961	3.67	3.66	3.60	3.57	3.47	3.81
1962	3.94	3.89	3.68	3.60	3.66	3.64
1963	3.58	3.66	3.68	3.74	3.72	3.81
1964	4.07	4.03	4.14	4.15	4.05	4.02
1965	4.10	4.15	4.15	4.15	4.15	4.15
1966	4.86	4.98	4.92	4.83	4.89	4.97
1967	4.70	4.74	4.54	4.51	4.75	5.01
1968	5.54	5.59	5.76	5.69	6.04	5.85
1969	6.25	6.34	6.41	6.30	6.54	6.75
1970	8.17	7.82	7.21	7.50	7.97	7.85
1971	5.89	5.56	5.00	5.65	6.28	6.53
1972	5.59	5.69	5.87	6.17	5.85	5.91
1973	6.34	6.60	6.80	6.67	6.80	6.69
1974	6.95	6.82	7.31	7.92	8.18	8.10
1975	7.41	7.11	7.30	7.99	7.72	7.51
1976	7.46	7.45	7.49	7.25	7.59	7.61
1977	6.58	6.83	6.93	6.79	6.94	6.76
1978	7.77	7.83	7.86	7.98	8.18	8.36
1979	9.20	9.13	9.20	9.25	9.24	8.85
1980	10.74	12.60	13.47	11.84	9.95	9.21
1981	12.77	13.41	13.41	13.99	14.63	13.95
1982	14.65	14.54	13.98	14.00	13.75	14.43
1983	10.03	10.26	10.08	10.02	10.03	10.63
1984	11.37	11.54	12.02	12.37	13.17	13.48
1985	10.93	11.13	11.52	11.01	10.34	9.60
1986	8.68	8.34	7.46	7.05	7.52	7.64
1987	6.64	6.79	6.79	7.57	8.26	8.02
1988	8.18	7.71	7.83	8.19	8.58	8.49
1989	9.15	9.27	9.51	9.30	8.91	8.29
1990	8.12	8.42	8.60	8.77	8.74	8.43
1991	7.70	7.47	7.77	7.70	7.70	7.94
1992	6.24	6.58	6.95	6.78	6.69	6.48
1993	5.83	5.43	5.19	5.13	5.20	5.22
1994	5.09	5.40	5.94	6.52	6.78	6.70
1995	7.76	7.37	7.05	6.86	6.41	5.93
1996	5.36	5.38	5.97	6.30	6.48	6.69
1997	6.33	6.20	6.54	6.76	6.57	6.38
1998	5.42	5.49	5.61	5.61	5.63	5.52
1999	4.60	4.91	5.14	5.08	5.44	5.81
2000	6.58	6.68	6.50	6.26	6.69	6.30
2001	4.86	4.89	4.64	4.76	4.93	4.81
2002	4.34	4.30	4.74	4.65	4.49	4.19
2003	3.05	2.90	2.78	2.93	2.52	2.27
2004	3.12	3.07	2.79	3.39	3.85	3.93
2005	3.71	3.77	4.17	4.00	3.85	3.77
2006	4.35	4.57	4.72	4.90	5.00	5.07
2007	4.75	4.71	4.48	4.59	4.67	5.03
2008	2.98	2.78	2.48	2.84	3.15	3.49
2009	1.60	1.87	1.82	1.86	2.13	2.71
2010	2.48	2.36	2.43	2.58	2.18	2.00
2011	1.99	2.26	2.11	2.17	1.84	1.58
2012	0.84	0.83	1.02	0.89	0.76	0.71
2013	0.81	0.85	0.82	0.71	0.84	1.20
2014	1.65	1.52	1.64	1.70	1.59	1.68
2015	1.37	1.47	1.52	1.35	1.54	1.68
2016	1.52	1.22	1.38	1.26	1.30	1.17
2017	1.92	1.90	2.01	1.82	1.84	1.77

* Source: Federal Reserve Bank of St. Louis, monthly data calculated as average of business days

5 YEAR TREASURY BOND YIELDS

JUL	AUG	SEP	OCT	NOV	DEC	
1.85	1.90	1.96	2.02	2.09	2.16	**1954**
2.72	2.86	2.85	2.76	2.81	2.93	**1955**
3.12	3.41	3.47	3.40	3.56	3.70	**1956**
4.00	4.00	4.03	4.08	3.72	3.08	**1957**
2.77	3.29	3.69	3.78	3.70	3.82	**1958**
4.58	4.57	4.90	4.72	4.75	5.01	**1959**
3.79	3.62	3.61	3.76	3.81	3.67	**1960**
3.84	3.96	3.90	3.80	3.82	3.91	**1961**
3.80	3.71	3.70	3.64	3.60	3.56	**1962**
3.89	3.89	3.96	3.97	4.01	4.04	**1963**
4.03	4.05	4.08	4.07	4.04	4.09	**1964**
4.15	4.20	4.25	4.34	4.46	4.72	**1965**
5.17	5.50	5.50	5.27	5.36	5.00	**1966**
5.23	5.31	5.40	5.57	5.78	5.75	**1967**
5.60	5.50	5.48	5.55	5.66	6.12	**1968**
7.01	7.03	7.57	7.51	7.53	7.96	**1969**
7.59	7.57	7.29	7.12	6.47	5.95	**1970**
6.85	6.55	6.14	5.93	5.78	5.69	**1971**
5.97	6.02	6.25	6.18	6.12	6.16	**1972**
7.33	7.63	7.05	6.77	6.92	6.80	**1973**
8.38	8.63	8.37	7.97	7.68	7.31	**1974**
7.92	8.33	8.37	7.97	7.80	7.76	**1975**
7.49	7.31	7.13	6.75	6.52	6.10	**1976**
6.84	7.03	7.04	7.32	7.34	7.48	**1977**
8.54	8.33	8.43	8.61	8.84	9.08	**1978**
8.90	9.06	9.41	10.63	10.93	10.42	**1979**
9.53	10.84	11.62	11.86	12.83	13.25	**1980**
14.79	15.56	15.93	15.41	13.38	13.60	**1981**
14.07	13.00	12.25	10.80	10.38	10.22	**1982**
11.21	11.63	11.43	11.28	11.41	11.54	**1983**
13.27	12.68	12.53	12.06	11.33	11.07	**1984**
9.70	9.81	9.81	9.69	9.28	8.73	**1985**
7.06	6.80	6.92	6.83	6.76	6.67	**1986**
8.01	8.32	8.94	9.08	8.35	8.45	**1987**
8.66	8.94	8.69	8.51	8.79	9.09	**1988**
7.83	8.09	8.17	7.97	7.81	7.75	**1989**
8.33	8.44	8.51	8.33	8.02	7.73	**1990**
7.91	7.43	7.14	6.87	6.62	6.19	**1991**
5.84	5.60	5.38	5.60	6.04	6.08	**1992**
5.09	5.03	4.73	4.71	5.06	5.15	**1993**
6.91	6.88	7.08	7.40	7.72	7.78	**1994**
6.01	6.24	6.00	5.86	5.69	5.51	**1995**
6.64	6.39	6.60	6.27	5.97	6.07	**1996**
6.12	6.16	6.11	5.93	5.80	5.77	**1997**
5.46	5.27	4.62	4.18	4.54	4.45	**1998**
5.68	5.84	5.80	6.03	5.97	6.19	**1999**
6.18	6.06	5.93	5.78	5.70	5.17	**2000**
4.76	4.57	4.12	3.91	3.97	4.39	**2001**
3.81	3.29	2.94	2.95	3.05	3.03	**2002**
2.87	3.37	3.18	3.19	3.29	3.27	**2003**
3.69	3.47	3.36	3.35	3.53	3.60	**2004**
3.98	4.12	4.01	4.33	4.45	4.39	**2005**
5.04	4.82	4.67	4.69	4.58	4.53	**2006**
4.88	4.43	4.20	4.20	3.67	3.49	**2007**
3.30	3.14	2.88	2.73	2.29	1.52	**2008**
2.46	2.57	2.37	2.33	2.23	2.34	**2009**
1.76	1.47	1.41	1.18	1.35	1.93	**2010**
1.54	1.02	0.90	1.06	0.91	0.89	**2011**
0.62	0.71	0.67	0.71	0.67	0.70	**2012**
1.40	1.52	1.60	1.37	1.37	1.58	**2013**
1.70	1.63	1.77	1.55	1.62	1.64	**2014**
1.63	1.54	1.49	1.39	1.67	1.70	**2015**
1.07	1.13	1.18	1.27	1.60	1.96	**2016**
1.87	1.78	1.80	1.98	2.05	2.18	**2017**

BOND YIELDS 🇺🇸 3 MONTH TREASURY

	JAN	FEB	MAR	APR	MAY	JUN
1982	12.92	14.28	13.31	13.34	12.71	13.08
1983	8.12	8.39	8.66	8.51	8.50	9.14
1984	9.26	9.46	9.89	10.07	10.22	10.26
1985	8.02	8.56	8.83	8.22	7.73	7.18
1986	7.30	7.29	6.76	6.24	6.33	6.40
1987	5.58	5.75	5.77	5.82	5.85	5.85
1988	6.00	5.84	5.87	6.08	6.45	6.66
1999	8.56	8.84	9.14	8.96	8.74	8.43
1990	7.90	8.00	8.17	8.04	8.01	7.99
1991	6.41	6.12	6.09	5.83	5.63	5.75
1992	3.91	3.95	4.14	3.84	3.72	3.75
1993	3.07	2.99	3.01	2.93	3.03	3.14
1994	3.04	3.33	3.59	3.78	4.27	4.25
1995	5.90	5.94	5.91	5.84	5.85	5.64
1996	5.15	4.96	5.10	5.09	5.15	5.23
1997	5.17	5.14	5.28	5.30	5.20	5.07
1998	5.18	5.23	5.16	5.08	5.14	5.12
1999	4.45	4.56	4.57	4.41	4.63	4.72
2000	5.50	5.73	5.86	5.82	5.99	5.86
2001	5.29	5.01	4.54	3.97	3.70	3.57
2002	1.68	1.76	1.83	1.75	1.76	1.73
2003	1.19	1.19	1.15	1.15	1.09	0.94
2004	0.90	0.94	0.95	0.96	1.04	1.29
2005	2.37	2.58	2.80	2.84	2.90	3.04
2006	4.34	4.54	4.63	4.72	4.84	4.92
2007	5.11	5.16	5.08	5.01	4.87	4.74
2008	2.82	2.17	1.28	1.31	1.76	1.89
2009	0.13	0.30	0.22	0.16	0.18	0.18
2010	0.06	0.11	0.15	0.16	0.16	0.12
2011	0.15	0.13	0.10	0.06	0.04	0.04
2012	0.03	0.09	0.08	0.08	0.09	0.09
2013	0.07	0.10	0.09	0.06	0.04	0.05
2014	0.04	0.05	0.05	0.03	0.03	0.04
2015	0.03	0.02	0.03	0.02	0.02	0.02
2016	0.26	0.31	0.30	0.23	0.28	0.27
2017	0.52	0.53	0.75	0.81	0.90	1.00

* Source: Federal Reserve Bank of St. Louis, monthly data calculated as average of business days

3 MONTH TREASURY BOND YIELDS

JUL	AUG	SEP	OCT	NOV	DEC	
11.86	9.00	8.19	7.97	8.35	8.20	**1982**
9.45	9.74	9.36	8.99	9.11	9.36	**1983**
10.53	10.90	10.80	10.12	8.92	8.34	**1984**
7.32	7.37	7.33	7.40	7.48	7.33	**1985**
6.00	5.69	5.35	5.32	5.50	5.68	**1986**
5.88	6.23	6.62	6.35	5.89	5.96	**1987**
6.95	7.30	7.48	7.60	8.03	8.35	**1988**
8.15	8.17	8.01	7.90	7.94	7.88	**1999**
7.87	7.69	7.60	7.40	7.29	6.95	**1990**
5.75	5.50	5.37	5.14	4.69	4.18	**1991**
3.28	3.20	2.97	2.93	3.21	3.29	**1992**
3.11	3.09	3.01	3.09	3.18	3.13	**1993**
4.46	4.61	4.75	5.10	5.45	5.76	**1994**
5.59	5.57	5.43	5.44	5.52	5.29	**1995**
5.30	5.19	5.24	5.12	5.17	5.04	**1996**
5.19	5.28	5.08	5.11	5.28	5.30	**1997**
5.09	5.04	4.74	4.07	4.53	4.50	**1998**
4.69	4.87	4.82	5.02	5.23	5.36	**1999**
6.14	6.28	6.18	6.29	6.36	5.94	**2000**
3.59	3.44	2.69	2.20	1.91	1.72	**2001**
1.71	1.65	1.66	1.61	1.25	1.21	**2002**
0.92	0.97	0.96	0.94	0.95	0.91	**2003**
1.36	1.50	1.68	1.79	2.11	2.22	**2004**
3.29	3.52	3.49	3.79	3.97	3.97	**2005**
5.08	5.09	4.93	5.05	5.07	4.97	**2006**
4.96	4.32	3.99	4.00	3.35	3.07	**2007**
1.66	1.75	1.15	0.69	0.19	0.03	**2008**
0.18	0.17	0.12	0.07	0.05	0.05	**2009**
0.16	0.16	0.15	0.13	0.14	0.14	**2010**
0.04	0.02	0.01	0.02	0.01	0.01	**2011**
0.10	0.10	0.11	0.10	0.09	0.07	**2012**
0.04	0.04	0.02	0.05	0.07	0.07	**2013**
0.03	0.03	0.02	0.02	0.02	0.03	**2014**
0.03	0.07	0.02	0.02	0.13	0.23	**2015**
0.30	0.30	0.29	0.33	0.45	0.51	**2016**
1.09	1.03	1.05	1.09	1.25	1.34	**2017**

MOODY'S SEASONED CORPORATE Aaa*

	JAN	FEB	MAR	APR	MAY	JUN
1950	2.57	2.58	2.58	2.60	2.61	2.62
1951	2.66	2.66	2.78	2.87	2.89	2.94
1952	2.98	2.93	2.96	2.93	2.93	2.94
1953	3.02	3.07	3.12	3.23	3.34	3.40
1954	3.06	2.95	2.86	2.85	2.88	2.90
1955	2.93	2.93	3.02	3.01	3.04	3.05
1956	3.11	3.08	3.10	3.24	3.28	3.26
1957	3.77	3.67	3.66	3.67	3.74	3.91
1958	3.60	3.59	3.63	3.60	3.57	3.57
1959	4.12	4.14	4.13	4.23	4.37	4.46
1960	4.61	4.56	4.49	4.45	4.46	4.45
1961	4.32	4.27	4.22	4.25	4.27	4.33
1962	4.42	4.42	4.39	4.33	4.28	4.28
1963	4.21	4.19	4.19	4.21	4.22	4.23
1964	4.39	4.36	4.38	4.40	4.41	4.41
1965	4.43	4.41	4.42	4.43	4.44	4.46
1966	4.74	4.78	4.92	4.96	4.98	5.07
1967	5.20	5.03	5.13	5.11	5.24	5.44
1968	6.17	6.10	6.11	6.21	6.27	6.28
1969	6.59	6.66	6.85	6.89	6.79	6.98
1970	7.91	7.93	7.84	7.83	8.11	8.48
1971	7.36	7.08	7.21	7.25	7.53	7.64
1972	7.19	7.27	7.24	7.30	7.30	7.23
1973	7.15	7.22	7.29	7.26	7.29	7.37
1974	7.83	7.85	8.01	8.25	8.37	8.47
1975	8.83	8.62	8.67	8.95	8.90	8.77
1976	8.60	8.55	8.52	8.40	8.58	8.62
1977	7.96	8.04	8.10	8.04	8.05	7.95
1978	8.41	8.47	8.47	8.56	8.69	8.76
1979	9.25	9.26	9.37	9.38	9.50	9.29
1980	11.09	12.38	12.96	12.04	10.99	10.58
1981	12.81	13.35	13.33	13.88	14.32	13.75
1982	15.18	15.27	14.58	14.46	14.26	14.81
1983	11.79	12.01	11.73	11.51	11.46	11.74
1984	12.20	12.08	12.57	12.81	13.28	13.55
1985	12.08	12.13	12.56	12.23	11.72	10.94
1986	10.05	9.67	9.00	8.79	9.09	9.13
1987	8.36	8.38	8.36	8.85	9.33	9.32
1988	9.88	9.40	9.39	9.67	9.90	9.86
1989	9.62	9.64	9.80	9.79	9.57	9.10
1990	8.99	9.22	9.37	9.46	9.47	9.26
1991	9.04	8.83	8.93	8.86	8.86	9.01
1992	8.20	8.29	8.35	8.33	8.28	8.22
1993	7.91	7.71	7.58	7.46	7.43	7.33
1994	6.92	7.08	7.48	7.88	7.99	7.97
1995	8.46	8.26	8.12	8.03	7.65	7.30
1996	6.81	6.99	7.35	7.50	7.62	7.71
1997	7.42	7.31	7.55	7.73	7.58	7.41
1998	6.61	6.67	6.72	6.69	6.69	6.53
1999	6.24	6.40	6.62	6.64	6.93	7.23
2000	7.78	7.68	7.68	7.64	7.99	7.67
2001	7.15	7.10	6.98	7.20	7.29	7.18
2002	6.55	6.51	6.81	6.76	6.75	6.63
2003	6.17	5.95	5.89	5.74	5.22	4.97
2004	5.54	5.50	5.33	5.73	6.04	6.01
2005	5.36	5.20	5.40	5.33	5.15	4.96
2006	5.29	5.35	5.53	5.84	5.95	5.89
2007	5.40	5.39	5.30	5.47	5.47	5.79
2008	5.33	5.53	5.51	5.55	5.57	5.68
2009	5.05	5.27	5.50	5.39	5.54	5.61
2010	5.26	5.35	5.27	5.29	4.96	4.88
2011	5.04	5.22	5.13	5.16	4.96	4.99
2012	3.85	3.85	3.99	3.96	3.80	3.64
2013	3.80	3.90	3.93	3.73	3.89	4.27
2014	4.49	4.45	4.38	4.24	4.16	4.25
2015	3.46	3.61	3.64	3.52	3.98	4.19
2016	4.00	3.96	3.82	3.62	3.65	3.50
2017	3.92	3.95	4.01	3.87	3.85	3.68

* Source: Federal Reserve Bank of St. Louis, monthly data calculated as average of business days

MOODY'S SEASONED
CORPORATE Aaa ▆▆▆ BOND YIELDS

JUL	AUG	SEP	OCT	NOV	DEC	
2.65	2.61	2.64	2.67	2.67	2.67	**1950**
2.94	2.88	2.84	2.89	2.96	3.01	**1951**
2.95	2.94	2.95	3.01	2.98	2.97	**1952**
3.28	3.24	3.29	3.16	3.11	3.13	**1953**
2.89	2.87	2.89	2.87	2.89	2.90	**1954**
3.06	3.11	3.13	3.10	3.10	3.15	**1955**
3.28	3.43	3.56	3.59	3.69	3.75	**1956**
3.99	4.10	4.12	4.10	4.08	3.81	**1957**
3.67	3.85	4.09	4.11	4.09	4.08	**1958**
4.47	4.43	4.52	4.57	4.56	4.58	**1959**
4.41	4.28	4.25	4.30	4.31	4.35	**1960**
4.41	4.45	4.45	4.42	4.39	4.42	**1961**
4.34	4.35	4.32	4.28	4.25	4.24	**1962**
4.26	4.29	4.31	4.32	4.33	4.35	**1963**
4.40	4.41	4.42	4.42	4.43	4.44	**1964**
4.48	4.49	4.52	4.56	4.60	4.68	**1965**
5.16	5.31	5.49	5.41	5.35	5.39	**1966**
5.58	5.62	5.65	5.82	6.07	6.19	**1967**
6.24	6.02	5.97	6.09	6.19	6.45	**1968**
7.08	6.97	7.14	7.33	7.35	7.72	**1969**
8.44	8.13	8.09	8.03	8.05	7.64	**1970**
7.64	7.59	7.44	7.39	7.26	7.25	**1971**
7.21	7.19	7.22	7.21	7.12	7.08	**1972**
7.45	7.68	7.63	7.60	7.67	7.68	**1973**
8.72	9.00	9.24	9.27	8.89	8.89	**1974**
8.84	8.95	8.95	8.86	8.78	8.79	**1975**
8.56	8.45	8.38	8.32	8.25	7.98	**1976**
7.94	7.98	7.92	8.04	8.08	8.19	**1977**
8.88	8.69	8.69	8.89	9.03	9.16	**1978**
9.20	9.23	9.44	10.13	10.76	10.74	**1979**
11.07	11.64	12.02	12.31	12.97	13.21	**1980**
14.38	14.89	15.49	15.40	14.22	14.23	**1981**
14.61	13.71	12.94	12.12	11.68	11.83	**1982**
12.15	12.51	12.37	12.25	12.41	12.57	**1983**
13.44	12.87	12.66	12.63	12.29	12.13	**1984**
10.97	11.05	11.07	11.02	10.55	10.16	**1985**
8.88	8.72	8.89	8.86	8.68	8.49	**1986**
9.42	9.67	10.18	10.52	10.01	10.11	**1987**
9.96	10.11	9.82	9.51	9.45	9.57	**1988**
8.93	8.96	9.01	8.92	8.89	8.86	**1989**
9.24	9.41	9.56	9.53	9.30	9.05	**1990**
9.00	8.75	8.61	8.55	8.48	8.31	**1991**
8.07	7.95	7.92	7.99	8.10	7.98	**1992**
7.17	6.85	6.66	6.67	6.93	6.93	**1993**
8.11	8.07	8.34	8.57	8.68	8.46	**1994**
7.41	7.57	7.32	7.12	7.02	6.82	**1995**
7.65	7.46	7.66	7.39	7.10	7.20	**1996**
7.14	7.22	7.15	7.00	6.87	6.76	**1997**
6.55	6.52	6.40	6.37	6.41	6.22	**1998**
7.19	7.40	7.39	7.55	7.36	7.55	**1999**
7.65	7.55	7.62	7.55	7.45	7.21	**2000**
7.13	7.02	7.17	7.03	6.97	6.77	**2001**
6.53	6.37	6.15	6.32	6.31	6.21	**2002**
5.49	5.88	5.72	5.70	5.65	5.62	**2003**
5.82	5.65	5.46	5.47	5.52	5.47	**2004**
5.06	5.09	5.13	5.35	5.42	5.37	**2005**
5.85	5.68	5.51	5.51	5.33	5.32	**2006**
5.73	5.79	5.74	5.66	5.44	5.49	**2007**
5.67	5.64	5.65	6.28	6.12	5.05	**2008**
5.41	5.26	5.13	5.15	5.19	5.26	**2009**
4.72	4.49	4.53	4.68	4.87	5.02	**2010**
4.93	4.37	4.09	3.98	3.87	3.93	**2011**
3.40	3.48	3.49	3.47	3.50	3.65	**2012**
4.34	4.54	4.64	4.53	4.63	4.62	**2013**
4.16	4.08	4.11	3.92	3.92	3.79	**2014**
4.15	4.04	4.07	3.95	4.06	3.97	**2015**
3.28	3.32	3.41	3.51	3.86	4.06	**2016**
3.70	3.63	3.63	3.60	3.57	3.51	**2017**

MOODY'S SEASONED CORPORATE Baa*

	JAN	FEB	MAR	APR	MAY	JUN
1950	3.24	3.24	3.24	3.23	3.25	3.28
1951	3.17	3.16	3.23	3.35	3.40	3.49
1952	3.59	3.53	3.51	3.50	3.49	3.50
1953	3.51	3.53	3.57	3.65	3.78	3.86
1954	3.71	3.61	3.51	3.47	3.47	3.49
1955	3.45	3.47	3.48	3.49	3.50	3.51
1956	3.60	3.58	3.60	3.68	3.73	3.76
1957	4.49	4.47	4.43	4.44	4.52	4.63
1958	4.83	4.66	4.68	4.67	4.62	4.55
1959	4.87	4.89	4.85	4.86	4.96	5.04
1960	5.34	5.34	5.25	5.20	5.28	5.26
1961	5.10	5.07	5.02	5.01	5.01	5.03
1962	5.08	5.07	5.04	5.02	5.00	5.02
1963	4.91	4.89	4.88	4.87	4.85	4.84
1964	4.83	4.83	4.83	4.85	4.85	4.85
1965	4.80	4.78	4.78	4.80	4.81	4.85
1966	5.06	5.12	5.32	5.41	5.48	5.58
1967	5.97	5.82	5.85	5.83	5.96	6.15
1968	6.84	6.80	6.85	6.97	7.03	7.07
1969	7.32	7.30	7.51	7.54	7.52	7.70
1970	8.86	8.78	8.63	8.70	8.98	9.25
1971	8.74	8.39	8.46	8.45	8.62	8.75
1972	8.23	8.23	8.24	8.24	8.23	8.20
1973	7.90	7.97	8.03	8.09	8.06	8.13
1974	8.48	8.53	8.62	8.87	9.05	9.27
1975	10.81	10.65	10.48	10.58	10.69	10.62
1976	10.41	10.24	10.12	9.94	9.86	9.89
1977	9.08	9.12	9.12	9.07	9.01	8.91
1978	9.17	9.20	9.22	9.32	9.49	9.60
1979	10.13	10.08	10.26	10.33	10.47	10.38
1980	12.42	13.57	14.45	14.19	13.17	12.71
1981	15.03	15.37	15.34	15.56	15.95	15.80
1982	17.10	17.18	16.82	16.78	16.64	16.92
1983	13.94	13.95	13.61	13.29	13.09	13.37
1984	13.65	13.59	13.99	14.31	14.74	15.05
1985	13.26	13.23	13.69	13.51	13.15	12.40
1986	11.44	11.11	10.50	10.19	10.29	10.34
1987	9.72	9.65	9.61	10.04	10.51	10.52
1988	11.07	10.62	10.57	10.90	11.04	11.00
1989	10.65	10.61	10.67	10.61	10.46	10.03
1990	9.94	10.14	10.21	10.30	10.41	10.22
1991	10.45	10.07	10.09	9.94	9.86	9.96
1992	9.13	9.23	9.25	9.21	9.13	9.05
1993	8.67	8.39	8.15	8.14	8.21	8.07
1994	7.65	7.76	8.13	8.52	8.62	8.65
1995	9.08	8.85	8.70	8.60	8.20	7.90
1996	7.47	7.63	8.03	8.19	8.30	8.40
1997	8.09	7.94	8.18	8.34	8.20	8.02
1998	7.19	7.25	7.32	7.33	7.30	7.13
1999	7.29	7.39	7.53	7.48	7.72	8.02
2000	8.33	8.29	8.37	8.40	8.90	8.48
2001	7.93	7.87	7.84	8.07	8.07	7.97
2002	7.87	7.89	8.11	8.03	8.09	7.95
2003	7.35	7.06	6.95	6.85	6.38	6.19
2004	6.44	6.27	6.11	6.46	6.75	6.78
2005	6.02	5.82	6.06	6.05	6.01	5.86
2006	6.24	6.27	6.41	6.68	6.75	6.78
2007	6.34	6.28	6.27	6.39	6.39	6.70
2008	6.54	6.82	6.89	6.97	6.93	7.07
2009	8.14	8.08	8.42	8.39	8.06	7.50
2010	6.25	6.34	6.27	6.25	6.05	6.23
2011	6.09	6.15	6.03	6.02	5.78	5.75
2012	5.23	5.14	5.23	5.19	5.07	5.02
2013	4.73	4.85	4.85	4.59	4.73	5.19
2014	5.19	5.10	5.06	4.90	4.76	4.80
2015	4.45	4.51	4.54	4.48	4.89	5.13
2016	5.45	5.34	5.13	4.79	4.68	4.53
2017	4.66	4.64	4.68	4.57	4.55	4.37

* Source: Federal Reserve Bank of St. Louis, monthly data calculated as average of business days

MOODY'S SEASONED CORPORATE Baa* BOND YIELDS

JUL	AUG	SEP	OCT	NOV	DEC	
3.32	3.23	3.21	3.22	3.22	3.20	1950
3.53	3.50	3.46	3.50	3.56	3.61	1951
3.50	3.51	3.52	3.54	3.53	3.51	1952
3.86	3.85	3.88	3.82	3.75	3.74	1953
3.50	3.49	3.47	3.46	3.45	3.45	1954
3.52	3.56	3.59	3.59	3.58	3.62	1955
3.80	3.93	4.07	4.17	4.24	4.37	1956
4.73	4.82	4.93	4.99	5.09	5.03	1957
4.53	4.67	4.87	4.92	4.87	4.85	1958
5.08	5.09	5.18	5.28	5.26	5.28	1959
5.22	5.08	5.01	5.11	5.08	5.10	1960
5.09	5.11	5.12	5.13	5.11	5.10	1961
5.05	5.06	5.03	4.99	4.96	4.92	1962
4.84	4.83	4.84	4.83	4.84	4.85	1963
4.83	4.82	4.82	4.81	4.81	4.81	1964
4.88	4.88	4.91	4.93	4.95	5.02	1965
5.68	5.83	6.09	6.10	6.13	6.18	1966
6.26	6.33	6.40	6.52	6.72	6.93	1967
6.98	6.82	6.79	6.84	7.01	7.23	1968
7.84	7.86	8.05	8.22	8.25	8.65	1969
9.40	9.44	9.39	9.33	9.38	9.12	1970
8.76	8.76	8.59	8.48	8.38	8.38	1971
8.23	8.19	8.09	8.06	7.99	7.93	1972
8.24	8.53	8.63	8.41	8.42	8.48	1973
9.48	9.77	10.18	10.48	10.60	10.63	1974
10.55	10.59	10.61	10.62	10.56	10.56	1975
9.82	9.64	9.40	9.29	9.23	9.12	1976
8.87	8.82	8.80	8.89	8.95	8.99	1977
9.60	9.48	9.42	9.59	9.83	9.94	1978
10.29	10.35	10.54	11.40	11.99	12.06	1979
12.65	13.15	13.70	14.23	14.64	15.14	1980
16.17	16.34	16.92	17.11	16.39	16.55	1981
16.80	16.32	15.63	14.73	14.30	14.14	1982
13.39	13.64	13.55	13.46	13.61	13.75	1983
15.15	14.63	14.35	13.94	13.48	13.40	1984
12.43	12.50	12.48	12.36	11.99	11.58	1985
10.16	10.18	10.20	10.24	10.07	9.97	1986
10.61	10.80	11.31	11.62	11.23	11.29	1987
11.11	11.21	10.90	10.41	10.48	10.65	1988
9.87	9.88	9.91	9.81	9.81	9.82	1989
10.20	10.41	10.64	10.74	10.62	10.43	1990
9.89	9.65	9.51	9.49	9.45	9.26	1991
8.84	8.65	8.62	8.84	8.96	8.81	1992
7.93	7.60	7.34	7.31	7.66	7.69	1993
8.80	8.74	8.98	9.20	9.32	9.10	1994
8.04	8.19	7.93	7.75	7.68	7.49	1995
8.35	8.18	8.35	8.07	7.79	7.89	1996
7.75	7.82	7.70	7.57	7.42	7.32	1997
7.15	7.14	7.09	7.18	7.34	7.23	1998
7.95	8.15	8.20	8.38	8.15	8.19	1999
8.35	8.26	8.35	8.34	8.28	8.02	2000
7.97	7.85	8.03	7.91	7.81	8.05	2001
7.90	7.58	7.40	7.73	7.62	7.45	2002
6.62	7.01	6.79	6.73	6.66	6.60	2003
6.62	6.46	6.27	6.21	6.20	6.15	2004
5.95	5.96	6.03	6.30	6.39	6.32	2005
6.76	6.59	6.43	6.42	6.20	6.22	2006
6.65	6.65	6.59	6.48	6.40	6.65	2007
7.16	7.15	7.31	8.88	9.21	8.43	2008
7.09	6.58	6.31	6.29	6.32	6.37	2009
6.01	5.66	5.66	5.72	5.92	6.10	2010
5.76	5.36	5.27	5.37	5.14	5.25	2011
4.87	4.91	4.84	4.58	4.51	4.63	2012
5.32	5.42	5.47	5.31	5.38	5.38	2013
4.73	4.69	4.80	4.69	4.79	4.74	2014
5.20	5.19	5.34	5.34	5.46	5.46	2015
4.22	4.24	4.31	4.38	4.71	4.83	2016
4.39	4.31	4.30	4.32	4.27	4.22	2017

COMMODITIES

OIL - WEST TEXAS INTERMEDIATE
CLOSING VALUES $ / bbl

	JAN	FEB	MAR	APR	MAY	JUN
1950	2.6	2.6	2.6	2.6	2.6	2.6
1951	2.6	2.6	2.6	2.6	2.6	2.6
1952	2.6	2.6	2.6	2.6	2.6	2.6
1953	2.6	2.6	2.6	2.6	2.6	2.8
1954	2.8	2.8	2.8	2.8	2.8	2.8
1955	2.8	2.8	2.8	2.8	2.8	2.8
1956	2.8	2.8	2.8	2.8	2.8	2.8
1957	2.8	3.1	3.1	3.1	3.1	3.1
1958	3.1	3.1	3.1	3.1	3.1	3.1
1959	3.0	3.0	3.0	3.0	3.0	3.0
1960	3.0	3.0	3.0	3.0	3.0	3.0
1961	3.0	3.0	3.0	3.0	3.0	3.0
1962	3.0	3.0	3.0	3.0	3.0	3.0
1963	3.0	3.0	3.0	3.0	3.0	3.0
1964	3.0	3.0	3.0	3.0	3.0	3.0
1965	2.9	2.9	2.9	2.9	2.9	2.9
1966	2.9	2.9	2.9	2.9	2.9	2.9
1967	3.0	3.0	3.0	3.0	3.0	3.0
1968	3.1	3.1	3.1	3.1	3.1	3.1
1969	3.1	3.1	3.3	3.4	3.4	3.4
1970	3.4	3.4	3.4	3.4	3.4	3.4
1971	3.6	3.6	3.6	3.6	3.6	3.6
1972	3.6	3.6	3.6	3.6	3.6	3.6
1973	3.6	3.6	3.6	3.6	3.6	3.6
1974	10.1	10.1	10.1	10.1	10.1	10.1
1975	11.2	11.2	11.2	11.2	11.2	11.2
1976	11.2	12.0	12.1	12.2	12.2	12.2
1977	13.9	13.9	13.9	13.9	13.9	13.9
1978	14.9	14.9	14.9	14.9	14.9	14.9
1979	14.9	15.9	15.9	15.9	18.1	19.1
1980	32.5	37.0	38.0	39.5	39.5	39.5
1981	38.0	38.0	38.0	38.0	38.0	36.0
1982	33.9	31.6	28.5	33.5	35.9	35.1
1983	31.2	29.0	28.8	30.6	30.0	31.0
1984	29.7	30.1	30.8	30.6	30.5	30.0
1985	25.6	27.3	28.2	28.8	27.6	27.1
1986	22.9	15.4	12.6	12.8	15.4	13.5
1987	18.7	17.7	18.3	18.6	19.4	20.0
1988	17.2	16.8	16.2	17.9	17.4	16.5
1989	18.0	17.8	19.4	21.0	20.0	20.0
1990	22.6	22.1	20.4	18.6	18.2	16.9
1991	25.0	20.5	19.9	20.8	21.2	20.2
1992	18.8	19.0	18.9	20.2	20.9	22.4
1993	19.1	20.1	20.3	20.3	19.9	19.1
1994	15.0	14.8	14.7	16.4	17.9	19.1
1995	18.0	18.5	18.6	19.9	19.7	18.4
1996	18.9	19.1	21.4	23.6	21.3	20.5
1997	25.2	22.2	21.0	19.7	20.8	19.2
1998	16.7	16.1	15.0	15.4	14.9	13.7
1999	12.5	12.0	14.7	17.3	17.8	17.9
2000	27.2	29.4	29.9	25.7	28.8	31.8
2001	29.6	29.6	27.2	27.4	28.6	27.6
2002	19.7	20.7	24.4	26.3	27.0	25.5
2003	32.9	35.9	33.6	28.3	28.1	30.7
2004	34.3	34.7	36.8	36.7	40.3	38.0
2005	46.8	48.0	54.3	53.0	49.8	56.3
2006	65.5	61.6	62.9	69.7	70.9	71.0
2007	54.6	59.3	60.6	64.0	63.5	67.5
2008	93.0	95.4	105.6	112.6	125.4	133.9
2009	41.7	39.2	48.0	49.8	59.2	69.7
2010	78.2	76.4	81.2	84.5	73.8	75.4
2011	89.4	89.6	102.9	110.0	101.3	96.3
2012	100.3	102.3	106.2	103.3	94.7	82.3
2013	94.8	95.3	92.9	92.0	94.5	95.8
2014	94.6	100.8	100.8	102.1	102.2	105.8
2015	47.2	50.6	47.8	54.5	59.3	59.8
2016	31.7	30.3	37.6	40.8	46.7	48.8
2017	52.5	53.5	49.3	51.1	48.5	45.2

* Source: Federal Reserve

OIL - WEST TEXAS INTERMEDIATE
CLOSING VALUES $ / bbl
COMMODITIES

JUL	AUG	SEP	OCT	NOV	DEC	
2.6	2.6	2.6	2.6	2.6	2.6	1950
2.6	2.6	2.6	2.6	2.6	2.6	1951
2.6	2.6	2.6	2.6	2.6	2.6	1952
2.8	2.8	2.8	2.8	2.8	2.8	1953
2.8	2.8	2.8	2.8	2.8	2.8	1954
2.8	2.8	2.8	2.8	2.8	2.8	1955
2.8	2.8	2.8	2.8	2.8	2.8	1956
3.1	3.1	3.1	3.1	3.1	3.0	1957
3.1	3.1	3.1	3.1	3.0	3.0	1958
3.0	3.0	3.0	3.0	3.0	3.0	1959
3.0	3.0	3.0	3.0	3.0	3.0	1960
3.0	3.0	3.0	3.0	3.0	3.0	1961
3.0	3.0	3.0	3.0	3.0	3.0	1962
3.0	3.0	3.0	3.0	3.0	3.0	1963
2.9	2.9	2.9	2.9	2.9	2.9	1964
2.9	2.9	2.9	2.9	2.9	2.9	1965
2.9	2.9	3.0	3.0	3.0	3.0	1966
3.0	3.1	3.1	3.1	3.1	3.1	1967
3.1	3.1	3.1	3.1	3.1	3.1	1968
3.4	3.4	3.4	3.4	3.4	3.4	1969
3.3	3.3	3.3	3.3	3.3	3.6	1970
3.6	3.6	3.6	3.6	3.6	3.6	1971
3.6	3.6	3.6	3.6	3.6	3.6	1972
3.6	4.3	4.3	4.3	4.3	4.3	1973
10.1	10.1	10.1	11.2	11.2	11.2	1974
11.2	11.2	11.2	11.2	11.2	11.2	1975
12.2	12.2	13.9	13.9	13.9	13.9	1976
13.9	14.9	14.9	14.9	14.9	14.9	1977
14.9	14.9	14.9	14.9	14.9	14.9	1978
21.8	26.5	28.5	29.0	31.0	32.5	1979
39.5	38.0	36.0	36.0	36.0	37.0	1980
36.0	36.0	36.0	35.0	36.0	35.0	1981
34.2	34.0	35.6	35.7	34.2	31.7	1982
31.7	31.9	31.1	30.4	29.8	29.2	1983
28.8	29.3	29.3	28.8	28.1	25.4	1984
27.3	27.8	28.3	29.5	30.8	27.2	1985
11.6	15.1	14.9	14.9	15.2	16.1	1986
21.4	20.3	19.5	19.8	18.9	17.2	1987
15.5	15.5	14.5	13.8	14.0	16.3	1988
19.6	18.5	19.6	20.1	19.8	21.1	1989
18.6	27.2	33.7	35.9	32.3	27.3	1990
21.4	21.7	21.9	23.2	22.5	19.5	1991
21.8	21.4	21.9	21.7	20.3	19.4	1992
17.9	18.0	17.5	18.1	16.7	14.5	1993
19.7	18.4	17.5	17.7	18.1	17.2	1994
17.3	18.0	18.2	17.4	18.0	19.0	1995
21.3	22.0	24.0	24.9	23.7	25.4	1996
19.6	19.9	19.8	21.3	20.2	18.3	1997
14.1	13.4	15.0	14.4	12.9	11.3	1998
20.1	21.3	23.9	22.6	25.0	26.1	1999
29.8	31.2	33.9	33.1	34.4	28.5	2000
26.5	27.5	25.9	22.2	19.7	19.3	2001
26.9	28.4	29.7	28.9	26.3	29.4	2002
30.8	31.6	28.3	30.3	31.1	32.2	2003
40.7	44.9	46.0	53.1	48.5	43.3	2004
58.7	65.0	65.6	62.4	58.3	59.4	2005
74.4	73.1	63.9	58.9	59.4	62.0	2006
74.2	72.4	79.9	86.2	94.6	91.7	2007
133.4	116.6	103.9	76.7	57.4	41.0	2008
64.1	71.1	69.5	75.6	78.1	74.3	2009
76.4	76.8	75.3	81.9	84.1	89.0	2010
97.2	86.3	85.6	86.4	97.2	98.6	2011
87.9	94.2	94.7	89.6	86.7	88.3	2012
104.7	106.6	106.3	100.5	93.9	97.6	2013
103.6	96.5	93.2	84.4	75.8	59.3	2014
50.9	42.9	45.5	46.2	42.4	37.2	2015
44.7	44.7	45.2	49.8	45.7	52.0	2016
46.6	48.0	49.8	51.6	56.6	57.9	2017

GOLD $US/OZ LONDON PM
MONTH CLOSE

	JAN	FEB	MAR	APR	MAY	JUN
1970	34.9	35.0	35.1	35.6	36.0	35.4
1971	37.9	38.7	38.9	39.0	40.5	40.1
1972	45.8	48.3	48.3	49.0	54.6	62.1
1973	65.1	74.2	84.4	90.5	102.0	120.1
1974	129.2	150.2	168.4	172.2	163.3	154.1
1975	175.8	181.8	178.2	167.0	167.0	166.3
1976	128.2	132.3	129.6	128.4	125.5	123.8
1977	132.3	142.8	148.9	147.3	143.0	143.0
1978	175.8	182.3	181.6	170.9	184.2	183.1
1979	233.7	251.3	240.1	245.3	274.6	277.5
1980	653.0	637.0	494.5	518.0	535.5	653.5
1981	506.5	489.0	513.8	482.8	479.3	426.0
1982	387.0	362.6	320.0	361.3	325.3	317.5
1983	499.5	408.5	414.8	429.3	437.5	416.0
1984	373.8	394.3	388.5	375.8	384.3	373.1
1985	306.7	287.8	329.3	321.4	314.0	317.8
1986	350.5	338.2	344.0	345.8	343.2	345.5
1987	400.5	405.9	405.9	453.3	451.0	447.3
1988	458.0	426.2	457.0	449.0	455.5	436.6
1989	394.0	387.0	383.2	377.6	361.8	373.0
1990	415.1	407.7	368.5	367.8	363.1	352.2
1991	366.0	362.7	355.7	357.8	360.4	368.4
1992	354.1	353.1	341.7	336.4	337.5	343.4
1993	330.5	327.6	337.8	354.3	374.8	378.5
1994	377.9	381.6	389.2	376.5	387.6	388.3
1995	374.9	376.4	392.0	389.8	384.3	387.1
1996	405.6	400.7	396.4	391.3	390.6	382.0
1997	345.5	358.6	348.2	340.2	345.6	334.6
1998	304.9	297.4	301.0	310.7	293.6	296.3
1999	285.4	287.1	279.5	286.6	268.6	261.0
2000	283.3	293.7	276.8	275.1	272.3	288.2
2001	264.5	266.7	257.7	263.2	267.5	270.6
2002	282.3	296.9	301.4	308.2	326.6	318.5
2003	367.5	347.5	334.9	336.8	361.4	346.0
2004	399.8	395.9	423.7	388.5	393.3	395.8
2005	422.2	435.5	427.5	435.7	414.5	437.1
2006	568.8	556.0	582.0	644.0	653.0	613.5
2007	650.5	664.2	661.8	677.0	659.1	650.5
2008	923.3	971.5	933.5	871.0	885.8	930.3
2009	919.5	952.0	916.5	883.3	975.5	934.5
2010	1078.5	1108.3	1115.5	1179.3	1207.5	1244.0
2011	1327.0	1411.0	1439.0	1535.5	1536.5	1505.5
2012	1744.0	1770.0	1662.5	1651.3	1558.0	1598.5
2013	1664.8	1588.5	1598.3	1469.0	1394.5	1192.0
2014	1251.0	1326.5	1291.75	1288.5	1250.5	1315.0
2015	1260.3	1214.0	1187.0	1180.3	1191.4	1171.0
2016	1111.8	1234.9	1237.0	1285.7	1212.1	1320.8
2017	1212.8	1255.0	1244.9	1266.4	1266.2	1242.3

* Source: Bank of England

GOLD $US/OZ LONDON PM MONTH CLOSE

COMMODITIES

JUL	AUG	SEP	OCT	NOV	DEC	
35.3	35.4	36.2	37.5	37.4	37.4	1970
41.0	42.7	42.0	42.5	42.9	43.5	1971
65.7	67.0	65.5	64.9	62.9	63.9	1972
120.2	106.8	103.0	100.1	94.8	106.7	1973
143.0	154.6	151.8	158.8	181.7	183.9	1974
166.7	159.8	141.3	142.9	138.2	140.3	1975
112.5	104.0	116.0	123.2	130.3	134.5	1976
144.1	146.0	154.1	161.5	160.1	165.0	1977
200.3	208.7	217.1	242.6	193.4	226.0	1978
296.5	315.1	397.3	382.0	415.7	512.0	1979
614.3	631.3	666.8	629.0	619.8	589.8	1980
406.0	425.5	428.8	427.0	414.5	397.5	1981
342.9	411.5	397.0	423.3	436.0	456.9	1982
422.0	414.3	405.0	382.0	405.0	382.4	1983
342.4	348.3	343.8	333.5	329.0	309.0	1984
327.5	333.3	326.5	325.1	325.3	326.8	1985
357.5	384.7	423.2	401.0	383.5	388.8	1986
462.5	453.4	459.5	468.8	492.5	484.1	1987
436.8	427.8	397.7	412.4	422.6	410.3	1988
368.3	359.8	366.5	375.3	408.2	398.6	1989
372.3	387.8	408.4	379.5	384.9	386.2	1990
362.9	347.4	354.9	357.5	366.3	353.2	1991
357.9	340.0	349.0	339.3	334.2	332.9	1992
401.8	371.6	355.5	369.6	370.9	391.8	1993
384.0	385.8	394.9	383.9	383.1	383.3	1994
383.4	382.4	384.0	382.7	387.8	387.0	1995
385.3	386.5	379.0	379.5	371.3	369.3	1996
326.4	325.4	332.1	311.4	296.8	290.2	1997
288.9	273.4	293.9	292.3	294.7	287.8	1998
255.6	254.8	299.0	299.1	291.4	290.3	1999
276.8	277.0	273.7	264.5	269.1	274.5	2000
265.9	273.0	293.1	278.8	275.5	276.5	2001
304.7	312.8	323.7	316.9	319.1	347.2	2002
354.8	375.6	388.0	386.3	398.4	416.3	2003
391.4	407.3	415.7	425.6	453.4	435.6	2004
429.0	433.3	473.3	470.8	495.7	513.0	2005
632.5	623.5	599.3	603.8	646.7	632.0	2006
665.5	672.0	743.0	789.5	783.5	833.8	2007
918.0	833.0	884.5	730.8	814.5	869.8	2008
939.0	955.5	995.8	1040.0	1175.8	1087.5	2009
1169.0	1246.0	1307.0	1346.8	1383.5	1405.5	2010
1628.5	1813.5	1620.0	1722.0	1746.0	1531.0	2011
1622.0	1648.5	1776.0	1719.0	1726.0	1657.5	2012
1314.5	1394.8	1326.5	1324.0	1253.0	1204.5	2013
1285.3	1285.8	1216.5	1164.8	1282.8	1206.0	2014
1098.4	1135.0	1114.0	1142.4	1061.9	1060.0	2015
1342.0	1309.3	1322.5	1272.0	1178.1	1145.9	2016
1267.6	1311.8	1283.1	1270.2	1280.2	1291.0	2017

FOREIGN EXCHANGE

US DOLLAR vs CDN DOLLAR
MONTHLY AVG. VALUES*

	JAN		FEB		MAR		APR		MAY		JUN	
	US / CDN		US / CDN		US / CDN		US / CDN		US / CDN		US / CDN	
	CDN	/ US	CDN	/ US	CDN	/US	CDN	/ US	CDN	/ US	CDN	/ US
1971	1.01	0.99	1.01	0.99	1.01	0.99	1.01	0.99	1.01	0.99	1.02	0.98
1972	1.01	0.99	1.00	1.00	1.00	1.00	1.00	1.00	0.99	1.01	0.98	1.02
1973	1.00	1.00	1.00	1.00	1.00	1.00	1.00	1.00	1.00	1.00	1.00	1.00
1974	0.99	1.01	0.98	1.02	0.97	1.03	0.97	1.03	0.96	1.04	0.97	1.03
1975	0.99	1.01	1.00	1.00	1.00	1.00	1.01	0.99	1.03	0.97	1.03	0.97
1976	1.01	0.99	0.99	1.01	0.99	1.01	0.98	1.02	0.98	1.02	0.97	1.03
1977	1.01	0.99	1.03	0.97	1.05	0.95	1.05	0.95	1.05	0.95	1.06	0.95
1978	1.10	0.91	1.11	0.90	1.13	0.89	1.14	0.88	1.12	0.89	1.12	0.89
1979	1.19	0.84	1.20	0.84	1.17	0.85	1.15	0.87	1.16	0.87	1.17	0.85
1980	1.16	0.86	1.16	0.87	1.17	0.85	1.19	0.84	1.17	0.85	1.15	0.87
1981	1.19	0.84	1.20	0.83	1.19	0.84	1.19	0.84	1.20	0.83	1.20	0.83
1982	1.19	0.84	1.21	0.82	1.22	0.82	1.23	0.82	1.23	0.81	1.28	0.78
1983	1.23	0.81	1.23	0.81	1.23	0.82	1.23	0.81	1.23	0.81	1.23	0.81
1984	1.25	0.80	1.25	0.80	1.27	0.79	1.28	0.78	1.29	0.77	1.30	0.77
1985	1.32	0.76	1.35	0.74	1.38	0.72	1.37	0.73	1.38	0.73	1.37	0.73
1986	1.41	0.71	1.40	0.71	1.40	0.71	1.39	0.72	1.38	0.73	1.39	0.72
1987	1.36	0.73	1.33	0.75	1.32	0.76	1.32	0.76	1.34	0.75	1.34	0.75
1988	1.29	0.78	1.27	0.79	1.25	0.80	1.24	0.81	1.24	0.81	1.22	0.82
1989	1.19	0.84	1.19	0.84	1.20	0.84	1.19	0.84	1.19	0.84	1.20	0.83
1990	1.17	0.85	1.20	0.84	1.18	0.85	1.16	0.86	1.17	0.85	1.17	0.85
1991	1.16	0.87	1.15	0.87	1.16	0.86	1.15	0.87	1.15	0.87	1.14	0.87
1992	1.16	0.86	1.18	0.85	1.19	0.84	1.19	0.84	1.20	0.83	1.20	0.84
1993	1.28	0.78	1.26	0.79	1.25	0.80	1.26	0.79	1.27	0.79	1.28	0.78
1994	1.32	0.76	1.34	0.74	1.36	0.73	1.38	0.72	1.38	0.72	1.38	0.72
1995	1.41	0.71	1.40	0.71	1.41	0.71	1.38	0.73	1.36	0.73	1.38	0.73
1996	1.37	0.73	1.38	0.73	1.37	0.73	1.36	0.74	1.37	0.73	1.37	0.73
1997	1.35	0.74	1.36	0.74	1.37	0.73	1.39	0.72	1.38	0.72	1.38	0.72
1998	1.44	0.69	1.43	0.70	1.42	0.71	1.43	0.70	1.45	0.69	1.47	0.68
1999	1.52	0.66	1.50	0.67	1.52	0.66	1.49	0.67	1.46	0.68	1.47	0.68
2000	1.45	0.69	1.45	0.69	1.46	0.68	1.47	0.68	1.50	0.67	1.48	0.68
2001	1.50	0.67	1.52	0.66	1.56	0.64	1.56	0.64	1.54	0.65	1.52	0.66
2002	1.60	0.63	1.60	0.63	1.59	0.63	1.58	0.63	1.55	0.65	1.53	0.65
2003	1.54	0.65	1.51	0.66	1.48	0.68	1.46	0.69	1.38	0.72	1.35	0.74
2004	1.30	0.77	1.33	0.75	1.33	0.75	1.34	0.75	1.38	0.73	1.36	0.74
2005	1.22	0.82	1.24	0.81	1.22	0.82	1.24	0.81	1.26	0.80	1.24	0.81
2006	1.16	0.86	1.15	0.87	1.16	0.86	1.14	0.87	1.11	0.90	1.11	0.90
2007	1.18	0.85	1.17	0.85	1.17	0.86	1.14	0.88	1.10	0.91	1.07	0.94
2008	1.01	0.99	1.00	1.00	1.00	1.00	1.01	0.99	1.00	1.00	1.02	0.98
2009	1.22	0.82	1.25	0.80	1.26	0.79	1.22	0.82	1.15	0.87	1.13	0.89
2010	1.04	0.96	1.06	0.95	1.02	0.98	1.01	0.99	1.04	0.96	1.04	0.96
2011	0.99	1.01	0.99	1.01	0.98	1.02	0.96	1.04	0.97	1.03	0.98	1.02
2012	1.01	0.99	1.00	1.00	0.99	1.01	0.99	1.01	1.01	0.99	1.03	0.97
2013	0.99	1.01	1.01	0.99	1.02	.098	1.02	0.98	1.02	0.98	1.03	0.97
2014	1.09	0.91	1.11	0.90	1.11	0.90	1.10	0.91	1.09	0.92	1.08	0.92
2015	1.21	0.82	1.25	0.80	1.26	0.79	1.23	0.81	1.22	0.82	1.24	0.81
2016	1.42	0.70	1.38	0.72	1.32	0.76	1,28	0.78	1.29	0.77	1.29	0.78
2017	1.30	0.77	1.32	0.75	1.33	0.75	1.37	0.73	1.35	0.74	1.30	0.77

Source: Federal Reserve: Avg of daily rates, noon buying rates in New York City for cable transfers payable in foreign currencies

US DOLLAR vs CDN DOLLAR
MONTHLY AVG. VALUES

JUL US/CDN	JUL CDN/US	AUG US/CDN	AUG CDN/US	SEP US/CDN	SEP CDN/US	OCT US/CDN	OCT CDN/US	NOV US/CDN	NOV CDN/US	DEC US/CDN	DEC CDN/US	Year
1.02	0.98	1.01	0.99	1.01	0.99	1.00	1.00	1.00	1.00	1.00	1.00	1971
0.98	1.02	0.98	1.02	0.98	1.02	0.98	1.02	0.99	1.01	1.00	1.00	1972
1.00	1.00	1.00	1.00	1.01	0.99	1.00	1.00	1.00	1.00	1.00	1.00	1973
0.98	1.02	0.98	1.02	0.99	1.01	0.98	1.02	0.99	1.01	0.99	1.01	1974
1.03	0.97	1.04	0.97	1.03	0.97	1.03	0.98	1.01	0.99	1.01	0.99	1975
0.97	1.03	0.99	1.01	0.98	1.03	0.97	1.03	0.99	1.01	1.02	0.98	1976
1.06	0.94	1.08	0.93	1.07	0.93	1.10	0.91	1.11	0.90	1.10	0.91	1977
1.12	0.89	1.14	0.88	1.17	0.86	1.18	0.85	1.17	0.85	1.18	0.85	1978
1.16	0.86	1.17	0.85	1.17	0.86	1.18	0.85	1.18	0.85	1.17	0.85	1979
1.15	0.87	1.16	0.86	1.16	0.86	1.17	0.86	1.19	0.84	1.20	0.84	1980
1.21	0.83	1.22	0.82	1.20	0.83	1.20	0.83	1.19	0.84	1.19	0.84	1981
1.27	0.79	1.25	0.80	1.23	0.81	1.23	0.81	1.23	0.82	1.24	0.81	1982
1.23	0.81	1.23	0.81	1.23	0.81	1.23	0.81	1.24	0.81	1.25	0.80	1983
1.32	0.76	1.30	0.77	1.31	0.76	1.32	0.76	1.32	0.76	1.32	0.76	1984
1.35	0.74	1.36	0.74	1.37	0.73	1.37	0.73	1.38	0.73	1.40	0.72	1985
1.38	0.72	1.39	0.72	1.39	0.72	1.39	0.72	1.39	0.72	1.38	0.72	1986
1.33	0.75	1.33	0.75	1.32	0.76	1.31	0.76	1.32	0.76	1.31	0.76	1987
1.21	0.83	1.22	0.82	1.23	0.82	1.21	0.83	1.22	0.82	1.20	0.84	1988
1.19	0.84	1.18	0.85	1.18	0.85	1.17	0.85	1.17	0.85	1.16	0.86	1989
1.16	0.86	1.14	0.87	1.16	0.86	1.16	0.86	1.16	0.86	1.16	0.86	1990
1.15	0.87	1.15	0.87	1.14	0.88	1.13	0.89	1.13	0.88	1.15	0.87	1991
1.19	0.84	1.19	0.84	1.22	0.82	1.25	0.80	1.27	0.79	1.27	0.79	1992
1.28	0.78	1.31	0.76	1.32	0.76	1.33	0.75	1.32	0.76	1.33	0.75	1993
1.38	0.72	1.38	0.73	1.35	0.74	1.35	0.74	1.36	0.73	1.39	0.72	1994
1.36	0.73	1.36	0.74	1.35	0.74	1.35	0.74	1.35	0.74	1.37	0.73	1995
1.37	0.73	1.37	0.73	1.37	0.73	1.35	0.74	1.34	0.75	1.36	0.73	1996
1.38	0.73	1.39	0.72	1.39	0.72	1.39	0.72	1.41	0.71	1.43	0.70	1997
1.49	0.67	1.53	0.65	1.52	0.66	1.55	0.65	1.54	0.65	1.54	0.65	1998
1.49	0.67	1.49	0.67	1.48	0.68	1.48	0.68	1.47	0.68	1.47	0.68	1999
1.48	0.68	1.48	0.67	1.49	0.67	1.51	0.66	1.54	0.65	1.52	0.66	2000
1.53	0.65	1.54	0.65	1.57	0.64	1.57	0.64	1.59	0.63	1.58	0.63	2001
1.55	0.65	1.57	0.64	1.58	0.63	1.58	0.63	1.57	0.64	1.56	0.64	2002
1.38	0.72	1.40	0.72	1.36	0.73	1.32	0.76	1.31	0.76	1.31	0.76	2003
1.32	0.76	1.31	0.76	1.29	0.78	1.25	0.80	1.20	0.84	1.22	0.82	2004
1.22	0.82	1.20	0.83	1.18	0.85	1.18	0.85	1.18	0.85	1.16	0.86	2005
1.13	0.89	1.12	0.89	1.12	0.90	1.13	0.89	1.14	0.88	1.15	0.87	2006
1.05	0.95	1.06	0.95	1.03	0.97	0.98	1.03	0.97	1.03	1.00	1.00	2007
1.01	0.99	1.05	0.95	1.06	0.95	1.18	0.84	1.22	0.82	1.23	0.81	2008
1.12	0.89	1.09	0.92	1.08	0.92	1.05	0.95	1.06	0.94	1.05	0.95	2009
1.04	0.96	1.04	0.96	1.03	0.97	1.02	0.98	1.01	0.99	1.01	0.99	2010
0.96	1.05	0.98	1.02	1.00	1.00	1.02	0.98	1.02	0.98	1.02	0.98	2011
1.01	0.99	0.99	1.01	.098	1.02	0.99	1.01	1.00	1.00	0.99	1.01	2012
1.04	0.96	1.04	0.96	1.03	0.97	1.04	0.96	1.05	0.95	1.06	0.94	2013
1.07	0.93	1.09	0.92	1.10	0.91	1.12	0.89	1.13	0.88	1.15	0.87	2014
1.29	0.78	1.31	0.76	1.33	0.75	1.31	0.76	1.33	0.75	1.37	0.73	2015
1.31	0.77	1.30	0.77	1.31	0.76	1.33	0.75	1.34	0.74	1.33	0.75	2016
1.25	0.80	1.25	0.80	1.25	0.80	1.29	0.78	1.29	0.78	1.25	0.80	2017

FOREIGN EXCHANGE — U.S. DOLLAR vs EURO MONTHLY AVG. VALUES

	JAN		FEB		MAR		APR		MAY		JUN	
	EUR / US	US / EUR	EUR / US	US / EUR	EUR / US	US / EUR	EUR / US	US / EUR	EUR / US	US / EUR	EUR / US	US / EUR
1999	1.16	0.86	1.12	0.89	1.09	0.92	1.07	0.93	1.06	0.94	1.04	0.96
2000	1.01	0.99	0.98	1.02	0.96	1.04	0.94	1.06	0.91	1.10	0.95	1.05
2001	0.94	1.07	0.92	1.09	0.91	1.10	0.89	1.12	0.88	1.14	0.85	1.17
2002	0.88	1.13	0.87	1.15	0.88	1.14	0.89	1.13	0.92	1.09	0.96	1.05
2003	1.06	0.94	1.08	0.93	1.08	0.93	1.09	0.92	1.16	0.87	1.17	0.86
2004	1.26	0.79	1.26	0.79	1.23	0.82	1.20	0.83	1.20	0.83	1.21	0.82
2005	1.31	0.76	1.30	0.77	1.32	0.76	1.29	0.77	1.27	0.79	1.22	0.82
2006	1.21	0.82	1.19	0.84	1.20	0.83	1.23	0.81	1.28	0.78	1.27	0.79
2007	1.30	0.77	1.31	0.76	1.32	0.75	1.35	0.74	1.35	0.74	1.34	0.75
2008	1.47	0.68	1.48	0.68	1.55	0.64	1.58	0.63	1.56	0.64	1.56	0.64
2009	1.32	0.76	1.28	0.78	1.31	0.77	1.32	0.76	1.36	0.73	1.40	0.71
2010	1.43	0.70	1.37	0.73	1.36	0.74	1.34	0.75	1.26	0.80	1.22	0.82
2011	1.34	0.75	1.37	0.73	1.40	0.71	1.45	0.69	1.43	0.70	1.44	0.69
2012	1.29	0.77	1.32	0.76	1.32	0.76	1.32	0.76	1.28	0.78	1.25	0.80
2013	1.33	0.75	1.33	0.75	1.30	0.77	1.30	0.77	1.30	0.77	1.32	0.76
2014	1.36	0.73	1.37	0.73	1.38	0.72	1.38	0.72	1.37	0.73	1.36	0.74
2015	1.16	0.86	1.14	0.88	1.08	0.92	1.08	0.92	1.12	0.90	1.12	0.89
2016	1.09	0.92	1.11	0.90	1.11	0.90	1.13	0.88	1.13	0.88	1.12	0.89
2017	1.06	0.94	1.07	0.94	1.07	0.94	1.07	0.93	1.11	0.90	1.12	0.89

Source: Federal Reserve: Avg of daily rates, noon buying rates in New York City for cable transfers payable in foreign currencies

US DOLLAR vs EURO
MONTHLY AVG. VALUES

FOREIGN EXCHANGE

JUL		AUG		SEP		OCT		NOV		DEC		
EUR / US	US / EUR	EUR / US	US / EUR	EUR / US	US / EUR	EUR / US	US / EUR	EUR / US	US / EUR	EUR / US	US / EUR	
1.04	0.96	1.06	0.94	1.05	0.95	1.07	0.93	1.03	0.97	1.01	0.99	**1999**
0.94	1.07	0.90	1.11	0.87	1.15	0.85	1.17	0.86	1.17	0.90	1.11	**2000**
0.86	1.16	0.90	1.11	0.91	1.10	0.91	1.10	0.89	1.13	0.89	1.12	**2001**
0.99	1.01	0.98	1.02	0.98	1.02	0.98	1.02	1.00	1.00	1.02	0.98	**2002**
1.14	0.88	1.12	0.90	1.13	0.89	1.17	0.85	1.17	0.85	1.23	0.81	**2003**
1.23	0.82	1.22	0.82	1.22	0.82	1.25	0.80	1.30	0.77	1.34	0.75	**2004**
1.20	0.83	1.23	0.81	1.22	0.82	1.20	0.83	1.18	0.85	1.19	0.84	**2005**
1.27	0.79	1.28	0.78	1.27	0.79	1.26	0.79	1.29	0.78	1.32	0.76	**2006**
1.37	0.73	1.36	0.73	1.39	0.72	1.42	0.70	1.47	0.68	1.46	0.69	**2007**
1.58	0.63	1.50	0.67	1.43	0.70	1.33	0.75	1.27	0.78	1.35	0.74	**2008**
1.41	0.71	1.43	0.70	1.46	0.69	1.48	0.67	1.49	0.67	1.46	0.69	**2009**
1.28	0.78	1.29	0.78	1.31	0.76	1.39	0.72	1.37	0.73	1.32	0.76	**2010**
1.43	0.70	1.43	0.70	1.37	0.73	1.37	0.73	1.36	0.74	1.32	0.76	**2011**
1.23	0.81	1.24	0.81	1.29	0.78	1.30	0.77	1.28	0.78	1.31	0.76	**2012**
1.31	0.76	1.33	0.75	1.34	0.75	1.36	0.73	1.35	0.74	1.37	0.73	**2013**
1.35	0.74	1.33	0.75	1.29	0.78	1.27	0.79	1.25	0.80	1.23	0.81	**2014**
1.10	0.91	1.11	0.90	1.12	0.89	1.12	0.89	1.07	0.93	1.09	0.92	**2015**
1.11	0.90	1.12	0.89	1.12	0.89	1.10	0.91	1.08	0.93	1.05	0.95	**2016**
1.15	0.87	1.18	0.85	1.19	0.84	1.18	0.85	1.17	0.85	1.18	0.84	**2017**